XIV

Human Diversity and Civil Society in *Paradiso*, VIII

Paradiso is the *cantica* of coherence and understanding. As Dante moves from the Moon out into the other heavens, themes that had been considered in other contexts earlier in the poem become juxtaposed in novel ways, the juxtaposition itself illuminating the themes so brought together. Elsewhere in the *Comedy*, Dante had discussed the problems of human individuation and the influences that shaped it, and he had spoken eloquently and somberly about the political culture of his own age. In *Paradiso* VIII, these and other themes are interwoven in a way that illuminates Dante's ideas of both.

Both the earliest and the most recent commentators on *Paradiso* VIII have noted the abundance and variety of subjects that Dante treats in the canto, the ornate and meticulous language, the extraordinary atmosphere of friendliness and courtliness that pervades the heaven of Venus, and the occasion of the canto for Dante's discussion of heredity, human nature, human freedom, and influence of the heavens on human beings. Faced with such an abundance, the earliest commentators either amplified the text by paraphrasing it or selected only one or two aspects of the canto for discussion. Pietro di Dante, for example, focused almost exclusively on Dante's astronomical references, while Benvenuto da Imola and others preferred to deal with the personal history of Charles Martel. Nineteenth-century critics focused on the elaborate poetics of the canto, the sentimental appeal of the figure of the king who died too young, or the increasing abstraction of the *Paradiso*.

The more sober and workmanlike literary-historical criticism of the early part of this century, best represented in the readings of Luigi Rocca

and Vittorio Vaturi, drew heavily on the pioneering historical research of Michelangelo Schipa of 1889–90 concerning the career of Charles Martel and the Angevin dynasty of Naples, noting the simultaneous expression of Dante's highest affection and deepest disdain throughout the canto; it also emphasized that the political concerns of *Paradiso* VIII were of a piece with Dante's larger political philosophy.

From the early work of André Pézard beginning in 1949, criticism has focused on the integration of themes in the *Comedy*, bringing to bear vast learning and considerable insight into both Dantean and thirteenth-century thought generally. Although Pézard's readings often seemed to reach too far in their imaginative speculation, they have influenced most later readings of both this particular canto and Dante's entire literary work. Subsequent readings have been selective in their emphasis, and their variety and perceptiveness reflects the extraordinary richness of Dante's text and thought and the critical discipline required to make sense of it.[1]

Like all the other cantos of the *Paradiso*, Canto VIII must be read in the matrix of the astonishing variety of perceptual transformations in the sensorium of the pilgrim, the highly detailed and specific theological and scientific accounts of the operations of the heavens, and the deliberate occasions for prolonged discussion and the final resolution of a series of topics that have been prominent so far in the *Paradiso*. The disposition of the souls in the first seven heavens (*Par.* I–XXII) represents both a concession to Dante's limited human powers of comprehension (*Par.* IV, 22–63) and an illustration of the first truth of Paradise, stated by Beatrice in Canto I:

> "Le cose tutte quante
> hanno ordine tra loro, e questo è forma
> che l'universo a Dio fa simigliante."
> (*Par.* I, 103–105)

This truth is repeated by Dante himself at the beginning of *Paradiso* X, (1–6), and it is directly addressed in Canto VIII.

Although the entire pilgrimage has prepared Dante for this truth, a number of Beatrice's statements in the first seven cantos of the *Paradiso* make it explicit. Beatrice first explains (*Par.* I, 103–135) that the light of God passes from sphere to sphere in differing intensities and that the

angelic orders within each sphere, perceiving forms in the mind of God, impart motion and power from sphere to sphere and from the spheres to the Earth in order to realize those forms. The realization of those forms is the purpose of the ordering of the universe, and the more forms that are realized the more the structure of the universe resembles God himself. In order to accomplish this, the principle of infinite diversity creates immense varieties of natures which

> più al principio loro e men vicine;
>   onde si muovono a diversi porti
> per lo gran mar de l'essere, e ciascuna
> con istinto a lei dato che la porti.
> (*Par.* I, 111–114)

Divine Providence has arrayed the universe in this way; therefore, all of the powers in the universe function for the good. But some creatures also possess the freedom and the power to "swerve elsewhere," and the benevolent purpose of the heavens may be thwarted by the behavior of humans. In *Paradiso* II, 112–148, Beatrice states that power is distributed throughout the heavenly order so that each part of the order may attain its aim within the great design. Each sphere bears the imprint of the sphere that stamped it and in turn stamps the one below it. Just as the human soul is shared by different organs, so Providence is shared by different celestial bodies, even though the Divine Intellect is a unity.

Following Piccarda's discussion of the harmony of diverse wills in the Divine Will in *Paradiso* III, Beatrice takes up (*Par.* IV, 22–63) Plato's suggestion in the *Timaeus* that individual souls descend from and return to particular planets whose Intelligences have given them their earthly characters. She explains that the way Dante perceives Paradise is merely a concession to the defective character of human sensory understanding, and then she suggests that the point made in the *Timaeus* may have some truth if it is taken, not literally, but as indicating that individual heavenly bodies do influence humans, and that that influence inclines humans to particular characters, in which they may either win salvation or not, and thus the honor or blame may be said to fall upon a heavenly body. But it remains an error to assume that gods dwell in the stars or to have named heavenly bodies for Jupiter, Mercury, or Mars. In Canto VI Justinian points out (echoing Beatrice in *Par.* I, 127–132) that human

desires may also be focused exclusively on earthly ends and therefore fail to mount to God with sufficient force. Finally, in Canto VII (124–148) Beatrice distinguishes between primary and secondary creation in order to explain the facts of coming into being and passing away. By Canto VII, then, Dante has not only been taught about human generation, ensoulment, freedom of the will and the inclinations of nature imparted by the stars and planets in such discourses as those of Marco Lombardo (*Purg.* XVI) and Statius (*Purg.* XXV), but he has also been assured by Beatrice that the heavenly influences are good and that diversity is an instrument to realize in actuality the infinity of forms in the mind of God. The inescapable and essential *fact* of diversity is thus accommodated to the equally inescapable and essential *necessity* of harmony in diversity in order to reflect the unity of the Divine Will.

These truths of Paradise are consistent with Dante's understanding of contemporary philosophical approaches to causation and cosmology. The thinkers to whose work Dante was most sympathetic argued that causation involves the transmission of a likeness from cause to effect; that causal agents act in ways that are "like" themselves; and that one may learn something about a cause by studying its traces (*vestigiae*) in its effects. The recipient of causality receives according to its capacity and disposition. The application of these doctrines to God's creation and design of the soul and the universe enabled Dante to use them as governing assumptions about the nature of Providence, human freedom, and the nature of heavenly influence on humans. Any interpretation of the universe and its order that fails to recognize these truths—whether this be the *antico errore* of pagans or what, as we will see, might be termed the *moderno errore* of contemporary Christians—will lead simply to intellectual and moral error, disordering the ordered universe and making more difficult the path from man to God.

Dante is in the heaven of Venus, the third heaven and the last that is still touched by the shadow of the Earth (*Par.* IX, 118–119). Both physically and formally the heaven of Venus draws to a close what some scholars have termed the Ante-Paradise, a structural parallel to the Ante-Inferno and the Ante-Purgatorio. Like its corresponding sections in the *Inferno* and the *Purgatorio*—the gate of the city of Dis (*Inf.* VIII) and the valley of the princes that precedes the dream of the Eagle and the flight to Purgatory proper with St. Lucy (*Purg.* VIII)—*Par.* VIII is what Rachel Jacoff has termed a "threshold Canto," completing the consid-

Livre dou Tresor, which also emphasized the civilizing and moral character of language), and Aristotle's medieval commentators, including Thomas Aquinas, Rhetoric served the political good, and the heaven of Rhetoric was an appropriate place for a discussion of one aspect of the political good, an aspect identified with the essence of human nature.

Dante orchestrates the full range of these identifications of Venus in *Paradiso* VIII. The topic of *folle amor*—that mad love which conquers both reason and will—had been considered earlier in *Inferno* V in the cases of Dido and Paolo and Francesca and on the terrace of the lustful who had repented in *Purgatorio* XXV–XXVII, and it is noted in the twelve-line introduction to *Paradiso* VIII. But this aspect of the planet is delayed by Dante until *Paradiso* IX, when Cunizza, Folco, and Rahab exemplify the "Venusian" souls who repented their mad love. In this sense, Cantos VIII and IX of the *Paradiso* may be said to reflect the problem of the "two Venuses" discussed earlier—the souls (and themes) of *Paradiso* VIII illustrating the first Venus, that of civic and cosmic harmony (and of cosmic harmony and benevolence in general), and those of *Paradiso* IX the second, the Venus of mad love and wantoness. This would explain neatly the topical differences between the two cantos devoted to the same heaven, but it would also explain Dante's rethinking of the "two Venus" problem. That is, for the poet there is only a single Venus, whose misunderstood force on the shaping of human character has led to the misconception of the second Venus. In *Paradiso* VIII Dante chooses to focus on the broader and more important aspects of Venus, the Principalities, and the art of Rhetoric: human nature and diversity, the necessary love that must bind citizens together in a state, and the art of speech that enables humans to understand themselves as individuals and as citizens. In one sense, *Paradiso* VIII may be read as Dante's complement to the great meta-history of the Empire delivered by Justinian in *Paradiso* VI. Charles Martel, like Brunetto Latini and Marco Lombardo, steps away from a specific location in order to apply a truth associated with that specific location to human life in general and to Dante's own life in particular.

A number of commentators, from Benvenuto da Imola to Aldo Vallone, have proposed different line-divisions for the complex sequence of subjects within the Canto. In this reading I have assumed a specifically defined twelve-line introduction (vv. 1–12) and a specifically defined (as a "corollary") twelve-line conclusion (vv. 137–148). The rest of the

Canto appears to use a module of about seventeen lines, either singly (vv. 13–30; 31–48) or in multiples to treat more extended topics (vv. 49–84; 85–114).

The rhetorical formality of the introduction echoes Beatrice's earlier discussion of pagan error (*Par.* IV, 22–24; 49–63) concerning the heavens' influence as well as Vergil's *Aeneid* (I, 657–660; 715–719), and in the latter reference reminds us of Dido in *Inferno* V. The first module describes the progressive changes that mark ascent through the heavens: the increase in Beatrice's beauty, the great speed and circular dance of the arriving souls (dramatically different from the mirrored faces of the Moon and the "fishpond" assembly of Mercury), and the greater intensity of the souls' synchronous movements with the angelic orders and their vision of the Divine Mind. Like sparks within a blaze or a single voice and choir in plainsong, the souls of Venus are described in metaphors of sound and light that characterize Dante's descriptions throughout the rest of the *Paradiso.*

The second module opens with the courteous and affectionate words of a still unidentified speaker (and visually unidentifiable—from Venus on, Dante is unable to distinguish the features of the bright souls whom he encounters) who assures Dante of his own and his fellow-spirits' delight in their meeting, of their identification with the angelic order of Principalities, and reminds Dante that Dante himself had once invoked that same order in his canzone "Voi che 'ntendendo il terzo ciel movete" (*Rime* 69; *Conv,* II, i). Given permission by Beatrice, Dante asks simply, but with *grande affetto,* "great love," "Who are you?" And, with gladness added to gladness making the spirit brighter, the spirit launches into its complex and intricate identification.

All commentators have remarked the spirit and language of genuine human friendliness and affection that characterize the heaven of Venus. And, as a nineteenth-century critic once observed, no one in Paradise is more well-intentioned toward Dante, politer, or more willing to accommodate the pilgrim's desires than Charles Martel.[6] A friend and patron of Dante in life, an exemplar of the best possible effects of the heaven of Venus in his own person, and a ruler characterized by the great love he bears his subjects, Charles Martel becomes Dante's spokesman (and heaven's) on the topics of human diversity, political necessity, and the relation between humans and the influences of the cosmos.

No figure ever stepped directly from history or memory onto any page of Dante, and Charles Martel is no exception. Historically, Charles

Martel (1271–1295) was the first son of Charles II of Anjou and Mary of Hungary and the grandson of Charles I of Anjou and Beatrice of Provence (one of the four daughters of Raymond Berenguer IV of Provence whom Romeo had [*Par.* VI] made queens). During his father's imprisonment by the Aragonese, Charles was appointed regent of the kingdom of Naples by Charles I (1285), and he served a second time as regent designated by his father in 1289. Heir to the county of Provence, the Kingdom of Naples, and actual king of Hungary, Charles was also the source (with his wife, Clemenza, daughter of the emperor Rudolph I of Habsburg) of the joining of the bloodlines of the two most eminent Guelf and Ghibelline families of his age. Had not Angevin misrule lost Sicily to Aragon after the Sicilian Vespers of 1282, Charles Martel would have ruled the united Kingdom of Sicily and Naples, and it is possible, as Vincenzo Mazzei has suggested, that Dante might, at the time of writing the *Paradiso,* have imagined him as once having been an ideal future emperor.

Certainly the contemporary chroniclers like Villani and the early commentators on the *Comedy* all agreed upon the sumptuousness, civility, obvious affection for Florence, and universal appeal of Charles Martel during his brief visit to Florence in March, 1294, the presumed occasion of his meeting with Dante and his hearing the *canzone* "Voi che 'ntendendo il terzo ciel movete." They and other sources tell of his just administration during his regencies, his own humility displayed in personally ascending Monte Morrone to bring the saintly hermit Pietro da Morrone to Naples and to the papal throne as Celestine V, and to the tragedy of his and his wife's untimely deaths.

Charles Martel's first words about himself, however, clearly touch a major concern of Dante: the effect upon Dante and the world of his untimely death. Twice Charles says, "If I had stayed [alive] longer . . . ," once to designate the evil now in the world that would not have existed, and the second time referring to the help that he would have given Dante personally. Like Brunetto Latini, who had said the same thing (*Inf.* XV, 55–60) to Dante, Charles Martel is the lost patron and protector, who here holds out the lost promise of well-ruled lands ringing northern and central Italy in the south, northwest, and northeast, uniting Guelf and Ghibelline in a rule animated by an equal love for all his subjects. Against this lost hope, Dante looked back from nearly two decades of political chaos in which Provence and Hungary passed to other lords, Sicily

remained in Aragonese hands, and the kingdom of Naples was snatched from the son of Charles Martel, Caroberto (cf. *Par.* IX, 1–6; *Par.* XIX, 115–148), by Charles' grasping and avaricious brother Robert of Naples. The failure and death of Henry VII in 1313, that of yet another potential patron and protector of the poet, sharpened Dante's regret, and his mind turned, as it did in a number of other places in the *Comedy,* back to the promising world of his youth in Florence, when prospects were bright, when the qualities and promise of *il buon tempo antico* still seemed alive. Then, learned teachers like Brunetto Latini and Remigio de' Girolami taught civilized citizenship, good judges like Nino Visconti (*Purg.* VIII, 53–81) visited the city and spoke of just law, and bright and glittering princes displayed generosity and affection to Florence's people and poets, showed exquisite taste in literature and music, and held out the promise of a well governed future.

Charles Martel is not, however, only an idealized personal memory. He is also a type of the eternal figure of the prince who dies too young—echoing Vergil's Marcellus (*Aeneid* VI, 890–892) and the Manfred of the *Purgatorio* (*Purg.* VI, 106–108) as well as the young Pedro of Aragon (*Purg.* VII, 115–117) who, if he, instead of his brother Alfonso III, had followed his father Pedro III on the throne, "then valor might have been poured from vessel unto vessel." But Charles is more; he is the perfect example of *adolescenza* turning into *giovinezza,* from the age governed by Venus to that governed by the Sun. Charles had reached the age when those characteristic virtues of *adolescenza*—obedience, charm, bodily development, and *vergogna* (a composite virtue consisting of a sense of wonder, becoming shyness, and an ability to feel shame at one's own or another's faults)—develop with proper instruction and guidance (*Conv.* IV, xxiv, 11–14) into the nobler virtues of *giovinezza*—temperance and strength (*Conv.* IV, xxvi), affection, courtesy, and legal-mindedness. In his discussion in the *Convivio* Dante cites Aeneas as the ideal *giovane,* and he is clearly thinking of Charles Martel as a type of Aeneas, both as a man and as a political leader. Aeneas, of course, was the son of Venus and Anchises. And as Bernard Silvestris had observed, this Venus is the *musica mundana* whose marriage with Anchises produces Aeneas, the human spirit in which Concord and Harmony are essential. Dante's own reading of Aeneas, as part of his meta-political rereading of Vergil generally, would have emphasized this aspect of the Trojan hero—one not only as the founder of a perfect political community and its just ruler

but a ruler characterized by the spirit of his divine mother—a spirit of loving affection for his subjects, one that the subjects themselves necessarily also had to possess for their ruler and for one another.[7] Book VIII of Aristotle's *Ethics* treats friendship and the benevolence of princes, (*Ethics* VIII. 1. 11–13), and Dante wrote often of that love of princes toward their people that is ideally expressed in affection and generosity (*Conv.* IV, xi, 14; *Mon.* I, ix, 3). Charles Martel here adds that dimension of affection to the portrait of the ideal emperor that is Dante's Justinian (*Par.* VI).

Idealized *adolescente/giovane,* idealized personal memory, and idealized prince, Charles Martel also exemplifies the bewildering effects of *Fortuna* (*Inf.* VII, 73–96; *Fortuna,* like the Principalities, influences the change of power from one people to another). How is it that he should be so unlike his father and brothers, and that men and women should differ from their parents and from their fellow-citizens so much? How, from gentle seed, may bitter fruit derive? Charles Martel's answer to Dante's question sweeps away both the *antico errore* of the pagans and modern misunderstanding of the nature of the heavens' influences on human character. Charles' answer to the pilgrim invokes Beatrice's earlier statements about the benevolent character of planetary influence. If benevolence did not rule the heavens, the heavens would be haywire, devoid of art (that is, of science and reason), and they would be ruins instead of works of perfect design. If such a thing were true, the minds that move the planets would be defective, and so would be the First Mind that made them and set them in motion.

Having stated the inescapable *fact* of benevolent celestial influences, Charles then takes up the *reason* for the diverse outcomes of the operation of Providence. He asks Dante,

> "Or dí: sarebbe il peggio
> per l'omo in terra, se non fosse cive?"
> (vv. 115–116)

This question, immediately following the contrast between *arti* and *ruine,* between a defective and a perfect Mind and that Mind's agents, anticipates a contrast between *cive* and something worse. Citizenship, the ideal state of humans, is so obvious a necessity for Dante that he assents without requiring proof. Yet citizenship does have an unacceptable

opposite, and Dante knew it. As a full reading of Dante's source for his statement, Aristotle's famous remark (*Pol.* I. ii. 8) that "man is an animal intended by nature to live in a polis," indicates the alternatives are that man must be either a beast or a god (*Pol.* II. ii. 14). Thus, for Aristotle and for Dante, the definition of man as a *zoon politikon* leaves room for no other definition of man that does not remove man from the definition of *human*. That is why Dante needs no proof. But why should Charles Martel ask Dante about citizenship when he has just begun to answer the larger question of the heavens' influence and the benevolence of Providence? Dante's reading of Aristotle and his commentators had led to his remarkable conviction that mankind has two distinct ends in life: that of earthly beatitude and that of heavenly beatitude (*Conv.* IV, xvii, 9–10). He expressed this idea forcefully at the end of the *Monarchia* (III, xv) and in Marco Lombardo's image of the two suns (*Purg.* XVI, 106–108). The topic of earthly beatitude is now linked to the problem of human individuation and freedom in a remarkable discourse on political anthropology that has no equal anywhere else in medieval political thought.

In the *Quaestio de aqua et terra,* said to have been delivered by Dante at Verona in 1320, Dante addressed the question whether water can be anywhere naturally above dry land. Dismissing a number of arguments drawn from theories of the proper spheres of the four elements (according to which earth should be lowest and fire highest), Dante (*Quaestio* 18) then turns to what, for him, is the basic physical principle of the universe:[8]

> Sed intentio Nature Universalis est ut omnes forme, que sunt in potentia materie prime, reducantur in actum. . . . Nam cum omnes forme, que sunt in potentia materie, ydealiter sint in actu in Motore celi . . . si omnes iste forme non essent semper in actu, Motor celi deficeret ab integritate diffusionis sue bonitatis.

> [The intention of universal nature is to realize in actuality all of those forms that exist potentially in prime matter . . . Since all forms that exist in potentiality in prime matter ideally exist in actuality in the [mind of] the Mover of the heavens, if all of these forms were not always being brought into actuality, the Mover of the heavens would be deficient in the diffusion of the integrity of his goodness.]

That is, the infinite diversity of nature is required to realize in the world all of the possible forms that already exist in the mind of God. As John North has pointed out, this is a religious answer to a question of natural philosophy, and it is remarkably similar to Charles Martel's explanation of the necessity of human diversity to civic completeness as a framework for considering the problems of human heredity and its purposes and the mechanisms by which it is achieved.

Put briefly, man achieves his greatest potentiality for earthly beatitude when he is a citizen; communities of citizens cannot exist, according to Aristotle, without the greatest possible diversity among those citizens; such societies require a Solon, a Xerxes, a Melchesidech, a Daedalus (the law-giver, the ruler who knows how to delegate power, the priest, and the engineer/artisan). Where can such diversity come from if universal nature does not interfere with the biological process of generation, according to which

> Natura generata il suo cammino
> simil farebbe sempre a' generanti,
> se non vincesse il proveder divino.
> (*Par.* VIII, 133–135)

in order to pursue its higher end, that of creating diversity among mortals? "Revolving nature" thus always works as it is obliged to by God, impressing characteristics on individuals that differentiate them from their parents and siblings, but it cannot afford to pay attention to biological descent. Hence, brothers like Jacob and Esau (and Charles Martel and Robert of Naples) are necessarily different from each other, and sometimes sons are so different from their fathers that it seems that their ignoble fathers could not have sired them (not their mothers—the male seed was thought to be the active principle forming the fetus). Men used to assume (another aspect of *antico errore*) that some heroes were the children of a god rather than their natural fathers, as the ancients said that Quirinus was (and as Homer had Priam suggest of Hector [*Iliad* XXIV] and Dante himself had once said about Gherardo da Cammino [*Conv.* IV, xiv, 12]).

This necessary diversity among parents and children presupposes a three-stage process of generation and ensoulment. The biological identity of parents and children is modified by the actions of the heavens

imparting diversity to humans, and the rational soul is directly imparted to this combination by God.

In this process, the cultivation of true individual natures becomes the task of societies, of laws, teachers, guidance, and advice, so that a Solon *in potentia* becomes a Solon *in esse.* The indiscriminate delight displayed by the soul early in life (*Purg.* XVI, 88–96) must be restrained, shaped, guided, taught, and directed according to its individual nature, by the development of those virtues appropriate to each of the stages of life. Charles Martel, a perfect example of this process at its best, becomes the spokesman of the process. Thus, he can afford to display a great indifference to the actual mechanics of celestial influence. Dante knew the details of the astrological literature well, but he also knew that these were merely a subordinate part of universal nature's greater purpose, important only in the fact that they contributed to the *how* of shaping different natures. The proper cultivation of individual natures realizes in the individual person that freedom that Dante calls God's greatest gift to rational creatures (*Par.* V, 19–24), and this enables humans to overcome the inclinations of their natures and places squarely upon each individual the responsibility for his actions.[9]

Charles then completes the Canto by "cloaking" Dante with a corollary, an additional conclusion legitimately drawn from the proof of another proposition.[10] Here, the proof had established that diversity in nature is essential; nature always operates in accordance with the divine mind and will, and that human natures will always move toward God. Thus, when a human nature goes astray in matters of natural character, it is the result of that nature having encountered unpropitious circumstances for its development (the result of *Fortuna*), just as a seed dropped outside its prepared seedbed will fail to grow into the true plant that was the seed's purpose. The image of mis-scattered seed recalls, as Pézard pointed out, the parable in Matthew 13, 4–9, and Luke 8–15.

The world, misunderstanding the truth about nature and its purposes—or diverted from that truth by greed—"corrupts" (*Purg.* XVI, 105), or, as here, "twists" individual natures away from their ideal forms and perverts them into paths that do not suit them. *Torcete,* "you twist," here suggests unnaturalness in the botanical sense of mis-sown seed or mis-nourished plants. Twisting is a favorite metaphor of Dante's (*Par.* XVI, 62–63; *Par.* IX, 10–12; *Par.* XXVI, 62–63), and here it is applied in a striking assertion of human individuality and freedom against those

forces in Dante's world—astrology, greed, family, ambition, and political alliance—that tended to suppress individual freedom in their own mistaken private or ideological interests. Thus, people "twist" to a life of religion one who was a natural soldier, and they "twist" into a king one who is better fit for making sermons. Dante's reference here is generally agreed to be to Charles Martel's brother, Robert of Naples, who published a vast number of his own sermons and considered himself an expert theologian; it has been suggested that the first of these references may be to Charles' other brother, St. Louis of Toulouse, that single generation of a single family exemplifying neatly the consequences of the combination of biological and celestial nature and human influence in different human beings.

Thus, as the last line of the Canto asserts, the track that humans take is off the road established by universal nature, and here Charles balances the *antico errore* of the ancients by condemning the *moderno errore* of contemporary Christians. Diversity indeed is achieved, but at the terrible price of mutated and twisted natures: it is rather an anti-diversity, a turning of Aristotle and universal nature (and hence the divine will) upside-down. Diversity is present, but it is a diversity that leads not to co-operation, natural affection, and individual and collective fulfillment, but to their opposites. And because it destroys the possibility of earthly beatitude, it makes more difficult, indeed, barely possible, the work of salvation.

In the first line of *Paradiso* I Dante has told his readers that it is God who moves everything in the universe; the last line of *Paradiso* XXXIII speaks of the *love* "that *moves* the Sun and the other stars." All other truths are necessarily subordinate to this truth, and in *Paradiso* VIII Dante has focused intensely on celestial influence as a reflection of the loving aspect of Divine Providence. He has dismissed the *antico errore* of pagans and the modern errors of his fellow-Christians, and he has also relegated the mechanics of astrology to an appropriate place, one that is well subordinate to the real importance of Venus and of the heavens generally in this regard. Dante may be said to have reunited Venus and to have explained the error of the "two Venuses" in mythography, but he has also explained the nature of celestial influence generally, and, more importantly, its purpose. With the understanding of that purpose at the end of *Paradiso* VIII, neither ancient nor modern error any longer has credibility. The theme broached by Marco Lombardo, and continued by

Statius and Beatrice, is here drawn to a close as in a dance—the dance of the souls in Venus and of the Principalities. It is the dance of *mundana musica,* a reflection in terms of earthly beatitude of that *musica celestis* that is heavenly beatitude.

At the end of *Paradiso* VIII Dante has not finished his work in the heaven of Venus, but he has elegantly and economically completed his own political vision and his consideration of those elements that link the high subject of empire with the very roots of human nature and the operation of the heavens. He has answered and expanded the problems raised by Marco Lombardo and Statius elsewhere in the *Comedy,* and he has realigned biology and astrology in an explanation of human nature, which for Dante, as for his master Aristotle and for Aquinas, is the elemental and free building block of a true political order.

NOTES

This *Lectura Dantis* is dedicated to the memory of my teacher, Thomas Goddard Bergin, and to my fellow student under *il maestro,* William D. Paden, Jr.

A slightly different version of this essay is to appear in the forthcoming *Lectura Dantis Californiana,* edited by Allen Mandelbaum and published by the University of California Press. I acknowledge the kind permission of the University of California Press for its prepublication here.

1. The text of the *Comedy* used here is the Petrocchi edition in Charles S. Singleton, ed., *The Divine Comedy,* 6 vols. (Princeton, New Jersey: Princeton University Press, 1970–1975). For a brief characterization of the tradition of commentary on the canto, see G. Mavaro and S. A. Costa, eds., *Motivi e Personaggi della Divina Commedia* (Firenze, 1968), pp. 547–548. Most of the scholarly discussion of *Paradiso* VIII is located in various *lectura Dantis.*

Lectura Dantis: Luigi Rocca, *Il canto* VIII *del Paradiso* (Firenze, 1903); Vittorio Vaturi, *Il canto* VIII *del Paradiso* (Firenze, 1923); André Pézard, "Vénus et Dante," *Revue des langues Romanes,* LXX (1949/1950), pp. 89–118; 199–225 (rpt. in Pézard, *Dans le sillage de Dante* [Paris, 1975], pp. 37–38); Pézard, *Il canto* VIII *del Paradiso* (Bologna, 1953; expanded version published as "Charles Martel au ciel de Vénus," in Vittorio Vettori, ed., *Lectura Dantis Internazionale,* Vol. III, *Letture del 'Paradiso'* [Milano, 1970], pp. 71–140); Aldo Vallone, "Lectura del canto VIII del Paradiso," *Humanitas,* XIV (1959), pp. 277–295 (rpt. in Vallone, *La critica dantesca nel Settecento ed altri saggi danteschi* [Firenze, 1961], pp. 119–136); Giovanni Fallani, *Il canto* VIII *del Paradiso* (Torino, 1964), in part rpt. in Fallani, *Dante Autobiografico* (Napoli, 1975), pp. 109–116; Carlo Muscetta, *Il Canto* VIII *del Paradiso* (Firenze, 1966); Vincenzo Cioffari, "Interpretazione del canto VIII del *Paradiso,*" *L'Alighieri,* XIII (1972), pp. 3–17 (English trans. "Lectura Dantis: *Paradiso* VIII," *Dante Studies,* XC [1972], pp. 93–108); Salvatore Accardo, "Il canto VIII del Paradiso," in *Nuove Letture Dantesche,* Vol. VI (Firenze, 1973), pp. 27–44 (rpt. in Accardo, *Capitoli Danteschi* [Roma, 1976], pp. 107–124); Rachel Jacoff, "The Post Palinodic Smile: *Paradiso* VIII and IX," *Dante Studies,* XCVIII (1980), pp. 111–122; Ettore Paratore, "Il canto VIII del Paradiso," *L'Alighieri,* XXVI (1985), pp. 33–52.

There is an extensive list of readings in Dante Alighieri, *La Divina Commedia,* Vol. III, *Paradiso,* ed. Aldo Vallone and Luigi Scorrano (Napoli, 1986), p. 141.

2. On the complex character of Venus, see Earl G. Schreiber, "Venus in the Medieval Mythographic Tradition," *Journal of English and Germanic Philology,* LXXIV (1975), pp. 519–535, and George D. Economou, "The Two Venuses and Courtly Love," in George D. Economou and Joan M. Ferrante, eds., *In Pursuit of Perfection: Courtly Love in Medieval Literature* (Port Washington, N.Y., 1975), pp. 17–50. There is an excellent example of the use of these aspects of Venus in art in Jack M. Greenstein, "The Vision of Peace: meaning and representation in Ambrogio Lorenzetti's *Sala della Pace* cityscapes," *Art History,* XI (1988), pp. 492–510.

On Venus in the *Convivio* and elsewhere in Dante, from the reference in *Convivio* II, see the important essay by Giuseppe Mazzotta, "The Light of Venus and the Poetry of Dante," in *Magister Regis: Studies in Honor of Robert Earl Kaske,* ed. Arthur Groos with Emerson Brown, Jr., Thomas D. Hill, Giuseppe Mazzotta, and Joseph S. Wittig (New York, 1986), 147–170.

3. On the vast topic of creation and generation in Dante and his readings, see the concise discussion by Patrick Boyde, *Dante Philomythes and Philosopher: Man in the Cosmos* (Cambridge: Cambridge University Press, 1981), Chs. 8–11, the last two chapters considering physical gestation in nature, including that of human beings. On the topic of astrology, however, Boyde should be supplemented by Richard Kay, "Astronomy and Astrology," in Giuseppe Di Scipio and Aldo Scaglione, eds., *The Divine Comedy and the Encyclopedia of the Arts and Sciences* (Amsterdam-Philadelphia: John Benjamins, 1988), pp. 147–162; and by John D. North, "Celestial Influence—the Major Premiss of Astrology," in Paola Zambelli, ed., *'Astrologi hallucinati:' Stars and the End of the World in Luther's Time* (Berlin-New York, 1986), pp. 45–100, esp. pp. 82-85; Valerie I. J. Flint, *The Rise of Magic in Early Medieval Europe* (Princeton, New Jersey: Princeton University Press, 1991); Richard Kay, *Dante's Christian Astrology* (forthcoming).

4. For the idea of the stages of human life in Dante, see Bruno Nardi, "L'arco della vita (Nota illustrativa al *Convivio*)," *Saggi di Filosofia Medievale,* 2nd ed. (Firenze, 1967), pp. 110–138, and in general Elizabeth Sears, *The Ages of Man: Medieval Interpretations of the Life Cycle* (Princeton, New Jersey: Princeton University Press, 1986).

On human gestation, see M. Anthony Hewson, *Giles of Rome and the Medieval Theory of Conception* (London: The Athlone Press, 1975), and for the medical astrology on the subject, Helen Rodnite Lemay, "The Stars and Human Sexuality: Some Medieval Scientific Views," *Isis,* LXXI (1980), 1272–1307, and idem, "Human Sexuality in Twelfth- through Fifteenth-Century Scientific Writings," in Vern L. Bullough and James Brundage, eds., *Sexual Practices and the Medieval Church* (Buffalo: Prometheus Books, 1982), pp. 187–205. For medicine generally, Nancy Siraisi, "Dante and the Art and Science of Medicine Reconsidered," in Di Scipio and Scaglione, *The Divine Comedy and the Encyclopedia of the Arts and Sciences,* pp. 223–245, and for matters of law, James A. Brundage, *Law, Sex and Christian Society in Medieval Europe* (Chicago: University of Chicago Press, 1987), esp. Ch. 9.

On the topic of ensoulment in Dante, the classic study is that of Bruno Nardi, "L'Origine dell'anima umana secondo Dante," in Nardi, *Studi di Filosofia Medievale* (Roma, 1960), 9–68.

5. *Commentum Bernardi Silvestris super Sex Libros Eneidos Virgilii,* ed. G. Riedel (Greifswald, 1924), 9, cited in Schreiber, "Venus in the Medieval Mythographic Tradition," 522.

6. On the historical Carlo Martello, see the comprehensive article by Raoul Manselli, "Carlo Martello," *Enciclopedia dantesca,* I, 841–843. The most detailed account in English of Angevin South Italy and Sicily remains that of Steven Runciman, *The Sicilian Vespers* (Cambridge: Cambridge University Press, 1958). More recent scholarship is summarized in Italian in Vol. III of the *Storia di Napoli, Napoli Angioina,* esp. chs. 2 and 3 (Napoli: Edizioni Scientifiche Italiane, 1969), and its cultural history in Francesco Sabatini, *Napoli Angioina. Cultura e Società* (Napoli: Edizioni Scientifiche Italiane, 1975); Vincenzo Mazzei, *Dante e i suoi amici nella Divina Commedia* (Milano, 1987), Ch. 9, "Carlo Martello (*Par.* VIII)," pp. 125–138. On Dante's attitude toward the Angevins see Paolo Brezzi, "Dante e Roberto d'Angio," in *Dante e l'Italia Meridionale. Atti del Convegno Nazionale di Studi danteschi a cura del Seminario di Studi danteschi di Caserta* (Firenze: Olschki, 1966),

and idem, "I cattivi Capetingi e Angioini," in Brezzi, *Letture dantesche di Argomento Storico-politico* (Napoli: Editrice Ferrari, 1983), pp. 47–66. The point of view of the Guelf alliance is excellently described in Norman Housley, *The Italian Crusades: The Papal-Angevin Alliance and the Crusades against Christian Lay Powers, 1254–1343* (Oxford, 1982).

7. The political theory worked into *Paradiso* VIII is integrated into the rest of Dante's political thought in Joan M. Ferrante, *The Political Vision of the Divine Comedy* (Princeton, New Jersey: Princeton University Press, 1984), esp. pp. 257–273. There is an important discussion of the place of love in thirteenth-century concepts of citizenship in Anthony Black, "The Individual and Society," in J. H. Burns, ed., *The Cambridge History of Medieval Political Thought* c. 350 – c. 1450 (Cambridge, 1988), pp. 588–606, at 597. On citizenship generally, see Peter N. Riesenberg, "Civism and Roman Law in Fourteenth-Century Italian Society," in David Herlihy, Robert S. Lopez, and Vsevolod Slessarev, eds., *Economy, Society and Government in Medieval Italy: Essays in Memory of Roger L. Reynolds* (Kent, Ohio: Kent State University Press, 1969), pp. 237–254.

8. *Questio de aque et terra*, ed. Francesco Mazzoni, in Dante Alighieri, *Opere Minori,* II (Milano-Napoli: Ricciardi, 1979), 758–760.

9. On the "theology" of love in Dante, with some discussion of the present canto, see Kenelm Foster, O.P., "Dante and Eros," in his *The Two Dantes and Other Studies* (Berkeley and Los Angeles: The University of California Press, 1977), pp. 37–55. Frank B. Ordiway has recently argued that the heavens of the Moon, Mercury, and Venus are ordered according to the principle of the marred, "earth-tainted" forms of the three theological virtues: faith, hope, and charity: Frank B. Ordiway, "In the Earth's Shadow: The Theological Virtues Marred," *Dante Studies,* C (1982), pp. 77–92.

10. There is a useful consideration of the medieval tradition of clothing metaphors, à propos *Paradiso* VIII, in Manfred Bambeck, "Un corollario voglio che t'ammanti (*Par.* VIII , 136–138)," in Bambeck, *Studien zu Dantes "Paradiso"* (Wiesbaden, 1979), pp. 39–43.

XV

The Shadowy, Violent Perimeter: Dante Enters Florentine Political Life

Dante is far better known as a philosopher and poet of politics than as a political figure himself. Yet at least seven important—and, as it turned out, highly formative—years of his life were spent in part, at least, in active participation in the governmental affairs of Florence, during much of this period as holder of elective and appointive offices. Most of our knowledge of this and every other phase of the *vita di Dante* rests upon the extensive archival and documentary research of the past century and a half. This enterprise has produced and is recorded in the histories of Davidsohn and Ottokar, the great enterprise of publication of the sources of Florentine history and the Dante life-records culminating in the *Codice Diplomatico Dantesco* of Renato Piattoli, the *Vita e tempi* of Nicola Zingarelli, and in the biographies by Paget Toynbee, Michele Barbi and Giorgio Petrocchi. It has informed such elegant analyses as Peter Herde's *Dante als florentiner Politiker*, and the two excellent recent essays in the *Cambridge Companion to Dante*—those by Giuseppe Mazzotta and John Najemy—which have intelligently summed up and advanced our knowledge of the life. One of them, Mazzotta's, has also given me the first part—and the governing theme—of the title of this essay.[1]

Mazzotta's terms are at first surprising, even arresting, but on reflection perfectly appropriate. In the mid-1290s Florentine political life was indeed shadowy—there were forces at work in it that are not clearly identified in or accounted for by any of the constitutional forms that the government took in those years; indeed violent—as Book I and the opening pages of Book II of Dino Compagni's *Cronica* and the sentences passed on

the exiled White Guelfs in 1302 amply attest; and indeed it was a perimeter—on the edges of Angevin, imperial, papal, and Valois affairs, and personally peripheral: prior and later ambassador though he briefly became, it is not at all clear that Dante was ever at the center of power during the most crucial episodes of Florentine life in a political career that lasted (even if one counts Dante's "official" service to the exiled White Guelfs, as I am inclined to do, and one further detail between 1302 and 1315 with which I will conclude), a bit more than seven years, but overall less than a decade.

How did this part of Dante's life look to those who first undertook to describe it? Later studies of the poet's *vita* have all greatly improved upon the work of the writer who originated them. Boccaccio is little help here, because although he bitterly criticized Dante's pursuit of *vani onori*, he nevertheless must have Dante at the very center, not at all on the periphery of Florentine government. He introduced the *Trattatello* with the anecdote of Solon's two legs of a commonwealth and berated the injustice with which Florentines treated Dante. But when he came to Dante's actual entry into political life, he treated it as he did Dante's marriage—an unfortunate and unpropitious thing for a philosopher and poet to do, but explainable by Dante's all too human thirst for honor and glory. And then—perhaps with somewhat more justification from the archives than his earlier remarks had—he elevates Dante into the role of the only political wise man in the Florentine government:

> Never an embassy was heard nor answered, never a law enacted nor cancelled, never a peace made, never a war undertaken, and in brief never a deliberation of any weight conducted, till he first had given his opinion thereon.[2]

Although there are reasonable grounds in the archives to confirm Dante's energetic participation in Florentine government between 1295 and 1301, these are probably not the basis for Boccaccio's remarks on the subject. Boccaccio rather wants some dramatic struggle troubling his hero. Employing all his wit, and every art and every study on their behalf, Boccaccio's Dante finds the Florentines intractable, proposes to withdraw from public life, but is held fast to it by his own longing for splendor, the favor of the people, the persuasions of his elders, and the conviction that he could do more good as a holder of power than as a private person. And he ends as leader of the mission to Rome and as the noblest of the exiles.

The *Trattatello* is not, on the whole, a particularly encouraging document for historical inquiry.[3]

Leonardo Bruni, on the other hand, will have none of the themes of Boccaccio's *Vita*: love, sighs, burning tears, and trivial matters.[4] Bruni's Dante is the brave soldier who left a (now lost) letter about and a drawing of the battle-plan for Campaldino (as Dante himself and Bruni indicate, Dante was both a scribe with an excellent script and a far better than average artist), the socializing, non-reclusive scholar who takes a wife, and the citizen "much employed by the commonwealth" and in 1300 elected, not chosen by lot (as Bruni says Dante would be in Bruni's own day), to the priorate.[5] Bruni's Dante in fact sounds very much like Hans Baron's Bruni, except for what Bruni considers Dante's regrettable lack of republican sentiments.[6]

But doing everything correctly and virtuously did not lead to good fortune. Bruni quotes another lost letter:

> All my ill and troubles had their cause and origin in the unfortunate meetings during my term as prior, of which although for my prudence I was not worthy nonetheless for my good faith and my age I was not unworthy, since ten years had passed since the battle of Campaldino, in which the Ghibelline party was almost entirely killed and undone; I went there not a boy in arms and there I experienced much fear and finally great joy, over the various developments of the battle.[7]

This certainly sounds authentic—Dante's Priorate, from June 15 to August 15, 1300, occurred historically just two or three months after the great events later described in the *Commedia*, in Holy Week, 1300. Might Dante's dating of the events in the *Commedia* thus be in some sense a retroactive validation of his political activities in 1300-1301? There is certainly enough else in the poem that constantly circles back to the historical Dante-life.[8]

Bruni knew why the election was ill-omened—the violent factionalism that destroyed the commonwealth in favor of private interests instrumentalizing state power and resources for their own narrow ends. Both he and Compagni knew well what he termed the *gara d'uffici*, heightened by the *inane partium studium*.[9] Then came the accusations of undue partisanship against Dante—both for suggesting the banishment of the leaders of the factions during the priorate of 1300 and later for the release of some of the banished leaders, the looting of his house, and the retroactive laws that resulted in criminal charges leading first to his own exile, then to that of

his sons, and finally the conviction for contumacy, and the sentence of death.[10] Then the political career continues, at first in Gargonza and Mugello with some of the other White exiles, among whom Dante was elected one of the twelve councillors and briefly chancellor of the *Universitas partis Alborum*, the Florentine government in exile (*Epistle* I)—yet other "public" offices, and impressive ones at that, although Dante later termed this company *malvagia e scempia* (*Par.* XVII, 62)—then the failed assault on Florence itself from Lastra, on 20 July 1304, the opening of Dante's private negotiations with the Florentine government and individual citizens (*Epistle* IX), finally interrupted by his association with Henry VII and the publication of the *Letter to the Florentines* (*Epistle* VI; which Bruni criticizes as improper on Dante's part and therefore justification of his continuing exile), and further negotiations for return and their repeated failure.[11] At some point in this sequence of events, Dante perforce ended his career as a political figure and became instead a political philosopher.[12] To fix the ills of Florence, the world had to be fixed. But that is the matter of another discussion, as are the story of Dante's invitation to Milan to work magic on an image of the pope, and Filippo Villani's account of Dante's last political role—as Guido da Polenta's frustrated ambassador who terrified the Venetians by the prospect of his eloquence.

Bruni knew all this because he had seen official Florentine documents and some of Dante's own documents, many now lost—he had been and was to be again after all, the chancellor himself. And he had already written the *Florentine History*.[13] And he had been visited by Dante's great-grandson, also named Leonardo, to whom he showed Dante's house and the scenes of his life, for young Leonardo and the rest of the family knew little of them, having long resided outside Florence in Verona. The personal connection, the account of documents of both Dante and the city, and the guided tour all tend to authorize Bruni's *Vita* over that of Boccaccio, as well as over the short account of the life in Giovanni Villani's *Cronica*, which itself has a few echoes in Bruni's own account.[14]

II

Thus far, Dante's entry into political life and what his first biographers subsequently made of it. It is time to look at the person and the process a little more closely.

The Shadowy, Violent Perimeter: Dante Enters Florentine Political Life

In the letter-fragment quoted by Bruni, Dante justified his eligibility for election to the Priorate by virtue of his "good faith and age" and by virtue of his experience at Campaldino. By good faith, we can perhaps expand a little to locate him in that segment of the *popolo* that was of old and respectable family, but certainly not of magnate status—certainly not in the class of the great *barone*, Corso Donati—and sufficiently prosperous to be trusted with public office, particularly during that segment of the 1290s when anti-magnate feeling was running high and successfully. Bruni tells us that although Dante came from an old and distinguished Florentine family (although he was its first member to be elected to the priorate), it was not one that possessed great wealth, nor yet was it poor, but "he had a middling patrimony that permitted him to live honorably."[15] Both Zingarelli and Petrocchi point out several moments of personal financial crisis in the later 1290s.[16] Dante had once been taunted by Forese Donati for his poverty and for unavenged insults to his father, who had died in 1283 (although the context of poetic invective in which these insults took place, probably in the period 1293-1295, must be considered in terms of a personal relationship between Dante and Forese and the conventions of literary flyting).[17] It seems to be something like an idealization of his own kind and level of material circumstances that Dante holds up for praise in the *buon tempo antico* of Cacciaguida's twelfth-century Florence.[18]

Dante was the eldest son of his father's first marriage. He married in 1285 (although his wife brought only a small dowry of 200 *libre*, and the status of Gemma Donati seems approximately to parallel that of Dante himself). He was the father of a young family, and he owned some property—half of Bruni's "very good house"—in fact, a rather modest house—in Florence, and other properties in Camerata, the Piacentina, and in Piano di Ripoli.[19] And there was the later confiscated property at Sant'Ambrogio.[20] Bruni locates the house in Florence (as does Villani) in the *sesto* of Porta San Piero in the parish of San Martino del Vescovo and locates it by reference to the nearby houses of the Sacchetti, Donati, and the Giuochi. Dante was thirty when he first entered political life, just turned thirty-five when elected Prior, also "*nel mezzo del cammin. . . .*"

Dante's association of his electoral qualifications with his experience at Campaldino in 1289 is perhaps more interesting than his modest, but respectable family and material qualifications. Both Bruni and the letter-fragment make much of it. Dante's one ancestor encountered or mentioned

in the *Commedia* was a knight, Cacciaguida. His uncle Brunetto was one of the *pediti del Carrocio* in 1260.[21] Both comments indicate that Dante did not consider himself—and apparently was not considered by others—as that kind of citizen criticized by Compagni as having played only a small part in the battle of Campaldino.[22] Dante fought, as both Bruni and Carol Lansing have pointed out, in the *feditori*, the picked cavalry most exposed to the enemy and led by Vieri de' Cerchi.[23] Dante's role at Campaldino also necessitates a biographical point about the poet's life in the 1280s—he must have spent some time training for mounted combat. No one fought a cavalry battle in the late thirteenth century without some earlier training. The prestige of *feditori* service at Campaldino under Vieri de' Cerchi proved long lasting and was certainly remembered into the mid-1290s. Vieri de' Cerchi's son (and Dante's companion in arms at Campaldino) Giano was the head of the citizens' delegation that greeted Carlo Martello in March of 1294 (*Par.* VIII).[24] Dante also fought in one of the inconsequential later wars against Pisa, and he was at least present at the taking of the castle at Caprona.[25] The victors of Campaldino who were not unregenerate *magnati* may well have appealed to the government of the *popolo* and the electorate because they had acquired military prestige close to that of the magnate heroes like Corso Donati. The *popolo* perhaps could not entirely do without such figures if it was to maintain its authority in a city containing *magnati* who continually scorned its non-noble pretensions, not least because of their own military skills.[26] Besides, there is considerable evidence that admiring memories even of the older generation of Ghibelline warriors were circulating in Florence at the time, and that Dante's Farinata (*Inf.* X) was not as unique as he might otherwise seem. Tegghiaio di Aldobrandi (*Inf.* XVI) was also remembered by Dante for his heroism.[27] Dante's ancient family, its traditions of military honor, and his own distinguished military experience are more than adequate to explain the chivalric dimension of much of his thought.

The political history of the Alighieri family is not as easily traceable as is that of greater Florentine families during the period of Guelf rule. Indeed, Dante's father seems to have been entirely apolitical. An Aligheri of Porta San Piero is listed as a member of the Council in 1278, and another in the Council of 1284.[28] Giovanni Villani's identification of Dante by *sesto* (Porta San Piero) and *parrocchia* (San Martino al Vescovo—Villani's own neighborhood: "*Questo Dante fue onorevole e antico cittadino di Firenze di Porta San Piero, e nostro vicino . . .*") may also be a political desig-

nation, or at least a designation that serves to locate Dante in terms of Florentine political geography.[29] Porta San Piero was also the *sesto* of Giano della Bella, Vieri de' Cerchi, and Corso Donati. It was the cockpit of Florentine politics. Bruni also makes much of Dante's connections with other Alighieri (in fact, the name in Dante's lifetime seems to have been Alaghieri; the form Alighieri seems to date only from Boccaccio) and with the more prominent Elisei.[30] Dante was only moderately materially well-off, related to noble folk more prosperous than himself, an established family man from an old and respectable line, a well-known poet (enjoying the friendship of Guido Cavalcanti, the literary relationships with Forese Donati and others, and the public reception of Carlo Martello in March, 1294), a protege of Brunetto Latini, who died in 1294, and a war-hero. These were his qualifications for political office.

From 1292 he had been reading Boethius and Cicero (*Conv.* II.xii.1-7), two writers who had had their own respectable political careers and opinions about them, attending the Mendicant *scuole* and the *disputazioni* of the philosophers (*Conv.* II.xii.7), constructing his own "Lady Philosophy," and writing the *Fiore*, *Il Detto*, and a number of philosophical poems. At least one of these, *Le dolci rime d'Amor*, introduces the topic of true nobility, a theme not entirely esoteric in the Florence of the 1290s, the Florence of the Ordinances of Justice of 1293, of Giano della Bella, and of Dino Compagni.[31] Among other poems of the period are the *rime petrose*, which Durling and Martinez date to 1296-1297.[32] 1294 also witnessed the visit of Carlo Martello to Florence, as well as both the election and the resignation of Celestine V and the subsequent election of Boniface VIII. These were events whose echoes in the letters, the *Commedia*, and the *Monarchia* all indicate a considerable impact on Dante, not only subsequently to his exile, but certainly at the time they occurred. Dante had clearly been thinking politics well before he enrolled in the *Arte dei Medici e degli Speziali*, probably in July of 1295, and was elected to the special council of the *Capitano del Popolo* in November, 1295.[33]

III

At the end of the thirteenth century Florence was a city developing at a pace that was virtually off the scale of contemporary European urbanization. Its immense size within the new walls, its recent population growth, scale of consumption, industrial and financial enterprise, and its

disparities of wealth and poverty provided both work and confusion for its government. Perhaps most striking is the material plasticity of the city. In Dante's lifetime, Florence continuously transformed its fabric and its geography. Richard Goldthwaite and Guido Pampaloni speak of its vast urban "program," the building and rebuilding of bridges, churches—including Santa Reparata, public buildings, and private palaces. Streets were straightened and widened. In 1297 the city even began construction of a heavily capital-intensive project unique in Europe—the first official municipal prison, Le Stinche.[34] The city cannot have looked the same from one year to the next.[35] And the towers of the *magnati* sometimes came down too, as in the case of the houses of the Galli in Por Santa Maria in 1293. The Florentine government had far more to attend to than the political antagonisms and instability of its most powerful and restless citizens, although as it turned out these alone (with the intervention of Boniface VIII and his Valois allies) were quite enough to subvert the government of the guilds, if not the city, that Dante came to serve.

The government of Florence at the time that Dante entered political life had been shaped in the 1280s, and especially by the Ordinances of Justice in 1293.[36] It consisted of an alien *podestà* who had two councils—one general with three hundred members, one special with ninety—a *capitano del popolo* who also had two councils—a general one of one hundred and fifty members and a special council of thirty-six—and a council of one hundred. The city had been governed by the priors of the guilds since 1282. Its security was supervised by a Standard-bearer of Justice, an office created by the Ordinances. All of the councils, the office of Standard-bearer, and the priorate were elective, and changing methods of electoral procedures occupied much of the time and political effort of the government during the 1280s and 1290s, particularly since elections had to be so frequent. The bishop of Florence was not politically prominent, although ecclesiastical wealth and property in the city and countryside was contended over by a number of political actors during Dante's lifetime, perhaps strengthening the poet's inclination to denounce ecclesiastical avarice both severely and often.[37]

But the year 1295 also saw the beginning of the demise of the vigorous government of the *popolo* that had created the Ordinances of Justice in 1293, as well as the exile of Giano della Bella, who had urged and engineered their rigorous enforcement, especially against the *magnati*, and an attempt on the part of the *magnati* to overturn the Ordinances. As a consequence, both

Dante and Dino Compagni state, the popular government rallied, but later weakened in the face of the increasing, ferocious, and eventually all-consuming factional divisions among the *magnati*. 1295 was hardly the most auspicious time for a learned, thoughtful, and civic-minded poet to enter Florentine political life.

Dante's political activities, especially the offices he held, are well-recorded between 1295 and 1298, but the gap in the records of the *Consulte* from 1298 to 1301 would, if filled, probably yield still others.[38] Dante took his political work seriously, and others seem to have taken him seriously.

Which others? Dante was elected to the council of thirty-six remarkably quickly following upon his enrollment in the guild at a time when he was entirely lacking in earlier political experience. This council seems to have had the main concern of electoral procedures concerning the priorate, virtually holding in its hands the constitution of Florence. It was thus particularly important at the time Dante was elected to it. It is not beyond possibility that Dante's candidacy appealed to those who wished the popular form of government to continue but realized that the position of Giano della Bella (and Dino Compagni) could not be sustained in that effort. Thus, Dante might have seemed to be a candidate with good *popolo* credentials, not unacceptable initially, at least, to some of the *magnati*, and not identified with the now-discredited position of Giano.

There is some support for such a view in two silences—or virtual silences. Dino Compagni mentions Dante only once, in his list of those condemned in 1302, when not mentioning Dante would not have been possible (II.25).[39] Dante in turn does not mention Dino or the Ordinances, nor does he mention Giano by name.[40] It would seem that Dante was clearly not a supporter of Giano, although still a supporter of the *popolo*. Surely not yet a White Guelf, possibly only a sympathizer of the Cerchi group, Dante had not yet shaped his contempt for the self-destruction and corruptibility of the popular government nor for the boundless violence of the *magnati*. The years 1295-1302 were important ones for shaping both Dante's later retrospective interpretation of Florentine politics and his later—perhaps initially desperate—turning to the figure of the ideal emperor.

But seven years is a long time. The power of Dante's post-exilic recollections and the direction in which they turned his thought are so compelling—in the letters, the *Monarchia*, and especially in the sixth canto of each of the three *cantiche* of the *Commedia*, that it is difficult to separate

them from the moment in 1295 when he first entered political life, when presumably none of the later anger and contempt had yet developed. *Inferno* VI, for example, reveals a Dante in 1300, a few months before his priorate, who still thought that Farinata, Tegghiaio, Jacopo Rusticucci, Arrigo and Mosca *fuor sì degni* and among *li altri ch'a ben far puoser li 'ngegni* (vv. 79-81). Ciacco bitterly disabuses the pilgrim. There are indeed two just men in Florence—here unnamed (but was one of them Dante?)—but those about whom Dante asks are condemned to worse punishments than Ciacco himself. Florentine political life, from the perspective of *Inferno* VI, had begun to unravel long before Dante entered it. Here, at the introduction of the great Florentine theme in the *Commedia*, the pilgrim expresses both civic and chivalric idealism—even ingenuousness—and he receives his answer from the most sordid of sinners, in comparison with whom no one in Hell suffers a more shameful punishment.[41] The pilgrim's ideal of Florentine chivalry is disabused by the politics of brutishness. There can be no sharper contrast between Dante's political enthusiasm in 1295, perhaps even in early 1300 (but could he still have been that ingenuous by the Spring of 1300?), and the reflections that culminate in that devastating scene in *Inferno* VI.

IV

Questo Dante. . . . Was he already in 1295, as Villani describes him, "*alquanto presuntuoso e schifo e isdegnoso, e quasi a guisa di filosafo mal grazioso non bene sapea conversare co' laici*"?[42] These are hardly political virtues, but the varied languages of the *Rime* suggest that Dante had many voices and that Villani's characterization may have come from later in Dante's life, but we cannot be certain. Villani knew Dante, as did Dino, and his account and estimation of the life are thorough, generally accurate, and still profoundly moving. The references to his political participation in the *Consulte* and the *Codice diplomatico* are too brief to answer the question.

The political career can be briefly summed up:

- On 6 July 1295, Dante may have spoken at the general Council of the Comune in favor of modifying the Ordinances of Justice.[43]
- Sometime in July, 1295, Dante matriculated in the *arte* of the *Medici e Speziali*.[44]

- From 1 November 1295 to 30 April 1296, Dante served on the special council of the *Capitano*. No instances of his speaking are recorded.[45]
- On 14 December 1295, Dante is recorded as having spoken, not as an official, but as a *sapiens et bonus vir*, to the Council of the Captain on the matter of electing the priorate.[46]
- From 1 May to 30 September 1296, Dante served on the Council of One Hundred.[47]
- On 5 June 1296, Dante spoke before the Council of One Hundred concerning the widening of the piazza of San Giovanni.[48]
- On 1 January 1297, Dante was probably elected to the Council of the Podestà.[49]
- In May, 1300, Dante served as an ambassador to San Gimignano.[50]
- From 16 June to 15 August 1300, Dante served as one of the six priors. During their priorate, the priors lived together, and their communication with others was restricted.[51]
- On 14 April 1301, Dante addressed the Council of the Captain concerning the electoral process for the priorate.[52]
- On 25 April 1301, Dante spoke on the widening of the Via San Procolo.[53]
- On 19 June 1301, Dante addressed the Council of the Captain opposing aid to Boniface VIII: "Let nothing be done in the matter of a subsidy for the pope".[54]
- On 13 September 1301, Dante spoke to the assembled Councils regarding electoral matters.[55]
- On 20 September 1301, Dante spoke in the Council of One Hundred on the matter of grain shipments from Bologna to Pisa.[56]
- On 28 September 1301, Dante addressed the Council of One Hundred, again on electoral matters.[57]
- In October, 1301, Dante was part of the embassy from Florence to Boniface VIII at Rome.[58]

Following his condemnations between 27 January and 10 March 1302, Dante joined the White exiles in Gargonza from January to March, 1302, and in Mugello from 8 June 1302. *Epistle* I, written in the name of all the White exiles to Cardinal Niccolò da Prato, seems to date from Arezzo in 1304, some few months before Dante's break with them. Among the exiles, Dante held several elective offices, including that of Chancellor.[59]

And that is the political life, except, of course, for any records no longer in existence, especially for the period from July, 1298, to February, 1301. It is worth pointing out that part of Dante's political activity consisted of routine government business, but that another substantial part appears to have focused on the vexing question of electoral forms for the priorate, forms that remained problematic in Florence into the fourteenth century. Besides the growing interests of Boniface VIII (Florence had sent a contingent of troops to the siege of Palestrina in 1297, but by 1301 Dante was firmly opposed to further Florentine cooperation with the pope) and the increasing hostility between the Donati and Cerchi factions, which became the *Bianchi* and *Neri* around 1300, Dante's political career also witnessed the scandal over the *podestà* Monfiorito da Coderta in 1299. Throughout this career, Dante rose steadily to higher offices, not only to the priorate itself, but to the roles of emissary to San Gimignano and to Rome.

V

Dante's personal pilgrimage to Rome during the Jubilee Year probably took place in the Fall of 1300.[60] Documents in the *Codice diplomatico* indicate his concerns with other affairs in this period, chiefly financial. These events, with the literary works more or less datable to the years 1295-1304, are all that we know and are likely to know of the poet's life during his political career. The greatest works lie in the future: the *De vulgari eloquentia* around 1302-1304, some of the commentaries, at least, and probably the idea of the *Convivio* a few years later (1304-1308), the *Commedia*, and the *De Monarchia*. Dante had begun with poetry, and later learned philosophy, and with poetry and philosophy he would end. The political years had ultimately been years of failure, not so much the particular personal failure of Dante and his political allies, but the failure of the governments of those years to prepare the *Bianchi* in the crucial months of the autumn of 1301 to resist the forces of Boniface VIII, Charles of Valois, and the returning *Neri*. The entry of Charles of Valois

and the *Neri* on 1 November 1301 sealed the fates of any *Bianchi* who had recently held public office or who had joined the initially voluntary exiles outside of Florence.

The *Neri*, now controlling the government of Florence as they had failed to do several times earlier, instituted the two last political roles of Dante—that of official among the exiled *Bianchi* and the final role, that of political criminal. Dante's political record moves from the *Liber Fabarum* to the *Libro del Chiodo*.

"All my woes and all my misfortunes had their cause and origin in my ill-omened election to the Priorate." So says the letter quoted by Bruni.[61] And indeed it seems to be to the period of Dante's priorate that the criminal charges of 27 January 1302 were aimed. Dante was charged *in absentia* with barratry, extortion, and resistance to Boniface VIII. The citation begins by stating that these offenses were committed while Dante (and those condemned with him) were priors or before or after their terms of office.[62] The last charge may derive from his remarks to the Council of the Captain on 19 June 1301, urging the discontinuance of financial aid to the pope, although they may equally refer to some unrecorded actions or words of his during the priorate. The first two charges are less clear. Starn has pointed out that some of them may derive from Dante's appointment to supervise the widening of the Via San Procolo.[63] For others there is simply no available information. Dante was charged with extortion, "by tacit promises or by tampering with public documents."[64] They were also charged with corrupting the election of new priors, accepting money for making appointments to civic office, the illegal appropriation of public funds, the illegal acceptance of money in negotiations for public works, the use of fraud and extortion to suborn resistance to the pope and Charles of Valois, and the plot to use public office in order to expel the Black Guelfs from Pistoia and to detatch Pistoia from its union with Florence. Dante was sentenced to two years of exile, a fine, and permanent exclusion from public office.

Not quite two months later, on 10 March 1302, Dante was sentenced to be burned to death, having failed to appear before his judges, thereby rendering himself contumacious. Then Florence began to feel the sting of Dante's pen, first with the letter to Cardinal Niccolò da Prato (*Epistle* I). On 31 March 1311, Dante dated *Epistle* VI to the Florentines, the letter that Bruni so bitterly regretted. And the pen stung. Five months later, on

2 September 1311, the Florentine government issued a partial amnesty to some of the exiles, but specifically excluded Dante.[65]

At some point during the next two years, however, an offer of conditional amnesty was apparently made to Dante, since the letter to a friend in Florence (*Epistle* IX) indicates that not only were some people in Florence working on the poet's behalf, but that an offer had actually been made:

> that . . . I may receive pardon and be permitted to return forthwith, on condition that I pay a certain sum of money, and submit to the stigma of the oblation. . . .

The latter was the public humiliation of "offering" oneself to the public authorities, and performing a degrading civic penance as a sign of *infamia*.[66] Exactly how harsh the *oblatio* might have been, however, is a matter of some debate. There is some evidence of its occasional *pro forma* character, at least for lesser criminals. Nevertheless, the potential for humiliating punishments both to become grotesque and to carry substantial civil consequences remained real, as discussions of punishments in the fourteenth and fifteenth centuries indicate.[67] In the event, Dante refused the offer:

> Far be from a familiar of philosophy such a senseless act of abasement as to submit himself to be presented at the oblation, like a felon in bonds, as one Ciolo and other infamous wretches have done! Far be it from the preacher of justice, after suffering wrong, to pay of his money to those that wronged him, as though they had deserved well of him! . . . But if no . . . path [which does not derogate from the fame and honor of Dante] can be found, then I will enter Florence never.[68]

In October, 1315, a renewed death sentence included Dante's two sons.[69] On 6 November 1315, the death sentence against Dante and his two sons was reiterated.[70] The only possible return would be the projects for returning Dante's remains to the city, projects later undertaken without success by both Leonardo Bruni and Michelangelo. Dante entered Florence never.

The Florentine political career—in office, in exile, and as a political criminal—was over. But Dante was hardly disheartened:

> Can I not anywhere gaze upon the face of the sun and the stars? Can I not under any sky contemplate the most precious truths, without I first return to Florence, disgraced, nay dishonored, in the eyes of my fellow citizens? Assuredly, bread will not fail me!

Indeed, bread did not fail him. But Romeo, another political exile, found that it sometimes had to be begged for. And Cacciaguida warned that it

would taste salty.[71] And Cacciaguida also warned that the steps to other men's houses were very steep.

NOTES

1. Robert Davidsohn, *Geschichte von Florenz*, 4 vols. (Berlin: Mittler, 1896-1925); Nicola Ottokar, *Il comune di Firenze alla fine del Dugento*, 2nd ed., E. Sestan (Torino: Einaudi, 1962); Paget Toynbee, *Dante Alighieri: His Life and Works*, rpt. of 4th ed., with an Introduction, Notes, and Bibliography by Charles S. Singleton (New York: Harper & Row, 1965); Michele Barbi, *Vita di Dante* (Firenze: Sansoni, 1961); Giorgio Petrocchi, "Biografia: attività politica e letteraria," *Enciclopedia Dantesca* (= *ED*), VI (Roma: Istituto della Enciclopedia Italiana, 1978), 1-53; idem, *Vita di Dante* (Bari: Laterza, 1986); Giuseppe Mazzotta, "Life of Dante," and John Najemy, "Dante and Florence," in *The Cambridge Companion to Dante*, ed. Rachel Jacoff (Cambridge: Cambridge University Press, 1993), pp. 1-13 and pp. 80-99. Mazzotta's phrase in my title is on page 4.

The most recent survey of Dante's Florence is that of Giovanni Cherubini, "La Firenze di Dante e di Giovanni Villani," in Cherubini, *Scritti toscani. L'urbanesimo medievale e la mezzadria* (Firenze: Salimbeni, 1991), 35-51. On the political transformations of the period 1260-1300, the best surveys are Sergio Raveggi, Massimo Tarassi, Daniela Medici, Patrizia Parenti, *Ghibellini, Guelfi e popolo grasso: I detentori del potere politico a Firenze nella seconda metà del Dugento* (Firenze: La Nuova Italia, 1978), and Massimo Tarassi, "Le famiglie di parte guelfa nella classe dirigente della città di Firenze durante il XIII secolo," in *I ceti dirigenti dell'età comunale nei secoli XII e XIII*, Comitato di studi sulla storia dei ceti dirigenti in Toscana, Atti del II Convegno: Firenze, 14-15 dicembre 1979 (Pisa: Pacini, 1982), 301-321. Also useful are Giovanni Fallani, *Dante autobiografico* (Napoli: Società Editrice Napoletana, 1975), and Jeremy Catto, "Florence, Tuscany and the World of Dante," in *The World of Dante: Essays on Dante and His Times*, ed. Cecil Grayson (Oxford: Clarendon Press, 1980), pp. 1-17.

There is a brief account of the history of the publication of the sources for Dante's life and Florentine politics and society in the introduction to Renato Piattoli, ed., *Codice diplomatico dantesco* (= CD) (Firenze: Gonnelli, 1950).

Peter Herde, *Dante als florentiner Politiker* (Wiesbaden: Steiner, 1976); Giorgio Petrocchi, *Politica e letteratura nella vita giovanile di Dante* (Roma: ELIA, 1974), 119-138 (later reworked into the *Vita di Dante*). Nicola Zingarelli, *La Vita, i tempi e le opere di Dante*, Storia Letteraria d'Italia, Vol. III, 3rd ed. (Milano: Vallardi, 1931).

2. Trans. in Philip Wicksteed, *The Early Lives of Dante* (London: Alexander Moring, 1904). All Boccaccio citations are from this translation. On other editions and translations of Boccaccio's *Trattatello*, see note 3.

3. Although the *codice diplomatico* does indeed bear out the fact that once Dante entered Florentine political life, he seems to have assumed a prominent position. This is the reading of most of the Dante-historians in Italy, as well as Haller, Schneider, and Herde, *Dante als florentiner Politiker*.

Boccaccio's text has been most recently edited by Paolo Baldan, *Vita di Dante di Giovanni Boccaccio* (Bergamo: Moretti & Vitali, 1991). The most recent English translation is that of Vincenzo Zin Bollettino: Giovanni Boccaccio, *The Life of Dante (Trattatello in Laude di Dante)* (New York: Garland, 1990). Bollettino translates the text from Pier Giorgio Ricci, *Trattatello in laude di Dante*, in Vol. III of *Tutte le opere di Giovanni Boccaccio* (Verona: Mondadori, 1965).

4. Leonardo Bruni Aretino, *Humanistisch-philosophische Schriften*, ed. Hans Baron (Leipzig: Teubner, 1928; rpt. Wiesbaden, 1969). The best English translation is that of Alan Nagel in *The Humanism of Leonardo Bruni: Selected Texts*, trans. and ed., Gordon Griffiths, James Hankins, and

David Thompson (Binghamton, New York: Medieval & Renaissance Texts & Studies, 1987), 85-95. Nagel's translation is cited here. There is a convenient old collection of relevant texts, chiefly from Boccaccio, in Oddone Zenatti, *Dante e Firenze: Prose antiche* (1902; new ed., Franco Cardini, Firenze: Sansoni, 1984).

5. On election by *imborsazione* (not by lot) and its rejection in 1292, see John Najemy, *Corporatism and Consensus in Florentine Electoral Politics, 1280-1400* (Chapel Hill: University of North Carolina Press, 1982), 30-42.

6. See now Paolo Viti, *Leonardo Bruni e Firenze: Studi sulle lettere pubbliche e private* (Roma: Bulzoni, 1992), esp. 78-82, 343-346, with extensive references. There is also a brief discussion in Catto, "Florence, Tuscany, and the World of Dante," p. 3. Dante himself termed this period in his life one of *cura familiare e civile* (*Conv*. I.i.4). There is an excellent discussion of Bruni's Dante in *The Humanism of Leonardo Bruni*, especially in the context of the *Dialogues* and the *History of Florence*.

7. Nagel, 88. Dante's reference to his own lack of prudence, may echo the third rubric of the Ordinances, which requires that those nominated to the priorate be "the most prudent, the best qualified, and the most law-abiding guild members of the city who are continuously engaged in the exercise of a profession or trade, and who are not knights." See Najemy, *Corporatism and Consensus*, 47. On the problem of continuous (i.e., active) engagement in a profession, see ibid., 47-49. In Dante's case in 1295, either the rule must have fallen into desuetude or Dante practiced the profession of his guild (which also included painters). The latter is extremely doubtful. Pasquale Villari (*The First Two Centuries of Florentine History*, trans. Linda Villari [4th ed. London: Unwin, 1908], 497) suggests that the *magnati*-dominated priorate elected on July 6, 1295 eliminated the requirement of continuous practice of the guild's art, basing his assumption on Villani, VIII.12. Cf. Herde, *Dante als florentiner Politiker*, 28, and Gaetano Salvemini, *Magnati e popolani in Firenze dal 1280 al 1295* (Firenze: Carnesecchi, 1899), 390.

8. A similar point is made by Najemy, "Dante and Florence," 80, 82. But Najemy also properly warns against reading too much of Dante's post-1302 characterization and criticism of Florence back into the pre-1302 period.

9. The prominence of factions in Dante's and Compagni's Florence, their destructive role in the commonwealth, and their competition for offices is outlined in Edward Peters, "*Pars, parte*: Dante and an Urban Contribution to Political Thought," in *The Medieval City* eds. Harry A. Miskimin, David Herlihy, and A. L. Udovitch (New Haven, Connecticut: Yale University Press, 1977), pp. 113-140, and in Daniel Bornstein's introduction to his translation of Compagni, cited in note 14. The best study of the impact of factionalism on the constitutional aspects of the electoral procedures of the priorate, with an extensive discussion of the sources, is that of John Najemy, *Corporatism and Consensus*, 1-78.

Compagni's only reference to Dante (II.25 as ambassador to Rome among those condemned in 1302), a figure who might be thought to deserve more prominence in the *Cronica*, may be attributable to Compagni's association with Giano della Bella, whom Dante does not mention, and Dante's association with Vieri de' Cerchi, who opposed Giano.

10. There is a reproduction of the formal sentence against Dante in Randolph Starn, *Contrary Commonwealth: The Theme of Exile in Medieval and Renaissance Italy* (Berkeley: University of California Press, 1982), Fig. 7, and an extensive discussion of Dante's exile, 60-85.

11. On the logic of the exile organization, see Starn, *Contrary Commonwealth*, 47: "The fact remains that the internal organization of companies in exile made no less (or more) historical sense than the structure of politics and society in the communal age." On Dante and republicanism, see Najemy, "Dante and Florence," 91-94, and Hans Baron, *The Crisis of the Early Italian Renaissance* (Princeton, New Jersey: Princeton University Press, 1966), 531-531.

12. Uberto Limentani, "Dante's Political Thought," in *The Mind of Dante*, ed. Uberto Limentani (Cambridge: Cambridge University Press, 1965), 113-137, at 116-117: "Given to speculation as he was [after 1304], he saw that his task was not so much to be active in practical affairs as to discover the ideal conditions for the happiness of humanity, to expound his system, and, by proving its truth, to persuade men to adopt it." The best recent survey of the later polit-

ical thought is that of Joan M. Ferrante, *The Political Vision of the "Divine Comedy"* (Princeton, New Jersey: Princeton University Press, 1984), esp. 44-75.

13. The imagined speech of Giano della Bella in Book IV has been translated in Renee Neu Watkins, *Humanism and Liberty: Writings on Freedom from Fifteenth-Century Florence* (Columbia: University of South Carolina Press, 1978), 69-73.

14. The relevant texts are conveniently translated in Wicksteed, *The Early Lives of Dante*. See also *Dino Compagni's Chronicle of Florence*, trans. Daniel E. Bornstein (Philadelphia: University of Pennsylvania Press, 1986).

15. *Vita di Dante*, 58: "Dante innanzi la cacciata sua di Firenze, con tutto che di grandissima richezza non fosse, niente di meno non fu povero, ma ebbe patrimonio mediocre e sufficiente a vivere onoratamente." On the family history, see Michele Barbi, "La condizione economica di Dante e della sua famiglia," in Barbi, *Problemi di critica dantesca*, Vol. I (Firenze: Sansoni, 1934), and Zingarelli, *Vita*, 54-87. For the documents, see Piattoli, CD docs. 1-46.

16. Petrocchi, *Politica e letteratura*, 135-136, particularly during 1297; Zingarelli, 390-391.

17. All citations to the *Rime* are to the edition of Kenelm Foster and Patrick Boyde, *Dante's Lyric Poetry*, 2 vols. (Oxford: Clarendon Press, 1967), by number. The exchanges with Forese are 72-74a.

18. See Charles T. Davis, "*Il Buon Tempo Antico* (The Good Old Time)," in Davis, *Dante's Italy and Other Essays* (Philadelphia: University of Pennsylvania Press, 1984), 71-93. Davis emphasizes the differences between Dante's locating the good old time of Florence in the virtuous, sober, and less wealthy twelfth century and his contemporaries' locating it later in a more prosperous period. Dante's emphasis on "austerity and a modest communal life" specifically criticizes the luxury and wealth that characterized the *magnati* of his own day. Such a sense surely lies behind Dante's famous argument about the nature of nobility. See Davis, "*Il Buon Tempo Antico*," 86-88, especially his remarks on 88, of which the discussion here is an expansion. Najemy ("Dante and Florence," 80) makes the point that since Dante was the first of his old family to be elected to the priorate, it may be assumed that the family lacked the prestige of the highest level of Florentine society.

19. On the "Casa di Dante," see the *codice diplomatico* edited by Emilio Frullani, *Della Casa di Dante. Relazione con documenti al Consiglio Generale del Comune di Firenze* (Firenze: Le Monnier, 1865), and Michele Barbi and Renato Piattoli, "La casa di Dante," *Studi danteschi*, XXII (1938). The strongest case for Dante's affections toward his wife and children has been made by Zingarelli, 370-371; cf. *Par.* XVII, 55-57.

20. Umberto Dorini, "Dei bene rurali confiscati a Dante," *Bulletino della Società Dantesca Italiana*, n.s. XII (1905), 34-39.

21. CD docs. 31, 32.

22. Compagni's comment, as well as the whole question of citizen combat, is considered in Carol Lansing, *The Florentine Magnates: Lineage and Faction in a Medieval Commune* (Princeton, New Jersey: Princeton University Press, 1991), 145-163. See also Daniel Waley, "The Army of the Florentine Republic from the Twelfth to the Fourteenth Century," in Nicolai Rubinstein, ed., *Florentine Studies: Politics and Society in Renaissance Florence* (Evanston, Illinois: Northwestern University Press, 1968), 70-108.

23. Lansing, *The Florentine Magnates*, 153. See also Daniel Waley, "The Army of the Florentine Republic."

24. Compagni, I.10. See Herbert L. Oerter, "Campaldino, 1289," *Speculum*, XLIII (1968), 429-450.

25. *Inf.* XXI, 94-96; *Inf.* XXII, 1-9.

26. Compagni, I.21.

27. Any echoes of Dante's martial adventures in 1289 in the *Commedia* have not been investigated. See Robert Hollander, "Dante and the Martial Epic," in *A Miscellany of Medieval and Renaissance Studies in Honor of Aldo S. Bernardo*, special issue of *Mediaevalia*, XII (1989), 67-92, and Jeffrey T. Schnapp, *The Transfiguration of History at the Center of Dante's "Paradise"* (Princeton, New Jersey: Princeton University Press, 1986). See also Gaetano Salvemini, *La dignità cavalleresca nel comune di Firenze e altri scritti* (rpt. Milano: Feltrinelli, 1972), Emilio Cristiani, "Sul valore politico

del cavalierato nella Firenze dei secoli XIII e XIV," *Studi medievali*, 3rd series, III (1962); Marvin B. Becker, *Florence in Transition*, Vol. I, *The Decline of the Commune* (Baltimore, Maryland: Johns Hopkins University Press, 1967), 11-15; Ruggero M. Ruggieri, *L'Umanesimo cavalleresco italiano: Da Dante all'Ariosto* (Napoli: Fratelli Conte, 1977), 50-101, and Lansing, *The Florentine Magnates*, 145-163.

28. Raveggi, et al., 162, 236.

29. Giovanni Villani, *Nuova Cronica*, ed. Giuseppe Porta, Vol. II (Parma: Guanda, 1990), X.136.

30. On the history of the name, see Herde, *Dante als florentiner Politiker*, p. 10, n. 34.

31. *Rime* 69 (*Conv.* IV). I agree here with George Holmes, *Dante* (New York: Hill and Wang, 1980), 22-23. For the political context of the debate on true nobility, see Lansing, *The Florentine Magnates*, 212-228, and *Conv.* III, *Mon.* II.iii.4, and *Par.* XVI. Bruno Maier, *Dante e la realtà politica del suo tempo tra Bonifacio VIII e Arrigo VII* (Milano, 1982), has a substantial comment on pp. 19-20; see also Davis, *Dante's Italy*, 178-186. On Dante's Cicero, see Davis, *Dante's Italy*, 173-178.

32. Robert M. Durling and Ronald L. Martinez, *Time and the Crystal: Studies in Dante's 'Rime Petrose'* (Berkeley: University of California Press, 1990). J. F. Took offers a persuasive chronology of some of the lyrics of this period in his *Dante, Lyric Poet and Philosopher: An Introduction to the Minor Works* (Oxford: Clarendon Press, 1990), 61-73.

33. Bruni's *vita* emphasizes that after Campaldino, Dante returned even more intensely to his earlier studies, but continuing them in the light of political concerns and activity: Viti, *Leonardo Bruni e Firenze*, 344-345. On the centrality of the *città* in Dante's thought, see A. P. d'Entrèves, *Dante as a Political Thinker* (Oxford: Clarendon Press, 1952), 1-25, and Charles T. Davis, *Dante's Italy*, 1-22. For Brunetto Latini, see Davis, *Dante's Italy*, 166-197.

34. Marvin Wolfgang, "Crime and Punishment in Renaissance Florence," *The Journal of Criminal Law and Criminology*, LXXXI (1990), 567-584. Among later prisoners were Matteo Villani, Benvenuto Cellini, and possibly Machiavelli. See also Laura Ikins Stern, *The Criminal Law System of Medieval and Renaissance Florence* (Baltimore, Maryland: Johns Hopkins University Press, 1994).

35. Richard Goldthwaite, *The Building of Renaissance Florence* (Baltimore, Maryland: Johns Hopkins University Press, 1980), and the references on p. 9 n. 4, especially to Guido Pampaloni, *Firenze al tempo di Dante: Documenti sull'urbanistica fiorentina*, Pubblicazioni degli Archivi di Stato, Fonti e sussidi, 4 (Roma, 1973). To these should be added Hagen Keller, "Das Stadtbild von Florenz im Zeitalter Dantes," in *Dante Alighieri* (Wurzburg: Leonhardt, 1966), and Franek Sznura, *L'espansione urbana di Firenze nel Dugento* (Firenze: La Nuova Italia, 1975), and Sznura, "Civic Urbanism in Medieval Florence," in *City-States in Classical Antiquity and Medieval Italy*, eds. Anthony Molho, Kurt Raaflaub, and Julia Emlen (Ann Arbor: University of Michigan Press, 1991), 403-418. Bornstein's Introduction to his translation of Compagni succinctly sums up the shape of Florence at the time. See also Ernesto Sestan and Ugo Proccaci, art. "Firenze," *ED*, II, 904-920, Paul G. Ruggiers, *Florence in the Age of Dante* (Norman: University of Oklahoma Press, 1964), and Giulio Tofanari, *Le lapidi dantesche: Pagine di storia fiorentina* (Prato: Edizioni del Palazzo, 1985). Jeffrey Schnapp, *The Transfiguration of History*, 36-69, offers an eloquent study of the anti-city of Dis in *Inferno* X.

36. For the text, see Salvemini, *Magnati e popoli*, 384-432.

37. See now George W. Dameron, *Episcopal Power and Florentine Society, 1000-1320* (Cambridge, Mass.: Harvard University Press, 1991). On Dante's ideal of ecclesiastical poverty, see Charles T. Davis, "Poverty and Eschatology in the *Commedia*," in Davis, *Dante's Italy*, 42-70. There is an excellent overview of the struggle between the popular government of the guilds and the *magnati* in John Najemy, "The Dialogue of Power in Florentine Politics," in *City-States in Classical Antiquity*, 269-288.

38. The *consulte* to 1298 have been edited by Alessandro Gherardi, *Le Consulte della Repubblica Fiorentina dall'anno MCCLXXX al MCCXCVIII*, 2 vols. (Firenze: Sansoni, 1896-1898). On the gaps in the records before 1298 that affect Dante, see Zingarelli, 374-375.

39. On the two figures, see Isidoro Del Lungo, *Dino Compagni e la sua Cronica*, Vol. I (Firenze, 1879), 14-18; Vol. II, 495-627, esp. 521-528, and Zingarelli, 403-404.

40. He seems to refer to him in *Paradiso* XVI, 131-132.

41. Najemy ("Dante and Florence," 82-85) offers a similar reading of *Inferno* VI.

42. Villani, x.136.

43. The name is not given entirely; the identification is simply. . . *herii.* See Cardini, 341. There is a brief summary in Fallani, 121-125, and a longer one in Herde, *Dante als florentiner Politiker*, 28-43. For convenience's sake, I usually cite immediately below only references from Cardini, CD, and Zingarelli.

44. CD 79.

45. Cardini, 342.

46. Cardini, 342; CD 53; Zingarelli, 375-376.

47. Zingarelli, 376-377; Cardini, 342.

48. CD 56; Cardini, 342.

49. Zingarelli, 379-380; Cardini, 342.

50. CD 73; Zingarelli, 389-390.

51. CD 75; Zingarelli, 390-392.

52. CD 81-82; Zingarelli, 400.

53. CD 60; Zingarelli, 401.

54. CD 83-84; Zingarelli, 401-402.

55. CD 86; Zingarelli, 404-405.

56. CD 87; Zingarelli, 405.

57. CD 88; Zingarelli, 405-406.

58. Zingarelli, 406-409.

59. CD 90-1, 106, 115; Zingarelli, 413-430; Starn, *Contrary Commonwealth*, Ch. 3. On the *Epistole*, see Manlio Pastore Stocchi, art., "Epistole," *ED*, II, 703-710.

60. Thus Zingarelli, 393-395. Petrocchi dates the pilgrimage to the spring of the year, before the mission to San Gimignano and election to the priorate (*Vita di Dante*, 78). Herde inclines toward Zingarelli's date (*Dante als florentiner Politiker*, 33 n. 161).

61. Cited above, p. 000.

62. CD 90-91; Starn, *Contrary Commonwealth*, 70. The trial of 27 January is analyzed in detail by Starn (*Contrary Commonwealth*, 67-76), with extensive references to the literature, esp. Bernardino Barbadoro, "La condanna di Dante e le fazioni politiche del suo tempo," *Studi danteschi*, II (1920), 5-74, and *Il processo di Dante*, ed. Dante Ricci (Firenze: Arnaud, 1967).

63. Starn, *Contrary Commonwealth*, 71-72.

64. Starn, *Contrary Commonwealth*, 70.

65. CD 106.

66. See Edward Peters, "Wounded Names: The Medieval Doctrine of Infamy," in *Law in Mediaeval Life and Thought*, eds. Edward B. King and Susan J. Ridyard (Sewanee: The Press of the University of the South, 1990), 43-89; Starn, *Contrary Commonwealth*, 84.

67. See Samuel Y. Edgerton, Jr., *Pictures and Punishment: Art and Criminal Prosecution during the Florentine Renaissance* (Ithaca, New York: Cornell University Press, 1985), esp. 58-90. On public humiliation in France, see now the splendid study of Mary C. Mansfield, *The Humiliation of Sinners: Public Penance in Thirteenth-Century France* (Ithaca, New York: Cornell University Press, 1995), esp. 262-269.

68. See the unsigned art., "Ciolo" in *ED*, II, 18. Dante at least claims that any form of *oblatio* (presumably whether *pro forma* or individualized and conspicuous) would result in a derogation of Dante's honor—legally, *diminutio capitis*.

69. CD 114.

70. CD 115.

71. *Par.* VI, 140-142; *Par.* XVII, 58-60; *Conv.* I.iii.3-5; *DVE* II.vi. See also F. M. Powicke, "Dante's Romeo," in his *Ways of Medieval Life and Thought: Essays and Addresses* (rpt. New York: Biblo and Tannen, 1964), 239-248.

XVI

THE VOYAGE OF ULYSSES AND THE WISDOM OF SOLOMON: DANTE AND THE *VITIUM CURIOSITATIS*

The damnation of Ulysses in Dante's Inferno, canto *26 is the result of a distortion of Ulysses's will which draws the hero into inappropriate undertakings, particularly undertakings inappropriate for a ruler. Ulysses is in many respects a* curiosus, *a man who has displaced natural and associational affections in favor of a passion which he could not or would not control. Dante contrasts Ulysses, the ruler who asks inappropriate questions, with Solomon (*Paradiso *13), who, in Dante's version, is praised because he did not ask questions of an academic kind, which are inappropriate for a ruler, but questions on how to be a good ruler. Ulysses is a* rex curiosus *not only because he pursues inherently forbidden objects, but because he engages in activities improper to a king.*

Odysseus wird in Dantes Inferno, canto *26 deswegen verdommt, weil ihn eine Verirrung seines Willens zu unangebrachten Unternehmungen veranlaßt, insbesondere zu Unternehmungen, die für einen Herrscher unpassend sind. Odysseus ist in mehrfacher Hinsicht ein* curiosus, *ein Mann, der natürliche und gesellschaftliche Bindungen einer Leidenschaft unterordnet, die er nicht kontrollieren kann oder will. Odysseus, dem Herrscher, der unangebrachte Fragen aufwirft, stellt Dante Salomo gegenüber (*Paradiso *13). Dieser wird von Dante gelobt, weil er keine Fragen akademischer Art stellte, die für einen Herrscher unpassend sind, sondern zu wissen wünschte, wie er ein guter Herrscher sein könne. Ein* rex curiosus *ist Odysseus nicht nur, weil er grundsätzlich verbotene Ziele verfolgt, sondern weil er Tätigkeiten nachgeht, die einem König nicht angemessen sind.*

The figures in Dante's *Inferno* are punished, not for *doing* something, but for *being* - or having made themselves - something. Those in the Malebolge and below (*Inferno* 18-34) are punished for being deceivers, that is, for having given themselves up to the willful perversion of the Aristotelian and Dantean quintessentially human powers of reason, will, and speech in order to confuse, deceive, and persuade, always for their own gain or the gain of a client or patron and another's loss. From the pimps to the traitors, from Geryon to Lucifer, Fraud is the worst of the human condition. Inherently monstrous itself, it is bracketed in Hell by monsters.

The damned are not only punished, but they are also convincingly punished. Dante's intended audience may not have known Latin (and hence the world of learning that Latin contained), but its members were not ignorant, and it is pointless to assume that Dante could have proposed to teach them the lessons that he did without convincing

them of the justice of the punishment of those he placed in Hell[1]. If modern readers have often failed to perceive this justice and the appropriateness of Dante's depiction of both character and punishment, that is hardly Dante's fault. We must assume that his readers did; otherwise, the poem would have been either solipsistic or pointless.

The case of Ulysses in *Inferno* 26:55-142 was once an episode that raised questions about the justice of Ulysses' damnation and of the possible ambiguities of Dante's representation of an otherwise heroic type seeking an otherwise laudable human goal. Although modern critics still debate the range and nuances of Dante's attitude toward Ulysses, the old romantic-Tennysonian view, in whatever modern theoretical garb it now parades, seems pretty much discredited. The best recent readings of *Inferno* 26 focus primarily on Ulysses' fault (or faults) in the light of Dante's conception of sin and on the structural-thematic importance of the Ulysses-figure and the issues it raises in the *Commedia* as a whole[2]. One reason for this change has been the slow but increasingly certain identification of Dante's literary and other sources and their place in the structure of the story as Ulysses himself tells it in *Inferno* 26[3]. A second reason, related

---

[1] The audience I assume here for the *Commedia* is that referred to in *convivio* I. ix. 4-5. See Maria PICCIO SIMONELI, Dante and His Public. In: Deutsches Dante-Jahrbuch 59 (1984) 37-54, and Richard LANSING, Dante's Intended Audience in the *Convivio*. In: Dante Studies 110 (1992). - An earlier version of this essay was delivered as a talk at the New College Conference of Medieval and Renaissance Studies at the University of South Florida, Sarasota, in 1994. I am grateful to Lee Daniel Snyder for his hospitality and to members of the audience who made helpful comments, as well as to Michael Ryan.

[2] See the brief discussion in Teodolinda BAROLINI, The Undivine Comedy: Detheologizing Dante, Princeton 1992, 48-58, and the references there cited. The most recent *lectura Dantis* reflects the point made above: Ruggero STEFANINI, Inferno XXVI. In: Lectura Dantis, Number 6, Supplement: Lectura Dantis Virginiana, Vol. I (1990) 332-350. Two studies that illustrate recent functions of Ulysses-criticism are those of Richard KAY, Two Pairs of Tricks: Ulysses and Guido in Dante's *Inferno* XXVI-XXVII. In: Quaderni d'italianistica 1 (1980) 107-124, and Peter S. HAWKINS, 'Out upon Circumference': Discovery in Dante. In: Discovering New Worlds: Essays on Medieval Exploration and Imagination, ed. by Scott D. WESTREM, New York/London 1991, 193-220. The most extensive recent reading, one with which I am in general agreement, is that of John A. SCOTT, L'Ulisse dantesco. In: ID., Dante Magnanimo: Studi sulla "Commedia", Florence 1977, 117-193. See also ID., *Inferno* XXVI: Dante's Ulysses. In: Lettere Italiane 23 (1971) 145-186, and ID., Dante and Philosophy. In: Annali d'Italianistica 8 (1990) 258-277. For the tradition of scholarship, see Anthony K. CASSELL, *Ulisseana*: A Bibliography of Dante's Ulysses to 1981. In: Italian Culture 3 (1981) 23-45. Most recently, see Werner ROSS, Der Held in der Hölle. Ein Versuch über den Odysseus-Gesang des Inferno. In: Deutsches Dante-Jahrbuch 64 (1989) 61-74, and Larry PETERMAN, Ulysses and Modernity. In: Dante Studies 113 (1995) 89-110.

[3] By this I mean not only the identification of Dante's general reading and the debates about what he could or might have known or not known, as, e. g., the Homeric text and its Latin retellings and revisions, but also specific readings that help to explain precisely why the Ulysses story begins where it does. See, for example, Barbara REYNOLDS, Dante's Tale of Ulysses. In: Istituto Universitario Orientale, Annali, Sezione Romanza. Vol. 2, ed. by Giuseppe Carlo Rossi, Naples 1960, 49-65, an article that brings into consideration Ovid's *Metamorphoses* XIV and convincingly explains why Ulysses' story begins as it does. At the same time, the splendid study of Giorgio PADOAN, Ulisse *fandi fictor* e le vie della

to the first, is the sharp distinction that we are now able to make between Dante's moral geography and that of the slowly expanding eastern Atlantic world from the mid-fourteenth century on. Dante's attitude toward the southern hemisphere and the problem of the Antipodes now seems much closer to that of Augustine than to that of Petrarch and Boccaccio, or to that of Benvenuto da Imola[4]. Finally, we have learned to look more closely at recurring themes within the *Commedia,* themes illuminated in different ways by different characters and different contexts in different parts of the poem.

But this last method too has its characteristic dangers. And one of them is the subject of this paper.

Ulysses is damned. I emphasize the obvious because his damnation is reflected in several distinct elements besides the one for which it is best known. He has deceived and misadvised both Greeks and Trojans - in the episodes cited by Vergil of the ambush from the Trojan horse, the discovery and enticement of Achilles, and the theft of the Palladium. He has continued to display *astutia* and *magnanimitas* at an age well beyond their appropriate use[5]. He has already lingered too long with Circe, a neglect of marital affection and duty. He has further displaced natural affections - those of a skipper for a crew, a king for a people, a child for his parent, a parent for his child, and a husband for his wife - in favor of a passion that he could not or would not control[6]. He has transgressed the limits set by Hercules (and by God) for human voyages to the west[7]. He has used an

---

sapienza. In: Studi Danteschi 37 (1960) 21-61, rpt. in ID., Il pio Enea, l'empio Ulisse: Tradizione classica e intendimento medievale in Dante, Ravenna 1977, 170-199, effectively summarized the literary sources and analogues up to the time of its appearance.

[4] For the change, see ID., Petrarca, Boccaccio e la scoperta delle Canarie. In: Italia medioevale e umanistica 7 (1964) 263-277, and ID., Cause, struttura, e significato del *De situ et figura aque et terre*, intro. to ID. (ed.), De situ et figura aque et terre, Florence 1967, rpt. in ID., Il lungo camino del 'poema sacro': Studi Danteschi, Florence 1993, 163-180. On the Antipode debate, see Valerie I. J. FLINT, Monsters and the Antipodes in the Early Middle Ages and the Enlightenment. In: Viator 15 (1984) 65-80, rpt. in EAD., Ideas in the Medieval West: Texts and Their Contexts, London 1988, IV.

[5] This is the argument of R. KAY (note 2) and of J. A. SCOTT, L'Ulisse dantesco (note 2) 172-175.

[6] On the nature of passion in Dante, although without particular attention to Ulysses, see Patrick BOYDE, Perception and Passion in Dante's Comedy, Cambridge 1993, 275-301. On Ulysses as king, see J. A. SCOTT, L'Ulisse dantesco (note 2) 186.

[7] I have dealt with the Pillars of Hercules elsewhere: The Desire to Know the Secrets of the World (forthcoming). See also P. S. HAWKINS (note 2) and PINDAR, Olympia, 3:43-45; Nemea 3:19-23; Nemea 4:69-70; Pythia 3:29-31. Adolf SCHULTEN, Die Säulen des Herakles. In: Otto JESSEN, Die Strasse von Gibraltar, Berlin 1927, 174-206. See also J. A. SCOTT, L'Ulisse dantesco (note 2) 163-4, and Piero BOITANI, Beyond the Sunset: Dante's Ulysses in Another World. In: Lectura Dantis 9 (1991) 34-53. On the intermittent citation of the Pindar-reference, see Earl ROSENTHAL, *Plus Ultra, Non Plus Ultra*, and the Columnar Device of Emperor Charles V. In: Journal of the Warburg and Courtauld

admirable and in other circumstances noble and proper argument (how else could he have convinced the crew to follow him?) to deceive those who have every reason to trust him both to speak the truth and to to see them home. He has deliberately delayed making that "little speech" until they are at the very pillars of Hercules. The speech was devised so to move them to the extent that they could neither control their response nor wait for a fair wind, making their oars into sails for the mad voyage. And the storm from the mountain destroys both himself and the crew he has deluded[8]. Who does not think of Ulysses, not only when reading *Purgatorio* 19 and *Paradiso* 27, but also *Purgatorio* 2?

Moreover, his last voyage begins in a sea in which it criscrosses (specifically in Ovid [*Metamorphoses* XIV:438-439] in the persons of Achaemenides and Macareus, which explain why Dante has Ulysses begin his narrative at the point he does) another voyage - that of Aeneas, one that, with but a single diversion, which in itself only underlines Aeneas' *pietas*, heads directly for its divinely ordained destination[9]. The other legitimate methods of reaching the only destination reachable in the southern hemisphere (besides the awful route Dante and Vergil take in *Inferno* 34) - that is, the ascension of Elijah in the whirlwind and the ship of the angel - are mentioned immediately preceding and shortly following Ulysses' account of his own misdirected voyage. And Ulysses tells his story to the guide of a real pilgrim, one who has already described himself as a victim of shipwreck and will use the imagery of the sea voyage again and again (surprisingly often, for an inland Tuscan) in the *Commedia*, including its use as an image of Dante's own presumptuous genius and the temerity of the entire project of the *Commedia*[10]. Dante's Ulysses, both in terms of what Dante chose to show of him (and to have Vergil remind us of things about Ulysses that we are expected to know) and in the moral-geographical context of his last voyage, is exactly where he ought to be when Dante meets him in the eighth *bolgia*. And Dante expected this to be clear to his readers, in the early fourteenth century as in the late twentieth. Ambiguous damnations make neither better Christians nor Florentines, and Dante had a considerable interest in making both.

Institutes 31 (1971) 204-228, and James D. ROMM, The Edges of the Earth in Ancient Thought, Princeton 1992, esp. 17-20

[8] On Dante's ideas and uses of storms, see Patrick BOYDE, Dante Philomythes and Philosopher: Man in the Cosmos, Cambridge 1981, 320-321, note 14.

[9] On the crossed tracks of the two voyages, pointed out by André Pézard, see the references in J. A. SCOTT, L'Ulisse Dantesco (note 2) 141, note 36.

[10] The most sensitive study of the relation between Dante the voyager and Ulysses is that of P. S. HAWKINS (note 2).

As if the sins listed above were not enough, a number of scholars have considered Ulysses in terms of yet another vice, the medieval *vitium curiositatis*, specifically in terms of Ulysses' own expressed *longing that I had to gain experience of the world, and of human vice and worth*, and his exhortation to the crew,

> *Choose not to deny experience, following the sun,*
> *of the world that has no people. Consider your origin:*
> *you were not made to live as brutes, but to pursue*
> *virtue and knowledge*[11].

For Dante there could be no relevant experience in a part of the world that had no people, and especially no experience of human vice and worth!

In medieval moral theology the *vitium curiositatis* was a vice far more complex than its usual characterizations by the terms "anti-intellectualism" or "primitivism" indicate. It had two aspects: the object sought and the attitude and motivation with which an object was sought. That is, some objects were inherently forbidden to human inquiry, while a disordered sense of inquisitiveness might be sinful even though its object might be neutral or good. In this sense the classical Augustinian formulation of forgetfulness of self might be just as powerful as the forbidden objects of inquiry[12]. *Curiositas* is much more an Augustinian than a Thomistic vice.

Most scholars who have addressed the problem of *curiositas* in *Inferno* 26, however, have made the same mistake that their predecessors used to make when they turned to Aquinas every time they found a theological crux in the *Commedia*. It is no more possible to understand Dante on moral theology merely by going to St. Thomas than it is to understand Dante on dogmatic theology. Yet most discussions of *curiositas* in connection with Ulysses turn precisely to the *Summa theologiae* IIa IIae, qq. 166-167,

---

[11] Most recently, Christian K. ZACHER, Curiosity and Pilgrimage: The Literature of Discovery in Fourteenth-Century England, Baltimore/London 1976, 18-41; Hans BLUMENBERG, Die Legitimität der Neuzeit, Frankfurt a. M. 1966, Eng. trans.: The Legitimacy of the Modern Age, trans. by Robert WALLACE, Cambridge, Mass. 1983, 338-342. There is an early and significant discussion of Ulysses and the *vitium curiositatis* in Rocco MONTANO, Il 'folle volo' di Ulisse. In: Suggerimenti per una Lettura di Dante, Naples 1957, 131-166, and in G. PADOAN (note 3) 185-186. There is a balanced discussion in J. A. SCOTT, L'Ulisse Dantesco (note 2) 117-193, and ID., *Inferno* XXVI (note 2).

[12] See Richard NEWHAUSER, Augustinian *Vitium Curiositatis* and Its Reception. In: Saint Augustine and His Influence in the Middle Ages, ed. by Edward B. KING and Jacqueline T. SCHAEFER, Sewanee 1988, 99-124. Richard Newhauser and I are collaborating on a study tentatively entitled "Curiosity and the Limits of Inquiry in the Western Tradition". A recent study by G. R. EVANS offers a

and remain satisfied with the limited and largely mechanical treatment of the vice that Aquinas provides.

From one perspective, of course, Ulysses seems the ideal *curiosus*, for he has a flawed and sinful curiosity to begin with, which he then devotes to the most forbidden of objects. But it may be wiser to postpone the characterization until we consider the vice in a broader Dantean (and other) context. Dante's notions of *curiositas* seem to function in ways largely peculiar to Dante and perhaps to his audience.

A consideration of the most important instances in which Dante uses terminology or scriptural references that are generally associated with the *vitium curiositatis* in twelfth- and thirteenth-century moral theology will illustrate the difficulty.

In *Vita nuova* IV Dante explains the necessity of using a certain lady as a *screen* - the pretended object of his obviously love-struck countenance and behavior - by stating that some people, *full of malicious curiosity, were doing their best to discover things about me which I particularly wished to conceal.* The curiosity of others then becomes something of a leitmotif throughout the next several sections of the *Vita nuova*, as indeed it does in other discussions of love in thirteenth- and fourteenth-century literary works. Dante here modifies the substantive *curiosity* by adding the term *malicious* - *curiosity* standing alone is not necessarily pejorative. Their curiosity is malicious because it focuses on something Dante wishes to conceal and because knowledge of the concealed subject will presumably harm Dante and the object of his love.

This is close to the kind of malicious interest in the affairs of others (the implication being that in taking such an interest one loses the essential spiritual concern for oneself) expressed by Sapia of Siena in *Purgatorio* 9:109-111:

> *Sapient was I not, although Sapia*
> *I was called, and took in others' ills*
> *more joy than in my own good fortune.*

Sapia may be being punished for envy, but here she demonstrates pure *Schadenfreude*, a dimension of *curiositas* long noted in classical and patristic literature[13].

---

useful taxonomy of the vice: What We Are Not Supposed to Know. In: The Joy of Learning and the Love of God: Studies in Honor of Jean Leclercq, ed. by E. Rozanne ELDER, Kalamazoo 1995, 309-326.

[13] See Paul ANTIN, Textes de St. Jerome (et d'autres) sur la joie du malheur d'autrui. In: ID.,

The examples of these aspects of *curiositas* in the *Vita nuova* and the *Purgatorio* represent what was probably for Dante and his readers the simplest and most common level of the vice: excessive and improper interest in the affairs of others, sometimes, perhaps usually, in conjunction with wishing - or wishing to hear about - harm to them. Elsewhere, Dante quotes a number of scriptural texts often associated with discussions of *curiositas* by scholars who have noted them. But these texts, too, need to be read in context.

In *Convivio* III.8.2, for example, Dante notes the difficulty of describing the perfect human being:

> *And if this creature is so wonderful, it is certainly*
> *a daunting task to treat of its various aspects not only*
> *in words but even in thought.*

A similar sentiment is expressed by the Sage [*Eccles*. 1:3, 3:22] where he says *Who will search the wisdom of God which existed before all things?* and elsewhere; *You shall not enquire about things too high for you, nor search after things beyond your reach; consider, rather, what God has commanded you, and do not be curious about His other works*, that is, do not concern yourself with them[14].

Earlier in Book III (III.4.9-12) Dante had spoken of the limits of the human intellect in acquiring certain kinds of knowledge, limits that are faultless, since they were placed upon the intellect by God, but nevertheless essential features of the human condition. The Ecclesiasticus text, often cited in terms of the *vitium curiositatis* in exegesis and moral theology, he here used merely to express a topos of difficulty in describing a complex subject. Dante does not cite it as the central point of his text. One need not seek *curiositas* where none is intended.

Another scriptural text frequently cited in connection with *curiositas* - Prov. 22:28, *Do not overstep the ancient bounds set by your fathers* - indeed occurs in *Convivio* IV.7.9, but in the context of a discussion of the greater guilt of an infamous person descended

---

Recueils sur saint Jérôme, Brussels 1968, 203-208.

[14] I cite here and below the translation of Christopher RYAN, Dante: The Banquet, Saratoga, Cal. 1989. See also John A. SCOTT, The Unfinished *Convivio* as a Pathway to the *Comedy*. In: Dante Studies 113 (1995) 31-56, at 41-45.

from noble ancestors and the greater fault of a person who gets lost when he has a guide. Dante emphatically does not cite the text in any sense resembling *curiositas*[15].

Far closer is the passage in *Convivio* IV.13.9, which takes place in a complex discussion of the human desire for knowledge. Dante's discussion here seems to follow directly from *Convivio* III.4.9-12 with its concerns about the degree of certainty that the human intellect can achieve in the light of its divinely imposed limitations. Citing Aristotle's observation in the *Ethics* (I.1) that, *The educated person wants to know things with the measure of certainty that their nature allows*, Dante comments:

> *[This] indicates that we must recognize that there is a limit set not only for the person desiring, but also for the object which he desires to know. Likewise Paul (Rom.12:3) says, "Do not strive to know more than is fitting; rather, strive to know according to the nature of man's capabilities."*

Once above the level of prying into the concealed business of others and that of rhetorical commonplace, Dante's concern with human *curiositas* is intimately connected to his idea of the limitations and proper activities of the human intellect[16]. Any consideration of Dante's concerns should begin with *Convivio* III.4.9-12 and *Convivio* IV.13.9.

Convivio III.4.9-12 argues that the human intellect is fundamentally limited, particularly in attempting to comprehend immaterial substances, since the power that *draws forth whatever it sees*, the imagination, is physical and cannot supply the necessary faculty to the intellect. Although we can speculate *somewhat* about immaterial things, we cannot know them directly or fully understand them: the imagination fails the intellect. Moreover, even when the imagination and intellect work perfectly (up to the limits of their capacities), their ability to express such understanding is further limited by their powers of language, which are necessarily narrower than the intellect, just as the powers of language themselves are broader than the powers of direct signification:

---

[15] On the exegetical history of the phrase, see my study, Transgressing the Limits Set by the Fathers: Authority and Impious Exegesis in Medieval Thought. In: Christendom and Its Discontents, 1000-1500, ed. by Scott L. WAUGH and Peter DIEHL, Cambridge/New York 1996, 338-362, which traces the usage of the Proverbs text from Origen to the fourteenth century. See also below, note 25.

[16] On the limitations of the intellect, see also Robin KIRKPATRICK, Dante's "Paradiso" and the Limitations of Modern Criticism: A Study of Style and Poetic Theory, Cambridge 1978, esp. 28-50, and John A. SCOTT, Dante and Philosophy. In: Annali d'Italianistica 8 (1990) 258-277, at 262-264.

So if any thought of ours, not only such as fails to attain a perfect understanding of its object but even such as does attain a perfect understanding, defeats our power of speech, we ourselves are not to be blamed, for it is not we who are the cause of that.

In the *Convivio* as in the *Commedia*, Dante rooted his representation of human nature in an articulated philosophical, theological, and biological anthropology, expressing in a social and political context a coherent and extensive version of human gestation, development, function, character, and personality, first laid out in the Fourth Book of the *Convivio* and then reiterated in *Purgatorio* 16, *Purgatorio* 25, and *Paradiso* 8[17]. His ideas about the nature and purpose of human knowledge are developed in the long discussion of nobility that constitutes most of *Convivio* IV. They draw upon contemporary medical, astrological, psychological, physiognomic, and biological thought, as well as upon moral theology and the work of Aristotle, chiefly the *Ethics* and the *De anima*. They provide a framework that accounts for the appropriate stage of human development at all points along what Dante termed *l'arco della vita*[18]. Properly achieved, that development will also locate people in the life-statuses that are appropriate for them and not in a status or occupation unsuited to their character. When the latter occurs, as it does, for example, in the cases of the sons of Charles II of Sicily in *Paradiso* 8, or in those of the women in *Inferno* 20 who have left their proper roles in order to tell fortunes, natures have become *twisted* (*torcete*, a favorite term of Dante's) and social and political roles are filled by people who are inappropriate for them and are thus unable to fulfill them properly.

In order to assess the virtuousness or viciousness of a figure in the *Commedia*, it is necessary to consider both the stage of life at which the figure has arrived (including the figure's astrological and other developmental history) and the use that the figure has made of the intellect and will in the status to which the figure has been called. In the case of *curiositas*, as in that of other vices, we must consider the *curiosus* or *curiosa* as central, rather than the object of curiosity. Dante is far more concerned with the functioning of *prudentia* - and not, as in Aquinas, with *temperantia* - as the intellectual virtue that guides and directs the moral virtues (*Convivio* IV.7.8) and its flowering in the third stage of human life (*Convivio* IV.27.1-11). Dante's examples here are Solomon and Cato, and especially in the figure of Solomon, both here and in its appearance

---

[17] I have traced the process and the literature in Human Diversity and Civil Society in Paradiso VIII. In: Dante Studies 109 (1991) 51-70.

[18] *Conv.* IV.23.6. See Bruno NARDI, L'arco della vita (Nota illustrativa al *Convivio*). In: Saggi di Filosofia Dantesca, 2nd ed., Florence 1967, 110-138.

in *Paradiso* 13, it is possible to identify Dante's idea of *curiositas* on a more complex political level than in most of the instances cited above.

In III *Regum* 3:5-12 God invites Solomon to ask of him what he will. Solomon responds that he is ignorant of ruling and requests the skills that a ruler needs. God answers that because he has not asked for a long life, riches, or the lives of his enemies, but rather for *sapientia ad discernendum iudicium*, God will give him a *cor sapiens et intelligens*, to such a degree that this had been possessed by no one before Solomon and would be possessed by none after. The last verse became the text explicated by Thomas Aquinas in *Paradiso* 13. Thomas changes one thing, however, in his retelling of the story from III *Regum*: instead of not having asked for long life, riches, or the lives of his enemies, Solomon is now praised for not having asked,

> *to know the number of the mover spirits here above,*
> *nor if necesse with a contingent ever made a necesse;*
> *nor si est dare primum motum esse; nor if in a*
> *semicircle a triangle can be so constructed that it*
> *shall have no right angle.*

Solomon's unique *regal prudenza* pertains properly, as Thomas says, only to kings. No second *king* ever arose with such wisdom. The gifts Solomon did not ask for are perfectly appropriate for others, but not kings. As scholars have noted, the unasked-for gifts are the answers to perfectly appropriate questions in the disciplines of theology, dialectic, physics, and geometry - but appropriate only for those whose proper business it is to investigate them at those levels.

The idea that only a certain kind of knowledge was appropriate for a king (and the lack of authority a king displayed when he pronounced on topics outside his proper sphere of expertise - as in Dante's discussion of the erroneousness of the definition of nobility attributed to Frederick II in *Convivio* IV.7f) was not original with Dante. Bede had glossed Isaiah 30:21 with *Romans* 12:3 as *declinat ad dexteram, qui vult plus sapere quam opportet sapere*[19]. More recently, however, in the rich thirteenth-century literature of advice to kings and courtiers, John of Limoges, abbot of the Cistercian monastery of Zirc in Hungary and formerly prior at Clairvaux, had written a treatise dedicated to Theobald IV of Champagne[20]. The treatise, *Morale Somnium Pharaonis*,

---

[19] BEDE, Super parabolas Salomonis allegorica expositio, I.4, PL 91:956.

[20] Johannis Lemovicensis, Abbatis de Zirc 1208-1218, Opera Omnia, ed. by Constantin HORVATH.

consists of a series of letters among Pharaoh, Joseph, and others (*Genesis* 41), in which Pharaoh is identified by John as a *rex curiosus* and Egypt represents a *typus cuiuslibet regni studiosi*[21].

Joseph's undertaking is to make the ruler a *rex rationabilis*, and when Pharaoh's courtiers point out to Joseph that they have urged the king to study and withdraw from the cares of the court (as Jaeger points out, creating a Prospero *avant la lettre)*, Joseph denounces the *rex curiosus*, who speculates and studies and does not attend to his kingly duties and cultivate the *virtutes civiles*.

Whether Dante knew of the work of John of Limoges is impossible to determine, but the sentiments of the *Morale* and *Paradiso* 13 are virtually identical, particularly when Dante has substituted the study of subjects in the *artes liberales* for the original unasked-for gifts in III *Regum*. The *rex* becomes *curiosus* not because he pursues inherently forbidden subjects or trivial studies, or even natural philosophy, but because he engages in activities improper for a king.

Here, it seems to me, is the essence of Dante's strongest sense of the *vitium curiositatis*: it is the pursuit of objects of knowledge that are improper *for the pursuer*. Dante is much more interested in lives led according to the proper observation of the ages of man (and woman) and to the status to which an individual has been called. Any violation of these (as in the *twisted natures* of *Paradiso* 8, or the case of Ulysses) will lead to the loss of *the good of the intellect* (*Inferno* 3:18), and only rigorous training and discipline can curb the appetites that, uncontrolled, lead to the manifestations of incontinence, violence, and fraud that place people in Hell.

Is Ulysses, then, a *curiosus* in this sense? As a number of scholars have pointed out, had Dante wanted to emphasize simply the kind of royal *curiositas* that is often attributed to Ulysses, he could have used a much better-known figure, Alexander the Great, as had moralists and poets from Pseudo-Callisthenes to Walter of Châtillon. In fact, the last verses of Book IX of Walter's *Alexandreis* which include Alexander's declaration

---

3 vols., Vesprem 1932. There is an excellent discussion of the treatise in C. Stephen JAEGER, The Origins of Courtliness: Civilizing Trends and the Formation of Courtly Ideals, 939-1210, Philadelphia 1985, 87-95. Jaeger further notes several unnoticed texts relevant to the figure of the "good" medieval Ulysses, 95-100, for which see also P. S. HAWKINS (note 2) 201.

of his purpose in sailing to the Antipodes and his stimulation of his crew sound very much like Dante's Ulysses, and it seems not impossible that they may be at least an analogue, if not a source, of Dante's Ulysses[22]. For Dante, however, the condition of the seeker of knowledge was more important than the object of knowledge. If Dante had followed Thomas Aquinas, he would have had to allow that the Thomistic alternative to *curiositas*, *studiositas*, would have been appropriately virtuous for both Solomon and Ulysses. No more than John of Limoges could Dante concede this point. Ulysses had subordinated both intellect and natural affection to fraud and deceit long before he was moved to sail west and south. Once the *ben de l'intelletto* has been lost, all choices are the wrong choices. An ordered intellect and ordered affections would have prevented the surrender to the last impulse because the last impulse would never have happened. But Ulysses had no defenses against it, and he perverted his leadership and oratorical skills in order to accomplish it.

In both the *Convivio* and the *Commedia*, Dante is too much the student of Aristotle (in whose work the Greek equivalents of various kinds of *curiositas* - *periergia*, *polypragmosyne*, and *tolma* - rarely appear) to condemn the human desire for knowledge. Even Adam, in *Paradiso* 26, points out that his fault was not the eating of the fruit of the tree of the knowledge of good and evil (medieval exegetes pointed out that such knowledge would have been imparted by God in other ways), but the *trapassar del segno* - the violation of God's command. What Dante does do - as did many late thirteenth and early fourteenth-century thinkers, is to make explicit - more in the case of Solomon than in that of Ulysses - that the desire for knowledge must be commensurate with the status, obligations, and capacities of the person desiring knowledge. In universities, as

---

[21] C. St. JAEGER (note 20) 89. Jaeger's suggestion of the resemblance of Joseph's Pharaoh to Shakespeare's Prospero in *The Tempest* should be modified somewhat in the light of my own study, *Rex curiosus*: A Preface to Prospero. In: Majestas 4 (1996) 61-84.

[22] This has been pointed out by a number of scholars, notably Silvio AVALLE D'ARCO, L'Ultimo Viaggio di Ulisse. In: Studi Danteschi 43 (1966) 35-67, and J. A. SCOTT, L'Ulisse dantesco (note 2) 129-132, and ID., *Inferno* XXVI (note 2) 151, note 18. There is an extensive discussion of the place of Alexander-stories in the history of *curiositas* in my The Desire (note 7). In addition to Silvio Avalle and Scott, see George CARY, The Medieval Alexander, ed. by David J. A. ROSS, Cambridge 1936, rpt. New York 1987; Paul GOUKOVSKY, Essai sur les origines du mythe d'Alexandre. Vol. 1, Nancy 1978; Hans HOLLÄNDER, Alexander: *Hybris* und *Curiositas*. In: Kontinuität und Transformation der Antike im Mittelalter, ed. by WILLI ERZGRÄBER, Sigmaringen 1989, 65-79. On Alexander, Cato, and Solomon, see especially J. A. SCOTT, *Inferno* XXVI (note 2) 151-183, and ID., Dante's Political Purgatory, Philadelphia 1996, 69-84. Cary's work does not mention Walter of Châtillon, although the poem was widely read and glossed from the late twelfth century on. See Galteri de castellione Alexandreis, ed. by Marvin COLKER, Padua 1978, and The "Alexandreis" of Walter of Châtillon: A Twelfth-Century Epic, trans. by David TOWNSEND, Philadelphia 1996, 166-184.

Heiko Oberman has suggested, this was accomplished by insisting upon the professional content of curricular subjects and faculties[23]. The opening of the condemnation of errors in natural philosophy and theology at Paris in 1277 spoke of the arts faculty as having exceeded the limits of its discipline. Late thirteenth-century political theory emphasized the importance of *ratio* in the exercise of rulership, and increasingly isolated the specifically kingly virtues[24]. Well before Dante impugned the philosophical authority of Frederick II, St. Bonaventure pointed out that even theologians may err when they assert opinions in areas where they have no disciplinary competence[25].

Ulisse curioso? If there is an instance of a uniquely Dantean *curiositas* in the *Commedia*, I would argue that it is illustrated in the gifts for which Solomon did *not* ask, gifts that would have been inappropriate to his condition and duty. The *curiositas* that might be attributed to Ulysses is merely the last fault in a profoundly disordered intellect, it is the fault that kills, but not the fault that damns him. The last voyage both anticipates the mountain of Purgatory virtually at the last possible moment in the *Inferno* and reminds the reader forcefully of the failure of the disordered intellect either to preserve life or to avoid damnation.

---

[23] Heiko OBERMAN, Reformation and Revolution: Copernicus's Discovery in an Era of Change. In: The Cultural Context of Medieval Learning, ed. by John R. MURDOCH and Edity DUDLEY-SYLLA, Dordrecht/Boston 1977, 397-435, and ID., Contra vanam curiositatem. Ein Kapitel der Theologie zwischen Seelenwinkel und Weltall, Zurich 1973. See also my Transgressing the Limits (note 15).

[24] To the references in my *Rex curiosus* (note 21), I would add the figure of Charles IV of Bohemia, on whom most recently, see Peter DEMETZ, Prague in Black and Gold: Scenes from the Life of a European City, New York 1997, 67-117, with further references.

[25] I have dealt with this reference in Transgressing the Limits (note 15), and in *Libertas inquirendi* and the *Vitium Curiositatis* in Medieval Thought. In: La notion de liberté au Moyen Age. Islam, Byzance, Occident, ed. by George MAKDISI, et al., Paris 1985, 89-98.

INDEX

eration of some themes in preparation for a major shift in concern from *Paradiso* X on. Of all the planets, Venus plays a particularly prominent part in the *Comedy.* It is the first star that Dante sees in Purgatory:

> Lo bel pianeto che d'amar conforta
> faceva tutto rider l'orïente,
> velando i Pesci ch'erano in sua scorta,
> (*Purg.* I, 19–21).

Helen Flanders Dunbar once plausibly suggested that Dante may have considered Venus his own "lord of the horoscope" and therefore particularly important in his own destiny (cf. *Inf.* XXVI, 21–24).[2]

In the case of Venus—both the goddess and the planet—Dante could also draw heavily upon material widely known to himself and his readers. Vergil's *Aeneid* and the work of the earlier and later mythographers dealt at great length with the characteristics of the goddess. Aristotle, Cicero, Ptolemy, and the Arab astronomers accounted for Venus' place in the sequence and order of the heavens. Literary and mythographical themes were prominent in much thirteenth-century literature, notably Jean de Meung's *Roman de la Rose* (where Venus is the natural enemy of chastity and reason), and the work of the astronomers powerfully influenced thirteenth-century physicians and astrologers as well, notably Dante's older contemporary Ristoro d'Arezzo. From the astronomers Dante knew that the motions of the Moon, Mercury, Venus, Mars, Jupiter and Saturn included epicycles, circular orbits whose center was on the great orbit of the planet's course through the heavens (hence Dante's use of the term "epicycle" to designate the greater orbit of Venus [*Par.* VIII, 2]), of the similarity of the orbits of Mercury and Venus to that of the Sun, and the fact that Venus is both a morning and an evening star, travelling sometimes before the Sun, and sometimes behind it (*Par.* VIII, 11–12). The characteristics of Venus in literature and mythology determined the character of the planet's influence on humans in the work of astrologers: Venus was the heaven of Rhetoric, as Dante had noted in the *Convivio* (II, xiii, 13–14) and thus associated with political and public order. But it was also the planet that sent down "mad love"—and in the crudest works of astrology, discussion of the planet's influence began and ended there.

XIV

In more detailed and learned works, however, Venus had other functions. Venus governed the fifth month of fetal life, influencing the configuration of the exterior members— ears, nose, fingers, and sexual organs—and removed excess from the fetus.[3] Although most Latin astrologers were careful not to imply astral determinism in their discussions, they could safely assert the influence of the planets on matter, including the material human body and the formation and exercise of the individual temperament, as does Marco Lombardo in his discussion of the topic in *Purgatorio* XVI. The planets were thought to influence human development before birth in an order beginning with Saturn and ending with the Moon. After birth the periods of influence were reversed, beginning with the Moon and ending with Saturn in old age. In many schemes of the ages of man, Venus ruled adolescence, in Dante the ages of nine to twenty-five. Dante's *adolescenza* then gives way to *giovinezza,* (ages twenty-five to forty-five) which is ruled by the Sun. As we will see, Charles Martel represents an ideal portrait of the youth turning from *adolescenza* to *giovinezza.*[4] Planets were also thought to influence non-human phenomena, Venus in particular associated with the rising of rivers (prominent in *Par.* VIII) and, in one treatise, with the climatic zone in which lie Sicily and South Italy, the chief geographical locations discussed in *Paradiso* VIII.

In the great encyclopedia of medieval mythographic thought, pagan gods and goddesses (as well as the planets and stars named after them) were exhaustively explained and allegorized, none so extensively as Venus. It is appropriate that Venus is the first heaven in which Dante takes up this theme, since Venus was not only of particular interest to him, but to many other thinkers as well. The characters of the Moon and Mercury are certainly noted in the poetry of the early cantos of the *Paradiso,* but it is in the heaven of Venus that Dante extensively addresses both mythology and astrology in categorical terms.

The double aspect of Venus was demonstrated, not only in the planet's dual character as a morning and an evening star

il vocabol de la stella
che 'l sol vagheggia or da coppa or da ciglio
(*Par.* VIII, 11–12)

but in the mythographic image of the "two Venuses." As Bernardus Silvestris had said in the twelfth century, "one lawful, and the other the goddess of wantonness." Bernard went on to explain that the "lawful" Venus was:

Legitimam Venerem dicimus esse mundanam musicam, i.e., aequalem mundanorum proportionem, quam alii Astream, alii naturalem iustitiam vocant. Haec enim est in elementis, in sideribus, in temporibus, in animantibus.[5]

[The harmony of the world, that is, the even portion of worldly things, which some call Astrea, and others call natural justice. This subsists in the elements, in the stars, in the seasons, in living beings.]

For Bernard, the "wanton" Venus was "carnal concupiscence since that is the mother of all fornications." The "harmony of the world" that Bernard attributed to the first Venus was the *musica mundana,* expressed for him and for later mythographers (and, by Dante, in the appearance and behavior of the souls in the heaven of Venus) in the image of the dance, of harmony and the co-ordination of order and reason. Cosmic and civic harmony thus both pertained to one of the "two Venuses" in the tradition as it reached Dante, and "mad love," wantoness, and fornication to the other.

Theologians, retaining the ancient names of the planets, preferred to consider the heavens in terms of the hierarchy of angelic orders. Gregory the Great (and, following Gregory, Dante himself in *Conv.* II, v, 13) had stated that the order of Thrones governed the third heaven (Gregory smiles at his error in *Par.* XXVIII, 133–139). But the treatise of Pseudo-Dionysius, whose influence had grown considerably from the twelfth century on, had identified the third heaven with the angelic order of Principalities. Like Venus in the sequence of heavens, the Principalities were the highest ranking order in the lowest triad of angelic orders. The functions of the Principalities were chiefly "political." As Thomas Aquinas, following Pseudo-Dionysius, described them (*Contra Gentiles* III, 80):

Nam in rebus humanis est aliquod bonum commune, quod quidem est bonum civitatis vel gentis, quod videtur ad principatuum ordinem pertinere. Unde et Dionysius in eodem cap. dicit, quod nomen principatuum designat *quoddam dominium cum ordine sacro* . . . et sic dispositio regnorum et mutatio dominationis a gente in gentem ad ministerium huius ordinis pertinere opportet. Instructio etiam eorum, qui inter homines existunt principes, de his quae ad administrationem sui regiminis pertinent, ad hunc ordinem spectare videtur.

[There is a certain common good in human affairs, and that is the good of the city or nation [Aquinas here cites Aristotle, *Ethnics* I. 2. 1094b] which seems to pertain to the order of Principalities. Therefore Dionysius in the same chapter says that the name Principalities designates *a power of government according to a sacred order*. . . . Thus the disposition of kingdoms, and the transfer of rule from one people to another is the fitting object of the ministry of this order. There also pertains to this order the instruction of those among men who are raised up to be princes, in those matters pertaining to the administration of their rule.]

Philosophical allegory, drawing chiefly from Aristotle (*Ethics* I. 1; *Pol.* II. ii. 15–16) also considered the order of the heavens according to the sequence of the arts and sciences. According to this set of references, which Dante himself had used in the *Convivio* (II, xiii, 13–14), Venus was the heaven of Rhetoric, a subject which Dante, under the influence of the thirteenth-century Aristotelian thought and such figures as Brunetto Latini, had come to identify with the civilizing process and to have a particularly important place in political life. Aristotle had stated that among humans language "serves to declare what is advantageous and what is the reverse, and it therefore serves to declare what is just and what is unjust" (*Pol.* I. ii. 12). Man alone possesses a perception of good and evil, of the just and the unjust, "and it is association in [a common perception] of these things which makes a family and a polis." Further, Aristotle emphasizes (*Pol.* II. ii. 15–16) that polis-life makes man the most perfect of animals, but that the wicked use of language makes man unjust, because it turns man's most distinctive and differentiating feature, which had been designed for moral prudence and virtue, into a weapon against these very qualities. Aristotle's principle of teleology dictated that he consider nature to have made nothing in vain. Since nature had given humans language, language must have a purpose. That purpose must be to distinguish the just from the unjust and to teach other humans. Language is therefore a natural characteristic of humans that exists primarily to establish justice among them, and hence Rhetoric is an art fundamental to human nature, which is political. In Dante's moral reading of Aristotle, other treatises on rhetoric (notably Brunetto Latini's

Also in the Variorum Collected Studies Series:

GÉRARD GIORDANENGO
Féodalités et droits savants dans le Midi médiéval

ANDRÉ GOURON
Droit et coutume en France aux XIIe et XIIIe siècles

KATHRYN L. REYERSON
Society, Law and Trade in Medieval Montpellier

ROBERT FEENSTRA
Legal Scholarship and Doctrines of Private Law, 13th–18th Centuries

RICHARD KAY
Councils and Clerical Culture in the Medieval West

JAMES A. BRUNDAGE
The Crusades, Holy War and Canon Law

JAMES A. BRUNDAGE
Sex, Law and Marriage in the Middle Ages

KATHERINE FISCHER DREW
Law and Society in Early Medieval Europe: Studies in Legal History

ROGER COLLINS
Law, Culture and Regionalism in Early Medieval Spain

PAUL FREEDMAN
Church, Law and Society in Catalonia, 900–1500

ANDRÉ GOURON
Juristes et droits savants: Bologne et la France médiévale

HENRY ANSGAR KELLY
Inquisitions and Other Trial Procedures in the Medieval West

RICHARD KAY
The Council of Bourges, 1225: A Documentary History

PIERRE LEGENDRE
Écrits juridiques du Moyen Age occidental

VARIORUM COLLECTED STUDIES SERIES

Limits of Thought and Power in Medieval Europe

Professor Edward Peters

Edward Peters

Limits of Thought and Power in Medieval Europe

Ashgate
VARIORUM

Aldershot · Burlington USA · Singapore · Sydney

Published in the Variorum Collected Studies Series by

Ashgate Publishing Limited
Gower House, Croft Road,
Aldershot, Hampshire GU11 3HR
Great Britain

Ashgate Publishing Company
131 Main Street
Burlington, VT 05401–5600
USA

Ashgate website: http://www.ashgate.com

ISBN 0–86078–847–4

British Library Cataloguing-in-Publication Data
Peters, Edward, 1936–
Limits of Thought and Power in Medieval Europe. – (Variorum Collected Studies Series).
1. Power (Social sciences)–Europe–History–To 1500.
2. Europe–History–476–1492
I. Title.
940.1

US Library of Congress Cataloging-in-Publication Data
Peters, Edward, 1936–
Limits of Thought and Power in Medieval Europe / Edward Peters.
p. cm. – (Variorum Collected Studies: CS721).
Includes bibliographical references.
1. Kings and rulers, Medieval. 2. Philosophy, Medieval. 3. Europe–Intellectual life. 4. Power (Christian theology). 5. Europe–Church history–600–1500. 6. Law, Medieval.
I. Title. II. Collected Studies: CS721.
D107. P48 2001
940. 1–dc21 2001132848

The paper used in this publication meets the minimum requirements of the American National Standard for Information Sciences – Permanence of Paper for Printed Library Materials, ANSI Z39.48–1984. ∞ ™

Printed by St Edmundsbury Press, Bury St Edmunds, Suffolk.

VARIORUM COLLECTED STUDIES SERIES CS721

CONTENTS

This volume contains xiv + 344 pages

PUBLISHER'S NOTE

The articles in this volume, as in all others in the Variorum Collected Studies Series, have not been given a new, continuous pagination. In order to avoid confusion, and to facilitate their use where these same studies have been referred to elsewhere, the original pagination has been maintained wherever possible.

Each article has been given a Roman number in order of appearance, as listed in the Contents. This number is repeated on each page and is quoted in the index entries.

INTRODUCTION

The research careers of some historians often seem not very different from the adventures of Alice in Wonderland, even though they are always much less interesting. A question raised in the research for one project that leads on to a slightly different one, the intellectual adventures of preparing classes and answering intelligent and unexpected questions from students, a chance invitation to lecture or write on a topic on the edge of a current project, or puzzles raised in a book review all slip the historian unawares from field to field, one project always apparently growing logically out of another, until he finds himself in a field that had never occurred to him and wonders how he ever got there. Is there any underlying logic in the publication history of a teaching, research, and writing career that has extended for more than thirty years (except for the incidental logic that the same scholar has taught, researched, and written it all), or is the historian too much swayed and directed, not by a disciplined calculus of research but by an undisciplined curiosity that results all too often in random encounters with the research equivalents of March Hares and White Knights?

My earliest research interests are represented by the essays in Part III of this book – comparative constitutional history and the problem of political and personal inadequacy on the part of rulers and how, or whether, these should be borne by the ruler's rivals and subjects, just what those rivals and subjects might and sometimes did do when they would no longer bear it, and by what authority? This was the topic of my earliest essays (VI, VII, and XI in this volume), some of which were incorporated into my first book, *The Shadow King: 'Rex inutilis' in Medieval Law and Literature, 750–1327* (New Haven/London, Yale University Press, 1970), now out of print, and also a topic to which I returned by a circuitous but logical route after some decades of only occasional consideration of the subject, in the essays printed here as V, VIII, and IX.

A doctoral thesis on a topic that spanned six centuries and much of a subcontinent, as well as the pedagogical obligations upon a teacher of the history of medieval Europe quickly provide sobering evidence of all the things that one needs to know and doesn't and about which one had better make some serious effort to learn. At the beginning of my teaching career at the University of California, San Diego a curricular misadventure (none of my own doing) forced me to teach – and quickly learn – Renaissance and Early Modern History rather than that of earlier Europe, an experience that provided even more sobering evidence of how much I had to learn. My subsequent move to the University of Pennsylvania, where for many years I was the only teacher of medieval western European history, and, alas, am again, pushed me into yet other research areas, since it seemed (and seems) a kind of iron law of pedagogy that one teaches best those subjects in which one has done at least some original research. Original research was easy, because of the marvelous resources of the libraries at Pennsylvania particularly those of the Henry Charles Lea Library, of which I became and remain the curator, and helpfulness of the library's staff. The ghost, or at least the books and manuscripts of Mr. Lea, have exerted a continuous influence on my own approach to history and choice of research subjects.

At the same time, the financially dire straits of the University of Pennsylvania Press resulted in my collaboration with its then director, the late Fred Wieck, and then with subsequent directors until 1995, to issue a series of historical documents in translation, based on the late nineteenth- and twentieth-century series issued originally by the Department of History of the University of Pennsylvania, the *Translations and Reprints from the Original Sources of European History*, with additional texts and updated bibliographies and new introductions. The series quickly grew into a line of translations and original studies under the series title *The Middle Ages*. For twenty-five years I read manuscripts submitted to the Press, more each year, dealing with a broad array of subjects, and this experience, along with the exigencies of having to teach a variety of different courses in the evenings and during summers in order to support a family, indicated how much more there was to learn even beyond my regular forays through medieval and early modern Europe. The process did me a world of intellectual good, although it did not always seem so at the time.

One result of the process was the publication of my survey of early European history, a book first called *The World of the Middle Ages* (Englewood Cliffs, NJ, 1977) and in subsequent versions *Europe and the Middle Ages* (1983; 2nd edn. 1989; 3rd edn. 1997; 4th edn. 2002). By the late 1970s I had decided that 'The Middle Ages' were the middle of nothing at all and that the period was in fact early European history. Early in the twentieth century Johan Huizinga, and later Jacques le Goff, both identified the 'long Middle Ages' as a respectable topic of historical periodization, and here I agree with them.

The elements of the original dissertation and first book that did not deal with constitutional history proper – notions on the part of chroniclers, jurists, and others concerning the human personality and how it seemed to function, palaeopsychology rather than psychohistory, led me into the latest research indicated here, the literature of the vices and virtues and the broad field of moral theology as the earliest European psychology. These essays focus mostly on the characteristic – sometimes a vice, sometimes not – of *curiositas* – an ancient and medieval term that requires considerable unpacking before it becomes our own term 'curiosity'. The essays on curiosity grew out of my intermediate work on heresy and the problems of sorcery and witchcraft and are preliminary and adjunct to a large work in progress, with Richard Newhauser, provisionally entitled *Curiosity and the Limits of Inquiry in the Western Tradition*, which will range from the pre-Socratics into the seventeenth century, and which, in the essay on Prospero (V in this volume), brought me back circuitously to my original research interest in useless kings – in this instance kings who were excessively curious about kinds of learning unsuitable for rulers, an encouraging sign of an internal logic to this research career, after all.

Much of my work, then, has always seemed to deal in one way or another with limits – limits of both thought and power in the pre-modern world of western Europe, examined across a broad spectrum of particular occasions and subjects.

Finally, thanks to a generous and stimulating graduate teacher, Thomas Goddard Bergin, and a dissertation adviser, Robert Sabbatino Lopez, both of whom greatly admired and taught the poet, I acquired early on a love and a frequent teaching experience of Dante and considerable respect for the philosophical moralist as well as the poet. Nothing, after all, prohibits historians from using poetry as a historical source if they pay proper attention to it. In his own life and writing Dante often, it seems to me, both probed and prescribed for the limits of the human intellect and will, and the seven essays reprinted here in Part III all deal with one or another aspect of Dante's perception of those limits.

These are the studies that may be most usefully included in a volume dealing with some limits of thought and power. Other concentrations of studies and fields of research require other collections. Gathering these has helped me make sense and order out of some of the most important aspects of my own professional career. I hope that they may be of use to others, whether they are interested in limits or think that I have exceeded my own.[1]

The book is dedicated to our children: Nicole Peters Kane, Moira Peters Pakulniewicz, and Edward M. Peters III.

EDWARD PETERS

The Lea Library,
University of Pennsylvana
May 2001

---

[1] For the sake of bibliographical thoroughness, there are two further essays on the topic not included in this volume. They are: "*Omnia permixta sunt*: Where's the Border?", *The Medieval History Journal* 4/1 (2001), 109–127, and "The Desire to Know the Secrets of the World", *Journal of the History of Ideas* (forthcoming).

ACKNOWLEDGEMENTS

Grateful acknowledgement is made to the following persons, journals, institutions and publishers for their kind permission to reproduce the papers included in this volume: the Augustian Historical Institute, Heverlee (I, II); Cambridge University Press (III); Société d'Édition 'Les Belles Lettres', Paris, (IV); Böhlau Verlag GmbH & Cie, Köln (V, XVI); Librairie Droz, S.A., Geneva (VI); Libreria Ateneo Salesiano, Rome (VII); Biblioteca Apostolica Vaticana, Vatican City (VIII); the Medieval Academy of America, Cambridge, Massachusetts (IX); the Pontifical Institute of Medieval Studies, Toronto (X); Edizioni Scientifiche Italiane, Naples (XI); Yale University Press, New Haven, Connecticut (XII); John Benjamins Publishing Co., Philadelphia, Pennsylvania (XIII); Professor Christopher Kleinhenz, Editor, *Dante Studies* (XIV, XV).

I

What was God doing before He created the Heavens and the Earth?*)

I

Throughout his long life as a Christian thinker and teacher, Augustine often returned to the opening verses of Genesis, more often, and with greater sophistication than any writer before him[1]). Some of the passion with which he expounded Genesis surely came from his first recorded encounters with Scripture, when under Manichaean direction the problems of the two genealogies of Christ, the Genesis account of creation, anthropomorphism, and the sinful lives of the partriarchs had diverted him from his search for wisdom and his initial identification of wisdom with the name of Jesus[2]). The account of his conversion to *philosophia* and his first turning to Scripture in *Confessions* III. 4-5,

*) Earlier versions of this study were very kindly read by my colleagues Ann Matter, James J. O'Donnell, Judah Goldin, and Alan Charles Kors. I am very grateful for their suggestions and assistance. The paper was read at the Patristic-Medieval-Renaissance Conference of Villanova University in September, 1983. I am also grateful to Thomas Losoncy for having given me the opportunity to participate.

[1]) There is a careful account in Aimé SOLIGNAC, "Exégèse et Métaphysique. Genèse 1. 1-3 chez saint Augustin", in *In principio. Interprétations des premiers versets de la Genèse*, Centre d'Etudes des religions du livre (Paris, 1973), 153-171. On Augustine's concern with these verses, see Jacques DE BLIC, "Le processus de création d'après saint Augustin", in *Mélanges offerts au R.P. Ferdinand Cavallera* (Toulouse, 1948), 171-189; William A. CHRISTIAN, "Augustine on the Creation of the World", *Harvard Theological Review* 46 (1953), 1-25; Gilles PELLAND, *Cinq études d'Augustin sur le début de la Genèse* (Toulouse-Montréal, 1972); Joseph MOREAU, "Le temps et la création selon S. Augustin", in MOREAU, *Stoicïsme, Épicurisme, Tradition Hellénique* (Paris, 1979), 167-181; E.P. MEIJERING, *Augustin über Schöpfung, Ewigkeit und Zeit. Das elfte Buch der Bekenntnisse* (Leiden, 1979).

[2]) These initial stumbling-blocks in Scripture are recorded in *Sermo* 51. iv. 5; *De Gen. contra Man.* I. ii. 3ff, and 1. 17. 27-8; *Conf.* III. 5-7. See the Introduction of A. SOLIGNAC to *Confessions, Livres I-VII*, Bibliothèque Augustinienne, Vol. 13 (Paris, 1962), 128-9. On Augustine's developing knowledge of Scripture, see G.L. BONNER in *The Cambridge History of the Bible*, edd., P.R. ACKROYD and C.F. EVANS (Cambridge, 1970), Vol. I, *From the Beginnings to Jerome*, 541-562, and, on Scripture generally, Peter BROWN, *Augustine of Hippo* (Berkeley and Los Angeles, 1969), 162-3, 180-1, 262-9. On Ambrose, from whom Augustine seems to have received his appreciation of Scripture which had been aborted by the Manichaeans in 373, see Jean PÉPIN, *Théologie cosmique et théologie chrétienne* (Paris, 1964). Eugene TESELLE, *Augustine the Theologian* (New York, 1970), 197-223, ranks Augustine's Genesis theology with that of Philo and Origen.

introduces, not only his discovery of wisdom, but his immature attempts to probe the veiled mysteries of Scripture first on his own initiative, and then at the instigation of the vain and empty words of the Manichaeans[3]). The history of Augustine's first experience with Scripture, particularly the ease with which he was misled by the Manichaeans, may help to explain his continual return to the text, and particularly his concern over the proper interpretation of the creation story, his sense that these verses were, as they had been for Philo, the key to wisdom[4]). Having rejected them once, Augustine kept returning to them, lest others fall into the errors that had once entrapped him.

Thus, not merely proper exegesis, but improper exegesis as well, characterized Augustine's approach to Scripture in general and Genesis in particular. Much of Book XI of the *Confessions*, the first of the three exegetical books on Genesis that conclude that great work, is framed, in fact, by an example of one of these improper exegetical questions. In XI. 10 Augustine cites the example of some people, *pleni vetustatis suae*, who ask

> What was God doing before he created the heavens and the earth? If he was resting, they say, and was not making anything, why not continue to do nothing as he had done in the past?

Augustine repeats the question in XI. 12 at the beginning of the long meditation on eternity and time which occupies the rest of Book XI, repeating the question for the last time at XI. 30. The question, then,

[3]) St. Augustine's interest specifically in Manichaean interpretations of the opening verses of Genesis is not always noted. See H.-C. PUECH, *Le Manichéisme* (Paris, 1949), 69-72, and esp. 157, n. 281. See also Geo WIDENGREN, "La sagesse dans le Manichéisme", in *Mélanges d'histoire des religions offerts à Henri-Charles Puech* (Paris, 1974), 501-515. Cf. *Conf.* XI. 13 and *De mor. eccl.* 18. 34; *De util. cred.* 1-2. BROWN, *Augustine*, 54. For the Manichaean myth, see François DECRET, *Aspects du Manichéisme dans l'Afrique romaine* (Paris, 1970), 185-252, and idem, *L'Afrique manichéene (IV-V siècles). Étude historique et doctrinale*, 2 vols. (Paris, 1978), esp. I, 239-352; M. TARDIEU, *Trois mythes gnostiques* (Paris, 1974), 49f; John P. MAHER, "Saint Augustine and Manichean Cosmogony", *Augustinian Studies* 10 (1979), 91-104; idem, *Saint Augustine's Defense of the Hexaemeron against the Manichaeans* (Rome-St. Meinrad, Ind., 1946).

[4]) PHILO, *De opif. mundi*, 54; cf. Arnold EHRHARDT, *The Beginning: A Study of the Greek Philosophical Approaches to Creation from Anaximander to St. John* (Manchester, 1968), 202; E. R. GOODENOUGH, *By Light, Light: The Mystic Gospel of Hellenistic Judaism* (New Haven, 1935), 121-126, 326-7, 345-7; H.A. WOLFSON, *Philo: Foundations of Religious Philosophy in Judaism, Christianity, and Islam*, Vol. I (Cambridge, Mass., 1968), 180, 295-324; Pierre GEOLTRAIN, "Quelques lectures juives et chrétiennes des premiers versets de la Genèse, de Quomran au Nouveau Testament", *In principio*, 47-60, at 51-55.

constitutes something of a leitmotif of Book XI, important in itself and also as an example of the wrong way to approach scripture, this one question standing as synecdoche for all wrong questions.

The answer that Augustine says that others sometimes give, but that he will not give — *alta scrutantibus gehennas parabat* — appealed to John Calvin and has delighted sceptics ever since. Martin Luther, in his characteristically explicit fashion, once cast the answer as: "God was sitting in a birch wood, making rods to beat people who ask impertinent questions" [5]).

Augustine offers two answers to the question: either, that *principium* refers to the *verbum*, Jesus, or that the question is improper because time itself was created and therefore is not predicable of the creator at all. This second answer was probably derived from Plotinus (*Enneads* III. 7), ultimately from Plato's *Timaeus* (37d-38b) and Parmenides[6]). In its Augustinian-Christian form, the doctrine became the orthodox Christian distinction between eternity and time. It was used by Eriugena to argue against Gottschalk on the possibility of predestination and occupies a prominent place in the *Summa theologiae* of Aquinas (I.q. 14 art. 13) and was echoed by Dante (*Paradiso* xvii. 18). Its philosophical source,

[5]) CHRISTIAN, "Augustine on The Creation of the World", 5-9, discusses *Conf.* XI. 10-13, citing the later interest of Calvin (*Institutes* I. 14.1, *Commentary on Genesis*) and Kant. See also Richard STAUFFER, "L'Exégèse de Genèse 1. 1-3 chez Luther et Calvin", *In principio*, 245-256, and E. P. MEIJERING, *Calvin wider die Neugierde* (Nieuwkoop, 1980), esp. 52-56. There is a merry meditation on the question in J. M. ROSS, "Continuation" in CICERO, *On the Nature of the Gods*, trans. H. C. P. MCGREGOR (Harmondsworth, 1972), 246-7, a hypothetical continuation of Velleius' line of Epicurean argument.

[6]) Augustine's rejection of *tempus* in favor of an eternal *nunc* for God and his qualitative distinction between succession in infinite time and non-durational eternity were necessary correlates of his other views of creation, particularly those which ran counter to widely-held philosophical doctrines, such as the *deus* (or *demiurgos*) *artifex* (with its corrolary of a superior model from which to create), the pre-existence of formless matter (cf. *De div. quaest.* 46. 2), the recurring cycles of creation and destruction, and the problem of an immaterial, immutable being creating a material, mutable cosmos. The relevant materials from classical philosophy are discussed below, n. 14. On *principium* and *Verbum*, see *De Gen. ad. litt.* I. 2. There are extensive discussions in J. GUITTON, *Le temps et l'éternité. chez Plotin et saint Augustin* (Paris, 1959); Werner BEIERWALTES, *Plotin über Ewigkeit und Zeit* (Frankfurt, 1967); Ernst H. KANTOROWICZ, *The King's Two Bodies* (Princeton, 1957), 275-280. The idea of non-durational eternity in earlier Greek thought has been treated by John WHITTAKER, *God Time Being: Two Studies in the Transcendental Tradition in Greek Philosophy*, Symbolae Osloenses Fasc. Supplet. XXIII (Oslo, 1971); PÉPIN, *Théologie cosmique*. Most recently, see G. J. P. O'DALY, "Augustine on the Measurement of Time: Some Comparisons with Aristotelian and Stoic Texts", in H. J. BLUMENTHAL and R. A. MARKUS, eds., *Neoplatonism and Early Christian Thought: Essays in Honor of A. H. Armstrong* (London, 1981), 171-179.

although not its doctrine of creation, thus appears to have been Neo-Platonist, and Neo-Platonism marked much of Augustine's thought between his separation from Manicheism and his assumption of the bishopric of Hippo[7]). Neo-Platonist critical techniques seem, as others have noted and as I hope to show elsewhere in connection with Augustine's early uses of the term *curiositas*, to have been an important instrument in Augustine's savaging of the Manichaeans and a principal vehicle of his own intellectual and spiritual return to orthodox Christianity.

Book XI of the *Confessions* was not, however, Augustine's first citation of the "Manichaean" question. The reason that we know that the Manichaeans are those who pose the question in *Confessions* XI is given in a passage in the *De genesi contra Manichaeos* (I. 1. 3)[8]). But even if the Manichaeans used the question, as Augustine implies that they did, they did not invent it, nor were they the first to apply it to Genesis. The same question (and a similar objection to its impropriety) is cited by Irenaeus (*Adversus haereses* II. 28. 4), and its raisers are not Manichaeans, but Gnostics. The role of Manicheism as in some ways the heir of Gnostic approaches to Christianity and Judaism is, of course, generally accepted, and it is understandable that the question might appeal to the former in much the same ways as it had appealed to the latter[9]). Between Irenaeus and Augustine, the question appears once in

[7]) The various specific neo-Platonists, whether Plotinus or Porphyry, have been discussed and considered from THEILER and ALFARIC to HADOT and O'CONNELL; the bibliography is large. In addition, see A. SOLIGNAC, "Doxographies et manuels dans la formation philosophique de saint Augustin", *Recherches Augustiniennes* 1 (1958), 113-148; P. HENRY, *Plotin et l'Occident* (Louvain, 1934), 78-95, and, most recently, Robert RUSSELL, "The Role on Neoplatonism in St. Augustine's *De Civitate Dei*", in *Neoplatonism and Early Christian Thought*, 160-170.

[8]) *De Genesi contra Manichaeos* I. 2. 3: *Primum ergo librum Veteris Testasmenti qui inscribitur Genesis sic solent Manichaei reprehendere. Quod scriptum est, In Principio fecit Deus caelum et terram, quaerunt, in quo principio, et dicunt: Si in principio aliquo temporis fecit Deus caelum et terram, quid agebat antequam feceret caelum et terram*? As will be seen immediately below, earlier citations of this question occur in Irenaeus and Origen. Was it still being asked, now by Manichaeans, in the late fourth century? Augustine certainly implies that it was. In this text (as in that of Irenaeus, cited below), the critics use the term *quid agebat*; in *Conf.* XI. 10 they ask *quid faciebat*. Thus, there might be a slight variation in meaning between "what was God doing" and "What was God making" between Irenaeus' Gnostics and Augustine's Manichaeans, although this possibility does not alter the significance or form of the question. If the question was in fact being asked by Manichaeans late in the fourth century, might it have been a question that the Manichaeans invited the young Augustine himself to ask about Genesis I. 1.?

[9]) On Manichaeans and Gnostics, see Kurt RUDOLPH, *Die Gnosis (Göttingen, 1977), 349-365*, with further references; *W. H. C. Frend*, "The Gnostic-Manichaean Tradition in

the writings of Origen, and it may be useful to consider these two earlier Christian usages before searching for the question's ultimate source.

II

Book I of Irenaeus' *Adversus haereses* consists of a series of descriptions of Gnostic beliefs. In Book II Irenaeus then refutes these doctrines one by one, criticizing Gnostic psychology and method as well as Gnostic error. In II. 24 he takes up the problem of Gnostic numerology. Perhaps exasperated by this time over Gnostic methods of explanation, Irenaeus then devotes four chapters (II. 25-28) to the problem of the proper and improper uses of the human intellect in terms of knowing God. Since man is infinitely inferior to God (II. 25, 3.) he therefore lacks the capacity to know all about God. Violating the proper order of human knowledge leads man to rise up against God Himself and fall into madness:

> It is better and more useful that men of little or no learning exist and become through charity alone the friends of God than for men to assert that they know much, and much about God, and become blasphemers, makers of another God the Father. Wherefore Paul says (1 Cor. 8. 1) *Knowledge puffeth up, but charity edifies* ... because he knew that some people, lifted up by their supposed knowledge, fell away from the love of God ... there is no greater puffing up than to think that one is better or more perfect than his Creator who shaped him and gave the breath of life and granted him the power To Be itself ... It is better, as I said, to know nothing at all, not even one cause of why any of the things that have been made have been

Roman North Africa", *Journal of Ecclesiastical History* 4 (1953), 13-26; Peter BROWN, "The Diffusion of Manichaeism in the Roman Empire", in BROWN, *Religion and Society in the Age of Saint Augustine* (New York, 1972), 94-118. A good recent survey of early Gnosticism is that of Edwin M. YAMAUCHI, *Pre-Christian Gnosticism: A Survey of the Proposed Evidences* (Grand Rapids, Mich., 1973), and RUDOLPH, *Die Gnosis*, 291-311. On the Christian encounter with these problems, see the sources cited above, n. 1, and J. C. M. VAN WINDEN, "In the Beginning: Some Observations on the Patristic Interpretations of Genesis 1. 1", *Vigiliae Christianae* 19 (1963), 105-121; idem, "The Early Exegesis of 'Heaven and Earth' in Genesis 1. 1", in *Romanitas und Christianitas. Studio Iano Henrico Waszink* (Amsterdam-London, 1973), 371-382; idem, "*Terra autem stupida quadam erat admiratione*: Reflexions on a Remarkable Translation of Genesis 1. 2a", in R. VAN DEN BROEK and M. J. VERMASEREN, eds., *Studies in Gnosticism and Hellenistic Religious Presented to Gilles Quispel* (Leiden, 1981), 458-467; Pierre NAUTIN, "Genèse 1. 1-2, de Justin à Origène", *In principio*, 61-94. The best introduction to the general subject is Gregory T. ARMSTRONG, *Die Genesis in der alten Kirche. Die drei Kirchenväter* (Tübingen, 1962), which considers Justin, Irenaeus, and Tertullian.

> made, and rather simply to believe God and to persevere in the love of Him, than to be puffed up by knowledge and to fall from His love, which gives man life. It is better to learn nothing except that Jesus Christ is the Son of God who was crucified for us, rather than by subtle questions and quibbling minutiae to fall into impiety.

Irenaeus then goes on to deal with the proper method of interpreting parables, emphasizing that since God has placed some things squarely within the power of humans to understand (II. 27. 1), it behooves humans to interpret parables rather in accordance with the rest of their knowledge than toward ambiguity. Moreover, ambiguity leads to diversity of opinion, and the example of the pagan philosophers' disagreements ought to caution Christians from their experience. Such a method would lead Christians to a state of always inquiring but never finding (Matt. 7. 7, a key text in early heresiology), and seeking in a manner contrary to the message of creation and revelation — that the two are in harmony (II. 27. 2). Since God has revealed enough of the truth to lead us to salvation (II. 28. 1), it is suitable that we should use the powers He gave us to increase love, rather than divide in disaffection.

We should leave difficult matters to God and dwell instead upon those things that lie "before our feet.": Irenaeus here cites a number of examples of earthly mysteries, beginning with the rising of the Nile (II. 28. 2), on which agreement has not yet been reached[10]). Some things are to be learned later, in a state of perfection, "so that God should forever teach and man should forever learn".

At this point (II. 28. 4) Irenaeus brings up the question under discussion:

> If, for instance, anyone asks, "What was God doing before He made the world?" we reply that the answer to such a question lies with God Himself. For that this world was formed perfect by God, receiving a beginning in time, the Scriptures teach us; but no Scripture reveals to us what God was employed about before this event. The answer, therefore, to that question remains with God, and it is not proper for us to aim at bringing forth foolish, rash, and blasphemous suppositions ...[11]).

[10]) Irenaeus' use here of a philosophical handbook for his list of examples has been discussed by GRANT and SCHOEDEL. The problem is considered extensively in VAN UNNIK, "Theological Speculation and Its Limits" (see next note).

[11]) *Adv. haer.* II. 28. 4: *Ut puta, si quis interrogat, Antequam mundum faceret Deus, quid agebat? dicimus quoniam ista responsio subiacet Deo. Quoniam autem mundus hic factus est apotelesticos a Deo, temporale initium accipiens, Scripturae nos docent: quid autem ante hoc Deus sit operatus, nulla Scriptura manifestat. Subiacet ergo haec responsio Deo.* Arthur

The remainder of II. 28 continues this theme, without, however, bringing up either of the answers that Augustine later offered to the same question.

Origen uses the text in a considerably different manner. Book III Chapter 5 of the *Peri archōn* treats the subject of the beginning of the world in time. III. 5. 1 and 2 deal with the scriptural citations of the world's beginning and end, and III. 5. 3 cites the question:

> But they are accustomed to meet us with this objection: "If the world had a beginning in time, what was God doing before the world began?" For it is alike impious and absurd to say that God's nature is to be at ease and never to move, or to suppose that there was a time when goodness did not do good and omnipotence did not exercise its power. They raise this objection when we say that the world began at a definite time and when in accordance with our belief in scripture we also calculate how many years old it is[12]).

Darby NOCK sees in Irenaeus' handling of the question an example of the saint's "robust common sense". See "Gnosticism", in NOCK, *Essays on Religion and the Ancient World*, ed. Zeph STEWART, Vol. II (Cambridge, Mass., 1972), 947-8. 959. William R. SCHOEDEL, "Philosophy and Rhetoric in the *Adversus haereses* of Irenaeus", *Vigiliae Christianae* 13 (1959), 22-32 at 32 suggests that Irenaeus' refusal to answer the question indicates his lack of interest in, and active hostility to, philosophy. W. C. VAN UNNIK, "Theological Speculation and Its Limits", in William R. SCHOEDEL and Robert L. WILKIN, eds., *Early Christian Literature and the Classical Intellectual Tradition in Honorem Robert L. Grant* (Paris, 1979), 33-44, properly cites this passage as an example of Irenaeus' distinction between things knowable by men and things knowable only to God, who created them. Only things set forth in scripture and things plainly observable in the world of experience deserve consideration. God has reserved the rest to Himself. On this aspect of Irenaeus' thought, see also F.-M. SAGNARD, *La gnose valentinienne et le temoignage de saint Irenée* (Paris, 1947), 278-282; A. BENOÎT, *Saint Irenée. Introduction à l'étude de sa théologie* (Paris, 1960); Norbert BROX, *Offenbarung, Gnosis und gnostischer Mythos bei Irenaus von Lyon* (Salzburg-Munich, 1966), 196-199; A. ORBE, *Parabolas evangelicas en San Ireneo*, Vol. I (Madrid, 1972), 34-74, à propos Matt. 7. 7; ARMSTRONG, *Die Genesis*, 52-72.

[12]) ORIGÈNE, *Traité des principes (Peri archōn)*, trad. Marguerite HARL, Gilles DORVAL, Alain LE BOULLUEC (Paris, 1976), 198-9; A. LE BOULLUEC, "La place de la polémique antignostique dans le *Peri archón*", in *Origeniana* (Bari, 1975), 47-61. Since the work of Irenaeus was known very early in Egypt, the question may have been borrowed by Origen from Irenaeus rather than from the actual polemical questions of contemporary third-century Alexandrian Gnostics. LE BOULLUEC makes a strong case for Origen's reading Irenaeus in a later study, "Y a-t-il des traces de la polémique antignostique d'Irénée dans le *Peri archōn* d'Origène?" in Martin KRAUSE, ed., *Gnosis and Gnosticism*, Papers read at the Seventh International Conference of Patristic Studies (Oxford, September 8th,-13th, 1975) (Leiden, 1977), 138-147. He does not mention Origen's use of *Adv. Haer.* II. 24. 2, which strengthens his case, but does not solve the problem of the source of Origen's use of the question. See also Marguerite HARL, "Pointes antignostiques d'Origène: le questionnement impie des Écritures", in VAN DEN BROEK and VERMASEREN, *Studies in Gnosticism and Hellenistic Religions presented to Gilles Quispel*, 205-217, who makes a case that Origen is

Unlike Irenaeus, however, Origen undertakes an answer: there were other worlds before this one existed, just as after the destruction of this world there will yet be others. Clearly, although not undertaking the philosophical approaches of Gregory of Nyssa and Augustine, Origen is willing (here as elsewhere) to go much further than Irenaeus, for example, would have permitted[13]).

Both Irenaeus and Origen, then, seem to treat a question that Gnostics did in fact ask. Whether Origen took the question from Irenaeus is not clear, although the text in *Peri Archōn* III. 5. 3. could be a criticism that Origen had himself heard from critics.

Besides the problem of the transmission of the question, there is also the question of its source. Assuming that Irenaeus and Augustine, if not Origen, accurately reported contemporary Gnostic and Manichaean polemical criticism of Genesis, one may ask whether or not the Gnostics originated the question. Gnosticism certainly drew upon a wide variety of ancient thought, and in the case of cosmogony, at least, it drew upon elements that reached far back in Greek and Latin philosophical polemic.

responding to earlier polemical arguments from the second half of the second century. In his striking answer to the *quid antequam* question, Origen may have had haggadic traditions in mind. See the work of VAJDA, cited below, n. 32. On the age of the world, see Karl-Heinz SCHWARTE, *Die Vorgeschichte der augustinischen Weltalterlehre* (Bonn, 1966), 65-70, 260-290. The problem of transmission from Irenaeus to Augustine is not clarified by Altaner's important studies of earlier patristic influences on Augustine, particularly those of Philo, Origen, Irenaeus, Eusebius, Gregory of Nyssa, and Basil. See B. ALTANER, *Kleine patristische Schriften* (Berlin, 1967), 181-334.

[13]) Further discussions of this and similar problems in the thought of the Greek Fathers may be found in Monique ALEXANDRE, "L'Exégèse de Gen. 1. 1-2a dans l'*In Hexaemeron* de Grégoire de Nysse; Deux approches du probleme de la matière", in Heinrich DÖRRIE, et al., eds., *Gregor von Nyssa und die Philosophie* (Leiden, 1976), 159-182. In the same volume, see also David BALAS, "Eternity and Time in Gregory of Nyssa's *Contra Eunomium*", 128-155, esp. 143, for a discussion of Eunomius' charge that "God begins to be *Demiurgos* from the time of creation". On 147 Balàs argues for Gregory's priority over Augustine as the first Christian thinker to adopt the idea of eternity in its non-durational sense. The continuity of this line of thought in the context of the divine names is noted in Stephen GERSH, *From Iamblichus to Eriugena* (Leiden, 1978), 156-7, and in terms of divine wisdom on 264-282. On the Syrian Fathers, see Abraham LEVENE, *The Early Syrian Fathers on Genesis* (London, 1941); T. HANSMA, "Investigations into the Early Syrian Fathers on Genesis", in B. GEMSER, et al., eds. *Studies in the Book of Genesis* (Oudtestamentische Studien, Deel XII (Leiden, 1958), 69-181, esp. 91-95; Antoine GUILLAUMONT, "Genèse 1. 1-2 selon les commentateurs syriaques", *In principio*, 115-132.

III

Any search for a *terminus post quem* must take into account such problems as the nature of the gods, time, eternity, creation and providence in early Greek thought[14]). The roots of such concepts lie in Anaximander's doctrine of the *apeirōn* and his and Melissus of Samos' use of the term *archē*, Xenophanes' de-anthropomorphizing of the gods, and his and Parmenides' idea of the one, with Parmenides' idea of durationless eternity. But these elements were uncombined in dogma and not even systematic in the age of Plato and Aristotle. Greek thinkers, moreover, were never reluctant to critize their predecessors' and contemporaries' opinions on such subjects, often in the spirit of raillery that would appall all but the most pugnacious modern philosophers. Xenophanes' *silloi* and Heraclitus' cryptic insults are but two examples of early stages of the process. The plays of Epicharmus and Aristophanes often deal very roughly indeed with contemporary philosophical and theological ideas. Yet nowhere in this early polemical literature does there seem to be an example of the question considered here.

Some aspects of early Greek theological polemic do seem to anticipate the question. Xenophanes criticized Hesiod for believing that the gods could have come into existence, and Epicharmus attacks the notion that Chaos should at one time not have existed[15]). Diogenes of Apollonia's idea of a purposeful creator, eternal and all-wise, and the general transition from *apeirōn* to *nous* which Jaeger traces through the Hellenistic period all point in a similar direction[16]). The appeal of such approaches to Jews and Christians is obvious, and some aspects of Jewish and Christian cosmogonies also seem to have appealed to Greeks. "Longinus", in his discussion of terms that are fitting to be attributed to the gods, praises "the lawgiver of the Jews, no ordinary person, having

[14]) The following remarks depend heavily upon EHRHARDT, *The Beginning*, and Werner JAEGER, *The Theology of the Early Greek Philosophers* (1946: rpt. Westport, CT, 1980). There is a convenient summary of pagan philosophical thought on some of these points in Jaap MANSFELD, "Bad World and Demiurge: A Gnostic Motif from Parmenides and Empedocles to Lucretius and Philo", in VAN DEN BROEK and VERMASEREN, *Studies in Gnosticism and Hellenistic Religions Presented to Gilles Quispel*, 261-314. Some of these questions, of course, need not have originated in theological discussion. SEXTUS EMPIRICUS, *Pros Logikous* I. 68 f discusses ideas of existence and non-existence, eternal versus created things in a purely logical context: I am grateful to Alan KORS for suggesting that I look at Sextus.

[15]) JAEGER, *Theology*, 67-8.

[16]) Ibid, 204-6, the long note on *tó Theion*.

formed a high conception of the power of the Divine Being, and gave expression to it when at the very beginning of his laws he wrote: 'God said' — what? 'Let there be light, and there was light; let there be land, and there was land'"[17]).

Yet the development of Greek theology, the cosmogonic myths of Plato and their criticism in Aristotle's *De caelo* do not seem in their turn to have generated the question. Objections to various theologies continued, of course, to be made, often loudly and vociferously. From Philo to Augustine thinkers who posited the Judaeo-Christian creation narrative had to deal with objections that had become virtually endemic in Greek thought, some dating from the pre-Socratics and some from contemporary Middle-Platonists like Celsus. To the successors of Xenophanes' de-anthropomorphizing of the gods, the story sounded all too bluntly like another tale of Hesiod, a cosmogony achieving only the introduction of one more deity flourishing a *technē* which used the crassest of materials for the most ignoble of purposes, the binding of immaterial spirits into a material universe. To those who had spent nearly as long removing the divine from the space and the purview of man, it revived echoes of the *deus curiosus*, for which the Epicureans had long scolded the Stoics. To the Stoics it imposed a linear story of creation and final judgement by a transcendent deity in place of the organic, cyclical recurrence of life and cosmos alike. To the interlocutors of Minucius Felix' *Octavius*, it offered the paradox of a creating deity at once so interfering and transcendent that it combined the *deus curiosus* of the Stoics with the *deus solitarius et destitutus* of the Jews[18]).

Of all theological polemic in the ancient world, the one school which seems most likely to have concerned itself with these problems is that which contended most vigorously with theological *dogmata* of all kinds, that of the Epicureans. Epicurus' dramatic rejection, not merely of divine providence, but of the very possibility of divine creation of the cosmos, is

[17]) T.S. DORSCH, trans., *Classical Literary Criticism* (Baltimore, 1965), 110 (LONGINUS, *De Sublimitate*, ix). GALEN once noted that the Jewish conception of a divine creator was more attractive than Epicurus' doctrine of creation by chance in his *On the Parts of the Human Body* 11. 14, but he found it incompatible with the Platonic and Aristotelian Demiurge, who "brings to reality only what reason evinces as being possible, and from all possibilities he always chooses the best one". Albrecht DIHLE, *The Theory of Will in Classical Antiquity* (California, 1982), lf; R. WALZER, *Galen on Jews and Christians* (Oxford, 1949).

[18]) *Octavius* X. 5; cf. *De nat. deorum* I. 154.

firm and categorical[19]). Epicurean physics rejected the possibility of divine creation since nothing can come into existence from non-existence and since all concepts (including that of a cosmos) derive from evidence of the senses and the mind, and then only when the senses and the mind (here also considered as a sense) are applied to existent objects, an argument similar to Plato's insistence upon patterns of a higher order needed to bring into existence things of a lower order (*Timaeus* 29a). Hence, "if nothing existed, no concept of a world would be found in the minds of the gods"[20]). In any case, as Lucretius maliciously remarks, if the world had been made by gods it would not have so many things wrong with it — *tanta stat praedita culpa* (*De rer. nat.* V: 199; cf. II; 177-181). Thus, Epicurean physics and theology, both deny not only divine creation, but providence, teleology, and divine retribution. The gods have nothing to do with earth, nor (against Plato, the early Aristotle, and the astral religion of Stoicism and others) with the stars. Happy and untroubled in the *intermundia*, the gods seek for neither more happiness nor trouble in the *cosmos*, and they certainly did not make it.

As unique and idiosyncratic as Epicurus' position was, on the matter of divine creation his position was consistent with what Joseph Moreau has called "la tradition la plus constante de la philosophie grecque, représentée notamment par Aristote, qui professe l'éternité du monde. La doctrine de la création, l'idée d'un commencement du monde, entendue superficiellement, heurte la raison philosophique et suscite des railleries des esprits forts"[21]).

Epicurus and his followers could, of course, and often did adapt existing cosmological arguments whenever they agreed with some position of their own or attacked a position they themselves wished to

[19]) The classic study is that of A. J. FESTUGIÈRE, *Epicurus and His Gods*, trans. C. W. CHILTON (Cambridge, Mass., 1956). See also Knut KLEVE, *Gnosis Theou. Die Lehre der natürlichen Gotteserkenntnis in der epikureischen Theologie*, Symbolae Osloenses, Fasc. Supplet. XIX (Oslo, 1963), and, more recently, Dietrich LEMKE, *Die Theologie Epikurs* (Munich, 1973). For the context of Epicurean thought generally, see J. M. RIST, *Epicurus: An Introduction* (Cambridge, 1973). A number of important Epicurean texts on the topic are conveniently gathered in C. J. DE VOGEL, *Greek Philosophy*, Vol. III, 2nd ed. (Leiden, 1964), 23-25. See also PÉPIN, *Théologie cosmique*, 103-124, 173-216. On similar questions in Stoicism, which do not come into this paper, see DE VOGEL, III, 64-85, and Myrto DRAGONA-MONACHOU, *The Stoic Arguments for the Existence and the Providence of the Gods* (Athens, 1976), on arguments from design, 88-96.

[20]) RIST, *Epicurus*, 148. Cf. MACROBIUS, *Sat.* 7. 16. I am grateful to James J. O'DONNELL for this reference.

[21]) MOREAU, "Le temps et la création", 168.

attack, as they did with Aristotle's criticism of Plato's *Timaeus* (*De caelo* 281b 25 ff). But Epicurus was an articulate and ready polemicist, and the evidence for his original criticism of his predecessors and contemporaries is abundant and persuasive. It may be an accident of reference- and text-transmission as well as a testimony to the religious character of contemporary Greek philosophy that makes Epicurus appear often as the first philosopher to express his doctrines chiefly in polemic and invective, but his successors sustained and kept up to date the master's polemical assaults on other dogmata. Metrodorus, Hermarchus, and the *meretricula* Leontium continued the master's tradition and style, and Colotes preserved the somewhat older literary tradition of satire and polemic that went back to Xenophanes and Epicharmus. Recent studies have shown that new theories were readily taken into account in this post-Epicurean polemic. In spite of some scholarly opinion to the contrary, even Lucretius occupies a prominent place in this, as in other Epicurean traditions [22]).

In the first century B.C. the most prominent targets of Epicurean polemic seem to have been Middle Platonic cosmology and the cosmogonical theory of Stoicism, which postulated creation, providence, and recurrence as fundamental cosmological principles. Stoic creation and providence doctrines seemed as wrong-headed to Epicureans as did Aristotle's doctrine of the eternity of the universe. Festugière long ago pointed out how, to Epicurean piety, the new astral religion seemed if anything more dangerous than the older cosmogonies and theogonies [23]). It is in this light that we must seek the earliest time our question was likely to have been formulated and the earliest shape it was likely to take.

In Book V of the *De natura rerum*, Lucretius takes up his attack on the doctrines of the eternity and divinity of the material universe. The gods do not live in any part of the cosmos (Epicurus posited the *intermundia* as the home of the gods, a description of which Lucretius promises in V. 155, but does not in fact give), nor do they nor have they ever done anything for the benefit of man: *quidve novi potuit tanto post ante quietos / inlicere ut cuperent vitam mutare priorem*? Indeed, newness is impossible for the gods. Lucretius goes on to ask:

[22]) The best recent account of the literature is that of Knut KLEVE, "The Philosophical Polemics in Lucretius. A Study of the History of Epicurean Criticism", in *Lucrece*, Fondation Hardt, Entretiens sur l'antiquité classique, XXIV (Geneva, 1977), 39-76.

[23]) FESTUGIÈRE, *Epicurus and His Gods*, 73 f.

exemplum porro gignundis rebus et ipsa
notities divis hominum unde est insita primum,
quid vellent facere ut scirent animoque viderent,
quove modost umquam vis cognita principiorum
quidque inter sese permutato ordine possent,
si non ipsa dedit specimen natura creandi?

(V. 181-186)

From whence did the example, pattern, and *notities* (concept, *prolēpsis*) occur to the gods so that they suddenly had the idea of creating, and where did they get the pattern of what it was they were going to create? "Creation" is simply the result of collisions of random atoms in their eternal fall. These lines, which echo other parts of the poem (e.g., II, 167f; I, 1024-1028), are Lucretius' prime expression of his rejection of the doctrine of creation, as V. 310f express his rejection of the world's eternity. If we accept the idea that except for the Jews no thinkers before the Stoics held such views in a way that required polemical dismantling by Epicurean critics, we can perhaps locate in these verses of Lucretius the approach that produced the question whose origins we have been seeking. Kleve suggests strongly that "Lucretius' attack on the view that the world is created for the sake of men ... cannot be found in any extant writings from Epicurus and his time"[24]). They are found, however, in Philodemus and Cicero, and although it is possible that they attack views similar to those held by Plato (Cic. *De natura Deorum* 1. 8) and therefore once attacked by Epicurus, no such text of Epicurus survives, and the topic is not taken up between Epicurus and Lucretius. Kleve further suggests that the whole Epicurean attack upon doctrines of eternity and creation was assembled in parts from Epicurus to Lucretius and his contemporaries, but in any case, "not fully assembled' until Lucretius and Philodemus[25]).

Lucretius' attack on creation and eternity theories is, on the whole, somewhat more restrained than those of other Epicureans, and far less restrained that some charges of Philodemus. In his discussion of the gods, Philodemus asks whether they have furniture or use the lavatory. If a case has been made in our search for a *terminus post quem*, it is unlikely that our question will have been asked (or, possibly, could have been asked) much before the time of Lucretius. It remains to link Lucretius

[24]) KLEVE, "The Philosophical Polemics", 66.

[25]) Ibid. 69. Some of these survived into Neoplatonic works. For PLOTINUS, see *Enn.* II. 9. 8-9.

and Augustine, or, rather, Lucretius and Irenaeus and the Gnostics whom Irenaeus accuses of having asked the question.

One possible connection is, of course, Book I of Cicero's *De natura Deorum*, in which Velleius the Epicurean offers both Epicurean doctrine and Epicurean polemic in generous measure. In Book I, 21 f of *De nat. deorum* Velleius raises the question: why did the makers of the world wake up suddenly after having slept for so many centuries[26])? Succeeding sections of the first book deal, in the customary manner of Epicurean polemic, which the opinions of others, from Thales to Diogenes of Babylon, raising such questions as: what is the way of life of the gods and how do they spend their time? These questions, sharing with *De rerum natura* V, 110 ff the general character of Epicurean polemic, are sharper and more dramatic, since they are raised as part of a lively dialogue and thus lack the restraint that Lucretius' somber discourse gives to his own treatment of the question.

Epicurean polemic, then, focuses upon certain aspects of creation and the nature of the divinity that had long been criticized in several major streams of Greek apophatic theology which, in Gnostic, Jewish, and Christian theology took the form of emphasis upon the unknowability, unnameability, and incomprehensibility of the divinity, developed largely as negative theology. Any criticism of anthropomorphism would have appealed to such thinkers without entailing their acceptance of the rest of Epicurus' theology. The syncretistic character of late antique thought in the first and second centuries opened the latter to Platonic influences. Earlier anthropomorphism had to be argued away by Jewish and Christian thinkers alike, allegorized and made suitable to the apophatic approach taken by most serious religious thinkers of the period.

In our consideration of Epicureanism thus far, we have noted that the *cur ante non* form of the argument is indeed Epicurean, and the *quid antequam* form may be, although it is not in Lucretius, other Epicurean polemic, or the *De natura deorum*[27]). Perhaps the most likely Epicurean

[26]) For other uses of the image of the sleeping gods, see ORIGEN, *Contra Celsum* VI. 78 (ed. H. CHADWICK, p. 391); EHRHARDT, *The Beginning*, 163, nn. 1-3. The Ciceronian text is annotated in A. S. PEASE, *M. Tulli Ciceronis De natura deorum* (Cambridge, Mass., 1955), *ad* I. 21 (pp. 187-191).

[27]) MEIJERING, in his extensive annotations to Book XI of the *Confessions* (*Schöpfung, Ewigkeit und Zeit*, 40-45, 105-108) argues unequivocally that "diese Frage is ursprünglich von den Epikureen aufgeworfen worden, für die sie eine wichtige Rolle in der Polemik gegen die Stoiker spielt ...", citing the *De natura deorum*, *De rerum natura*, and

source for it would be Philodemus, particularly when we consider the tone and character of some of Philodemus' other questions in a similar vein. But Cicero was familiar with the work of Philodemus and would probably have had no hesitation about using the *quid antequam* form if he had found it *apud* Philodemus. Thus, Philodemus himself remains an unlikely source.

Epicurean polemic seems to have been satisfied with its notion of sleeping gods, or, in the polemic of Philodemus and Colotes, of gods using furniture and lavatories. There is really no reason why an Epicurean polemicist would have thought to ask what the gods were doing before they created heaven and earth because Epicureans were perfectly satisfied with the random events that the descent of the stream of atoms produced. Epicureanism approached creation from the point of view of providence and retribution, not cosmogony. The *quid antequam* question, however, seems to indicate not simply another approach to polemic, but a serious interest precisely in the nature of creation itself.

IV

Although Epicurean polemic was certainly known to the Gnostics who asked Irenaeus the *quid antequam* question, there is no certainty that the *quid antequam* form was Epicurean. In order to turn the one into the other (and there is much to suggest that Epicurean polemic shaped the original form of the question, even if it did not transform it), there must have been a scenario of pre-creation activity in whose interest it was to do so. There were, in fact, two scenarios. The first of these was Jewish, the second Gnostic.

The Jewish source was not Philo, since Philo's extensive discussion of Genesis and related topics do not include the *quid antequam* form of

AETIUS, *Placita* in support. However, as we argue here, the Epicurean *cur ante non* form of the question never, in Epicurean polemic becomes the *quid antequam* form. The case for an Epicurean origin of the *type* of question is much more solid. MEIJERING does not note Irenaeus' or Origen's citation of the question. The origin of the *quid antequam* form in gnostic circles seems clear. The question then becomes why did Gnostics modify the Epicurean polemical question? The following pages suggest one possible answer. There are, of course, other aspects of early Genesis-questions that this paper does not discuss. For Augustine and Epicurus, see H. HAGENDAHL, *Augustine and the Latin Classics*, Studia Graeca et Latina Gothoburgensia, XX (Göteborg, 1967), with significant additions in James J. O'DONNELL, "Augustine's Classical Readings", *Recherches Augustiniennes* 15 (1980), 144-175, at 161-2.

the question[28]). But Midrashic testimonies do in fact discuss a pre-creation scenario, not to be sure, a Gnostic type, but one which invited consideration from anyone interested in the creation story. The Midrashic account of creation, based upon Genesis 1. 1, rather prolongs the story, separating the creation of the first seven things — Torah, the divine throne, Paradise, Hell, the name of the Messiah, the celestial sanctuary, and the Voice that cries aloud, "Return, ye children of men" — from the creation of the heavens and the earth two thousand years later. Within this two thousand year period, God took counsel with Torah (identified with the divine Wisdom, although Tertullian, *Adversus Praxean* 16, indicates a Jewish tradition of God's consulting with angels in order to avoid Trinitarian implications), created several worlds before the present one, was petitioned by the letters of the alphabet to permit each one to be the agent of creation, and tempered justice with mercy in order to permit the world to survive[29]). In one sense, then, Midrash does offer an account of "what God was doing before He created the heavens and the earth—." but it is not an account that violates Genesis, rather prolonging and expanding the act of creation itself.

Assuming as seems likely, that the *cur ante non* form of the question was one basis for the *quid antequam* form, and that Midrashic commentary offered a much more prolonged scenario for creation than did

[28]) Besides the studies listed above, n. 4, see Arnold EHRHARDT, "Creatio ex nihilo", *Studia Theologica* 4 (1950), 13f, rpt. in EHRHARDT, *The Framework of New Testament Studies* (Manchester, 1964), 200-233; idem, *The Beginning*, 162-171; Gerhard MAY, *Schöpfung aus dem Nichts* (Berlin-New York, 1978); WOLFSON, Philo, I, 204 ff, 303; David WINSTON, "Philo's Theory of Cosmogony", in Birger A. PEARSON, ed., *Religious Syncretism in Antiquity: Essays in Conversation with Geo Widengren* (Missoula, Mon., 1975), 157-172. As WINSTON points out (p. 162), PHILO does remark that "time there was not before there was a world", in *De opif.* 26, 67; *Leg. all.* I. 2; *Sacr.* 65. but Philo is speaking of time, not the deity, See also below nn. 31-32.

[29]) Louis GINZBERG, *The Legends of the Jews*, Vol. 1 (Philadelphia, 1913), 3-8, and Vol. V (Philadelphia, 1925), 3-5. I am grateful to Judah GOLDIN for this reference. On the background, see John BOWKER, *The Targums and Rabbinic Literature: An Introduction to Jewish Interpretations of Scripture* (Cambridge, 1969), 95-109, and Geza VERMES, "Bible and Midrash: Early Old Testament Exegesis", in VERMES, *Post-Biblical Jewish Studies* (Leiden, 1975), 59-91. For Christian adaptation of some of these Midrashic accounts, see Louis GINZBERG, *Die Haggada bei den Kirchenvätern und in der apokryphischen Literatur* (Berlin, 1900), 2-14. On the continuity of these problems in Judaism, see E. E. URBACH, *The Sages: Their Concepts and Beliefs*, 2 vols. (Jerusalem, 19), Ch. 9, 161-189. I am grateful to Michael PANITZ for this reference. See also Saul LIBERMAN, Hellenism in Jewish Palestine (New York, 1962). I am grateful to Michael Kaplowitz for this reference. See also below, n. 32.

Genesis itself, it becomes possible to ask how, and by whom, did the *cur ante non* form of Lucretius, Velleius, and Philodemus become the *quid antequam* form of Irenaeus' Gnostic and Augustine's Manichaean opponents? How did the Epicurean *deus dormiens* become the *deus* (or *demiurgos curiosus* of the Gnostics? How would Gnostics look at Genesis 1. 1 in the light of both Epicurean *cur ante non* anti-creation polemic and the Midrashic doctrine of the pre-existence of the seven things[30])?

Both Gnostics and Manichaeans knew very well what the divinity and its enemies were doing before the creation. The Gnostic myth of material creation as a final stage in the falling-away of the Archons as described in the *Apocryphon of John* or the untitled tract in the Nag Hammadi collection commonly called "On the Origin of the World" both provided ample scenarios of divine and semi-divine activity which attacked the principle of creation as found in Genesis[31]). To ask the question "What was God doing before He created the heavens and the earth", was to indict Genesis for failing to account, first, for the true nature of God in the "Age Before" and, second, of failing to recognize

[30]) The best study of Gnostic polemic is now Klaus KOSCHORKE, *Die Polemik der Gnostiker gegen das kirchliche Christentum* (Leiden, 1978). Koschorke does not, unfortunately, note the question discussed here. The differences between Epicureanism and Gnosticism are outlined by A. H. ARMSTRONG, "Gnosis and Greek Philosophy", in B. ALAND, ed., *Gnosis. Festschrift fur Hans Jonas* (Göttingen, 1978), 91-2. There is some discussion of Gnostic use of Epicurean polemic in MEIJERING, *God Being History*, 31-8. IRENAEUS, much concerned with the philosophical origins of heresy (*Adv. haer*. II. 14. 2-6) did not link our question to Epicurus (or to Anaximander, whom he seems to have mistaken for Epicurus); see R. M. GRANT, "Early Christianity and Pre-Socratic Philosophy", *Harry Austryn Wolfson Jubilee Volume* (Jerusalem, 1965), 1, 357-384, at 366. For some Gnostic questions, *ap*. CLEMENT OF ALEXANDRIA, see *Ex. Theodoto* 78. 2. One of the staunchest Christian opponents of Epicureanism seems to have been Dionysius of Alexandria, *ap*. EUSEBIUS, *Praeparatio Evangelica* XIV. 23. Besides such writers as Arnobius and Lactantius, Eusebius seems to have been one of the chief sources for the fourth-century fathers' information concerning ancient philosophy. For cosmological inquiry, see *Pr. Ev*. I. 7-8; XIV. 16-27. On Christian ideas of creation, see VII, ii- XI. 31.

[31]) On Gnostics' finding the Demiurge in Old Testament texts, see Orval WINTERMUTE, "A Study of Gnostic Exegesis of the Old Testament", in James M. EFIRD, ed., *The Use of the Old Testament in the New and Other Essays: Studies in Honor of William Franklin Stinespring* (Durham, N. C., 1972), 241-70, citing particularly the untitled "On the Origin of the World", Codex II. 5 of the Nag Hammadi library. On the cosmogonic importance of the same text, see Michel TARDIEU, *Trois mythes gnostiques* (Paris, 1974), 49 ff. See also A. E. SEGAL, *Two Powers in Heaven: Early Rabbinic Reports about Christianity and Gnosticism* (Leiden, 1977) Nils A. DAHL, "The Arrogant Archon and the Lewd Sophia: Jewish Traditions in Gnostic Revolt", in Bentley LAYTON, ed., *The Rediscovery of Gnosticism*, 2 vols. (Leiden, 1981), II, 689-712; Ithamar GRUENWALD, "Aspects of the Jewish-Gnostic Controversy", ibid. 713-723.

creation as a flaw rather than as a significant and benevolent act. In short, to both Gnostics and Manichaeans Genesis provided an erroneous and misleading account of a history, the accurate understanding of which was crucial to true Gnosis.

The long debate on the relation between Jewish thought and early Gnosticism is not over, nor is there a general consensus on the question of the influence of Gnostic polemic on rabbinic literature in the first three centuries of the common era[32]). The variety of rabbinic opinion on such matters as creation *ex nihilo*, the emanation of light, pre-existent matter, Torah, and the angels shows traces both of Gnostic influence and anti-Gnostic polemic. In the light of the history of discussions of gods and creation, Gnostic approaches to the opening verses of Genesis seem, in fact, to be the most likely occasion for the transformation of the Epicurean *cur ante non* polemical question to the later *quid antequam* form. That the question was in fact a Gnostic adaptation of the Epicurean form may be further indicated by the absence of the *quid antequam* question from later Midrashic literature; that is, it was probably not a question that originated within Jewish thought.

Gnostic cosmogonies are well-enough known to scholars so that they do not have to be recounted here. From Marcion on, Gnostic denial that the creator god of the Old Testament was the high god forced Christian thinkers to evaluate and re-evaluate the place of the Old

[32]) The argument here is separate from the most vexing question of the Jewish origins of Gnosticism. For the latter, see YAMAUCHI, *Pre-Christian Gnosticism*, 143-162, with references; the most recent case has been made by Birger A. PEARSON, "Jewish Elements in Gnosticism and the Development of Gnostic Self-Definition", in E. P. SANDERS, ed., *Jewish and Christian Self-Definition* (Philadelphia, 1980), 151-160, with further references. Arthur Darby NOCK has linked Gnostic speculation with particular scriptural texts which Jewish thinkers prohibited to those with immature minds, for example, Ezekiel's vision of the chariot and the Genesis account of creation: "Gnosticism" (above, n. 11), 947-8. The Ezekiel text, of course, also got PETER ABELARD into some difficulties many centuries later. In addition to the studies cited here and in note 28, there are important observations in A. ALTMANN, "Gnostic Themes in Rabbinic Cosmology", in I. EPSTEIN, et al., eds., *Essays in Honor of the Very Rev. Dr. J. H. Hertz* (London, 1942), 19-32; idem, "A Note on the Rabbinic Doctrine of Creation", *Journal of Jewish Studies* 7 (1956), 195-206, rpt. in Alexander ALTMANN, *Studies in Religious Philosophy and Mysticism* (Ithaca, N. Y., 1969), 128-138. Georges VAJDA, "Notice Sommaire sur l'interprétation de Genèse 1. 1-3 dans le judaïsme post-biblique", *In principio*, 23-35, at 32, has pointed our the function of anterior worlds in the Haggadic anti-gnostic polemic. See also David WINSTON, "The Book of Wisdom's Theory of Cosmogony", *History of Religions* 11 (1971), 185-202, with further citations from rabbinic discussions of *creatio ex nihilo*, and WINSTON, ed., *The Wisdom of Solomon*, The Anchor Bible (New York, 1979), 38-42.

Testament in relation to the New, indeed, to create the New. The texts linked in Genesis 1. 1, Proverbs 8. 22-31, Ps. 110. 3, and Isaiah 53 offered plenty of room for this debate. Marcion and the development of his anti-creationist doctrine became the fundamental targets of later ecclesiastical thinkers analyzing heresy. Such arguments, especially when focused upon the nature of Christ, became the foundation for later Christological heresy as well, and contributed to the *zetēma-quaestio* genre in literature[33]).

[33]) Some, but not all of these polemical questions seem to have become part of the *zetēma-quaestio* genre in fourth-century Christian literature begun by Eusebius and Acacius of Caesarea and earlier, by Philo, in Jewish exegesis. See G. BARDY, "La littérature patristique des *Quaestiones et responsiones* sur l'Écriture sainte", *Revue biblique* 41 (1932), 210-236, 341-369, 515-537; 42 (1933), 14-30, 211-229, 328-352; cf. esp. Vol. 41, p. 347, citing the *quaestiones* of AMBROSIASTER: *Quid opus erat per Moysen, et non antea, exordium mundi et ordinem naturae exponere?* cf. p. 555; for AUGUSTINE's *Quaestiones*, pp. 514-537. In the work of JEROME, the *Quaestiones hebraicae in Genesim*, rabbinic questions enter the genre, and for Augustine's comments on these, see pp. 356-69, 520-1. On the later treatment and conception of these and similar questions, see Bardy's citation of the *Quaestiones* of the fifth-century THEODORET OF CYRRHUS, Vol. 42, p. 220: "Above all, we must realize that not all writers have the same purpose in undertaking their inquiries. Some pose their questions with impiety and seek to argue with Scripture, sometimes by arguing that Scripture does not teach the truth, sometines insisting that Scripture contains contradictions. Other writers inquire out of love for knowledge and the desire to find what it is they seek. With the grace of God we will shut up the blaspheming mouths of the first, and we will demonstrate the harmony of Holy Scripture and the truth of its teaching. To the second, we will bring, as far as we are able, the solution to their difficulties" (PG 80: 76). The two problems with Bardy's work are his neglect of pagan and heretical polemic on the one hand, and the tradition of rabbinic *quaestiones* on the other. The problem of the relations between earlier polemic, whether pagan, Jewish, or Christian, and the emergence of *zetēmata*, *quaestiones disputatae*, is complex, involving the *Testimonies* of early Christian literature as well as pagan and Jewish polemic. On the evidence of the *Testimonies* for some of the questions considered here, see, for example, James Rendel HARRIS, *Testimonies*, Vol I (Cambridge, 1916), 71-74, à propos IRENAEUS, *Apostolical Preaching*, c. 43 (ed. Joseph P. SMITH [Westminister, Md., 1952]). See also Jaroslov PELIKAN, *The Emergence of the Catholic Tradition* (100-600), Vol I of his *The Christian Tradition: A History of the Development of Doctrine* (Chicago, 1971), 78-81, 175-195, and Leo SCHEFFCZYK, *Creation and Providence*, trans. Richard STACHEN (New York-London, 1970), esp. 97-104. Pierre COURCELLE, "Propos antichrétiens rapportés par saint Augustin", *Recherches Augustiniennes* 1 (1958), 148-186; idem, "Critiques exégètiques et arguments antichrétiens rapportés par Ambrosiaster", *Vigiliae Christianae* 13 (1959), 135-169; idem, "Anti-Christian Arguments and Christian Platonism: from Arnobius to St. Ambrose", in A. MOMIGLIANO, ed., *The Conflict Between Paganism and Christianity in the Fourth Century* (Oxford, 1963), 151-192, all with extensive notes and references. In the second of these studies, Courcelle cites a criticism taken up by AMBROSIASTER about the date of Moses' writing: (p. 139) *Quaestio* III ... *Quid opus erat per Moysen, et non ante, exordium mundi et ordinem creaturae exponere?* Cf. the parallel question cited in the first study (p. 159 n. 54): *Quare non ante venit Christus?* The *non ante* objection seems related to the *antequam*

For Gnostics, the Old Testament recounted the creating activities of an inept and evil demiurge, a lower form of being than the highest deity, who was transcendent, passive, in fact rather Epicurean. To such a school of thought, such ideas as benevolent creation *ex nihilo*, the pre-existent Logos, and the dignity of material creation itself were anathema.

Thus, unlikely though it may have been for an Epicurean polemicist to ask the *quid antequam* form of the question, there is reason to expect that a Gnostic — probably not Marcion, but possibly Valentinus or Ptolemaeus or one of their followers — would have found that by turning the *cur ante non* Epicurean question into a *quid antequam* form he could indict the Old Testament creation story and the Christian doctrine of Christ as Logos and at the same time imply a secret knowledge of exactly what it was that "God" was doing before he created the heavens and the earth. It would be nice to find such a text in Gnostic literature rather than in Irenaeus, particularly since historians casually designate the question as "hoary" and a "stock" question, but no such text has so far been found. But Irenaeus' testimony is weighty, and if he cites the question in a Gnostic context, he had perhaps better be believed. And we may only suggest that that was where it originated in the *quid antequam* form.

V

It is readily understandable how the question in such a form might appeal to Manichaeans as readily as it evidently had to Gnostics. The heresiologists of the early church had their complex work cut out for them, and they employed doctrine, piety, rhetoric, and the same tone of satirical invective which they had encountered in their opponents. They also found a quick-witted response to the question. For although Augustine himself did not give the answer, "God was making hell for those who presumptuously scrutinize his secrets", and if he himself did not invent it, others had, and Augustine could at least remind his readers of that answer. Common sense is one of the least noted, but not one of the least important and appealing qualities of the early Latin fathers.

question dealt with here. Cf. "The Anti-Christian Arguments" p. 172, no. 57; "Ambrosiaster", p. 136 n. 17; p. 139 n. 31. See also Robert L. WILKEN, "Pagan Criticism of Christianity: Greek Religion and Christian Faith", in William R. SCHOEDEL and Robert L. WILKEN, eds., *Early Christian Literature and the Classical Intellectual Tradition: In Honorem Robert M. Grant* (Paris, 1979), 177-132.

Against these scenarios, Augustine later turned the very talents that had once led him astray. Criticizing the Manichaean term "The Father of the Happy Enlightenment", Augustine disingenuously asked: *Quibus ergo erat ille pater aut cuius erat pater, quem modo patrem nominavit? Si enim nihil genuerat, pater esse non poterat* (*C. Fel.* I. 18. 82). The answers of Felix and Faustus did not stand up to such questioning, which was, in fact, Augustine's skillful turning of a Manichaean rhetorical and polemical technique against the Manichaeans themselves. Those who depend upon metaphor must be prepared to defend metaphorical language more skillfully than did Augustine's Manichaean opponents and teachers. In fact, the technique works far better as polemic than as dogmatic assertion, as Augustine realized with increasing certainty and success, when he finally articulated his disillusionment with the once-enchanting myth of Manicheism: *fabula illa est longa et vana.* (*C. Faustum* XIII. 6)[34]).

The answer which Augustine says that he will not give, although others do — *alta scrutantibus gehennas parabat* — deserves a concluding comment. In Augustine's vocabulary, *altus* generally means either an attribute of God or the improper object of human attention[35]). In *Confessions* X. 8 (a passage later made famous by Francesco Petrarca) Augustine notes that men look at high mountains (*alta montium*) and forget what is in themselves. In *C. Faustum* XXI. 3, he notes:

> *Occultum est, altum est; inaccessabili secreto ab humana cogitatione seclusum est, quemadmodum Deus et damnet impium, et justificet impium.*

[34]) Here and elsewhere, Augustine charged the Manichaeans with understanding neither the function of language nor the nature of reality. Thus, his citation of this question as a leitmotif of Book XI is part of what Marcia COLISH has called Augustine's "redemption" of language. COLISH, *The Mirror of Language: A Study in the Medieval Theory of Knowledge* (New Haven, 1968), 24-82. I am grateful to Ann MATTER for this reference. On Christian polemic, see now Ilona OPELT, *Die Polemik in der christlichen lateinischen Literatur von Tertullian bis Augustin* (Heidelberg, 1980).

[35]) David LENFANT, *Concordantiae Augustinianae* (Paris, 1666; rpt. Brussels, 1963), sv. *altus*. Several exceptions to this generalization have kindly been pointed out to me by James J. O'DONNELL: *Conf.* VI. 7; IX. 1; IX. 4, but these do not affect the generalization itself.

[36]) For PETRARCH, the *locus* is *Rerum familiarum* IV. 1. See B. Martinellli, "L'ascensione al Monte Ventoux", *Studi in onore di Alberto Chiari* (Brescia, 1973), 369-377. and John E. WRIGLEY, "Petrarch, Saint Augustine, and the Augustinians", *Augustinian Studies* 8 (1977), 71-90. Interestingly, the Petrarchan text makes it clear that Petrarch opened his copy of the *Confessions* to X. 8. 15 "by chance", another Augustinian touch.

Scrutare (or, perhaps more commonly, *perscrutare*) *alta* was, of course, a classical and hellenistic commonplace, condemning all human intellectual seeking after the unattainable, echoed in Scripture and in patristic literature. It appeared familiarly in Ecclus. 3. 22: *altiora te ne quaesieris*, and Romans 11. 20: *noli altum sapere*. The phrase became attached to the late antique condemnation of one kind of intellectual curiosity and therefore plays a long and interesting role in later intellectual history[37]).

In Augustine, however, the commonplace had perhaps a second meaning, a more literal one. The Manichees had attracted him in the first place with their claims of explaining *alta*, and, like their Gnostic predecessors, claimed to be higher than other beings themselves, higher indeed than the demiurge of the Old Testament. Augustine here is not criticizing just anyone who scrutinizes the heavens or asks questions about the meaning of Genesis, but specifically those who scrutinize *alta*, those realms from which the eye of the flesh is excluded. For Augustine had discovered the trap into which such delusions might lead, and he knew the dangers they entailed. As he said elsewhere (*Ep*. 89. 9. 2): *Expedit ab imo surgere, quam ex alto cadere.*

[37]) There is a large literature on the subject. In the context of *curiositas* alone, see Hans BLUMENBERG, *Der Prozess der theoretischen Neugierde* (Berlin, 1973); Heiko Augustinus OBERMAN, *Contra vanam curiositatem* (Zurich, 1973); Carlo GINZBURG, "High and Low: The Theme of Forbidden Knowledge in the Sixteenth and Seventeenth Centuries", *Past and Present* 73 (1976), 28-41, and the work of MEIJERING, *Calvin wider die Neugierde* (Nieuwkoop, 1980). Richard NEWHAUSER and I are presently at work on a more thorough study of the ideas of curiosity and forbidden knowledge; cf. Richard NEWHAUSER, "Towards a History of Human Curiosity: A Prolegomenon to its Medieval Phase", *Deutsche Vierteljahrschrift* 56.4 (1982), 559-575; Edward PETERS, "*Libertas inquirendi* and the *vitium curiositatis* in medieval Thought", in George Makdisi, ed., *La notion de la liberté au moyen âge.Islam, Byzanze, Occident* (Paris: forthcoming) and idem, "*Aenigma Solomonis*: Manichaean anti-Genesis Polemic and the *Vitium Curiositatis* in *Confessions*, III. 6.". *Augustiniana*: forthcoming. For later medieval interest in some of the questions raised here, see Richard C. DALES, "Discussions of the Eternity of the World during the First Half of the Twelfth Century", *Speculum* 57 (1982), 495-508; M.-D. CHENU, "The Platonisms of the Twelfth Century", in L. K. LITTLE and Jerome TAYLOR, trans., *Nature, Man and Society in the Twelfth Century* (Chicago, 1968), with some additional comments in Stephen GERSH, "Platonism — Neo-platonism — Aristotelianism : A Twelfth Century Metaphysical System and Its Sources", in R. L. BENSON and Giles CONSTABLE, eds., *Renaissance and Renewal in the Twelfth Century* (Cambridge, Mass., 1982), 512-536. The larger role of creation in twelfth century thought is discussed in G. R. EVANS, *Old Arts and New Theology* (Oxford, 1980), 167-192. Our question is echoed in BEDE's Augustinian commentary on Genesis (*In pentateuchem commentarii* 1: PL 91; 189-190); and Bede may have the final word: *Utique non in principio temporis, Deus enim facit tempora. Et ideo antequam Deus faceret tempora, non erant tempora Non ergo possumus dicere quomodo Deus nondum aliquid fecerat.*

II

Aenigma Salomonis: Manichaean Anti-Genesis Polemic and the Vitium curiositatis in Confessions III. 6

Book III of St. Augustine's *Confessions* depicts the bleakest moments in a willful and erring life and, in two important places, the first signs of change in that life. After the description of his vicious student conduct in Carthage in III. 1-3, Augustine describes his conversion to *philosophia* after reading Cicero's *Hortensius* (III. 4), his turning to scripture and failure to understand it (III. 5), and his subsequent fall into Manichaean sympathies (III. 6-10). Book III concludes with the second sign of change, after the conversion to *philosophia*, the hopes expressed in the dream of Monica and the promise of the nameless bishop: *fieri non potest, ut filius istarum lacrimarum pereat* (III. 11-12). The narrative structure of Book III thus consists of the two courses of sin, at Carthage and among the Manichaeans, punctuated by the first conversion and concluded by the hope of a second conversion. Although the conversion to *philosophia* divides the two courses, it does not dissolve the link between them. The link is structural, and it had been established in the meditation on the psychology of sin in Book II (II. 4-10).

Book III. 4-5 and *Sermo* 51 describe the illumination and fear that combine, for the first time, to instill hope and a more complex sense of purpose in the young and successful student [1]). Having imbibed the name of Jesus with his morther's milk and determined that *philosophia* and Jesus must be one and the same, Augustine turns to scripture, whose truth he fails to perceive because of its lack of *Tulliana dignitas*. The student of rhetoric, brought to Cicero by the requirements of the study of rhetoric, is struck, not by Cicero's rhetoric, but by his great message, and, turning to that place where wisdom is in fact to be found, misses it because of his intellectual unpreparedness and superficial rhetorical expectations.

[1]) This was illustrated by Pierre COURCELLE, *Recherches sur les Confessions de saint Augustin* (Paris, 1950), 60-67, and developed by A. SOLIGNAC in his introduction to the *Confessions, Œuvres de saint Augustin*, Vol. 13, *Les Confessions, livres I-VII* (Paris, 1962), 125-132.

It is no wonder that Augustine then succumbs to the "empty language", "glib delirium", and "vain fables" of the Manichaeans. He does not say whether they offered *Tulliana dignitas* (although he later mentions Faustus' pleasing speech), but they certainly offered something as inviting and persuasive to both his pride and his anxiety[2]). Specifically, they offered a resolution of Augustine's problem of the identity of *philosophia* and Jesus in a way that did not disturb his inability to perceive spiritual meaning in scripture. They discarded, repudiated, or allegorized those parts of scripture which had offended Augustine in III. 5 and dressed the remainder and their own explanatory writings in fable and myth. Manichaean "solutions" to the problems of the two genealogies of Christ, the Genesis creation narrative, the anthropomorphic depiction of the deity, the wickedness of the patriarchs, and the divine and human natures of Christ are noted in the *Confessions* and in other early writings of Augustine[3]). In the *Confessions*, Book III. 6 discusses Manichaean cosmology and cosmogony, and III. 7 considers Manichaean theodicy.

As Peter Brown has pointed out, "in [the *Confessions*] one constantly senses the tension between the 'then' of the young man and the 'now' of the bishop"[4]). Book III. 8-10 constitutes just one example of the bishop's mind at the time of writing rushing in to deal directly with the problems of justice, goodness, and evil that Manichaean teachings contain, as if it were not satisfied by the exposition in the *De Gen. c. Man.*, the *De moribus Man.*, or other anti-Manichaean writings. The two final sections indeed raise the hope of conversion, appropriately enough, not in the mind of the young Augustine, but in the tears of Monica and in the promises of Christ and the bishop.

Of the two courses of sin divided by the ambiguous conversion of III. 4, the second is both more and less serious than the first. Following the conversion to *philosophia*, Augustine falls into greater, because more intellectual error concerning God among the Manichaeans, but at the same time he is at least moving the right direction. He is seeking the right thing, *philosophia*, in the right place, the name of Jesus. By a long and

[2]) *Conf.* V. 6; cf. SOLIGNAC, 131.

[3]) SOLIGNAC, 128-9. For the two genealogies, see *Sermo* 51; on anthropomorphism, *De Gen. c. Man.* I. 17. 27-8, *Conf.* III. 7. 12; on the sins of the patriarchs, *C. Faust* VI. II, *Conf.* III. 7. 13, V. 10. 19, V. 14. 24; on Creation, *De Gen. c. Man.* I. II. 3; *Conf.* XI-XIII; and as this article argues, *Conf.* III. 6.

[4]) Peter BROWN, *Augustine of Hippo* (Berkeley and Los Angeles, 1969), 164.

circuitous route, he will eventually find it, and the rest of the *Confessions* constitutes a description and verification (in the last three books) of that journey.

The appropriateness of the final three books of the *Confessions*, the exposition of the opening verses of Genesis, has been debated many times. Modern scholarly consensus has determined, rightly, I think, that the Genesis-exposition is indeed an integral part of the work and not an appendage. This study proposes to suggest the place of *Confessions* III. 6, or rather the events unclearly described therein, in Augustine's later studies on Genesis, and in fact in Augustine's attitude toward Genesis throughout the rest of his life as a Christian thinker and teacher. Its thesis is that *Confessions* III. 6, neither the clearest nor the most explicit part of the work, is a criticism and description of Manichaean attacks on Genesis and Christian cosmogony and cosmology, just as III. 7 is clearly a critique of Manichaean theodicy.

There are important links between III. 1-3 and III. 6-7, most notably in Augustine's virtuoso use of the *vitium curiositatis* to describe both his earlier and later sympathies and affections. The Manichaeans are, structurally at least, parallel to the *eversores*; they too are "overturners" and "wreckers". They too attract the weak and the morbid interest of those who, like Augustine himself, can admire, if not wholeheartedly join them. The admirer of the *eversores* and the "Hearer" of the Manichaeans is the same man, and the final lack of commitment to the former may prefigure an eventual lack of commitment to the latter. There are indeed a few rays of hope in Book III, but they are not many, and they are not soon realized.

To be converted to a life of *philosophia* in fourth-century North Africa, whether by the *Hortensius* or anything else, was to be converted to a way of life, a religious calling to free the soul from earthly attachments so that it might know its true nature and mount up to its celestial home[5]). Manichaeism, like Gnosticism before it, rejected any alternative cosmology, particularly the Jewish and Christian cosmology and cosmogony as told in Genesis and referred to elsewhere in scripture and haggadah[6]). Although Augustine fell in with a group of particularly

[5]) BROWN, *Augustine*, 40-45; Anne-Marie MALINGREY, *Philosophia. Étude d'un groupe de mots dans la littérature grècque des Présocratiques au IVe siècle après J.-C.* (Paris, 1961); Solignac, 86.

[6]) These themes may be traced in the work of FESTUGIÈRE, PUECH, A. H. ARMSTRONG, Georges VAJDA, and others. Much of it is cited in my study, "What Was God Doing Before He Created the Heavens and he Earth?" cited below n. 22.

intellectualist Manichaeans, his story is not a warning simply to any bright young man with a yearning for philosophical wisdom. For Augustine regarded his conquest by the Manichaeans as something to which he was particularly vulnerable precisely at the moment he met them. The encounter, and the beginning of the Manichaean theme that extends through Books Three, Four and Five, does not occupy a separate book, but takes up the second part of a book that details at its outset a notably distinctive and personal set of experiences, from Augustine's return to Carthage to his fascination with the *eversores*. In Augustine's mind the two episodes are connected. The conversion to *philosophia* and the prophecies at the end of the book punctuate, but do not dissolve the unity of conscience and the powerful and accusatory sense of self that works in the book from beginning to end. It remains to determine exactly what kind of conscience and sense of self that Augustine regarded himself as having brought, first to the conversion, and then to the Manichaeans.

A close reading of Book III. 1-2 reveals that it is not only the sins of lust, voyeurism, and academic pride that Augustine confesses, but his own psychological preparedness for and enjoyment of them. Anticipating the later sections, III. 1 begins with a description of the young Augustine searching madly and unsatisfactorily for love, as he was later to search for *philosophia*. Dreams of love, "fables and fictions", and the illusions of the theater reveal a young man who is guilty not simply of lust and voyeurism, but one who is attracted to these expressions of sin because of a particular personality history that finds these as the natural and adequate expressions of its fault. The fault, in III. 3, is *sacrilega curiositas*, a vice, I will argue, that Augustine regards as especially characteristic of his own moral condition, not to the exclusion of pride and *concupiscentia carnis*, but in his own case as an organizing and dominant vice, linking his student rioting with his inability to understand scripture and finally with his fascination for and vulnerability toward the fables of the Manichaeans.

Augustine's concept of *curiositas* is the subject of a respectable literature. He was, in fact, the third Latin writer, after Apuleius and Tertullian, to make extensive use of the term[7]). Arguments deriving

[7]) H.-I. MARROU, *Saint Augustin et la fin de la culture antique* (Paris, 1938), 148-57, 277-80, 350-52; Hans BLUMENBERG, "Augustins Anteil an der Geschichte des Begriffs der theoretischen Neugierde", *Revue des Études Augustiniennes* 7 (1961), 35-70; idem, "*Curiositas* und *veritas*. Zur Ideengeschichte von Augustin, *Confessiones* X. 35", *Studia*

Augustine's concept and usage of the term from either or both of his fellow North African writers (whose work he knew) have not, however, been uniformly persuasive. Moreover, most Augustinian scholarship focuses upon Augustine's use of the term in *Confessions* V. 3, where he finally condemns Manichaean cosmological speculations as well as pagan astronomy generally, and X. 35, where Augustine emphatically links *curiositas* with *concupiscentia carnis* and *superbia vitae* as the three great sins catalogued in 1 John 2. 16. The extensive scholarship of Hans Blumenberg on the subject has focused chiefly upon Augustine's condemnation of astrological and astronomical speculation, and although Heiko Oberman has emphasized the individual moral dimension of *curiositas* in Augustine and his relation in this to earlier Christian writers, Greek and Latin, few writers on the Augustinian sense of *curiositas*, except for the purpose or cataloguing Augustine's usage of the term, have considered *Confessions* III. 3 and III. 6[8]).

As I hope to argue elsewhere, Augustine's usage of *curiositas* from its first occurence in the *De musica* (VI. 13. 39) to the passages concerning his own youth in the *Confessions* are specialized and personal. They may derive somewhat from Apuleius and Tertullian (particularly the former), but in these early works, particularly those written about the Manichaean period during the Neoplatonist period, *curiositas* is not yet the broad vice that it becomes in later Augustinian and general Christian usage. The later bishop deals with the term as a category of moral theology and describes it in ways that are applicable to Christians generally. But not all, nor most Christians will be as vulnerable to the vice as was the young Augustine. The spiritual autobiographer is specific and individual; he knows himself as he was, and the keys to his own soul.

From the end of *Confessions* V, Augustine is guided, first by the example of Monica and then by the example and preaching of Ambrose,

Patristica 6 (1962), 294-302; Pierre COURCELLE, *Les Confessions de Saint Augustin dans la tradition litteraire* (Paris, 1963), 101-109; Hans BLUMENBERG, *Die Legitimität der Neuzeit* (Frankfurt, 1966), Part III; idem, *Der Prozess der theoretischen Neugierde* (Berlin, 1973), Heiko Augustinus OBERMAN, *Contra vanam curiositatem* (Zurich, 1973). André LABHARDT, "*Curiositas*. Notes sur l'histoire d'un mot et d'une notion", *Museum Helveticum* (1960), 206-224, is a catalogue rather than an analysis. R. JOLY, Curiositas, *L'Antiquité Classique* 30 (1961), 33-44. H. J. METTE, Curiositas, *Festschrift Bruno Snell*, München, 1956, 227-235. And see below, n. 18.

[8]) An exception in this regard is Robert J. O'CONNELL, *St. Augustine's Early Theory of Man, A.D. 286-391* (Cambridge, Mass., 1968), 146-183. Cf. COURCELLE, *Les Confessions*, 100-109.

further and further away from his Manichaean sympathies, from which he had originally begun to be dislodged by his own intellectual abilities, critical intelligence, and conscience. Although he confessed to a tendency toward *curiositas* at later periods in his life, that *curiositas* is treated more as a tendency towards distraction and thoughtless preoccupation, a somewhat generalized intrusion of the senses upon the mind[9]). Thus, Augustine seems to be essentially freed from the most personal and destructive consequences of the vice when he is freed from the Manichaeans. The *curiositas* peculiar to the young Augustine is a dominant theme only during the nine years between his student days at Carthage and the drawn-out final years of the tiring hearer of the Manichaeans. *Curiositas* in III. 3-6 is not the later, generalized vice applicable to the Christian Everyman, but the unique state of mind and morals, sense impressions and intellect, of the young North African rhetorician and pupil of Manichaean *philosophia*.

The reluctance of some modern commentators on the *Confessions* to appreciate Augustine's sense of the character of his personal moral state in Book III has sometimes led to their underestimating his catalogue of sins in Carthage, just as it has sometimes led to an underestimation of his obsession with the theft of the pears. Augustine, according to these views, is confessing relatively trivial and routine actions of a privileged fourth-century student at Carthage, perhaps out of an overscrupulous converted conscience. But Augustine seems not to be confessing specific acts as much as he confesses his own psychological sympathies with the evils those acts represent. He is drawn to them because of his temperament. His temperament creates a particular attitude toward them, and that attitude and the ensuing vulnerability it creates is Augustine's concern.

Confessions III. 3. 5 contains Augustine's indictment of his actions described in the immediately preceding sections:

> *Et circumvolabat super me fidelis a longe misericordia tua. In quantas iniquitates distabut et sacrilega curiositate secutus sum, ut deserentem te deduceret me ad ima infida et circumventoria obsequia daemoniorum, quibus immolabam facta mea mala, et in omnibus flagellabas me.*

These are not new and otherwise unspecified sins, but the *curiositas* behind the lust, voyeurism, and academic pride that he has already

[9]) Cf. *Conf.* X. 35; Brown, *Augustine*, 180.

recounted; these are his "sacrifices" to demons. Scholarly pride lies behind his rejection of scripture, and scholarly pride and hunger for *philosophia* (an ambivalent *curiositas*, both good and evil) make him prey to the *curiositas* of the Manichaeans.

These parts of *Confessions* III are, as Courcelle remarked, "*peu clair*". But several points ought to be remembered as one approaches them. First, as all Augustinian *curiositas* scholarship on *Confessions* V. 3 and X. 35 agrees, both the separation from Manicheism, and the later conviction of the importance of 1 John 2. 16 are associated particularly with the kind of errors Manichaeans make. It is not, given Augustine's style and method, unlikely, then, that the beginning of his association with Manicheism will also deal with *curiositas* and that *curiositas* is a personal link between the sins of Carthage in the academy and those with the Manichaeans. Indeed, *Confessions* III. 8. 16 already explicitly remarks the triadic sin of 1 John:

> *Haec sunt capita iniquitatis, quae pullulant principandi et spectandi et sentiendi libidine aut una aut duabus earum aut simul omnibus, et vivitur male adversus tria et septem, ...* [10])

With these suggestions in mind, and the reference to 1 John 2. 16 already clearly set out in Book III, we may approach III. 6 with an eye to both *curiositas* and the problem of Genesis.

Augustine, on the proper track of *philosophia* and Jesus, failed to find wisdom in Scripture, because:

> *tumor meus refugiebat modum eius et acies mea non penetrabat interiora eius.*

Pride as a scholar and rhetorician and intellectual inadequacy combined to deflect Augustine from the proper search for truth. For Scripture did not open itself to the wisdom of the world, which Augustine had applied to it, and it concealed deep truths and veiled mysteries behind apparent rough texture and simple narrative. Thus the Manichaeans became the perfect guides for such a personality, driven by *bona curiositas* and misled by *mala curiositas*. The pride of the scholar is indeed *superbia*, but it does not necessarily lead to the worst or most characteristic forms of *superbia vitae*, the *libido dominandi* or *principandi* of the political man. Nor is the

[10]) Evidence elsewhere in Book III is noted in R. J. O'CONNELL, *St. Augustine's Confessions: The Odyssey of a Soul* (Cambridge, Mass., 1969) 51 f.

scholar's lust simply for the flesh of others. In the academic *curiosus* these become subordinated to that one of the three great vices that most effectively enables them to injure the soul, *curiositas*, the lust for and pride in knowledge that points to nothing beyond itself, the desire vicariously to experience not merely the flesh, but the emotions of others, real or imagined, desirous of learning the secrets of the universe and the soul but improperly equipped and disciplined for learning that for which pride and lust drive him on. Such was Augustine when he met the Manichaeans[11]).

Arthur Darby Nock pointed out some years ago the interest that gnostics and Manichaeans took, precisely in those parts of scripture which Jewish scholarship had reserved for the study only of those with mature minds[12]). The opening verses of Genesis, the vision of Ezekiel, and other strategic parts of the Old Testament were not to be discussed before the uninitiated or immature. For these, one required age and experience. But these were often the very first targets of gnostic and later Manichaean exegesis. Irenaeus and Tertullian had cautioned both Christians and heretics to avoid putting questions to certain parts of scripture and, in the case of Irenaeus, to leave certain questions to God which someday, perhaps, He may see fit to divulge to humans in another state, "so that God may everlastingly teach, and men may everlastingly learn"[13]). Augustine's own lament in *Confessions* III. 7-9 is precisely over his own intellectual and spiritual incapacity to perceive the Manichaeans' presumptuous and erroneous treatment of these difficult questions and texts.

Augustine's first observation about the Manichaeans concerns their proud and carnal talkativeness. The snares of the devil were in their mouths, and although they mixed the syllables of the names of the Father, Son, and Holy Spirit, these were merely mixings of sounds from their mouths, not sentiments from their hearts. They spoke of Truth, but truth was not in them, merely a word in their many and clever books. Here Augustine, the proud rhetorician, hears his own unredeemed

[11]) SOLIGNAC, Introduction, 126-8.

[12]) Arthur Darby NOCK, "Gnosticism", in NOCK, *Essays on Religion and the Ancient World*, ed. Zeph STEWART, Vol. II (Cambridge, Mass., 1972), 947-8.

[13]) IRENAEUS, *Adv. Haer* II. 28. 2. See W. C. VAN UNNIK, "Theological Speculation and Its Limits", in William R. SCHOEDEL and Robert L. WILKEN, eds., *Early Christian Literature and the Classical Intellectual Tradition in Honorem Robert L. Grant* (Paris, 1979), 33-44; and Jean DANIÉLOU, "Recherche et tradition chez les pères", *Studia Patristica* 12 (1975), 3-13.

language, in Colish's phrase, echoed in the equally fallen language of the Manichaeans[14]). And he is seduced by the latter, as he had taken improper pride in the former.

The rest of *Confessions* III. 6 describes the further illusions of Manichaean teaching. They tell Augustine of the Creator and the first principles of creation. Their false language taught Augustine Manichaean cosmology, "the sun and moon, great works of yours, but not you, not even the greatest of your works". The sun and moon of the Manichaeans are compared to false food that does not satisfy the real hunger of the starving man. The images of sun and moon, celestial lights, false food, and perverted language all suggest that the III. 6 recounts Manichaean challenges to Genesis' account of creation and cosmology.

Augustine then applies to himself the image of the prodigal son in Luke 16, who desired even the *siliquae porcorum* which swineherds fed to the pigs, a reference which, as Bernhard Blumenkranz long ago showed, was consistently interpreted as profane learning in both Jewish and Christian haggadah[15]). Augustine twists the reference, for he states that he was not even able to eat the *siliquae*. That is, to believe the fables and

[14]) Marcia L. COLISH, *The Mirror of Language: A Study in the Medieval Theory of Knowledge* (New Haven, 1968), 24-82.

[15]) Exegetical criticism of worldly learning has been traced by Bernhard BLUMENKRANZ, "*Siliquae porcorum* (cf. Luc, XV, 16). L'Exégèse mediévale et les sciences profanes", *Mélanges ... Louis Halphen* (Paris, 1951), 11-17. Blumenkranz traces the early medieval exegesis on Luke's story of the prodigal son's wishing that he could have even the slops that a man fed his pigs in terms of the Fathers' and later commentators' understanding of the *siliquae* as signifying profane learning. Ambrose, offering *inanis philosophia* as one possible interpretation of the text (gluttony being the other), probably derived this suggestion from Origen. Origen may have inspired Jerome as well, although Blumenkranz suggests that one of Jerome's Jewish Hebrew teachers my have suggested a Talmudic text to illustrate the significance. Other Talmudic discussions of this theme are in I. EPSTEIN, ed., *The Babylonian Talmud. Seder Mo'ed.* Vol. IV (London, 1938): *Hagigah*, trans. I. Abrahams, pp. 59-104. Chapter II of the *Hagigah* is an important commentary on Jewish theories of esoteric learning and its place in Talmudic study. The Mishnah states that "Whosoever speculates upon four things, a pity for him | He is as though he had not come into the world. [to wit] what is above, what is beneath, what before, what after. And whosoever takes no thought for the honour of his maker, it were a mercy if he had not come into the world". The defense of esoteric knowledge in this text is emphasized by its citation (infrequent in the Talmudic literature although popular generally) of Ecclus. 3. 21-22: "Seek not things that have been permitted thee, think thereupon; thou hast no business with the things that are secret". (p. 73). I am grateful to Michael PANITZ of the Jewish Theological Seminary for discussion of this reference. On food imagery in the *Confessions*, see Leo C. FERRARI, "The 'Food of Truth' in Augustine's *Confessions*", *Augustinian Studies* 9 (1978), 1-14.

lies of the pagan writers would have been had enough, but he did not believe these. But the fables of the Manichaeans he did believe.

Augustine's blindness in *Confessions* III. 6-7 is not simply the result of intellectual unpreparedness. After all, he had penetrated to the great message of Cicero's *Hortensius* through the routine rhetorical expectations he and others brought to it. He pointedly contrasts his scepticism toward the literary fables of the poets with his succumbing to the fables of the Manichaeans. He avoided the trap, pointed out by both Cicero and St. Paul, of falling into step with one another philosophical school, and he aims directly at *philosophia* itself. These were considerable intellectual achievements in the fourth century, as they would have been in the first. Augustine's *acies* was sufficient to prevent him from falling into quite common intellectual traps, but it was not sufficient to open the veiled mysteries of Scripture to him, and this particular failure made him the prey of Manichaeans. It was a particular quality of Augustine's mind and spirit, not its intellectual incapacity, that led to his errors in III. 6-7[16]).

In Books IV and V there is more of this. In IV. 2, Augustine rejects the advances of a sorcerer who offered him success in a rhetorical competition. In IV. 3 he flirted with astrology and *sortes*, but he was advised by a friendly physician to avoid the errors of astrology and did. In IV. 16, unlike others who merely praise it, Augustine read and digested Aristotle's *Categories*, as he also read and easily understood other works on rhetoric, logic, geometry, music, and mathematics[17]). These last works may have been the "scientific books" which Augustine notes that he had read and later brought to bear in his encounter with Faustus (V. 3). The authors of these works did not know God, and, in an echo of Tertullian, became obsessed with the works of the Creator rather than adoring the Creator Himself[18]). And yet, even these books of the *curiosi* could easily overcome the smooth, but utterly unlearned doctrines of Faustus (III. 7.)[19]). Finally, just before his encounter with Ambrose

[16]) SOLIGNAC, Introduction, 85-93.

[17]) Ibid. 166-67.

[18]) TERTULLIAN, *Ad nat.* II. 4. 19. The most extensive discussion of Tertullian's use of the term is that of Jean-Claude FREDOUILLE, *Tertullien et la conversion de la culture antique* (Paris, 1972), 412-442. Fredouille, however, focuses somewhat too narrowly upon Tertullian's use of *curiositas* exclusively as a criticism of polymathy.

[19]) It should be noted that Augustine appreciates the scholarly accuracy of his sources and their intellectual competence, which was superior to that of the Manichaeans. His criticism is therefore not of learning itself, but learning detached from the ultimate

(V. 13–14: deftly introduced as a repetition of Augustine's initial encounter with Faustus), Augustine is moved further from Manicheism by his interest in Academic scepticism and by the dexterity of his friend Elpidius in attacking Manichaean scriptural exegesis. Throughout the experiences described in Books III-V, Augustine's intellectual astuteness brings him rewards and recognition: teaching in Carthage, the move to Rome, and the call to Milan. These constitute an external recognition of the intellectual skills which were not only not dulled, but actually developed (and emphasized in the *Confessions*) during the period of his Manichaean sympathies.

Augustine's wits are sufficiently sharp and his learning sufficiently broad to achieve success in a world with both very high critical standards and very many intellectual and spiritual traps. These are no small attributes, even though they prevented Augustine from accepting the teachings of Ambrose (VI. 4) at first, because, although Ambrose indeed lifted the *velamentum* from Scripture (cf. *velata mysteriis*, III. 5), Augustine could not then accept a new criterion for *certitudo*, and his perplexity became more intense. In the course of Book VI, however, the Manichaean period is over, and the sceptical period is waning. We must now turn back to the problem of Manichaean *curiositas*.

Book III. 6, when set against the problems that Augustine says the Manichaeans claimed to "solve", says nothing about the two genealogies of Christ, the anthropomorphic representation of the deity, the sins of the patriarchs, or the two natures of Christ, although, to be sure, these are considered elsewhere in the anti-Manichaean writings[20]). It does, however, describe and criticize in figurative language some aspects of Manichaean cosmology, introduced by the reference to Manichaean teaching *de te ... sed etiam de istis elementis mundi, creatura tua*. Out of their *libris multis et ingentibus*, the dishes out of which false food was served, the Manichaeans offered Augustine accounts of the sun and the moon, *pulchra opera tua, sed tamen opera tua, non tu, nec ipsa prima*.

Since Schmidt's discovery of the *Kephalaia* of Mani in 1930, much of Augustine's frame of reference in III. 6 can be understood more clearly[21]). The pre- and creation-narrative of the Manichaeans was the

purpose of learning. This is the substance of his attacks upon the *curiosi* in V. 3. Like the Romans and the earthly city, these thinkers have their value, but it is of a different order from that seeking which leads to salvation.

[20]) Above, n. 2.

[21]) There is a large bibliography on the subject, from John P. MAHER, *Saint*

foundation of their dualistic beliefs and must have been asserted, as Gnostic precreation scenarios also were, against the creation narrative of Genesis and the precreation scenarios contained in Midrash[22]). The sun and the moon are the outposts of the kingdom of light, created as a result of the first great battle between representatives of light and darkness, out-posts to be explained and revered by those aware of the particles of divinity in themselves and of the evil nature of the dark bodies in which those particles were entombed.

These, then, are the *phantasmata splendida*, the *fabula longa et vana*, the Manichaean alternative to the Genesis creation narrative. Here, for the first time, Augustine encountered Genesis through the eyes of its Manichaean opponents. It is the occasion of his fall away from the road to truth and already points toward the redemptive exegesis in the last three books of the *Confessions*.

All of this error, and in III. 6 it seems to be the error of Manichaean anti-Genesis polemic, Augustine says, came from his improper carnal use of senses given to all humans by God. The use of the intellect, by which God intended humans to be superior to beasts, was distorted by the senses. This is Augustine's essential definition of *curiositas*.

At the end of III. 6, Augustine offers a striking image that draws together these earlier themes and images:

> *Offendi illam mulierem audacem, inopem prudentiae aenigma Salomonis, sedentem super sellam in foribus et dicentem,* panes occultos libenter edite, et aquam dulcem furtivam bibite, *quae me seduxit quia invenit foris habitantem in oculo carnis meae et talia ruminantem apud me, qualia per illum vorassem.*

Augustine's Defense of the Hexaemeron against the Manichaeans (Rome-St. Meinrad, Ind., 1946), and H.-Ch. PUECH, *Le Manichéisme* (Paris, 1949), to François DECRET, *L'Afrique manichéenne (IV-V siècles). Étude historique et doctrinale*, 2 vols. (Paris, 1978), esp. I, 239-352.

[22]) I have considered this topic in much greater detail in my study "What Was God Doing Before He Created the Heavens and the Earth?" *Augustiniana* 34 (1984), 53-74. To the Augustinian texts cited in that study, I must now add a reference to *Contra Adversarium legis et prophetarum libri duo*, PL 42, 603-666. This work refutes the arguments of a book that Augustine found, *concurrentibus turbis periculosa curiositate et delectatione legeretur*. The work attacks Genesis, not only, "as do the Manichaeans", merely the law and the prophets, but in its doctrine of *Deum mundi fabricatorem*. In I. 2. 2 Augustine notes: *Quaerit ergo*: Quo principio? eiusne quo idem Deus esse coepit, an ex eo quo illum esse vacuum taeduit? *Cui respondetur, quia nec Deus esse coepit, nec eum vacationis suae taeduit, qui neque aliquando non fuit, nec cessando torpuit, nec operando laboravit: nec sine coelo sedis indiquit, nec facto coelo sedem tanquam finitis erroribus peregrinus invenit*. Augustine seems to suggest that the work may be of Marcionite origin. I am grateful to James J. O'Donnell for providing me with this reference.

The text is a pericope of Prov. 9, 13-18 (cf. Prov. 7. 24-7):

> A foolish woman, clamorous and full of allurements and knowing nothing at all, sat in the door of her house upon a seat, in the high place of the city, to call to them who pass on the way and go about their own business. "He that is a little one, let him turn to me", and to the fool she said, "Stolen waters are sweeter, and hidden bread is more pleasant". And he did not know that the dead are there, and that her guests are in the depths of Hell.

In the Hebrew text, the woman is Folly herself, the opposite of Wisdom, whose house, banquet and invitation to eat and drink so as to overcome ignorance are described in the parallel text in Prov. 9. 1-6. The *Aenigma Salomonis*, then, would seem to be for Augustine, as it had been for the writers of Proverbs, Dame Folly personified.

But *Confessions* III. 6 is not Augustine's only usage of the reference[23]). In the *De Gen. contra Man.* II. 27. 41, Augustine refers to the false food that is the *fallacia haereticorum* and then explains the reference to Proverbs 9:

> Haereticorum quippe superba et curiosa cupiditas in libro Proverbiorum clamat sub mulieribus imagine et dicit: *Qui stultus est, divertat ad me ...*

Elsewhere he mentions *fallax doctrina imagine sedens mulier*[24]). In the *Tractatus* 97 on the Gospel of John, the woman represents the *vanitas impiorum*, as La Bonnardière suggests, the followers of magicians. *Aenigma* was a technical term in Greek and Latin, associated with other terms designating riddle, parable, allegory, and mystery[25]). In scripture, it was a technique particularly associated with Solomon, especially in Ecclus. 47. 17 and III Kings 10. 1-10. *Confessions* III 6 uses this kind of

[23]) See the references in A.M. LA BONNARDIÈRE, *Biblia Augustiniana. A. T. Le Libre de Proverbes* (Paris, 1975), 51-54.

[24]) Ibid. 52. Cf. *Tract. in ep. Ioh.* II. 13.

[25]) T I. 985-7, s.v. *aenigma*, citing particularly *QUINTILIAN*, *Inst.* 8.6. 52: *allegoriae ... obscurior*; TERTULLIAN, *Scorp.* 11: *ut allegoriae, ut parabolae, ut aenigmata.* For general late antique use, see Jean PÉPIN, *Mythe et allégorie* (Paris, 1976). The pejorative sense of Quintilian, or the neutral classical usages were perhaps modified by the famous use of the term in the Greek text of 1 Cor. 13. 12. Augustine's usage of the term is much wider than the L'Enfant concordance suggests. Until the full Augustine concordance appears from Eindhoven, consult particular recent concordances to individual works. For later use of these images, see the studies collected in Edouard JEAUNEAU, *'Lectio philosophorum' Recherches sur l'École de Chartres* (Amsterdam, 1973), and Peter DRONKE, *Fabula: Exploration into the Uses of Myth in Medieval Platonism* (Leiden-Cologne, 1974), 32-47.

terminology more than once. Failing to understand that scripture is "veiled in mysteries", *velatam mysteriis*, Augustine succumbs to the *fabulae* of the Manichaeans, and finally becomes the prey of the *Aenigma Salomonis*. Not until his encounter with Ambrose (VI. 4) will Augustine see the *velamentum* lifted from scripture. To those whose intellect is distorted by the senses, who seek to pierce mysteries with the *oculus carnis* rather than the *oculus mentis*, the world will always be full of deceptive mysteries, veils, fables, and myths[26]).

The *Aenigma Salomonis* calls up images of unschooled childhood, foolishness, and deceptive, illusory food — *panis absconditus et aquae furtivae* — which exclude the seeker after wisdom from the banquet which Wisdom has prepared in Prov. 9. 1-6 and are associated with the Manichaean "carnal" approach to the mysteries of creation. Augustine had used such imagery elsewhere. In the *De musica* (VI. 13. 39) his first use of the term *curiositas* associates it with the process by which the soul turns away from eternal things out of love for *vanissima cognitio* and turns to sensual things. In the *De Gen. c. Man.* (II. 17-26 — II., 18. 30) he associates *curiositas* which God's curse upon the serpent, that it shall crawl on breast and belly and eat earth, "for whoever eats earth penetrates into profound and shadowy things, temporal and earthly". In *De vera rel.* (III. 4) Augustine addresses to the *curiosi* the words of 2 Cor. 4. 18:

> Seek not after those things which are seen, but after those which are not seen. For those which are seen are temporal, and those which are not seen are eternal.

Although it is not possible to demonstrate it here, this early and specialized usage of *curiositas* may be closely related to Augustine's Neoplatonic readings, particularly Neoplatonic explanations for the falling away, descent, and separation from the One, a topic very close to the center of Plotinus' conflict with gnosticism. The Greek terms applied to those souls who turn to the sensual world — *tolma*, *periergia*, *polupragmosune* — each convey a combination of pride, audacity, and inquisitiveness that their Latin equivalents — *superbia*, *audacia*, and *curiositas* — usually do not[27]).

[26]) On this distinction, see, most recently, Karl F. MORRISON, "'From Form into Form': Mimesis and Personality in Augustine's Historical Thought", *Proceedings of the American Philosophical Society*, 124 (1980), 276-294, at 281.

[27]) See O'CONNELL, *Early Theory of Man*, 146-83.

Since Augustine's other usages of the figure of the *Aenigma Salomonis* identity her, not as Folly, but sometimes as the error of heretics, *fallax doctrina*, and the *vanitas impiorum*, his citation of the figure in *Confessions* III. 6 suggests a somewhat more specialized meaning than personified Folly. From Apuleius to Tertullian, *curiositas* had been associated with magic and heresy. Earlier, Augustine had accused himself of *curiositas* during his student days, and *curiositas* had entangled him with Manichaean fables and myths. Summing up his youthful and then his Manichaean errors, Augustine evokes the image of the *aenigma* in Prov. 9, I suggest, as *curiosa cupiditas, concupiscentia oculorum, curiositas*, diverting those who mind their own business (a traditional sign of *periergia* and *polupragmosune* in Greek), promising wisdom to the unlearned, offering a banquet of false food, and sitting at the doorway, not of the seven-pillared mansion, but of the house of death. Augustine, after Plutarch and Apuleius, thus contributed a striking image to the early iconography of *curiositas*[28]).

This vice, developed during his student days at Carthage, strengthened and redirected in his search for *philosophia* and his presumptuous misreading of scripture, led him straight into the maze of Manichaean fables, from which he was to take nine years to extricate himself. In the concept of *curiositas*, which had a longer Greek than Latin history and possessed no consistent meaning or importance to most of the Latin Fathers after Tertullian, certainly not to Arnobius, Lactantius, or Ambrose, Augustine found one of the keys to his great dilemma, the condition and character of his mind and life before the conversion in Milan[29]). It served him well. It also served him uniquely, because his later treatment of the vice broadened its senses so as to make it applicable to more aspects of Christian life than simply his own experience. From some of his later works, and particularly from the thought of John Cassian, *curiositas* entered the vocabulary of monastic

[28]) Interesting use of the image has been made by Richard KAY, *Dante's Swift and Strong* (Lawrence, Kan., 1978), 300-306. For APULEIUS, see the *Metamorphoses*; for PLUTARCH, *Moralia* 515B-523B. There is a large literature on both works; see the study of LABHARDT (above, n. 7), and more recently, J. L. PENWILL, "Slavish Pleasures and Profitless Curiosity: Fall and Redemption in Apuleius' *Metamorphoses*", *Ramus* 4 (1975), 49-82.

[29]) ARNOBIUS, *Adv. Nat.* II. 57. 17; AMBROSE, *De Int. Iob et David* I. 9. 28 f. Cf. G. MADEC, *Saint Ambroise et la philosophie* (Paris, 1974), 177-246, esp. 181-2. In a work in progress, Richard NEWHAUSER and I will survey the history of the idea and term *curiositas* from its Greek origins to the nineteenth century.

psychology, where it generally remained until the theology of St. Anselm and the new intellectual circumstances of the twelfth and thirteenth centuries restored to it some of its earlier Augustinian features[30]).

Augustine was a careful and systematic writer. Looking back from the time of writing the *Confessions*, after the years of thinking about the life they described, he perceived to his own satisfaction what had happened to him and why his life had taken the shape it had. Illusion, deception, fable, and myth were the early lot of one who was unprepared, uninstructed, and possessed of a proud and concupiscent spirit. And this lot was introduced, not only by the particular qualities of his riotous living at Carthage, but by the traps of the Manichaeans, by their theodicy in III. 7, but most dramatically and crucially in their cosmogony and cosmology in III. 6. The young man who failed to perceive the veil of scripture was trapped in yet other veils. At the end of his Manichaean period Augustine could freely accuse himself and the Manichaeans of *curiositas*, not merely because of excessive attention to learning about the created world and not about its creator, but more profoundly, in that combination of ignorance, willfulness, and desire that necessarily prevents the soul from approaching God.

At the end of the *Confessions*, the exposition of the opening verses of Genesis testified to the redemption of this part of his life. Genesis became clearly the great door to Christian belief and, as it had been for Philo, the beginning of wisdom[31]). To repair the errors about Genesis that Augustine and the Manichaeans had made in *Confessions* III. 6, the first chapter of Genesis and its proper exposition had perhaps become a credo, or rule of faith, particularly important in the case of a former hearer of the Manichaeans whose first recorded contact with them had led directly into a sympathy for their false and "carnal" anti-Genesis polemic and their substitute cosmogony. For the Christian Augustine, scripture was "the countenance of God", and when, in the *De Trinitate*, Augustine urged his readers with him to "enter the path of charity, in search of Him of whom it is said: *Seek His face evermore*", both seeking and the countenance were intended to be conducted and understood in

[30]) See Richard NEWHAUSER, "Towards a History of Human Curiosity: A Prolegomenon to its Medieval Phase", *Deutsche Vierteljahrschrift* 56 (1982), 559-575.

[31]) PHILO, *De opif. mundi.* 54; Pierre GEOLTRAIN, "Quelques lectures juives et chrétiennes des premiers versets de la Genèse, de Quomran au Nouveau Testament", in *In principio. Interprétations des premiers versets de la Genèse*, Centre d'Études des religions du livre (Paris, 1973), 47-60.

terms of the proper exposition and understanding of scripture, the place where God's countenance was to be found, but with the *oculus mentis*, not the *oculus carnis*[32]). *Curiositas* had blocked that door once for Augustine, and no earthly sciences had been able to open it. For they too, unless conducted in the right spirit, were also manifestations of *curiositas*. Like the earthly city, their knowledge pointed to nothing beyond itself. Setting out in search of Wisdom, indeed, invited by Cicero and St. Paul to her banquet and house built upon seven pillars, Augustine had mistaken for her the *aenigma Salomonis* and had mistaken the book of Genesis for a rough and offensive account of ignorance. Following the prophecies and vision at the end of Book III, the remainder of the *Confessions* is an account of how long and complex was the journey to the house of Wisdom and how far from the right road Augustine, misled by *curiositas*, had originally wandered.

[32]) BROWN, *Augustine of Hippo*, 162, 262-3, 270-80.

III

Transgressing the limits set by the fathers: authority and impious exegesis in medieval thought

Some discontents of Christendom

Fundamental to any conception of *Christianitas*, whether as polity or order (including intellectual order), was the distinction between orthodoxy and heterodoxy and the role of authority in establishing and maintaining that distinction. Heterodoxy represented one of the most dangerous manifestations of discontent, as Chenu once argued, because it attacked two vital structural principles of *Christianitas*: the proper bond between the individual Christian and God and the common fraternal bonds among believing individuals in the Christian community.[1] Both kinds of violation are iterated in the famous definition of heresy attributed by Matthew Paris to Robert Grosseteste and discussed by Chenu "Haeresis est sententia humano sensu electa, scripturae sacrae contraria, palam edocta, pertinaciter defensa."[2] The last two parts of Grosseteste's four-part definition address heresy as an offense against the community – the heretic's defiant public teaching of destructive error after formal, authoritative instruction and condemnation. The first two parts address the individual and his or her cognitive and moral fault – he has, by the exercise of his own powers of understanding (which were universally understood to be differentiated among humans according to differing proportions of faith and grace), reached an opinion concerning religious truth that is contrary to scripture, the only measure of religious truth.

From the Pauline and Pastoral Epistles to the Reformation it is in discussions of the misuse of scripture, measured according to juridical and magisterial tradition, that we often find characterizations of moral psychology and

I would like to thank Richard Newhauser, James J. O'Donnell, Karl F. Morrison, and the anonymous reader for the University of California Press for their generous readings of earlier drafts of this essay. Their advice saved it from much incoherence, if not from all remaining errors, which are entirely my own responsibility.

1 Chenu (1963), repr. in Le Goff 1968: 9–14, most recently discussed in Vauchez 1990, in Mollat du Jourdin and Vauchez 1990: 320–51. For its use as early as Gregory the Great, see Straw 1988: 80.

2 Le Goff 1968: 10; Matthew Paris 1880: 401, *ad an.* 1253. For other categorizations, particularly those of canonists, see Hageneder 1976, and in general, Grundmann 1963.

intellectual error that could apply to a wide variety of discontent. As Chenu shrewdly remarked of the first part of Grosseteste's definition,

> The [heretic's fervent] faith has released in his spirit – and, transcending his intellect itself, in his entire mental behavior – an avid curiosity to penetrate the mystery, to have of it, in the obscurity of its transcendence, certain knowledge, understanding, *intellectus fidei*. The intimacy of this demand is the moving grandeur of the heretic, even though it is sometimes effected by a certain psychological disequilibrium.[3]

Before the heterodox thinker was pertinacious, before he even took his convictions public, before he revealed himself as a *superbus*, he was first, therefore, a kind of *curiosus*.

Although *curiositas* never became one of the major vices that, with the virtues, stand at the root of Christian moral theology and palaeopsychology, it was frequently discussed by early Christian writers, sometimes attached to a major vice such as pride, avarice, or sloth, and built into the characterization of certain kinds of dissent, notably heresy and the practice of magic. From Tertullian on, it was regularly attributed to heterodoxy.[4] A particularly troublesome scriptural text in this regard was Matt. 7.7, *zetete kai euersete*, "seek and ye shall find," which, as Tertullian bitterly proclaimed, had been appropriated by every heresiarch in the first two centuries, particularly the Gnostics, out of a fatal spirit of *curiositas*. *Cedat curiositas fidei*, proclaimed Tertullian; after the epiphany of Christianity such seeking as Tertullian denounced was invariably a sign of *sacrilega curiositas*. The proneness of the human intellect, dominated by a Pauline "lower nature," abounding in curiosity and pride, and unaided by adequate faith or grace, to err in spiritual matters was a prominent concern of Pauline anthropology and one echoed by other early Christian writers besides Tertullian. Jerome and Augustine insisted that the intellect had to be supplemented by revelation itself, by the Spirit which was its author, by grace in proportion as God had given it, and by *auctoritas*, i.e., the interpretive construction given to revelation by those who were regarded as authoritative interpreters of its meaning and the rules of belief and practice they prescribed.

Concerning the general problem of human intellectual and spiritual capacity

3 Le Goff 1968: 10. The intellectual passion of heterodox thinkers – as well as their apparent righteousness – led critics from Ambrose on to imply that their claims were based on *dissimulatio*, thus introducing the accusation, and assumption, of heterodox "hypocrisy" into patristic and later debates. Early writers did not neglect this "heroic" aspect of heterodox thinkers; cf. Grundmann 1963: 151 n. 55 on Augustine. For a full discussion of the *typus*, see Grundmann 1927 and Moore 1976.

4 Newhauser 1982. There is growing literature on the varying concepts of *curiositas* in antique and medieval thought. See the studies of Newhauser, Oberman, Peters, and Blumenberg, cited below. For Tertullian, see especially Frédouille 1972: 427; Barnes 1971. Richard Newhauser and I are completing an extensive study of the term and its history.

in the face of the profound mysteries of revelation, as well as that of the limits that God had set to legitimate spiritual and intellectual inquiry, early Christian writers drew on a set of images from scripture and elsewhere and their elaboration in later exegesis. For example, the Pauline dicta, *noli altum sapere* (Rom. 11.20), *Non plus sapere quam opportet sapere* (Rom. 12.3), and *Scientia inflat* (1 Cor. 8.1), could be readily joined to such phrases from the wisdom literature as *Altiora te ne quaesieris* (Ecclus. 3.22) or to such tags from non-Christian morality as the alleged "Socratic dictum" of Lactantius: *Quae supra nos, nihil ad nos*, and other similar phrases.[5] In such imagery there is implied an "above" that is not a legitimate concern of humans. The precise nature of the "above and below" or "high and low" might be a matter of debate, but such imagery in any case governed the metaphorical nature and terms of any debate. In other related imagery, the *patres* were depicted as having provided all essential teaching in an exegetical aggregate from which it was forbidden to subtract and to which it was forbidden to add (Deut. 4.2, 13.1; Apoc. 22.18–19), or of having laid out a road from which deviation to the left or right was forbidden (Num. 21.21–2; 1 Sam. 6.12; Isa. 30.21). Images of high and low, unalterable aggregate of wisdom, and linear rectitude occur again and again in debates about the nature of theological/exegetical speculation, its proper and improper objects, the spirit in which it is undertaken, and the nature of the authority that must guide and judge it, not only in exegesis, but also in terms of dogma, liturgy, and canon law.

Such imagery did much to shape the mental perceptions of the problem of speculative exegesis and its limits, especially when raised in the context of other Pauline considerations such as those distinguishing *sapientia* from *scientia* (1 Cor. 12.8) or that calling the wisdom of this world "foolishness" in the eyes of God (1 Cor. 3.19).

The magisterial and juridical history of another image, that of "limits (or boundaries) set by the Fathers," *termini positi a patribus* (Prov. 22.28), offers a perspective from which a number of aspects of such debates may be considered. The exegetical fortunes of a particular biblical verse are not inherently compelling objects of study and do not always offer a coherent history, of course, but the case of this verse illustrates the intertwining of the juridical and magisterial dimensions of authority in Christendom that were so often brought to bear on troubling problems of exegesis and other disciplinary matters in which ancient and authoritative tradition needed to be invoked. Originally, this was cited in discussions of exegesis, in the formulation of dogma, and in matters of ecclesiastical tradition, largely in the texts of early canon law. By the middle of the twelfth century it came to be routinely and more narrowly cited in the case of exegesis and intellectual speculation. Thus,

[5] Some of these and their histories are discussed in Oberman 1973a and Ginsburg 1976.

the exegetical history of the verse offers materials for considering some characteristic discontents that the question of human intellectual capacity, its characterization in scriptural imagery, and its application to scripture generated. That is, the exegetical history illustrates equally the response to authority to heterodox devotional forms and to the misuse of the intellect that had generated them.

Prov. 22.28 and its analogous texts (Deut. 19.4, 27.17; Hos. 5.10; Job 24.2) originally described the sacrality of ancient boundary stones, a common concern of ancient Mediterranean societies. Similar texts are found in Egyptian literature, the laws of various Greek city states, in Plato's *Laws* (VIII 842e–843), and in Festus's citation of an ancient law of Numa.[6] The Romans even possessed a god named Terminus, of whom both Erasmus and Gibbon made good use.[7] In all of its citations, the injunction emphasized the sacrality of boundaries set in antiquity and the audacity of those who crossed or moved them.

In order to appreciate the importance of Prov. 22.28 between the ninth and the fourteenth centuries, it is necessary first to consider its exegetical history in the early Church, when ideas of authority and tradition were being shaped; that is, to consider the various early meanings of the term *patres* and the nature of the *termini* they were thought to have set.

Patres and *termini*

The term *patres* possessed a variety of meanings in the first few Christian centuries, from the general sense of "teachers" in Paul (1 Cor. 4.15) and others, to the more specific sense of the apostles and their successors as receivers of divine inspiration in the thought of a number of Greek Christian writers.[8] This characterization lay at the root of the concept of ancient tradition and its double role in the early Church; on the one hand, scripture, divinely inspired, was interpreted for the apostles by Jesus and for others by the apostles. Therefore, authentic exegesis had to derive from and coincide spiritually with this authentic tradition. On the other hand, the apostles were also taught how to live by Jesus, and their practices were also transmitted to their followers. The centrality to Christian identity of both interpretation and practice were strongly (and often equally) emphasized by second-century Christian writers, thus

6 Scott 1965: 135–8; Festus 1913: 505 (attested only by Paul the Deacon); for Chios, Humphreys 1988: 470–1.

7 Gilmore 1963: 141; Allen and Allen 1928: 430–2; Festus 1913: 505; Wind 1937–8: 66–9; den Boeft 1988: 19–23; for Gibbon, many editions, ch. 1.

8 General accounts in Quasten 1966: 9–12; Amann 1933: 1192–215; de Ghellinck, 1948: 19–23. On the formation of tradition, see Van den Eynde 1933; Morrison 1969; Pelikan 1973; Brandmüller 1987.

establishing firmly the principles of antiquity and continuity that constituted an interpretive standard against which other interpretations and practices might be judged. Those found wanting by these standards could be dismissed and condemned as deriving from "one's own opinion," and therefore an illegitimate "novelty" (*chainautonomia*: 1 Tim. 6.20).

Both interpretations and practices are the *termini* set by the *patres* according to Papias, Polycarp, Origen, and Eusebius. The *patres* came to be understood as having possessed the authority – as heirs and interpreters of the apostolic tradition (*paradosis*) – to expound the rules of Christian life and the norms of the interpretation of scripture. But the opinions of individual *patres* were not considered sufficient in themselves to later writers. From Eusebius to Maximus the Confessor there emerged the idea of the consensus of the *patres* which regulated the proper investigation (*zetesis*) of scripture and determined which interpretations and practices were inconsistent with the patristic consensus and were therefore to be condemned as individual innovations, even when these might be the opinions of one or another individual *pater*. The first Christian writers who cited Prov. 22.28, Origen and Eusebius, understood the *patres* to have been the apostles and those of their successors who had been guided by the Holy Spirit, and the *termini* set by them to be the essentials of Christian belief.[9]

Augustine, whose own enthusiastic citations of Matt. 7.7 suggest how much more confident and hopeful Christian hermeneutics had become since the days of Tertullian, considered the *patres* primarily the figures of the Old and New Testaments – he referred to *patres temporis novi testamenti* and to *patres temporis veteris testamenti*, to *sancti antiqui patres* and *Hebraei patres*, and this understanding continued down to Isidore of Seville, whose *De ortu et obitu patrum* ended with the apostles and missionaries mentioned in the Pauline Epistles and Acts.[10]

The first Latin citation of Prov. 22.28, however, that of Siricius I in his *Ep.* 6.1.2 *Ad diversos episcopos*, added a new dimension to earlier, largely exegetical usage. Siricius cited the Proverbs text in conjunction with 2 Thes. 2.14, the Pauline command to hold fast to *traditiones*, a text that, with 1 Tim. 6.20, constituted another Pauline dimension of the discussion of ancient authority and boundaries.[11] Siricius was particularly disturbed at the variety of

[9] Pelikan 1973; Pelikan 1974: 52–3; Morrison 1969: 59–64, 71, 113–15; and especially Danielou 1975.

[10] Augustine, *De bono conjugali*, 18, 32; *Contra Faustum*, 22, 76.

[11] The earliest references to patristic citations of Prov. 22.28 are to those of Origen and Eusebius: Allenbach 1980a: 206; 1980b: 193. Virtually no scholarly research is cited in Sieben 1980 and 1983. It seems that the Prov. 22.28 text was first cited as a challenge to Jesus made by the scribes and Pharisees. Matt. 15.2, "quare discipuli tui transgrediuntur traditionem seniorum." Cf. Mark 7.1–23.

practices in the scattered churches of Christendom, and although he recognized much of the validity of local custom, he also warned against local presumption and observed that both local and universal traditions had to concur in belief and practice. The letter of Siricius added the dimension of orthopraxy to the earlier hermeneutic of Origen and Eusebius. Siricius's letter did not remain an isolated utterance; it was taken up in later canonical collections, notably those of Pseudo-Isidore and Regino of Prüm, and it gained particular currency in the divided world of Carolingian and post-Carolingian Europe.[12]

The themes worked out in early patristic literature and canon law, were taken up and transmitted to later ages by Vincent of Lerins, Cassiodorus, and Gregory the Great, which may be said to have completed the construction of the image of *patres* and *termini* in the early Church. Those who ventured to cross or remove these *termini*, whom Gregory identified as both heterodox dissenters and immoderate exegetes, shared the same trait: *plus quaerunt sentire quam capiunt*. In his *Moralia in Job* and elsewhere in his writings, Gregory explicitly identified those who transgressed the limits set by the *patres* with those who violated the *constitutiones patrum*. Gregory's focus upon the heretic's denial of faith and reason, his willfulness, and his meaningless isolation, reflects one of his central beliefs; as Carole Straw has characterized it, "For Gregory, self-sufficient autonomy is the true evil, the fatal mistake of seeking to stand in oneself (*stare in semetipso*)."[13] *Propria desideria, proprius sensus*, these are Gregory's characteristic explanations of the inappropriate address to exegesis.[14] This approach may explain why Gregory was more concerned with the heretic's willfulness, his *superbia*, than with his *curiositas*; that is, pride is the fundamental fault, *curiositas* being in this case a manifestation of underlying pride.

The various usages of Prov. 22.28 from Siricius to Gregory were put to active use between the late eighth and the early twelfth centuries. Carolingian scholars, eager to identify their own programs with authentic tradition, transformed the scattered dossiers of patristic texts into canon law, the regulation of monastic life, and the basis of a literary education. Having recovered a very wide range of patristic opinion, they brought the full weight of what they understood to be tradition – but which was just as often selective use of particular *patres* or local custom – to bear in their assertions of traditional

[12] *PL* XIII.1187–8; there is a brief discussion in Morrison 1969: 80–1. For later citations see Hinschius 1963: 524, and below, p. 344.

[13] Straw 1988: 79–80. Gregory's characterization of the misuse of scripture and the psychology of the misuser, with his descriptions of heterodox beliefs, were transmitted to Carolingian and later Europe by the *Moralia*, but also by his *Register* and by the *Dialogues*. For Vincent, see *PL* L.637–86; Madoz 1933; de Ghellinck 1935: 404 n. 5. For Cassiodorus, see Cassiodorus 1937: *Praef.*; Morrison 1969: 166; O'Donnell 1979. Cf. *Moralia in Job* 16. 4. 56; 20. 8. 18; de Lubac 1961: 99–128; Dagens 1977: 216–18, 340–2.

[14] Gregory, *Moralia*, 30.1; de Lubac 1961: 301–17.

authority in the attack on Adoptionism and especially in their dispute with their Byzantine opposite numbers in the matter of iconoclasm, emphatically in the *praefatio* to the *Libri Carolini* and the canons of the Council of Frankfurt of 794, which confidently cited Prov. 22.28, and in the Pseudo-Isidorean decretals, which relied very heavily upon an alleged ecclesiastical tradition having the authority of antiquity to argue its ninth-century case.[15] In letters forged under the names of Victor, Alexander, and Calixtus, Prov. 22.28 is cited, and in letters attributed to Fabianus and Eusebius the analogous text of Deut. 27.17 conveys the identical sense. In addition, Pseudo-Isidore also includes the authentic letter of Siricius I with its own citation of Prov. 22.28.[16] The Pseudo-Isidorean forger knew perfectly well how effective appeals to such a notion of tradition and patristic authority might be in ninth-century Francia.

Carolingian authorities also cited Prov. 22.28 in their debates over the Eucharist and the doctrine of double predestination, over proper and improper exegesis, and over the allegorical interpretation of the liturgy provoked by the work of Amalarius of Metz. The prominence of Prov. 22.28, its analogous texts, and the Carolingian elevation of patristic authority generally help to explain the important citation of the text in the *De synodalibus causis* of Regino of Prüm.[17] In the letter to Hatto of Mainz that prefaces the *De synodalibus causis*, Regino states that although the faith is universal, joining all Christians in the *societas christiana*, it nevertheless lives according to different customs in different places. Just as diverse *nationes* of peoples differ from one another in kind, morals, languages, and laws – *genere, moribus, lingua, legibus* – so also different ecclesiastical provinces require suitable customs, addressing "modern" problems, but also consistent with the common *termini* set by the Fathers. Scripture warns that the *termini* – that is, the *leges et decreta* – that the Fathers have set, must in all cases be observed, and only with the most presumptuous *temeritas* may they be transgressed. Regino, following his predecessors, has laid out these and the modern *termini* in order. The judgment

[15] On Adoptionism, see Alcuin, *Ep.* 23; Bullough 1983; Riché 1981: 736–7. Cavadini 1993 is a major contribution to the subject. On the *Libri Carolini*, see Bastgen 1924: 3. For the Council of Frankfurt, Brandmüller 1987. For Pseudo-Isidore, see Hinschius 1963: 95, 128, 139, 162, 238, 524. On canon law in general, see Munier 1957. The text of the *Collectio canonum Hibernensis*, the first collection to use patristic material, is in Wasserschleben 1885. The best recent discussion is that of Reynolds 1983. On *florilegia* as dossiers against particular heresies, see Riché 1981: 726–9. Generally, see McKitterick 1977; Wallace-Hadrill 1983; Riché 1981; Contreni 1983; Bullough 1983.

[16] There is a brief discussion in Morrison 1969: 236–40. See Hinschius 1963: 95, 128, 139, 163, 238, 524.

[17] For the text of Amalarius, see Hanssens 1948–50. The case has often been misunderstood as an example of general ecclesiastical anti-intellectualism. Regino's text is in Wasserschleben 1840. On Regino's importance in early discussions of "national" identities, see the essays in Beumann 1978. On the frequency of references to *leges*, *statuta*, and *decreta patrum*, see de Lubac 1959: 282 n. 1.

of Hatto must decide which are to be chosen and approved for the province of Mainz. In Regino's thought fundamental and authoritative tradition remained crucial, but it also had to allow for regional variation in some practices and usages, a dilemma that characterized a number of thinkers in the tenth, eleventh, and twelfth centuries.

For Carolingian thinkers, such images as that of the *termini* set by the *patres* were not necessarily metaphors. The collections of individual patristic texts grew in number during the ninth century, as did those of dossiers and *florilegia*, collections of excerpts from the writings of the Fathers.[18] Before the eleventh century it really was possible to believe that one had the *termini* set by the *patres* in front of one as one read or wrote. As Chenu and others have pointed out, by the ninth century patristic *texts* themselves came to be understood as possessing an *auctoritas* that "no longer signifies the personal worth of a Gregory or an Augustine, but rather designates a *text* of Gregory or Augustine."[19]

The wide figurative uses of Prov. 22.28 in exegesis, authoritative custom, and the idea of tradition that were exercised in Carolingian and post-Carolingian Europe retained their versatility in the eleventh and early twelfth centuries, when boundaries and limits of many kinds were being sorely tested. Radulphus Glaber, for example, wrote of flying boundary stones in a territorial dispute between one family and its neighbors. Fulbert of Chartres and Berno of Reichenau cited the Proverbs text to justify, respectively, a procedure in a case of homicide and the insistence upon observing the rules of cult.[20] Still others – Abbo of Fleury, Cardinal Humbert, *The Collection in 74 Titles*, and Ivo of Chartres – cited Prov. 22.28 to emphasize the integrity of episcopal jurisdiction, sometimes literally in geographical and territorial terms.[21]

Between the fourth and the twelfth centuries, then, Prov. 22.28 had proven to be an extremely useful text in a number of different contexts: canon law, scriptural and liturgical exegesis, and the developing concept of authoritative tradition. The term *patres* itself had broadened to include not only apostolic Fathers, early councils and popes, and such figures as Ambrose, Augustine, Jerome, and Gregory, but later thinkers as well, beginning with Bede. The term proved versatile in matters of canonical authority, ecclesiastical practice and discipline, doctrinal disputes, and the cognitive limits of exegesis. In all cases

18 See McKitterick 1977: 154–83.

19 Chenu 1976: 355.

20 For Glaber, see Fichtenau 1991: 101–9; for Fulbert, see Behrends 1976: 58–9; Peters 1990. For Berno, see de Lubac 1961: 36–41. The *glossa ordinaria* to the Bible allowed for both kinds of interpretation: *PL* CXIII.1106A, "Non transgrediaris terminos Catholicae fidei, quos ab initio statuere doctores."

21 For Ivo, see *MGH LdL* II.642–55; Morrison 1969: 309–10. See also Robinson 1983; Mostert 1987: 115–19; Morris 1989: 219–26; for Abbo's (and generally monastic) versatility in justifying a status quo by appealing to patristic literature, see Fichtenau 1991: 286–9.

the temerity of the act of transgression and the audacity of the alleged transgressor remained a principal component of the image.

The very versatility of the verse, however, suggests the eagerness with which Carolingian and post-Carolingian thinkers seized upon patristic authority and tradition to control a diverse and rapidly changing world of thought and practice in the absence of any clear-cut contemporary central authority and in the actual existence of "the Church," outside of theoretical ecclesiology and polemic, as many local churches whose eleventh- and early twelfth-century disputes could only be settled by appeals to a universally recognized tradition and the authority it entailed. Beginning in the mid-eleventh century, however, just such an authority was formulated in the reform papacy of Leo IX and his successors. In matters of canon law and ecclesiastical discipline, although the papacy certainly acknowledged and claimed to incorporate tradition, the growing presence and enforceability of *auctoritas romana* came to determine definitions of those *termini* that had once and for a long time been left in the hands and diverse texts of the *patres*.[22] Perhaps the inherent lack of specificity in the phrase from Proverbs as well as the increasing academic awareness of the variety and apparent internal contradictions in the patristic corpus led to its disuse, particularly in those contexts in which efficient and comprehensive collections of authoritative texts were now available – the *glossa ordinaria* to scripture, Gratian's *Decretum*, Peter Lombard's *Liber senteniarum*, and the decretals and canons of twelfth-century popes and councils. But it survived in one earlier function, indeed came to be used more frequently – that of characterizing impious or erroneous exegesis, its old cognitive role, applied from the eleventh century on to the world of the new schools, first to the use of the liberal arts in interpreting scripture, and later to the interpretation of doctrine by techniques developed in natural philosophy.

Patres, *termini*, and *magistri*

One of the chief concerns in the cautionary citation of Prov. 22.28 in matters of exegesis had long been the ecclesiastical – chiefly, but certainly not exclusively monastic – distaste for the use of the *artes liberales* and the kinds of interpretive questions they raised in a hermeneutic enterprise that was thought to require spiritual, rather than primarily intellectual understanding. Although Augustine and Jerome had struck a widely accepted compromise between the two kinds of effort, subsequent thinkers, including Bede, had renewed the debate, and the question was only temporarily settled by

[22] Kuttner 1982; Morris 1989; Gratian, C. 24 q. 3 cc. 26–31.

Carolingian thinkers.[23] The Carolingian balance struck between the *artes* and contemplative reading of scripture was lost during the tenth and early eleventh centuries, and the debate was renewed in earnest in the eleventh and twelfth centuries. The *artes* survived in the external schools of some monasteries, in cathedral schools, and in some urban schools in northern Italy. Nor were the *artes* entirely unattractive to monastic scholars, although their reappearance during the early eleventh century certainly did not please all monks.

The new prominence of the propaedeutic studies – the *artes* – in monastic learning and exegesis shaped the legend of Gerbert and elicited the doubts and stinging protests of Otloh of S. Emmeram, Peter Damian, and Manegold of Lautenbach, as well as the revival of the Augustinian sense of *curiositas* in the *De similitudinibus* long attributed to Anselm.[24] In the light of the instrumental use of grammar and dialectic in shaping the new academic forms of *quaestio* and *disputatio*, the monastic *lectio*, "oriented," as Jean Leclercq had said, "toward the *meditatio* and the *oratio*," stood in sharper and sharper contrast to the new methods and the new *theologia* that they purported to teach.[25] The monastic *lectio* fed memory and imagination, and when it inquired, its *quaerere* was a *studium* that came from the heart and sought God, not from the intellect seeking knowledge, nor, for that matter, teaching, preaching, and fighting heresy.

The Carolingian and later monastic deference to the *patres* here had to perform yet stronger service. In the late eleventh and twelfth centuries there was no longer a question of a few isolated debates concerning the correct interpretation of matters that had never been authoritatively settled, as there had been in the ninth century. Instead, the renovation of the curriculum of the *artes* brought them to bear consistently and in an original manner upon problems of exegesis and led ultimately to the discipline of theology. This new role of the *artes* was far removed even from the misgivings of Otloh and the outright hostility of Peter Damian. Although the reformed monastic tradition certainly did not entirely give way before it – indeed the greatest years of that tradition lay ahead during the twelfth century – it could, and did, reemphasize the *auctoritas patrum* as a means of control over what it considered the most extreme or superfluous manifestations of the new exegesis. Monastic critics took St. Paul's complaint about "novelties" straight to the new treatment of scripture, from the desacralization of the physical text to the new manner of disputing and expounding it.

23 Riché 1981; Contreni 1983; de Lubac 1961: 50–3, 381–93; D'Onofrio 1986; Gibson 1981, 1982; Wallace-Hadrill 1983; Sullivan 1989; d'Alverny 1946; Smalley 1983.

24 On Otloh, Evans 1980b: 60–2; Resnick 1987; on Peter Damian, Cantin 1975; Morrison 1983; on Manegold, Hartmann 1970; on Gerbert, Riché 1985. On the Anselmian *De similitudinibus (De Humanis moribus)*, see Southern and Schmitt 1969.

25 Leclercq 1982: 72.

Central to both monastic consciousness and to the adaptation of the new learning to monastic standards, although often neglected in studies of monastic attitudes toward the new schools, was the form of the exposition of scripture. As John Van Engen has succinctly put it:

> While a certain dialectic between reason and authority permeated this development, becoming especially prominent in public doctrinal controversies, the most fundamental change, overlooked in much of the older literature . . . was that which transformed Holy Scripture, the divine repository of sacred dogma, kissed, incensed, and invoked each day at mass, into a textbook routinely lectured upon in the schools and haggled over in public disputes.[26]

Central to monastic attitudes toward the new learning, and central to monastic self-awareness, was the *lectio divina* – the study and contemplation of scripture. Monastic discussions of the proper and improper approaches to scriptural exegesis formed the vocabulary applied by monastic critics and scholars to learning in general and to the new learning of the eleventh and twelfth centuries and to the problem of the *artes liberales*. From the tenth century on, monastic writers had readier access to patristic literature and regularly invoked it – and its heresiology – in a wide range of situations, not all of which appear to have borne on doctrine at all.

The *artes* in the eleventh and early twelfth centuries posed only one problem to the defenders of orthodoxy, as orthodoxy had come to be defined by 1100. A second, very old and potentially equally serious question, was the argument that scriptural exegesis could legitimately be extended beyond the comments of the *patres*, if it was inspired by the Holy Spirit. Origen had argued vigorously for an expanded exegesis, and even Augustine's and Jerome's tempering of Origen's enthusiasm allowed for an ongoing improved hermeneutic. Gregory the Great had anticipated an even clearer understanding of scripture in the future, and even Carolingian authorities allowed for a kind of *pia curiositas*, as long as it was accompanied by grace – as in Ambrosius Autpertus's remark that he had "added from my own resources, or rather from the gift of the grace of God, many things in which the *patres* seem to be deficient." Amalarius of Metz ran afoul of the irascible Florus of Lyons and the Council of Quierzy in 835 because he had omitted the qualifying "from the gift of the grace of God" when he explained that he had gotten many of his allegorical interpretations of the liturgy, "from inside myself" – Florus could then charge him with having displayed *ex proprii sensus temeraria praesumptio*. As Robert Lerner has pointed out, preserving the saving clause "with the aid of the Holy Spirit" led to the development of the "ecstatic

[26] Van Engen 1983: 97. See also Evans 1980b; Chenu 1968; Ferruolo 1985; Fichtenau 1992.

defense" of individual exegesis that might legitimately proceed *ultra patres*.[27]

This line of reasoning proved to be safest, however, in a monastic setting, more controversial in the schools, and most controversial when argued by individual dissenters, especially when these appeared to run afoul of monastic claims to intercessory functions or to challenge canonical authority of any kind. Within the monastic context the best – and one of the earliest – examples of this uneasiness is the reception of the work of Rupert of Deutz, his vast scriptural commentary produced in the first two decades of the twelfth century. Familiar with more of the exegetical tradition and literature than any writer before him, Rupert remained firmly within a distinctly monastic tradition of exegesis. Rupert's grand thematic focus on the Trinity and the Holy Spirit – as well as his involvement in disputes about specific doctrinal issues – made earlier commentaries less than useful for him, and his novel definition of monastic life as contemplation of scripture gave to the encounter between the individual monk and scripture a direct validity that ultimately reduced the role of the Fathers to a single stage of instruction; a monastic reader might very well find "more useful" meanings in his own encounters with the text of scripture than the Fathers themselves had produced.[28]

The scale and originality of Rupert's work drew from monastic critics the complaint that such a display of learning violated the warning of I Cor. 8.1, *scientia inflat*, as well as the charge from secular masters and their disciples that Rupert's ambitious commentary needlessly increased the literature in which the *patres* had said all that was sufficient. Rupert's Prologue to his commentary on the Apocalypse suggests strongly that he had been accused of going *ultra patres*, having produced superfluous exegetical material, offensive to the memory and judgment of the *patres*, a product of vainglory rather than piety.[29]

Rupert retorted, echoing Origen, that although the *patres* had opened one or two wells from which to draw the living water, he was opening new ones, as

[27] Origen, *De principiis*, *Praefatio*, 3; Danielou 1975: 11. Augustine, *Confessions*, xiii, 18–24; Gregory, *Homil. in Ezech.* 2. 4. 10–12 (*PL* LXXXVI.979–81). On Ambrosius see Pelikan 1978: 9–23 at n. 10. For Amalarius and Florus, see Cabaniss 1954; McKitterick 1977: 149–53; Hanssens 1948–50: 19; de Lubac 1961: 40, 99–128. In addition , a number of exegetes pointed out that the heretics' misuse of scripture forced orthodox Christians to examine scripture more closely (Grundmann 1963), increasing the inherently and properly tantalizing invitation. See de Lubac 1961: 305 n. 3; Lerner 1992.

[28] Van Engen 1983: 80.

[29] Rupert, *Comm. in Apoc.*, *Praef.* (*PL* CLXIX.825–8). See also Lerner 1992; Van Engen 1983: 71, 239–40, 343, 346. One of Rupert's critics, Alger of Liege, very carefully insisted that he did not interpret scripture "in my own sense," but in that of the Fathers. See Van Engen 1983: 171. Further on not proceeding *ultra patres*, Van Engen 1983: 184, 210, 219, 351; de Lubac 1959: 78–9, 84; de Lubac 1961: 219–38; Evans 1980: 57–79; de Ghellinck 1948: 250–77. On the image in Origen and Isidore see Gregoire 1965: 158.

had Isaac, when he opened new wells because the Philistines had closed the wells of Abraham.[30] For Rupert, such activity, because it lay at the heart of monastic life, could not repudiate the *patres*, but built upon and added to their work. His work expressed the matter better and more fully (*melius et compendiosius*). Rupert, "an ardent contemplative whose faith delighted in mystery," saw no conflict with the *patres* in what was, for him, a common enterprise.[31]

By the early twelfth century the concern over deviating from the *patres*, adding to or subtracting from their work in exegesis, had become a commonplace; it is interesting to note that criticism of this kind came to Rupert from fellow monks as well as secular masters, among the latter no less than Anselm of Laon and William of Champeaux, who professed to build their own commentaries squarely upon the bases laid by the *patres*. But the prospects opened up with such obvious delight and devotion by Rupert of Deutz and other monastic exegetes were too bright to be dimmed by criticism that they consisted of a presumptuous rejection of the *patres*. Thus, Richard of St. Victor regarded such criticism as an excuse for laziness: "For our part, however, let us take with all greediness what the *patres* have discussed; let us offer with all generosity the fruits of our research, that we may fulfill that which is written: Many shall pass over, and knowledge shall be manifold [Dan. 12.4]."[32] Elsewhere Richard repeated this idea – the *patres* had left many things unsaid; they were interested chiefly in allegorical problems; as in Origen, they had deliberately left things for later commentators to find: "Do you wish to honor and defend the authority of the *patres*? We cannot honor the lovers of truth more truly than by seeking, finding [Matt. 7.7], teaching, defending, and loving the truth. Do not ask whether what I say is new, but whether it is true."[33] Such sentiments as those of Rupert and Richard ring with the delight that the new exegesis had instilled in diligent mock-scholars, still secure in the monastic tradition, still confident that such seeking and finding would only redouble contemplative joy.

The defenses of Rupert and Richard appear to have succeeded, chiefly because of the popularity of their work in the world of monks and canons regular. But the practices of the masters in the schools soon passed well beyond the limited claims of Anselm of Laon and William of Champeaux, and many writers, notably St. Bernard, expressed great concern over the freedom with which the *mundanae artes* could be applied to the sacred pages. Here there

30 Van Engen 1983: 71; Gregoire 1965: 158.

31 Chenu 1968: 270–330; Chenu 1976: 351–65.

32 Smalley 1983: 107–8; Chenu 1968: 310; de Lubac 1959: 109–10.

33 Smalley 1983: 109. On defenses of *libertas inquirendi*, see McLaughlin 1977; Peters 1985. The forthcoming study of academic heresies by H. M. M. J. Thijssen properly criticizes the application to such conflicts of the modern term "academic freedom."

was less toleration for the ecstatic defense. The generation of Peter Abelard produced both praise of the new learning and bitter condemnations of it. In his own defense of his teaching at the Council of Reims in 1148, Gilbert of Poitiers claimed that he held the same faith as the Fathers, and that he knew their works not from *florilegiae* and excerpts, but from having read their entire books. It was the best defense that he could have offered.[34]

A related concern is that of spending too much time and energy on preliminary disciplines. The *Metalogicon* of John of Salisbury, with its criticism of students and masters who spend all of their lives on what ought to be a propaedeutic study, that of logic as one of the *artes*, is a well-known example. But excessively prolonged study of any one of the *artes* was only one kind of objection to the twelfth-century schools. The application of dialectic was not merely a tool for studying scripture and doctrine but also a principle of ordering the faith itself, a principle that insisted upon the debating of *quaestiones*, the puzzles of *sophismata*, the demystifying of the essential mystery of faith. There was little room here for the monastic *meditatio* or for the hieratic function of scripture. *Profanae novitates* appeared to critics to abound, not only in the schools, but in the character of heresies themselves. Thinkers during the second half of the twelfth century cited Prov. 22.28 again and again, not always from the same perspective, and not always with the same purposes, but from a general anxiety that old certainties were being discarded or ignored and that new approaches to scripture and its meaning were causing more discontent and anxiety than offering anything resembling new certainties. In many respects, the faith itself seemed to be becoming contingent, authority less fixed, and individual opinion, countered by other individual opinions, to be the chief medium of dialogue about matters essential to the salvation of mankind.

To others, however, far less secure in an intellectual and devotional tradition than Richard of St. Victor, the right to question, debate, and investigate was essential, even in matters of theology. In spite of the continuing assertion of patristic authority and tradition, some thinkers readily allowed for the importance of contemporary styles of thought and argument. From Abelard on, despite the occasional setbacks of condemnation and criticism, the new thinkers appropriated the title of *magistri*, and were acknowledged as such by their contemporaries.

Monastic culture could indeed contain the intellectual adventures of such figures as Rupert of Deutz and Richard of St. Victor, imbued as both were with its deepest spirit. In the case of monks going to the schools, however, and in the case of masters of the *artes* boldly undertaking the exposition of scripture with

[34] Otto of Freising 1974: I. 58 (59). For other defenses, see Peters 1985.

the tools of Aristotle, by the second half of the twelfth century many of the traditionalist advocates of the *patres* had turned against the *magistri*, and their opposition has been eloquently traced by Chenu and others, most recently by Stephen Ferruolo and Heinrich Fichtenau.[35]

Partly against the misuse of the *mundanae artes*, especially *disputatio*, in the exposition of scripture, St. Bernard launched his elaborate reconstruction of Augustinian *curiositas*, possibly through the medium of the Anselmian *De similitudinibus*. Gerhoch of Reichersberg cited Rupert of Deutz against the *magistri* and condemned *novitates* as violently as had any earlier exegete. Robert of Melun, Peter of Celle, Stephen of Tournai, and others took up the attack and its main themes. William of St. Thierry warned against ignoring "the limits of that faith that our *patres* established, nor to disregard them in any way."[36]

Within these contexts, the "novelties" condemned in 1 Tim. 6.20 and elsewhere in scripture and patristic literature figured prominently. Beryl Smalley traced the early medieval adventures of the idea and the term some years ago.[37] A term of opprobrium in 1100 (and for several decades after), "novelty" had become a largely honorific term by 1250. Smalley by no means insisted that *auctoritas antiqua* disappeared between 1100 and 1250, but that its privileged (and functional) place was modified in order to accommodate some concepts of a legitimate "novelty".

Throughout the twelfth century the debates concerning the limits of inquiry thus invoked Prov. 22.28 and the image of authority it conveyed more frequently and in more forms than had the juridical citations of the phrase and image between the fourth and the early twelfth centuries. The term was also apparently to be applied to intellectuals rather than to dissenters in general. It does seem to turn up in discussions of heterodoxy outside the schools. In spite of the many charges against heterodox thinkers outside the schools that they displayed considerable exegetical skills, even for rustics, the verse from Proverbs remained leveled primarily at early scholastic thinkers, not at dissenters with large "popular" followings. By the end of the twelfth century a contemporary and indisputable source of authority was in place – the papacy and its institution of judges-delegate. As in the case of Valdes, dissenters could be heard, their opinions assessed, and a confession of faith required – and given or not. If such assent were not forthcoming, the heretic could then be accused of pertinacity, increasingly the most important legal element in the charge of heresy. Heterodoxy then became the denial of legitimate contemporary

[35] Chenu 1976; Ferruolo 1985; Fichtenau 1992.

[36] Newhauser 1987; Leclercq 1982; Stock 1975; de Lubac 1961: 583–6.

[37] Smalley 1975. For an earlier manifestation of this spirit in episcopal circles see Fichtenau 1991: 286–7.

authority. There was no need to observe that Waldensians, Cathars, or others had transgressed the limits established by the Fathers. They had in any case transgressed the contemporary authority that mattered.

At the same time, scholars with opinions of the kind that had troubled William of St. Thierry, William of Champeaux, Bernard of Clairvaux, and others were not as readily controlable. The university was rapidly becoming, as Smalley observed, "a fact of life." The institution offered advantages to popes and rulers whose cultivation required considerable restraint on the part of authority, and permitted – sometimes grudgingly – considerable freedom within its relatively closed society. In the light of the new presence of the universities, once such charges as secret teaching and esoteric doctrines had been obliterated by public teaching and collegial familiarity, scholars were for the most part safe from the kind of exercise of authority that troubled dissenting groups outside the precincts of the universities.

On the other hand, the papacy of the twelfth and early thirteenth centuries took time to catch up with the thought of the scholars. Until it did, it could still resort to the last usage of the text from Proverbs. The limits set by the Fathers could still be invoked until the emergence of a concept of professional discipline in the thirteenth century. Withal, the form of earlier *auctoritas* itself was changed – into individual texts, propositions, and statements of doctrine excerpted in specialized, systematic, and increasingly authoritative collections of texts, usually according to the principles of one or another of the *artes*, chiefly logic. This was a far different use of *ratio* than the Carolingian exegetes had defended, or that even the best-intentioned early theological dialecticians would have allowed. It took time for the new theology to acquire respectability – and security – and to escape from the charges of introducing novelties and transgressing the limits set by the *patres*. The acknowledgment of ancient *auctoritas* survived into the textbooks and teaching of the later twelfth and thirteenth centuries, but it was an acknowledgment of a far different concept of *auctoritas* from that of the Carolingians, or even of Lanfranc. It did not refer to the compilation of patristic literature, but to patristic thought, which had to be arrayed side by side with the full apparatus of rational inquiry developed in the twelfth-century schools.

Peter Lombard concluded his prologue to the Books of Sentences with the insistence that his work echoes those of the Fathers, *non a paternibus discessit limitibus*. Although the contents of Peter's work most certainly did proceed well beyond the range of patristic exegesis, it is arguable that Peter's cautionary self-defense was not merely a *captatio benevolentiae*, but the expression of a genuine belief that his work was consistent with a constant tradition and that the phrase from Proverbs had by the mid-twelfth century lost some of its sharper overtones, at least in the schools.

Such a conclusion fits well with the first commentary on Peter's work, that of Peter Comestor.[38] In his commentary on the prologue, Peter Comestor interpreted the limits set by the Fathers not in terms of Proverbs 22.28 at all, but in terms of Exodus 19 and 24, the story of Moses placing boundaries around the mountain of the Lord. These images had long been a part of Jewish thought concerning tradition and the nature of authority. Exodus 19 and 24 provided the source for the expression "fences around the law" that is found in the Pirke Abot and echoed in Maimonides, where the phrase was understood to refer to the authority of sages to adapt the rules of Torah to particular circumstances.[39] It is possible that Peter Comestor knew something about this, since there had been increasing contact between Jewish and Christian scholars during the twelfth century, and the wisdom literature provided a ground more common to the two religions than many other parts of scripture. Whether he drew upon Jewish sources or not, Peter Comestor was certainly more concerned with the difficulties of intellectual motivation and effort than he was with any dangers that the hermeneutical *termini* might pose to ambitious students of theology. The mountain, Peter says, stands for the two testaments; the *limites* are the writings of the Fathers, who themselves could cross the *termini* because they were directly inspired by God. Others in the story are also allegorized in the spirit of the new learning; the elders who approach the *termini* and give up are those not sufficiently diligent in studying scripture. Others are lazy and do not even bother to begin the study of the Fathers. The work of the *patres* here seems to be rather an impenetrable forest than prohibitive boundaries, and Peter is far less concerned with transgressing hermeneutic limits than he is with the difficulties of understanding scripture and patristic literature concerning the exegesis of scripture. For Peter Comestor the purpose of Lombard's work was precisely the overcoming of this difficulty. Comestor is more concerned with lazy or insufficiently diligent scholars than with presumptuous ones.

The age of the new legitimacy of novelty, characterised by Comestor's distinctive reading of Peter Lombard's citation of Prov. 22.28, came to something of an end in the disputes between Mendicants at the University of Paris in the middle of the thirteenth century, in a revived Augustinian criticism of Aristotelian scholastic theology, in the condemnations of 1277, and in the new intellectual temper of the fourteenth century. Many of the themes and images considered already in this essay come together in the letter sent by Gregory IX on 17 July 1228, to the regent masters in theology at the University of Paris.[40] Old images usually applied to the study of secular literature – those of the spoils of the Egyptians (Exod. 3.21–2), the purified and shorn Egyptian

[38] Martin 1931.

[39] See Daly 1957 for a possible connection between Comestor and the Jews of his native Troyes. On the Jewish image see Neusner 1990.

[40] Denifle 1889: no. 59, 114–16; de Lubac 1959: 116. The forthcoming study by H. M. M. J. Thijssen on academic heresies will greatly illuminate a presently obscure subject.

handmaid (Deut. 21.11–13), and the children of Hagar (Gen. 17.20–7) – and other topoi from earlier Christian literature are all invoked to warn the masters that

> It has reached our ears that some among you, distended like a skin by the spirit of vanity [1 Cor. 8.1], are working with profane *novitates* [1 Tim. 6.20] to pass beyond the *positi a patribus termini*, the understanding of the heavenly pages limited by the fixed *termini* of expositions in the study of the holy Fathers, *quos transgredi non solum est temerarium, sed prophanum*, inclining toward the philosophical doctrine of natural things.

They are doing this, not for their students' profit, but only for a show of knowledge, so that they might be thought to be God themselves. They should expound scripture according to the approved traditions of the saints, rather than by carnal means, but instead they reverse a natural hierarchy – they force the queen to be a servant to the handmaid. They confuse the realms of grace and nature, and thereby violate the strictures of 1 Tim. 6.20. Gregory commands them to teach theological purity, not adulterating the word of God with the figments of philosophers, but abiding by the *termini* established by the *patres*.

Gregory is here summing up a century of criticism of the misuse of the intellect and the confusion of disciplines that had characterized Latin theological studies from the days of Rupert of Deutz. It was illustrated not only in the quarrels between monks, but between monks and masters and between masters and masters, finally among popes, bishops, and masters. But Gregory's apparatus of scriptural references already sounds dated. Although the problem he addressed was a real one – and one that continued to be debated for the next half-century – its solution was not to be reached by the repetition of the familiar scriptural injunctions, but by the internal development of the schools themselves. By the end of the thirteenth century monks were no longer at the center of intellectual debates, and although the mendicant professors had appropriated some of the arguments of earlier monastic critics, they were themselves too involved in the intellectual life of their world to be as effective as the eleventh and early twelfth-century monastic critics had been. Moreover, the cognitive world of the late thirteenth and early fourteenth centuries had developed stability and internal rules of its own; it had become, as Miss Smalley suggested, a "fact of life." And it settled its cognitive and epistemological problems not by invoking either a set of undefined "limits" set by Fathers or the rhetoric of Gregory IX. Rather, it developed a line of argument that ran from Augustine to Aquinas and consisted of defining humility as being contained within one's own limits, and extending this definition to the idea of individual academic disciplines. The opening of the condemnation of the errors in the confusion of natural philosophy and theology at Paris in 1277 spoke of the arts faculty as having exceeded the proper limits of its discipline.[41]

From the limits of patristic authority to the limits of an academic discipline is a conceptual step that effectively characterizes the achievement of the twelfth- and thirteenth-century schools. Gregory IX cited Prov. 22.28 and other scriptural texts in a language and style characteristic of twelfth-century critics of the schools, but his citation was aimed at practitioners of a particular discipline, that of theology. Within the academic disciplines, of course, the sense of *terminus* itself resonated differently, since it too was a term of art – terminist logic had insisted that areas of thought, too, possessed *termini*, "limits" or "boundaries" that contained the rules, proper subject-matter, and specificity of each discipline. The Aristotelianism of Aquinas and other thirteenth-century thinkers was perfectly at home with such a notion, and remained at home with it until the debates of the later thirteenth and fourteenth centuries challenged the new theology in the name of a revived Augustinianism and a new anxiety about the limitations upon the omnipotence of God potentially posed by that theology.

But the later medieval debates about the integrity of theology did not void the sense of the limits of disciplines as characterizing the authority of those disciplines. Indeed, the safety of the schools proved remarkable in the face of ecclesiastical and temporal authority's assault on manifestations of religious discontent in the world outside the schools. Although individual masters ran the occasional risk of condemnation of their doctrines, not until the fourteenth century did any run the risk of the most severe punishments inflicted upon heretics convicted in spiritual or temporal courts, and then only rarely. Jan Hus was, after all, the first doctor convicted and executed for heresy. This remarkable – and quite practical – demonstration of academic freedom indicates one of the roles played by the schools of the twelfth and thirteenth centuries: what might be culpable *curiositas* and *superbia* in non-academics could be considered well within the limits of an academic discipline. As Heiko Oberman has pointed out, these notions of individual and professional limits ran down to the days of Jean Calvin:

> To stay within one's personal limits – the medieval definition of humility and the alternative to proud curiosity – means now to stay within the limits of one's field of competence. The medieval differentiation between the university faculties – pragmatically transcended in the preceding stages of the Renaissance – is here recaptured by Calvin to defend and respect the different methods of illuminating the common object, the glory of God.[42]

[41] Denifle 1889: no. 473, 543.

[42] Oberman 1973b: 403. Oberman's study is a critique of the work on the subject by Blumenberg 1983.

Long before Calvin, St. Bonaventure had pointed out that even theologians may err when they assert opinions in areas where they have no disciplinary competence.[43]

In the fourteenth and fifteenth centuries, the notion of disciplinary competence attracted the attention of skeptics, critics of speculative theology, practical moralists like Jean Gerson, and humanist critics of scholastic thought generally. The images and scriptural armory of Cassiodorus and Gregory the Great had served a long and complex task, being invoked again and again in utterly different contexts in order to assert the existence, continuity, and authority of tradition, first in law and ecclesiastical politics, later in the study of theology, and finally in the restricted area of individual and professional capacities.

Oberman has suggested that nominalist thought, particularly the work of Nicole Oresme, in its restriction of the term *experientia*, either to recorded collective experience in the historical record or the use of inductive reasoning to produce general conclusions and the discovery of physical laws, constituted a revolution in the history of attitudes toward speculative thought. Lacking actual experience, we are permitted to use imagination until it is verified or refuted by actual experience: "In the field of theology, this would be vain curiosity; in the field of natural philosophy, this is research, *investigation*."[44] For expanding the concept of the universe to include natural philosophy, the heavens themselves became acceptable objects for human inquiry:

> For Oresme as well as for those who stand in his tradition, the issue of the heavenly movements – of the orbits of the sun, the moon, the moving stars, and the earth – is no longer to be solved in terms of a deductive speculative cosmo*logy*, but in terms of an experimental inductive cosmo*nomy* – with the aid of imagination, but without claim on scientific accuracy until the mental experiments are confirmed by experience.[45]

For Oberman, such a transformation freed valid *curiositas* (the appropriate attitude for investigating the whole order of nature, now including both earth and heaven) from *vana curiositas*, the pointless attempt to penetrate the unknown and unknowable realm of God omnipotent. The *termini* set by the Fathers now applied to a *disciplina*, the discipline of theology, but the province of theology had been redefined and that of natural philosophy expanded. The uncertainties of the twelfth and thirteenth centuries were past, and the adventures of the modern world yet to come.

43 Peters 1985: 94; Berubé 1976: 130–62.

44 Oberman 1973b: 409; Oberman 1973a: 33–8.

45 Oberman 1973b: 410–11.

REFERENCES

Allen, P. S. and Allen, H. M. 1928 *Opus Epistolarum Des. Erasmi Roterodami*, Tom. VII, 1527–8. Oxford: Clarendon Press.

Allenbach, J. 1980a *Biblia Patristica*, vol. III. Paris: Editions du Centre national de la recherche scientifique.

1980b *Biblia Patristica*, vol. IV. Paris: Editions du Centre national de la recherche scientifique.

d'Alverny, M.-T. 1946–9 La Sagesse et ses sept filles: recherches sur les allégories de la Philosophie et des arts liberaux du IXe au XIIe siècle. In *Mélanges dédiés à la mémoire de Félix Grat*, I: 245–78. 2 vols. Paris: Pecquer-Grat.

Amann, E. 1933 Pères de l'Eglise. *Dictionnaire de théologie catholique*, vol. XII.1: cols. 1192–215. Paris: Letouzet et Ane.

Barnes, Timothy David 1971 *Tertullian: A Historical and Literary Study*. Oxford: Oxford University Press.

Bastgen, Hubertus, ed. 1924 *Libri carolini, sive Caroli Magni Capitulare de imaginibus*. *MGH Leges* sec. 3, 2.

Behrends, Frederick 1976 *The Letters and Poems of Fulbert of Chartres*. Oxford: Clarendon Press.

Berubé, C. 1976 *De la philosophie à la sagesse chez Saint Bonaventure et Roger Bacon*. Rome.

Beumann, Helmut with Schröder, W. 1978 *Nationes. Historische und philosophische Untersuchungen zur Enstehung der europäischen Nationen im Mittelalter*. Sigmaringen.

Blumenberg, Hans 1983 *The Legitimacy of the Modern Age*. Trans. Robert Wallace. Cambridge, Mass.: MIT Press.

Blumenthal, Uta-Renate 1983 *Carolingian Essays: Andrew W. Mellon Lectures in Early Christian Studies*, Washington, DC: Catholic University of America Press.

Brandmüller, Walter 1987 *Traditio Scripturae Interpres*: The Teaching of the Councils on the Right Interpretation of Scripture Up to the Council of Trent. *Catholic Historical Review* 73: 523–40.

Bullough, Donald 1983 Alcuin and the Kingdom of Heaven: Liturgy, Theology and the Carolingian Age. In Blumenthal 1983: 1–69.

Cabaniss, Allen 1954 *Amalarius of Metz*. Amsterdam: North Holland Publishing Company.

Cantin, André 1975 *Les Sciences seculières et la foi: les deux voies de la science au jugement de S. Pierre Damien (1007–1072)*. Spoleto: Centro Italiano di Studi sull'alto Medioevo.

Cassiodorus 1937 *Cassiodori Senatoris Institutiones*. Ed. R. A. B. Mynors. Oxford: Clarendon Press.

Cavadini, John 1993 *The Last Christology of the West: Adoptionism in Spain and Gaul 785–820*. Philadelphia: University of Pennsylvania Press.

Chenu, Marie-Dominique 1968 *Nature, Man, and Society in the Twelfth Century: Essays on New Theological Perspectives in the Latin West*. Trans. Jerome Taylor and Lester K. Little. Chicago: University of Chicago Press.

1976 *La Théologie au douzième siècle*. Paris: J. Vrin.

Contreni, John J. 1983 Carolingian Biblical Studies. In Blumenthal 1983: 71–98.

Dagens, Claude 1983 *Saint Grégoire le Grand. Culture et experience chrétiennes.* Paris: Etudes Augustinienne.

Daly, Saralynn R. 1957 Peter Comestor: Master of the Histories. *Speculum* 31: 62–75.

Danielou, Jean 1975 Recherche et tradition chez les pères. *Studia Patristica* 12: 3–13.

den Boeft, J. 1988 *Illic aureum quoddam ire flumen*: Erasmus' Enthusiasm for the *Patres*. In J. S. Weiland and W. Th. M. Trijhoff, eds., *Erasmus of Rotterdam: The Man and the Scholar*, 172–81. Leiden and New York: E. J. Brill.

Denifle, H. 1889 *Chartularium Universitatis Parisiensis*, with A. Chatelain, vol. I. Paris: ex typis Fratrum Delalain.

D'Onofrio, Giulio 1986 Dialectic and Theology: Boethius' *Opuscula sacra* and their Early Medieval Readers. *Studi Medievali* 3rd ser. 27.1: 45–67.

Evans, G. R. 1980a *Old Arts and New Theology: The Beginnings of Theology as an Academic Discipline.* Oxford: Oxford University Press.

1980b *Anselm and a New Generation.* Oxford: Oxford University Press.

Ferrulo, Stephen C. 1985 *The Origins of the University: The Schools of Paris and their Critics, 1100–1215.* Stanford: Stanford University Press.

Festus 1913 *Sexti Pompeii Festi De verborum significatu quae supersunt cum Pauli Epitome.* Ed. W. M. Lindsay. Leipzig: B. G. Teubueri.

Fichtenau, Heinrich 1991 Die Ketzer von Orléans. In Klaus Herbert, Hans Henning Kortüm, and Carlo Servatius, eds., *Ex ipsis rerum documentis. Beiträge zur Mediävistik. Festschrift für Harald Zimmermann zum 65. Geburtstag.* Sigmarigen: Thorbecke.

1992 *Ketzer und Professoren. Häresie und Vernunftglaube im Hochmittelalter.* Munich: C. H. Beck.

Frédouille, Jean-Claude 1972 *Tertullien et la conversion de la culture antique.* Paris: Etudes Augustinienne.

de Ghellinck, Joseph 1935 Patristique et argument de tradition au bas moyen âge. In A. Lang, ed., *Aus der Geisteswelt des Mittelalters. Beiträge zur Geschichte der Philosophie und Theologie des Mittelalters*, 403–26. Texte und Untersuchungen, Supplementband III.1. Munster: Ock Aschendorff.

1948 *Le Mouvement théologique du XIIe siècle.* Brussels and Paris: Editions "De Tempel."

Gibson, Margaret 1981 *Boethius: His Life, Thought and Influence.* Oxford: Blackwell.

1982 Boethius in the Carolingian Schools. *Transactions of the Royal Historical Society* 5th ser. 32: 43–56.

Gilmore, Myron P. 1963 *Humanists and Jurists: Six Studies in the Renaissance.* Cambridge, Mass.: Harvard University Press.

Ginzburg, Carlo 1976 High and Low: The Theme of Forbidden Knowledge in the Sixteenth and Seventeenth Centuries. *Past & Present* 73: 28–31.

Grégoire, Reginald 1965 *Bruno de Segni exégète médiéval et théologien monastique.* Spoleto: Centro Italiano di Studi sull'alto Medioevo.

Grundmann, Herbert 1927 Der Typus des Ketzers in mittelalterlicher Anschauung. In *Kultur- und Universalgeschichte. Walter Goetz zu seinem 60. Geburtstag* (Leipzig) 91–107.

1963 *Opportet et haereses esse.* Das Problem der Ketzerei im Spiegel der mittelalterlichen Bibelexegese. *Archiv fur Kulturgeschichte* 45: 129–64.

Hageneder, Othmar 1976 Der Häresisbegriff bei den Juristen des 12. und 13. Jahrhunderts. In Lourdaux and Verhelst 1976: 42–103.

Hanssens, J. M. 1948–50 *Amalarii Episcopi Opera Liturgica Omnia*. Studi e Testi 138–40. Vatican City: Biblioteca apostolica vaticana.

Hartmann, Wilfried 1970 Manegold von Lautenbach und die Anfänge der Frühscholastik. *Deutsches Archiv* 26: 47–149.

Hinschius, Paul 1963 *Decretales Pseudo-Isidorianae et Capitula Angilramni*. Repr. Aalen: Scientia Verlag.

Humphreys, S. C. 1988 The Discourse of Law in Archaic and Classical Greece. *Law and History Review* 6: 465–93.

Kuttner, Stephan 1982 On "Auctoritas" in the Writing of Medieval Canonists: The Vocabulary of Gratian. In G. Makdisi, Dominique Sourdel, Janine Sourdel-Thomine, eds., *La Notion d'autorité au Moyen Age. Islam, Byzance, Occident*, 69–81. Paris: Presses Universitaires de France.

Leclercq, Jean, O.S.B. 1982 *The Love of Learning and the Desire for God*. Repr. New York: Fordham University Press.

Le Goff, Jacques, ed. 1968 *Hérésies et sociétés dans l'Europe pré-industrielle 11e–18e siècles*. Paris and La Haye: Mouton.

Lerner, Robert 1992 Ecstatic Dissent. *Speculum* 67: 33–57.

Lourdaux, W., and Verhelst, D., eds. 1976 *The Concept of Heresy in the Middle Ages (11th–13th c): Proceedings of the International Conference Louvain May 13–16 1973*. Louvain: Louvain University Press.

de Lubac, Henri 1959 *Exégèse médiévale. Les quatre sens de l'écriture*. Première Partie, I. Paris: Aubier.

1961 *Exégèse médiévale. Les quatre sens de l'écriture*. Seconde Partie, I. Paris: Aubier.

McKitterick, Rosamund 1977 *The Frankish Church and the Carolingian Reforms*. London: Royal Historical Society.

McLaughlin, Mary Martin 1977 *Intellectual Freedom and its Limitations in the University of Paris in the Thirteenth and Fourteenth Centuries*. New York: Arno Press.

Madoz, Jose 1933 *El Concepto de la Tradicion en S. Vincente de Lerins: Estudio Historico-Critico del "Commonitorio"*. Analecta Gregoriana, vol. V. Rome: Pontificiae Universitatis.

Martin, R.-M. 1931 Notes sur l'oeuvre littéraire de Pierre le Mangeur, *Recherches de théologie ancienne et médiévale* 3: 54–66.

Matthew Paris 1880 *Matthaei Parisiensis Chronica Majora*, ed. H. R. Luard, vol. V. London; repr., Wiesbaden, 1964.

Mollat du Jourdin, Michel, and Vauchez, André 1990 *Un temps d'épreuves*. Vol. VI of *Histoire du christianisme*. Paris: Fayard.

Moore, R. I. 1976 Heresy as Disease. In Lourdaux and Verhelst 1976: 1-11.

Morris, Colin 1989 *The Papal Monarchy: The Western Church from 1050 to 1250*. Oxford: Oxford University Press.

Morrison, Karl F. 1969 *Tradition and Authority in the Western Church, 300–1140*. Princeton: Princeton University Press.

1983 Incentives for Studying the Liberal Arts. In David L. Wagner, ed., *The Seven Liberal Arts in the Middle Ages*, 32–57. Bloomington: Indiana University Press.

Mostert, Marco 1987 *The Political Theology of Abbo of Fleury*. Hilversum: Verloven.

Munier, Charles 1957 *Les Sources patristiques du droit de l'église du VIIIe au XIIIe siècle*. Mulhouse: Salvator.

Neusner, Jacob, ed. and transl. 1990 *Scriptures of the Oral Torah: Sanctification and Salvation in the Sacred Books of Judaism*. Atlanta: Scholars Press.

Newhauser, Richard 1982 Towards a History of Human Curiosity: A Prolegomenon to its Medieval Phase. *Deutsche Vierteljahrschrift* 56: 559–75.

1987 The Sin of Curiosity and the Cistercians. In John R. Sommerfeldt, ed., *Erudition at God's Service*, 71–95. Cistercian Studies Series, 98. Kalamazoo.

Oberman, Heiko 1973a *Contra vanam curiositatem. Ein Kapitel der Theologie zwischen Seelenwinkel und Weltall*. Zurich: Theologischer Verlag.

1973b Reformation and Revolution: Copernicus's Discovery in an Era of Change. In John B. Murdoch and Edith Dudley Sylla, eds., *The Cultural Context of Medieval Learning*, 397–435. Dordrecht and Boston: D. Reidel Publishing Company.

O'Donnell, James J. 1979 *Cassiodorus*. Berkeley and Los Angeles: University of California Press.

Otto of Freising 1974 *Gesta Frederici seu Rectius Chronica*. Ed. G. Waitz, B. Simpson, F.-J. Schmale, Ausgewahlte Quellen sur Geschichte des Mittelalters, Band XVIII. Darmstadt: Wissenschäftliche Buchgesellschaft.

Pelikan, Jaroslav 1973 Council or Father or Scripture? The Concept of Authority in the Theology of Maximus the Confessor. In David Neiman and Margaret Schatkin, eds., *The Heritage of the Early Church: Essays in Honor of the Very Reverend Georges Florovsky*, 277–88. Rome: Institutum Studiorum Orientalium.

1974 *The Spirit of Eastern Christendom (600–1700)*. Chicago: University of Chicago Press.

1978 *The Growth of Medieval Theology (600–1300)*. Chicago: University of Chicago Press.

Peters, Edward 1985 *Libertas Inquirendi* and the *Vitium curiositatis* in Medieval Thought. In G. Makdisi, J. Sourdel Thomine, D. Sourdel, eds., *La Notion de liberté au moyen âge*, 89–98. Paris: Société d'Editions les Belles Lettres.

1990 The Death of the Subdean: Ecclesiastical Order and Disorder in Eleventh-Century Francia. In Bernard S. Bachrach and David Nicholas, eds., *Law, Custom, and the Social Fabric: Essays in Honor of Bryce Lyon*, 51–71. Kalamazoo: Medieval Institute Publications, Western Michigan University.

Quasten, Johannes 1966 *Patrology*, I: *The Beginnings of Christian Literature*. Utrecht and Antwerp: Spectrum.

Resnick, I. M. 1987 *Scientia liberalis*, Dialectics, and Otloh of St. Emmeram. *Revue bénédictine* 97: 241–52.

Reynolds, Roger E. 1983 Unity and Diversity in Carolingian Canon Law Collections: The Case of the *Collectio Hibernensis* and its Derivatives. In Blumenthal 1983: 99–135.

Riché, Pierre 1981 *Divina Pagina, Ratio et Auctoritas* dans la théologie carolingienne. In *Nascità dell'Europa ed Europa Carolingia: un'Equazione da Verificare*, II.719–63. Settimane di Studio del Centro Italiano di Studi sull'Alto Medioevo. Spoleto: Presso la Sede del Centro.

1989 *Ecoles et enseignement dans le Haut Moyen Age. Fin du Ve siècle–milieu du XIe siècle*. 2nd edn. Paris: Picard.

Robinson, I. S. 1983 Political Allegory in the Biblical Exegesis of Bruno of Segni. *Recherches de théologie ancienne et médiévale* 50: 67–98.

Scott, R. B. Y. 1965 *The Anchor Bible. Proverbs and Ecclesiasticus.* Garden City, N.Y.: Doubleday.

Sieben, Hermann Josef 1980 *Voces. Eine Bibliographie zu Worten und Begriffen aus der Patristik (1918–1978).* Berlin and New York: W. de Gruyter.

1983 *Exegesis Patrum: Saggio bibliografico sull'esegesi biblica dei Padri della Chiesa.* Rome: Institute Patristico Augustinianum.

Smalley, Beryl 1975 Ecclesiastical Attitudes to Novelty, c. 1100–c. 1250. *Studies in Church History* 12: 113–31.

1983 *The Study of the Bible in the Middle Ages.* 3rd edn. Oxford: Blackwell.

Southern, R. W., and Schmitt, F. S. 1969 *Memorials of St. Anselm,* Auctores Britannici Medii Aevi, vol. I. London: published for the British Academy by Oxford University Press.

Stock, Brian 1975 Experience, Praxis, Work, and Planning in Bernard of Clairvaux: Observations on the *Sermones in Cantica.* In John Murdoch and Edith Dudley Sylla, eds., *The Cultural Context of Medieval Learning,* 219–68. Dordrecht and Boston: Reidel Publishing Company.

Straw, Carole Ellen 1988 *Gregory the Great: Perfection in Imperfection.* Berkeley, Los Angeles, and London: University of California Press.

Sullivan, Richard E. 1989 The Carolingian Age: Reflections on its Place in the History of the Middle Ages. *Speculum* 64: 267–306.

Van den Eynde, Damien 1933 *Les Normes de l'enseignement chrétien dans la litterature patristique des trois premiers siècles.* Gembloux and Paris: J. Duculot.

Van Engen, John 1983 *Rupert of Deutz.* Berkeley and Los Angeles: University of California Press.

Vauchez, André 1990 Contestations et hérésies dans l'église latine. In Mollat du Jourdin and Vauchez 1990: ch. 6.

Wallace-Hadrill, J. M. 1983 *The Frankish Church.* Oxford: Oxford University Press.

Wasserschleben, F. G. A. 1840 *Reginonis Abbatis Prumiensis Libri Duo de Synodalibus Causis et Disciplinis Ecclesiasticis.* Leipzig: Sumptibus G. Engleman.

Wasserschleben, Hermann 1885 *Die irische Kanonensammlungen.* Leipzig, Tauchnitz.

Wind, Edgar, 1937–8 *Aenigma Termini. Journal of the Warburg and Courtauld Institutes* 1: 66–9.

Zimmermann, Albrecht, ed. 1973 *Antiqui und Moderni. Traditionsbewusstsein und Fortschrittsbewusstsein im späten Mittelalter.* Miscellanea Medievalia, Band 9. Berlin and New York: de Gruyter.

IV

Libertas Inquirendi *and the* Vitium Curiositatis *in Medieval Thought*

Since the eighteenth century the western world has identified the discovery of truth with the unfettered play of the mind, and it has formalized this identification in the terms "intellectual freedom" and "academic freedom". Yet in spite of their idealized value, these freedoms have generally existed, where they have in fact existed, rather as a compromise between contending ideologies and powers than as goods pursued and sustained for their own sake. Much of the academic freedom of the medieval universities was the result of the dangers that popes, kings, and masters perceived from each other and from other institutions in the twelfth and thirteenth centuries — from bishops, chancellors, and monasteries to heretics and townspeople. Even the famous principles of *Lehren — Lern —* and *Wertfreiheit* developed in nineteenth-century German universities and given a liberal philosophical justification by Max Weber, have recently been termed a "hot-house flower", growing precariously between the potentially revolutionary stimuli of philosophical publicism and social science on the one hand, and the powers of the absolute state on the other.[1]

For these reasons, most of the history of intellectual and academic freedom has focused upon freedom for the thinker or the academy from external threat.[2] The interior dimensions of these freedoms, aside from recent studies of professional consciousness, *Berufsbewusstsein*, have received somewhat less attention.[3] But as two recent numbers of *Daedalus* and a few other publications show, the inner limits upon thought and research have recently become the object of a good deal of discussion and concern.[4] And so an ancient debate which began with patristic discussions of *paradosis* and *zetesis* continues in the twentieth century, and the intrinsic freedom of the thinker is still a matter of debate and challenge.[5]

In the world of medieval thought the corporate entity of the university possessed *de facto* liberties that nearly equalled the great *libertas* of kings and clergy.[6] Yet corporate agreement in defense of particular privileges and liberties did not necessarily entail epistemological agreement about the nature of study and teaching, the divisions within the organization of knowledge, the dividing-line between *sapientia* and *scientia*, and the subjects upon which dispute could and could not be entertained. From the eleventh century on, these questions constituted the landmarks of the inner history of the freedom of thought, a history that is at least as interesting as — and somewhat more difficult to trace than — the institutional struggles by which its extrinsic history has customarily been examined. For the new learning of the twelfth and thirteenth centuries successfully challenged the traditional curricular content of monastic and literary schools, criticizing both their theory of knowledge and the place of learning and speculation in the Christian life itself. The history of this process has been extensively studied. More important for the purposes of this paper are the kinds of defense and criticism of the new learning, its claims to — and practical expression of — freedom of inquiry, and the role of the vice of *curiositas* in the criticism of inquiry, constituting as it were a kind of negative definition of *libertas inquirendi* on the basis of moral theology.

From St. Paul's observation in 2 Cor. 3. 17: *Ubi spiritus Domini, ibi libertas*, to later theologians' distinctions between *libertas libera* = freedom to do evil, and *libertas liberata* = freedom to do good, Christian discussions of *libertas* focused upon the *libertas* of the *arbitrium*, freedom of the will.[7] Conventional associations of *libertas* with study and thought are generaly found in the twelfth century in discussions of the *artes liberales* and the semantic associations of *liberalis* and *liber*, for example in the work of Conrad of Hirsau and John of Salisbury.[8] But these brief discussions usually refer to *libertas* in a Ciceronian sense of freedom from the cares of this world or freedom to follow virtue. A second association of *libertas* with study occurs in a more pragmatic sense of freedom from coercion. This is the better known *libertas scholastica*, the total of rights and privileges of masters and students as members of corporate groups, not generically different from the privileges and liberties of other corporate groups in the twelfth and thirteenth centuries.[9]

These three different kinds of *libertas* do not lead very far toward an abstract theory of liberty of thought and expression, for the expression of freedom of inquiry was more a matter of practical experience than of theorizing. In twelfth- and thirteenth-century Europe the scale of organized life was very small, and outside of conventional structures of power which touched relatively few areas of life and thought, there was considerable room for the exercise of freedom in practice, and the schools were the example of such empirical *libertas* par excellence. Although they seem to have coined no term for their inner freedom distinguishable from other senses of *libertas*, their critics did. They often designated it *curiositas*, thus giving a new function to an old and relatively restricted term from moral theology.

Curiositas came down to twelfth-century thinkers from two patristic sources, St. Augustine and John Cassian.[10] In his commentary on 1 John 12, 15-16,

Augustine had designated *curiositas* along with pride and lust, as three broad categories of sin, among which *curiositas* signified particularly the indulgence of the senses for the corruption of the mind. Augustine saw this character in God's curse upon the serpent, that he shall eat earth, and by the fish in the depths of the sea who see only *inania* and *praeterfluentia.*[11] Augustine's wide range of meanings for *curiositas* included both forbidden intellectual inquiry and the more domestic vices of neglect of self and excessive interest in the affairs of neighbours. John Cassian, writing for a different audience, emphasized the latter aspect of *curiositas* in making the vice a subdivision of sloth and focused upon its place in monastic psychology. Gregory the Great, while preserving some of Augustine's senses, was closer to that of Cassian, as were most monastic commentators from the seventh to the twelfth centuries. Isidore of Seville transmits the two different senses of *curiositas* in the *Etymologiarum Libri XX* in two different places.[12] Augustine had also spoken of the moral danger of *curiositas* in denying the need for salvation, because it forced the *curiosus* to neglect his own faults and interest himself only in the faults of others. This last aspect permitted Augustine to link *curiositas* to other groups of vices, as did Cassian, Gregory, and other thinkers.

Although Carolingian writers preserved the Augustinian/Isidorean criticism of excessive zeal for learning (and learning things that were forbidden), the first criticism of the new learning in the eleventh century did not focus primarily upon the *curiositas* of the dialecticians. The often-cited uses of the term by Peter Damian are not in his major criticisms of the use of learning by monks, and it is likely that Damian's sense of *curiositas* designates superficial arrogance, in the manner of Papias, rather than exceeding the limits of inquiry.[13] It is quite otherwise, however, with St. Anselm's *De humanis moribus (De similitudinibus).* In his discussion of *propria voluntas,* which, Anselm says, is possible only for God, he remarks that the assumption of *propria voluntas* by man takes three forms : in *delectatione, aut exaltatione aut curiositate. Curiositas est studium perscrutandi ea, quae scire nulla est utilitas.*[14] Anselm then goes on to identify forty-four *genera curiositatis* which range from careful study to learn the secrets of others to "numbering, measuring and considering by how much the sun and moon are distant from Earth, or how great the sun and moon are". The *De similitudinibus* reunited the two strands of *curiositas,* identified a wide range of behavior as *curiositas,* and reformulated the Augustinian triad of vices in the language of twelfth century monasticism.

From Anselm on, the vice of *curiositas* attracted particular monastic attention, particularly in the work of St. Bernard, who orchestrated *curiositas* into a major force in monastic psychology. In letters, sermons, the *Liber de modo bene vivendi,* the *De consideratione,* and especially in the *De gradibus humilitatis et superbiae,* Bernard made *curiositas* the first and most elaborately described step on the monastic ladder of *superbia.* Even Bernard's criticism of elaborate architecture, dress, ceremony and learning are linked to the theme of *curiositas* as a distraction from the monk's primary duty.[15] Thus, shaped in a monastic context, *curiositas* was revived in twelfth-century discourse and reassumed a prominent place in moral theology, from which it was later applied to circumstances outside the monastic world.

For Bernard and others also criticized the new schools. These had not, at first, challenged the meditative theology of monastic learning, but had begun among the grammarians and logicians of Tours, Chartres, Orleans, Laon, and Paris to revise the content and method of the liberal arts and only later to apply the results of their study to the exegesis of scripture and the exposition of theology.[16] Criticism of the intrusion of the new learning upon the province of theology is evident in the complaints of William of Champeaux and William of St. Thierry and in the defense of Peter Abelard. William of Conches once castigated his critics :

> Ignorant themselves of the forces of nature and wanting to have company in their ignorance, they do not want people to look into anything (*nolunt eos aliquid inquirere)* ; they want us to believe like peasants and not ask the reason behind things (*nec rationem quaerere*)... But we say that the reason behind everything should be sought out (in *omnibus rationem esse quaerendum*)... If they learn that anyone is so inquiring (*si inquirentem aliquid sciant*), they shout that he is a heretic, placing more reliance on their monastic robes than on their wisdom.[17]

Quaerere, inquirere, inquirens : these are the terms that William of Conches used to describe himself and others like him on the quest of the intellectuals. As Miss Smalley has demonstrated, not everyone in the twelfth century condemned the idea of novelty, and the twelfth century also witnessed the first references to curious readers in European history.[18] By the late twelfth century, the early monastic concerns of St. Bernard had spread to such non-Cistercian critics as John of Salisbury, Rupert of Deutz, and Stephen of Tournai. Monastic vision-stories were transformed into moral *exempla* critizing the *curiositas* of scholars, and even some of the new theologians criticized *supervacua vanitas* and *noxia curiositas,* both the arrogance and the pride of scholars.[19] Alexander Nequam summed up a century of criticism in the lines : *O vanitas ostentationis ! O laudis ambitus ! O inutilis curiositas.*[20] Stephen of Tournai linked conventional discussions of the theme of *libertas* in connection with the *artes liberales* to *servitudo* in what he regarded as the presumption and audacity of Parisian masters.[21] Several recent studies have been inclined to dismiss much of this criticism as superficial, but the different levels of meaning which *curiositas* had come to possess by the end of the twelfth century suggest that the criticism was more profound than is usually assumed.[22] Moreover, *curiositas* also circulated in the twelfth century to describe other kinds of intellectual activity that were clearly forbidden. The use of *curiositas* to describe heretics dates to Irenaeus and Tertullian, but such use of the term increased in the twelfth and thirteenth centuries. So strong was it that St. Bonaventure found himself called upon to defend the study of heretical beliefs in order to refute them, because some of his critics, probably thinking of St. Bernard's remark that to study evil was *curiositas*, accused heresiologists of the vice. A second meaning, one dating back to Apuleius and Augustine, associated *curiositas* with the study and practice of — and even interest in — magic. This connection appeared in several twelfth-century literary contexts, notably in Guibert of Nogent and William of Malmesbury, but by the beginning of the thirteenth century, as I have noted elsewhere, the use of *curiositas* to designate the practice of magic became more frequent, particularly in the work of William of Auvergne and Raymond of Peñaforte.[23]

By the end of the twelfth century, then, the relatively obscure and restricted term *curiositas* had come to acquire new prominence, first in the revival of Augustinian thought in Anselm's *De similitudinibus*, in St. Bernard and other Cistercian moral theologians, and then in discussions of superfluity in the arts and scholarship, in discussions of heresy and magic, and in the criticism of the schools. It had become a formidable accusation, losing many of its earlier honorific and neutral senses in the process, and it regularly came to be used against certain kinds of thinkers and teachers in the universities of the thirteenth and fourteenth centuries.

For the universities after 1200 were conspicuous, influential, and proud institutions. Their extensive *libertates* protected individual masters, and, as McLaughlin has pointed out, not until after the condemnations of the Amauricians in 1210 did a process of attempting to regulate the content of teaching really begin.[24] Its paths are well known, and so are its most conspicuous landmarks : the decretals *Super speculam* of Honorius III and *Ab Aegyptiis* of Gregory IX a few years later ; the conflict between Mendicants and the secular masters ; and the condemnations of 1270 and 1277. But these attempts at controlling teaching seem to have done little to stop a process that kept spilling beyond the tidy confines of philosophy and theology and carefully drawn schemes of the organization of knowledge. The great transformation of the liberal arts, the growing dominance of philosophy, the intermingling of philosophical techniques with theological study, and the reciprocal flow of Aristotelianism into philosophical discourse all sharpened problems of inquiry and exposition. For the universities witnessed not only an explosion of knowledge and speculation, but the most efficient means of gathering and disseminating them ever devised. To control such an explosion authorities had only the power to define limits to areas of teaching, to condemn the content of particular propositions, and the accusation of *curiositas* and *superbia* against those who ignored them.

The very method of study and teaching contributed to the lack of control by authorities. Gradually, teaching had ceased to consist of the meticulous following of a text, an *auctoritas*, in favor of inquiry *per modum quaestionis*. As McLaughlin and others have pointed out, "A master might venture almost any idea or opinion *narrando, dubitando, inquirendo* or *querendo*".[25] Here is the case of a development in pedagogical technique opening great vistas without positing any particular theory of its freedom to do so. Siger of Brabant and Boetius of Dacia, for whom the speculative intellect led to the knowledge of the truth and pleasure in it, boldly claimed the *studium sapientiae* as the philosopher's, not the theologian's duty. By positing a purely natural order, accessible to rational inquiry, as the province of the philosopher, Boetius and others, although they do not seem to have used an abstract sense of *libertas*, certainly claimed, as did Godefroid des Fontaines, that the philosopher "should not be silent" about such things, that it was "expedient" that even errors be read and discussed, that it was the philosopher's duty to consider everything within the province of logic and the natural order.[26]

But theologians too developed a speculative bent, and they too increased the number and range of subjects that their discipline touched. Although earlier legislation had sometimes prohibited the study of the liberal arts and such other *negotia saecularia* as alchemy, law, and medicine to theologians, in this field too pedagogical techniques often permitted what was otherwise forbidden. As scriptural study was increasingly restricted to the *sensus litteralis*, speculative theology was freed to deal with *quaestiones*, broad problems of interpretation and definition. The new *quaestiones disputatae* freed philosophical and theological speculation and at the same time drew down upon theologians the criticisms of popes and others for their "curious and futile questions".[27] Theologians too proceeded *per modum inquirendi*, "for the sake of inquiry and for the subtilizing of the intellect".[28]

Thomas Aquinas' well known summary of the moral dimensions of *curiositas* (which Thomas discussed in connection with *temperantia*) represents the content of moral theology rather than particular attention to thirteenth-century circumstances.[29] Much more responsive to contemporary circumstances, and more influential on later thinkers, however, was the discussion of St. Bonaventure. In his *Collatio* on the gifts of the Holy Spirit, and in other works, Bonaventure not only subordinates philosophy to theology, but theology itself to Scripture. Of these, Scripture is the only intellectual source that does not fail or fall into error. God has provided the human intellect with adequate knowledge to perceive the divine wisdom insofar as it is knowable in created things. To investigate by reason beyond the point of adequate knowledge is to move away from divine wisdom and be guilty of *curiositas*. Reason that is not illuminated by faith will be overshadowed by the senses, become darkened, be deceived by illusions, and fall into error. *Ecclesiasticus* 3. 22, *Altiora te ne quaesieris*, applies particularly to learned men, when it warns them of this kind of *curiositas*, which is a species of idolatry. Even theologians may err when they assert opinions in areas where they have no disciplinary competence. The *curiosi*, who lack devotion, abandon *pietas* and come to resemble the scribes and Levites : *isti nesciunt Christum propter curiositatem*.[30]

By widening the sense of *curiositas* to include the improper study of theology as well as philosophy, Bonaventure opened a door to fourteenth-century critics of intellectual inquiry of many different kinds, from Duns Scotus to Gerson, Spiritual Franciscans, representatives of the *Devotio moderna*, mystics, nominalists, and humanists. Michalski has pointed out the degree to which a lack of confidence in human cognitive powers is a characteristic of fourteenth-century scepticism, and Glorieux has demonstrated the extent to which Nicholas de Clamanges, Pierre d'Ailly, and Gerson himself were troubled, less by the subtleties and quibbling of tiresome pedants than by the serious moral and spiritual consequences of futile research and the dilettantism of disputations merely for the sake of disputation.[31] These movements, as well as dramatic tensions within the religious life (which, as Constable has shown, led to a revival of interest in the very twelfth-century spiritual writers who had first enunciated a theory of *curiositas* in their criticism of the schools), and a revived Augustinianism also characterize the fourteenth and fifteenth centuries and shape their continued use of *curiositas.*[32]

By the sixteenth century, *curiositas* had retained some of the semantic resonance of each of its earlier meanings. It did not mean simply transgressing the limits set upon human knowledge nor the study of magic, but a state of the passions that could entail both sensitive and intellective faults. It was a vice that essentially meant neglect of self and a turning outward, whether to neighbor or knowledge. It still possessed something of the air of arrogance and superficiality, but it had been strengthened and deepened by Bonaventure and Gerson, and later by humanist critics of scholasticism generally, into a term that served to criticize pretensions to knowledge of many kinds.[33] And for a time it succeeded. On the title-page of the first *Historia* of Faust, printed in Frankfurt in 1587, Faust is held up as an example of two of the three types of Augustinian sin, pride and curiosity. Faust's perversion of the gifts of *ingenium* and *memoria* through his long study of philosophy and theology led him to *curiositas* — an overripe example of the medieval academic vice, rather than the herald of a new age of intellectual freedom.[34]

Yet two years after the publication of the first Faust book, in 1589, another philosopher left Wittenberg. Giordano Bruno left Faust's town and university to seek, as he said, *philosophica libertas.* With Bruno, a name was finally put to a practice developed in the twelfth and thirteenth-century schools.[35] Two decades after Faust and Bruno, a series of struggles in the United Provinces over the interpretation of Calvinism raised once again the question of how much debate in theological matters could be tolerated by a European society. Isaac Casaubon wrote to Hugo Grotius, urging that "curious theologians" be silenced for the sake of social peace. But a wiser and more pragmatic Conrad Vorstius of Leiden took a different view. Writing to Casaubon around 1615, Vorstius stated : *Hic vero libertas aliqua inquirendi, aut etiam dissentiendi doctis omnino concedenda est.*[36] Otherwise, Vorstius remarked, "it will look as if we were stopping the slow march of truth." The linking of *libertas inquirendi* with "the slow march of truth" touched a part of the western consciousness that never relinquished the association, at least as an ideal, no matter how dangerous and troublesome the connection between freedom of thought and its institutionalization proved to be. And so men of the seventeenth century came to give a name at last to a practice long exercised during the twelfth and thirteenth centuries in the religious life and in the life of the universities. *Libertas... concedenda est* : the phrase comes from the old vocabulary of "conceding" particular liberties and privileges. But what *libertates* are conceded in Vorstius' phrase ! *Libertas inquirendi, libertas dissentiendi,* once conceded to the learned, soon became the right of Everyman, at least in a few societies for a few centuries.

NOTES

1. Max WEBER, "Science as a Vocation", in H.C. GERTH and C. WRIGHT MILLS, From *Max Weber : Essays in Sociology,* New York, 1947 ; Joseph BEN-DAVID and Awraham ZLOCZOWER, "The Universities and Academic Systems in Modern Societies," *Archives of European Sociology,* III, 1962, p. 45-84. On freedom of thought and speech in antiquity, see Enrico BERTI, "Ancient Greek Dialectic as Expression of Freedom of Thought and Speech", *Journal of the History of Ideas,* 39, 1978, p. 347-370. For the general problem in medieval usage, see Herbert GRUNDMANN, "Freiheit als religiöses, politisches und persönliches Postulat im Mittelalter", *Historische Zeitschrift,* 183, 1957, p. 23-53.

2. The finest study of the subject is Mary Martin MCLAUGHLIN, *Intellectual Freedom and Its Limitations in the University of Paris in the Thirteenth and Fourteenth Centuries,* New York, 1977, with a full bibliography and generous citation of texts.

3. See the studies in *Miscellanea Mediaevalia* III : *Beiträge zum Berufsbewusstsein des mittelalterlichen Menschen,* 1964, and A. MURRAY, *Reason and Society in the Middle Ages,* Oxford, 1978, p. 213-316 ; John W. BALDWIN, *Masters, Princes and Merchants,* Princeton, 1970, Vol. I, p. 63-170.

4. *The Limits of Scientific Inquiry, Daedalus : Proceedings of the Academy of Arts and Sciences,* Vol. 107, N° 2, 1978 ; *Intellect and Imagination : The Limits and Presuppositions of Intellectual Inquiry, Daedalus,* Vol. 109, N° 2, 1980 ; Robert S. LOPEZ, "Wisdom Science and Mechanics : The Three Tiers of Medieval Knowledge and the Forbidden Fourth", in Karl DEUTSCH and Andrew MARKOWITS, *Fear of Science / Trust in Science,* Cambridge Mass., 1980, p. 15-23.

5. Jean DANIÉLOU, "Recherche et tradition chez les pères", *Studia Patristica,* 12, 1975, p. 3-13.

6. H. GRUNDMANN, "*Sacerdotium — Regnum — Studium.* Zur Verwertung der Wissenschaft im 13. Jahrhundert", *Archiv für Kulturgeschichte,* 34, 1951, p. 5-21.

7. See the general discussion in O. LOTTIN, *Psychologie et morale au* XIII*e siècle,* Vol. 1, 2 ed., Louvain-Gembloux, 1954, p. 41.

8. R.B.C. HUYGENS ed., Conrad de Hirsau, *Dialogus super auctores,* Coll. *Latomus* XVII, Brussells, 1955, 23.4 (p. 16) ; 67. 15f ; 74-5 (p. 58) ; John of SALISBURY, *Metalogicon,* ed. C.C.J. WEBB, Oxford, 1929, p. 31.

9. Laetitia BOEHM, "*Libertas scholastica* und *Negotium scholare.* Entstehung und Sozialprestige des Akademischenstandes im Mittelalter", in H. RÖSSLER and G. FRANZ ed., *Universität und Gelehrtenstand 1400-1800,* Limburg an der Lahn, 1970, p. 15-61 ; *Chartularium Universitatis Parisiensis* I, N°s 64, 72.

10. There are general, but not complete discussions in Hans BLUMENBERG, *Der Pro-*

zess der theoretischen Neugierde, Berlin, 1973 ; Heiko Augustinus OBERMAN, *Contra vanam curiositatem*, Zurich, 1973. I am presently collaborating with Richard NEWHAUSER, of the Universities of Pennsylvania and Tübingen on a larger history of *curiositas*.

11. Augustine, *De genesi contra Manichaeos* II, 18, 27 ; *Ennar. in Ps*, VIII, 13.

12. *Etymologiarum Libri XX*, II, 52 ; II, 71 (PL 83 : 857, 861).

13. See André CANTIN, *Les sciences séculières et la foi. Les deux voies de la science au jugement de S. Pierre Damien (1007-1072)*, Spoleto, 1975, p. 151-180 ; PL 144 : 258C ; PL 145 : 831 ; PL 145 : 603C.

14. R.W. SOUTHERN and F.S. SCHMITT, *Memorials of St. Anselm*, Auctores Britannici Medii Aevi, vol. 1, London, 1969, p. 47-50.

15. See the discussion in C.K. ZACHER, *Curiosity and Pilgrimage*, Baltimore, 1976, p. 23-27 ; Meyer SCHAPIRO, « On the Aesthetic Attitude in Romanesque Art », *Romanesque Art : Selected Essays*, vol .1, New York, 1977, p. 1-27 ; BALDWIN, *Masters, Princes and Merchants*, I, p. 66-69 ; E. de BRUYNE, *Études d'esthétique médiévale, II, L'Époque Romane* Bruges, 1946, p. 133-172. The most sensitive study of the monastic concept of the vice in this context is that of Jean LECLERCQ, *The Love of Learning and the Desire for God : A Study of Monastic Culture*, transl. Catherine MISRAHI, 3rd. ed., New York, 1982, p. 193-235.

16. See M.-D. CHENU, *Nature, Man and Society in the Twelfth Century*, transl. J. TAYLOR and L.K. LITTLE, Chicago, 1968, p. 300-309 ; *Arts libéraux et philosophie au Moyen Age*, Actes du Quatrième Congrès International de Philosophie Médiévale, Montréal-Paris, 1969.

17. *Max. Biblioth. Patrum*, vol. XX, Lyon, 1667, 1002. Cf. John HOLMBERG ed., *Das Moralium Dogma Philosophorum des Guillaume de Conches*, Uppsala, 1929, p. 11 ; E. JEAUNEAU, *« Lectio philosophorum » : Recherches sur l'école de Chartres*, Amsterdam, 1973, p. 131.

18. B. SMALLEY, « Ecclesiastical Attitudes toward Novelty, c. 1100 — c. 1250 », *Studies in Church History*, 13, 1975, p. 113-131. For « curious » readers, see PL 188 : 1120 ; PL 182 : 531.

19. T.F. CRANE ed., *The Exempla of Jacques de Vitry*, rpt. Nendeln/Liechtenstein, 1967, p. 12-13, 145-6 ; BALDWIN, *Masters, Princes and Merchants*, I, p. 78-83 ; 96-107.

20. See E. GILSON, in CHENU, *Nature, Man and Society*, ix-xiii.

21. CUP I, N° 48.

22. MURRAY, *Reason and Society*, p. 213-316 ; J.H. MUNDY, *Europe in the High Middle Ages, 1154-1309*, New York, 1973, p. 464-483.

23. E. PETERS, *The Magician, the Witch and the Law*, Philadelphia, 1978, p. 89-90.

24. MCLAUGHLIN, p. 19-20.

25. *Ibid.*, p. 65, 182.

26. *Ibid.*, p. 85f.

27. CUP II, N° 1125.

28. MCLAUGHLIN, p. 193-221.

29. *Summa Theologiae*, IIa IIae, qq. 166-167.

30. There is a good discussion in C. BERUBÉ, *De la philosophie à la sagesse chez Saint Bonaventure et Roger Bacon*, Rome, 1976, p. 130-162.

31. Konstanty MICHALSKI, *La Philosophie au XIV*e siècle, Frankfurt, 1969, p. 38-9, 170-1 ; P. GLORIEUX, « Le Chancellier Gerson et la réforme de l'enseignement », *Mélanges offerts à Étienne GILSON*, Toronto-Paris, 1959, p. 285-298 ; BERUBÉ, *De la philosophie à la sagesse*, p. 312-319 ; GLORIEUX, « Gerson et Saint Bonaventure », *S. Bonaventure 1274-1974*, Rome, 1974, vol. IV, p. 773-791 ; Heiko A. OBERMANN, « Fourteenth Century Religious Thought : A Premature Profile », *Speculum*, 53, 1978, p. 80-93 ; idem, *Contra vanem curiositatem*, p. 33-38.

32. Giles CONSTABLE, « The Popularity of Twelfth-Century Spiritual Writers in the Late Middle Ages, » in A. MOLHO and J.A. TEDESCHI eds., *Renaissance : Studies in Honor of Hans Baron*, Dekalb Ill., 1971, p. 3-28.

33. Wilhelm KÖLMEL, « *Scolasticus literator* : Die Humanisten und ihr Verhältnis zur Scholastik, » *Historisches Jahrbuch*, 93, 1973, p. 307-335.

34. J. SCHEIBLE, *Das Kloster*, vol. II, Stuttgart, 1846, p. 933. Cf. Erich HELLER, « Faust's Damnation : The Morality of Knowledge », *The Artist's Journey to the Interior and Other Essays*, New York, 1976.

35. Robert H. SUTTON, « The Phrase *Libertas philosophandi* », *Journal of the History of Ideas*, 14, 1953, p. 310-316.

36. *Praestantium ac eruditorum virorum Epistolae...*, ed. C HARTSOEKER and P. von LIMBORCH, 2nd ed., Amsterdam, 1684, p. 288, 492, 378. Discussed in Carlo GINZBURG, « High and Low : the Theme of Forbidden Knowledge in the Sixteenth and Seventeenth Centuries », *Past & Present*, 73, 1976, p. 28-41.

V

REX CURIOSUS: A PREFACE TO PROSPERO

This article focuses on the magical interests and actions of Shakespeare's Prospero in The Tempest *to consider medieval and early modern ideas of appropriate and inappropriate royal learning. The article begins with a consideration of the play itself and then treats some contemporary cases in Shakespeare's world, e.g. James VI & I, Rudolf II, and the sixteenth-century literature on the civic purpose of learning on the part of courtiers and rulers. It then goes on to survey the problem of royal learning and the terms used to describe it from Charlemagne and Alfred to the seventeenth century. It argues that most thinkers approved royal patronage of learning as well as a kind of practical royal wisdom that expanded greatly from the twelfth through the fourteenth centuries. But no thinker (outside the occasional esoteric tradition) recommended intense royal study, because this would remove the king from the active governance of the kingdom.*

Cette étude part des intérêts et des actions magiques du Prospéro de Shakespeare dans La Tempête *pour examiner les idées du Moyen-Age et de la Renaissance sur le caractère approprié ou non de l'instruction des rois. Commençant avec le drame même, elle traite quelques cas tirés du monde contemporain de Shakespeare, comme Jacques VI et I et Rodolphe II, ainsi que la littérature du XVIe siècle sur le but civique de l'instruction pour les courtisans et les dirigeants. Elle donne ensuite un aperçu du problème de l'instruction des rois et des termes utilisés pour la décrire depuis Charlemagne et Alfred d'Angleterre jusqu'au XVIIe siècle. Elle soutient que la plupart des penseurs étaient favorables au patronage royal du savoir et à une sorte de sagesse pratique royale, qui a connu un fort développement entre le XIIe et le XIVe siècles. Mais aucun penseur n'a recommandé l'étude intensive pour les rois, car ceci les aurait éloignés de leur tâche active en tant que gouvernants du royaume.*

The hour's now come;
This very minute bids thee ope thine ear.
Obey, and be attentive.

After several earlier false starts that have left Miranda with only a *bootless inquisition*, Prospero finally tells her his (and her own) tale, or history, in the second scene of Act One of *The Tempest*. He draws forth from *the dark backward and abyss of time* (in fact, twelve years) the story of the widowed, excessively studious Duke of Milan, his treacherous brother Antonio, his enemy Alonso the King of Naples, the kindly and protective counsellor Gonzalo, the two-year old daughter, and the abandonment of father and daughter far out to sea in *a rotten carcass of a butt*, lacking tackle, rigging, sail, and mast, but containing, as we all know, a number of interesting items of baggage - including a staff, a cloak and some books[1].

It is a long story. Prospero later observes to Alonso (V.i.163-165):

> *... 'tis a chronicle of day by day,*
> *Not a relation for a breakfast, nor*
> *Befitting this first meeting.*

To Miranda, Prospero tells his history with considerable care and also with considerable indignation and moral commentary, frequently reminding Miranda - and the audience - to pay attention. *Be attentive* the episode begins, and it continues: *Dost thou attend me? - Thou attendest not! - I pray thee mark me. - Dost thou hear? - Your tale, sir, would cure deafness*[2].

The explicit themes of Prospero's tale - injustice, treachery, treason, magic, and general foul play directed at the once and future duke and his little daughter - amply engaged early critics and directors of the play. To more recent critics and theatrical directors many of these themes have been subordinated to others: racism, imperialism, colonialism, Eurocentrism, and post-modern cultural and political incorrectness. These latter are not the subject of this essay; the former are. I propose to offer a kind of genealogy of Prospero because in this, as in some other instances, Shakespeare touches on and draws together themes that were originally not related and were often incompatible, but

---

[1] *The Tempest*, ed. by Stephen ORGEL, The Oxford Shakespeare, Oxford 1987, I.2.33-184. On the contents of the boat, see below, n.7. - I am grateful to Barbara and Daniel Traister and Phyllis Rackin for their helpful and encouraging comments on earlier drafts of this essay. This essay was originally presented as a plenary lecture at the joint meeting of the Haskins Society and MAJESTAS at Houston in November, 1995. I am grateful to Sally Vaughan and Richard Jackson of the University of Houston for the opportunity to deliver it to an ideal audience, and to colleagues at the conference, particularly Janet L. Nelson, for their comments and advice. The essay is dedicated to the memory of Robert L. Benson, long an academic Prospero of sorts himself.

[2] This anxiety for Miranda's attention seems to be related to Prospero's acute sense of the passing of time and the need to accomplish his work in a very short space of it. On this theme, see Barbara TRAISTER, Heavenly Necromancers: The Magician in English Renaissance Drama, Columbia, Missouri 1984, 136-146. As Phyllis Rackin has kindly reminded me, these interjections may very well also be Shakespeare's acknowledgment to the audience of the length and theatrically static character of the scene. On the relations between masques and royalty, see Stephen ORGEL, Illusions of Power: Political Theater in the English Renaissance, Berkeley/Los Angeles 1975, 37-87.

which also take on a vividness and immediacy in the context of Shakespeare's imagination, text and stagecraft[3]. In the case of Prospero the cause of his deposition will also turn out to be the means of his and Miranda's restoration[4]. Prospero's fault and means of restoration may be, from one perspective, a cobbling together of quite distinct themes. From another, however, it is a marvelously competent aesthetic resolution of essentially disparate themes that need to be traced out. That is the subject of this paper.

Let us recall the original fault:

> *My brother, and thy uncle, called Antonio -*
> *I pray thee mark me, that a brother should*
> *Be so perfidious - he whom next thyself*
> *Of all the world I loved, and to him put*
> *The manage of my state, as at that time*
> *Through all the signories it was the first,*
> *And Prospero the prime duke, being so reputed*
> *In dignity, and for the liberal arts*
> *Without a parallel; those being all my study,*
> *The government I cast upon my brother,*
> *And to my state grew stranger, being transported*
> *And rapt in secret studies.*
> (I.2.66-77)

Antonio so managed Prospero's state that *He did believe / He was indeed the duke,* and Prospero,

> *... thus neglecting worldly ends, all dedicated*
> *To closeness and the bettering of my mind*
> *With that which, but by being so retired,*
> *O'er-prized all popular rate, in my false brother*

---

[3] E.g., in the multifaceted figure of Joan of Arc in *Henry VI,* a figure which draws upon several quite distinct Joan-traditions in constructing a single character. I would not go so far as to say that in *The Tempest* Shakespeare succeeds in this as well as Ernst Kantorowicz claims that he does in *Richard II.* See Ernst KANTOROWICZ, The King's Two Bodies, Princeton 1957, 24-41.

[4] There is a useful, recent, and brief inventory of critical approaches to Prospero in David DANIELL, The Tempest, Atlantic Highlands, N.J. 1989, 79-81, but see also William Shakespeare's 'The Tempest', Modern Critical Interpretations, ed. by Harold BLOOM, New York/Philadelphia 1988.

> *Awaked an evil nature ...*
> (I.2.89-93)

And so the treachery was accomplished, its purpose foiled only by Gonzalo's provisioning the boat with *Rich garments, linens, stuffs, and necessaries / Which since have steaded much* ... (I.2.163-165). Generous and foresighted indeed, for among the garments and necessaries (at least in my view) were a staff and the cloak of Prospero's "Art", and,

> *Knowing I loved my books, he furnished me*
> *From mine own library with volumes that*
> *I prize above my dukedom.*
> (I.2.166-168)

Although he will not prize those volumes above his dukedom for long, Prospero has already begun when the play opens to put staff, cloak and some of those volumes to both restorative and punitive use.

Which introduces a dilemma: if study, and then the study of magic (both improper for a ruler, the former if done in excess and the latter morally and religiously objectionable in any case), have cost Prospero real power in Milan, what is it that justifies (and makes efficacious) his using magic to regain that power, to make himself once more *Milan* as he does in V.i.86? Perhaps the answer is that, stripped of political power and society and left only with magic, Prospero has reflected upon the incompatibility of the two and therefore determines to re-secure political power by means of a magic that is indeed his only tool, but which he now sees as his only means of becoming a better duke than he had been. The civic obligation drives the magic (a reversal of earlier events, when the magic had driven out the civic [and domestic] obligations). Thus, the magic of the plot of *The Tempest* may be regarded as a magic used only in the degree necessary to achieve morally desirable political ends (*absunt* all other possibilities) and to achieve *only* those ends before being discarded. The limited degree and purpose of the play's magic may thus be considered as justifying its last use.

But prizing volumes above his dukedom is hardly the sign of a proper duke, and neither is so egregiously misunderstanding Antonio (who surely cannot have changed character significantly from Prospero's early reign to the stony, unrepenting despot of the play) and giving him such power of *potestas* and *administratio* as historically had tempted far better-disposed *curatores* than Antonio to take the drastic next step[5]. And whatever the arts to which Prospero devoted his ducal and intellectual energies, they were not merely the "liberal" ones he claims - we have already begun to see them in operation, and we know that they are magic and have been long before he first set foot on the island. Rich garments, stuffs, linens, necessaries, and books seem to indicate that Prospero had been studying magic in Milan before his deposition, but perhaps was not very far advanced. The cloak surely could not have come from the island, and the staff appears rather more finished and technical than the island was likely to provide. It is not a piece of driftwood of which Prospero has become inordinately fond. The books, too, must have come from Milan. It is likely that the twelve years of isolation developed Prospero's magic well ahead of the stage it had reached in Milan, when it could not (or at least did not) save Prospero and Miranda from the power of Antonio. *Rough magic* though he later calls his arts (V.i.50), they are nevertheless distinct, of course, from the other magic of *The Tempest*, that of Sycorax, because they employ a considerable degree of moral self-discipline, enlightenment, serious book-learning, and some elaborate *materia magica* of a technical kind, and they do not invoke demons, produce monsters, or shut up spirits of the air in trees[6]. As

---

[5] On the legal/constitutional terminology, see Edward PETERS, The Shadow King: 'Rex inutilis' in Medieval Law and Literature, 751-1327, New Haven/London 1970. Later scholarship is conveniently discussed in Helmut G. WALTHER, Depositions of Rulers in the Later Middle Ages: On Theory of the 'Useless Ruler' and its Practical Utilization. In: As Relacões de Poder no Pensamento Politico da Baixa Idade Media: Homenagem a João Morais Barbosa (Revista da Faculdade de Ciências Sociais e Humanas), 7, Lisbon 1994, 157-168. - On the whole, the fifteenth and sixteenth centuries were much concerned about regencies and curatorships, and with good reason. Shakespeare takes up the theme in *Measure for Measure*, with the same disastrous results that Prospero had when he appointed Antonio. Shakespeare's *Richard II*, along with *Henry VI* is the other play dealing with a *rex inutilis*. I am grateful to Phyllis Rackin for reminding me of both these last instances.

[6] On the differences and similarities between the magics of Prospero (who eloquently sums up his achievements in this area in the speech in V.i. 33-50) and Sycorax, there is useful discussion and set of references in St. ORGEL (note 1) 21-23, esp. 22, n.1. To any contemporary of Shakespeare's the differences would be far more obvious than they can be to modern

Caliban says (I.2.372-374), Prospero's

> *Art is of such power*
> *It would control my dam's god, Setebos,*
> *And make a vassal of him.*

But they are part of the broad and worrisome spectrum of early modern magic nonetheless. Four-faulted Prospero: neglecting his domestic and political duties toward his only child; neglecting his responsibilities of state; misinterpreting the character of Antonio, and devoted to magic. Miranda - and Milan - needed a better father and duke than that[7]. Medieval and early modern political theorists would not have required an Antonio or an Alonso waiting in the wings to justify getting Milan a better ruler.

---

scholars who do not specialize in sixteenth-century ideas of magic. This point has been made by Frances Yates, "Prospero: The Shakespearean Magus," Ch. 15 of Frances YATES, The Occult Philosophy in the Elizabethan Age, London/Boston 1979, 159-163. On the emergence of the secluded study in the sixteenth century, see J. R. HALE, The Civilization of Europe in the Renaissance, New York/London 1993, 397-398, and for the ideal secluded scholar (although not magician), see E. F. RICE, Jr., Saint Jerome in the Renaissance, Baltimore/London 1985. - The most sensitive study of both the magic and the magicians in the play, as well as of the Elizabethan and Jacobean stage-magician generally, is that of B. TRAISTER (note 2) esp. 125-149, the central argument for Prospero is reprinted in H. BLOOM (note 4) 113-130 . There is a review of the two kinds of magic in Michael SRIGLEY, Images of Regeneration: A Study of Shakespeare's 'The Tempest' and Its Cultural Background, Uppsala 1985, 141-166. There is a good brief treatment of some of the themes in this essay in D. G. JAMES, The Dream of Prospero, Oxford 1967, 45-71. But James' focus on the magical tradition out of which the figure emerged is here set beside the tradition of attitudes toward royal learning that James does not consider. James (pp. 63-64) and I disagree on the source of Prospero's staff and cloak and on the nature of the books that Prospero had in his boat. More satisfying is the argument of John S. MEBANE, Renaissance Magic and the Return of the Golden Age, Lincoln 1989, 174-199, whose focus is on the restorative and fruitful purposes and results of Prospero's magic, as well as upon Prospero's recognition of the limits of self-assertion, the necessity of self-mastery, the power wrought by self-knowledge in these contexts, and the compassion - indeed, compassionate pedagogy - that results. - The texts of the conventional "sources" of and analogues to the play are printed in Geoffrey BULLOUGH, Narrative and Dramatic Sources of Shakespeare. Vol. 8, London/New York 1975, 237-339. - There are several interesting observations on analogies between Prospero's noble magic and Vergilian themes in the *Aeneid* in Donna B. HAMILTON, Virgil and 'The Tempest', Columbus, Ohio 1990, esp. 106-109.

[7] B. TRAISTER (note 2, pp. 137-138) makes several of these points in terms of Prospero's growing (before the start of the play) awareness of limitations, including his understanding of "upsetting the proper balance between contemplation and action", of placing excessive trust in Antonio, and of the proper and improper uses of power. But Prospero's earlier errors in this direction were failings of study, character estimation, and political power. He did not use his magic in Milan to prevent his expulsion.

Rulers who were accused of attending too much to the acquisition of knowledge not essential to proper rulership were not exactly in short supply or obscurity in the sixteenth and early seventeenth centuries. Although we must distinguish between excessive study on the one hand, and the actual pursuit of magic on the other, at times in the later sixteenth and seventeenth centuries the two were hard to separate. James VI and I was a king who feared and despised magic (and, with his bride, once escaped a magically-conjured storm at sea himself), but certainly gave his attention to other intellectual matters in such a way as to elicit both admiration and criticism[8]. The spectacular and well known case of Rudolf II was another, known in England through the reports of Sidney and Wotton and the employment of Dr. John Dee at Rudolf's court[9]. Rudolf, after all, was accused of neglecting his governmental duties, studying magic and alchemy, and was replaced by his brother, Matthias. Sharp judgments on similar kings in the past also appeared in the sixteenth century. Juan de Mariana's *Historia de rebus Hispaniae*, published in Madrid in 1592, criticized Alfonso X of Castile to the effect that: *While he contemplated the heavens and*

---

[8] Eg., in *Basilikon Doron*, ed. by Charles Howard MCILWAIN, 1918, and *Daemonologie* of 1597, for which see Stuart CLARK, King James's *Daemonologie*. In: The Damned Art, ed. by Sidney Anglo, London 1977, 156-181, which effectively criticizes much earlier scholarship, e.g., David Harris WILLSON, King James VI and I, London 1956, rpt. 1967, 308-312. For James, the besetting sin of anyone interested in magic was *curiositas*, although, as D. G. JAMES (note 6) 61 points out, for King James the *curiositas* of magicians represented a "genuine labor after divine things". St. ORGEL (note 1) 22 reproduces the image of what he calls "a royal magician-scientist" from Henry Peacham's manuscript emblem book "based on the treatise [*Basilikon Doron*] of James I", which Peacham entitled 'Inopportuna Studia'. The possibility of a pictorial influence on the figure of Prospero (and perhaps on Ariel and Caliban as well) from the emblem tradition, including that of alchemical imagery, has not yet been explored. On the magically-conjured storm at sea, see News from Scotland, London 1591, esp. 16-17, briefly discussed in P. M. RATTANSI, Alchemy and Natural Magic in Raleigh's *History of the World*. In: Ambix 13 (1965) 122-138, at 124. On the *Daemonologie* and *The Tempest*, see Jacqueline E. M. LATHAM, 'The Tempest' and King James's 'Daemonologie'. In: Shakespeare Survey 28 (1975) 117-123. On Bacon's conversion of James as Hermes Trismegistus to James as the king of man and natural knowledge, see D. G. JAMES (note 6) 70-71. See also Louis MARIN, Les pouvoirs de l'image: Gloses, Paris 1993, 159-168.

[9] In general, see R. J. W. EVANS, Rudolf II and His World: A Study in Intellectual History, Oxford 1973, corrected paperback edition, Oxford 1984. There is little on Rudolf's interest in learning and the occult in H. C. Erik MIDELFORT, Mad Princes of Renaissance Germany, Charlottesville 1994, 125-143. There is considerably more in M. SRIGLEY (note 6) 122-140. Most recently on Rudolf, see the studies of Thomas DACOSTA KAUFMANN, The Mastery of Nature: Aspects of Art Science, and Humanism in the Renaissance, Princeton 1993.

observed the stars ... [he] lost his earthly realm[10].

Nor, since we learned long ago that discussions of royalty in medieval and renaissance Europe were often based upon or were considered analogous to discussions of traits found in nobles, prelates, popes, and other figures possessing specific kinds of authority and public responsibility, should we be surprised that Prospero's case echoes those of earlier figures who were not kings or dukes, perhaps most strikingly that of Gerbert of Aurillac, the history of whose legend as a *curiosus* and magician has been brilliantly traced by Massimo Oldoni[11]. But the point that popes, prelates, kings, dukes, and others were criticized for various kinds of excessive study indicates that the case of Prospero really poses two problems, originally quite unrelated. One is the problem of the figure with public responsibilities of any kind undertaking studies of a kind that require *otium* and disengagement from public affairs that are incompatible with public responsibilites, a topos at least as old as Cicero[12]. An ideal classical combination of study, learning, and effective rulership may be found in Ovid's portrait of Numa in Book XV of the *Metamorphoses*, and in the accolades later lavished on Hadrian[13]. Roman emperors might even work

---

[10] Juan de MARIANA, *Historia de rebus Hispaniae,* Madrid 1592, 649. Cited in Joseph F. O'CALLAGHAN, The Learned King: The Reign of Alfonso X of Castile, Philadelphia 1993, 272. O'Callaghan considers Alfonso's learning generally, 270-282.

[11] Massimo OLDONI, Fantasmi e fantasia nel Medioevo. Gerberto e il suo doppio, Naples 1987. The *locus classicus* for the topic is Johann Josef Ignaz von DÖLLINGER, Papst-Fabeln des Mittelalters. Ein Beitrag zur Kirchengeschichte, 2nd ed., Munich 1863, 155-159, eng. trans. by Alfred PLUMMER, Fables Respecting the Popes of the Middle Ages: A Contribution to Ecclesiastical History, by John J. Ign. von DÖLLINGER, London 1871, 265-270. On later accusations of papal magic, see William R. JONES, The Political Uses of Sorcery in Medieval Europe. In: The Historian 34 (1972) 670-687, and K. EUBEL, Vom Zaubereiwesen anfangs des 14. Jahrhunderts. In: Historisches Jahrbuch 18 (1897) 608-631, as well as Edward PETERS, The Magician, the Witch, and the Law, Philadelphia 1976. The vulnerability of popes to accusations of magic seems to parallel the vulnerability of secular rulers to charges of heresy or of failing to eradicate heresy. Both increased after the early thirteenth century. For a later case, see Margaret HARVEY, Papal Witchcraft: The Charges against Benedict XIII. In: Sanctity and Secularity: The Church and the World, ed. by Derek BAKER (Studies in Church History 10), Oxford 1973, 109-116. Harvey's title is misleading. The phenomena she describes constitute papal magic, not "witchcraft".

[12] See Eugene F. RICE, Jr., The Renaissance Idea of Wisdom, Cambridge, Mass. 1958, esp. 30-57.

[13] See L. K. BORN, The Perfect Prince According to the Latin Panegyrists. In: American Journal of Philology 55 (1934) 20-35; E. GALLETIER, Panégriques latines. 3 vols., Paris 1949-

miracles, but they were not to study excessively, and they might use magicians, but not practice magic themselves[14]. A sixteenth-century example occurs in Thomas Starkey's *A Dialogue between Reginald Pole and Thomas Lupset* when Lupset denies Pole's suggestion, *that the contemplative life may be a legitimate end for a nobleman's education*. Elsewhere in the sixteenth century, "Osorius in his book of *Civil Nobility* speaks slightingly of those who take their learning with them into seclusion and do not employ the benefits of their arts and sciences to the avail and commodity of the commonwealth"[15]. By the later sixteenth century - in fact well before it - the learning of the nobility and of its rulers was supposed to serve the commonwealth. When it did not, the commonwealth was likely to fall into the hands of what Jack Hexter has called, "the banalities of Renaissance despots and a monstrous nobility, half court insect and half bucolic vegetable"[16]. In fact, Hexter's phrase fits the Milanese and the Neapolitan contingents in *The Tempest* (with the exceptions of Ferdinand and Gonzalo and perhaps the reformed Alonso) very nicely.

But Cicero, Pole and Osorius were speaking of something different from the

---

1955. On conflicting views of Julian's learning, see The Emperor Julian: Panegyric and Polemic, ed. by Samuel N. C. LIEU, Liverpool 1989.

[14] On miracle-working emperors, see Howard Clark KEE, Miracle in the Early Christian World, New Haven/London 1983, 180-183. The miracles associated with later medieval kings were specifically those of a kind of thaumaturgy. On potentially magical aspects of royal blood in early medieval Europe, see V. I. J. FLINT, The Rise of Magic in Early Medieval Europe, Princeton 1991, 350-354, 381-386.

[15] Both cited in J. H. HEXTER, The Education of the Aristocracy in the Renaissance. In: IDEM, Reappraisals in History, Chicago 1961, 1979, 67, citing Thomas STARKEY, A Dialogue between Reginald Pole and Thomas Lupset, ed. by K. M. BURTON, London 1948, 21-26. The reference to Osorius is from Ruth KELSO, The Doctrine of the English Gentleman in the Sixteenth Century, Urbana, IL 1929, rpt. Gloucester, Mass. 1964, 125. Kelso summarizes sixteenth-century English attitudes toward the gentleman's learning on pp. 49-57, and the debates on his education on pp. 111-129. These debates certainly lasted into the seventeenth century, since, as Kelso points out (p.113), Bacon himself took great pains to counter criticisms of the gentleman's learning in *The Advancement of Learning*. For Osorius, see KELSO, No. 664a: OSORIUS, Hieronymous (OSORIO DA FONSECA, Jeronimo), *Hieronymi Osorii ... de nobilitate civili, libri duo*, Lisbon 1542, and No. 97, BLANDY, William, The five bookes of the famous, learned, and eloquent man, Hieronimus Osorius, contayninge a discourse of civill, and Christian nobilitie, London 1576.

[16] J. H. HEXTER (note 15) 69. On the ideal of *prudentia* rather than *scientia* as the norm of learning for those who govern, see E. F. RICE (note 12) 72-85, 163-170. Rice also catalogues alternative views of the ideal wisdom of rulers; cf. 117-123.

second problem posed by the case of Prospero. They were raising the question of the place of study and learning and their conventional location in the contemplative life, and they were certainly not talking about seclusion for the purpose of studying magic. In Prospero's case two initially different problems of royal learning came to coincide. I must consider these in sequence. Neither was entirely new in the sixteenth century.

Among the books that Prospero probably did *not* have in his library (or if he had them, he had certainly not read them, or if he had and read, then he had certainly forgotten) were Nicole Oresme's *Tractatus contra iudiciarios astronomos* and *Livre de divinacions*, as well as the little tract presented to John the Fearless of Burgundy in 1411 advising princes against dabbling in fortune-telling, the *Somnium Pharaonis* of John of Limoges, all of which explicitly warned rulers against indulging, not only in astrology and magic, but excessive study in general, and Dante's *Paradiso*, whose *canto* XIII spoke eloquently about those things which it was fitting for a king to know (and those whose study did not befit a king)[17]. Long before Ralegh, Bacon, and James VI and I himself had described the ideal content and limits of royal wisdom, a number of medieval thinkers from Bede to Oresme had addressed the same subject.

A number of instances of excessive royal interest in learning survived from antiquity - the Stoic criticism of Alexander the Great, anecdotes concerning Tiberius and Nero, Tertullian's criticism of Hadrian as *omnium curiositatum explorator*, Tertullian's and other Christian writers' category of *sacrilega curiositas*, and the figures of the Magi, the first magician-kings before Prospero whose arts resulted in good[18]. Especially in the case of Alexander, later medieval writers often made a particular point of his intellectual arrogance

[17] On Oresme, see the reference to the work of Susan M. BABBITT, Oresme's "Livre de Politiques" and the France of Charles V (Transactions of the American Philosophical Society 75), Philadelphia 1985. On the tract for John the Fearless, see Richard VAUGHAN, John the Fearless, New York 1966, 235. On John of Limoges and Dante, see below.

[18] On the Magi, see Hugo KEHRER, Die heiligen drei Könige in in der Legende und in der deutschen bildenden Kunst bis Albrecht Dürer. 2 vols. Leipzig 1908, Alexander MURRAY, Reason and Society in the Middle Ages, Oxford 1978, 118, in connection with Otto III, and V. I. J. FLINT (note 14) 364-375.

and audacity, a point to which I will return.

But we must begin with kings whose problem was quite the opposite of Prospero's or Reginald Pole's - rulers like Einhard's Charlemagne and Asser's Alfred who desperately sought for a minimum of competence in *grammatica* and *rhetorica* with what Asser calls *royal greed* (c. 78), and ultimately achieved a good deal of it, but no more, we are reminded, than was suitable for kingship[19]. Even Alfred's translations emphasized the social value of the work. The absence of learned men deprived the kingdom of one of its two components, warfare and wisdom: *Remember what punishments befell us in this world when we ourselves did not cherish learning nor transmit it to other men*[20]. They were patrons of scholars, not necessarily scholars themselves. Not by accident does Asser liken Alfred to Solomon (c. 76)[21]. But Alfred is a distinctly Carolingian

[19] Of the Germanic rulers before Charlemagne, only Theoderic appears to have proposed to put aside his public duties in order to study with Cassiodorus. See the discussion in Pierre RICHÉ, Education and Culture in the Barbarian West from the Sixth through the Eighth Century, trans. by John J. CONTRENI, Columbia, South Carolina 1976, 53-78, at 57-8, citing Cassiodorus, *Variae*, IX.24. Other rulers might be patrons, and occasionally, as in the case of Sisebut in Visigothic Iberia, actively learned in their own right, and they were not generally criticized for it. See RICHÉ, 258-262, and Peter GODMAN, Poets and Emperors: Frankish Politics and Carolingian Poetry, Oxford 1987, 16-21. Bede's exegesis of the phrase *via regia* in Num 21:22 and Isaiah 30:21, which he glossed with the Pauline precept on not knowing more than was fitting to know (Rom 12:3), does not seem to have been intended to apply to kings but to reflect Bede's profound distrust of the *artes liberales*, especially dialectic. BEDE, *Super parabolas Salomonis allegorica expositio*, I.4, PL 91:956. On the capacities and limits of the royal office, see J. M. WALLACE-HADRILL, The *Via Regia* of the Carolingian Age. In: Trends in Medieval Political Thought, ed. by Beryl SMALLEY, New York 1965, 22-41, and more recently, Janet L. NELSON, Kingship and Empire. In: The Cambridge History of Medieval Political Thought c. 350 - c. 1450, ed. by J. H. BURNS, Cambridge 1988, 211-251. - Carolingian panegyric could indeed be quite lavish in praise of Charlemagne's and other emperors' learning. See, e.g., the *Karolus Magnus et Leo Papa*, 53-87, in Peter GODMAN, Poetry of the Carolingian Renaissance, Norman, Okla. 1985, 200-202, and Godman's remarks on the prefatory verses to the Godescalc lectionary in Poets and Emperors, 46-47, and on *Karolus Magnus et Leo Papa*, 82-85.

[20] From the Prose Preface to Alfred's translation of Gregory the Great's *Pastoral Care*, in Alfred the Great, Asser's "Life of King Alfred" and other contemporary sources, trans. by Simon KEYNES and Michael LAPPIDGE, London/New York, 1983, 125. The best study of Alfred's wisdom is now that of Janet L. NELSON, The Political Ideas of Alfred of Wessex. In: Kings and Kingship, ed. by Anne DUGGAN, London 1993, 125-158.

[21] The scriptural Solomon was the archtype of idealized Christian kingship under the Carolingians, although he did not early necessarily represent royal wisdom. See Hans Hubert ANTON, Fürstenspiegel und Herrscherethos in der Karolingerzeit (Bonner Historische

Solomon. The figure itself suggested a number of different interpretations over the course of many centuries, just as the term *sapientia* also meant different things at different times. Einhard also indicates another important feature of the Carolingian idea of royal wisdom (c. 25) when he describes Charlemagne's own modest learning in conjunction with his ability to attract learned advisers. These, far more learned than the king, were the king's repository of wisdom and removed the need for the king personally to acquire and possess more learning than he needed to[22].

Although Stephen Jaeger has traced the emergence of a new courtly ideal of episcopal, aristocratic, and royal learning from the mid-tenth century, the Carolingian model of royal wisdom survived in some places into the eleventh and early twelfth centuries and can still be seen in Adalbero's *Carmen ad Robertum Regem* and narrative accounts of royal conduct in which kings, informed of problems but personally and properly lacking the *scientia* to understand and solve them, bring them to their wise and learned (and clerical) advisers, receive answers, and then act upon the advice they have received[23].

Forschungen 32), Bonn 1968, 76, 93, 233 n. 475. In this respect Solomon was the morally ideal pious ruler, like Josias and David. See ANTON, 420-432. With Charlemagne, the ruler assumes the wisdom characteristics of Solomon (ANTON, 98-99, 255-258). Anton points out that *Sapientia*/Wisdom "fades into the background" during the reign of Louis the Pious, but returns in that of Charles the Bald (ANTON, 255-257). See also Rosamond MCKITTERICK, The Palace School of Charles the Bald. In: Charles the Bald: Court and Kingdom, ed. by Margaret T. GIBSON and Janet NELSON, 2nd ed. Aldershot 1990, 326-347, and in general, the essays in the volume Carolingian Culture: Emulation and Innovation, ed. by Rosamund MCKITTERICK, Cambridge 1994, and Nikolaus STAUBACH, Rex Christianus. Hofkultur und Herrschaftspropaganda im Reich Karls des Kahlen. 2 vols., Cologne 1981, and below, n.27. See also P. GODMAN (note 19) 175-176, and ANTON, 346-349. Other aspects of this theme in ruler panegyric were also continued. See GODMAN (note 19) 136, for Walafrid Strabo's application to Louis the Pious of Alcuin's evocation of the Boethian philosopher-king, originally written to Charlemagne, a text that somewhat qualifies Anton's conclusion cited above.

[22] The shift from Carolingian ideals of royal learning to a courtly model is traced by C. Stephen JAEGER, The Envy of Angels: Cathedral Schools and Social Ideals in Medieval Europe, 950-1200, Philadelphia 1994.

[23] Johannes FRIED emphasizes this aspect of the relationship between rulers and advisers in: Endzeiterwartung um die Jahrtausendwende. In: Deutsches Archiv 45 (1989) 381-473. On the tendency among twelfth-century exegetes to exclude the prince from their own special province of learning, see Philippe BUC, *Principes gentium dominantur eorum*: Princely Power between Legitimacy and Illegitimacy in Twelfth-Century Exegesis. In: Cultures of Power:

A wise king is a king with wise advisers to whom he listens in matters beyond his individual and proper sphere of understanding.

Wilhelm Berges, who does not identify what I have termed the Carolingian model, suggested that the twelfth century made rather different demands upon kings. Berges identified both a courtly ideal of royal rulership and the ideal of the *rex litteratus*[24]. But the companion notion of the *rex ilitteratus est quasi asinus coronatus* did not necessarily mandate extensive royal learning. The ideal is laid down in John of Salisbury's *Policraticus* (IV.6), which recommends not only literacy, but the attending to the advice of wise counsellors (V.6) and specific learning in law and military science (VI.2), as well as in Gerald of Wales' *De principis instructione*, which also recommends literacy, general learning, and the knowledge of history[25]. Berges' courtly model required the king to be familiar with the arts of language and history, particularly that of

Lordship, Status, and Process in Twelfth-Century Europe, ed. by Thomas M. BISSON, Philadelphia 1995, 310-328, at 318-319.

[24] Wilhelm BERGES, Die Fürstenspiegel des hohen und späten Mittelalters (Schriften der Monumenta Germaniae Historica 2), Leipzig 1938, 66-70. On the maxim, *rex illiteratus*, see BERGES, 50-51. On the broader aspects of the twelfth-century view of kingship and learning, see also C. St. JAEGER (note 22) and IDEM, The Origins of Courtliness: Civilizing Trends and the Formation of Courtly Ideals, 939-1210, Philadelphia 1985, as well as Alexander MURRAY, Reason and Society in the Middle Ages, Oxford 1978, 110-137. - Berges begins with John of Salisbury; however, a number of John's themes, including the learning of rulers, appear earlier, notably in Bernard Silvestris, *Cosmographia*, for which see Winthrop WETHERBEE, The 'Cosmographia' of Bernardus Silvestris. A Translation with Introduction and Notes, New York 1973, 1990, 58. On the role of Alain de Lille's *Anticlaudianus* in the tradition of imperial intellectual perfection (including that of Charlemagne - see above, n.19), see Marie TANNER, The Last Descendant of Aeneas: The Habsburgs and the Mythic Image of the Emperor, New Haven/London 1993, 45-51, and in general, Michael WILKS, Alan of Lille and the New Man. In: Studies in Church History 14 (1977), 137-157, esp. 143, n.34 on philosopher-kings, including Frederick Barbarossa and Henry VI. Alain's scepticism about contemporary theories of learning is well known. See G. R. EVANS, Alan of Lille: The Frontiers of Theology in the Later Twelfth Century, Cambridge 1983.

[25] See the discussion in L. K. BORN, The Perfect Prince: A Study in Thirteenth- and Fourteenth-Century Ideals. In: Speculum 3 (1928) 470-504, at 472-473 (John of Salisbury; for whom see W. BERGES [note 24] 131-143) and 476 (Gerald; for whom see W. BERGES [note 24] 143-150). - There is a stimulating discussion of these themes in Sverre BAGGE, The Political Thought of the King's Mirror, Odense 1987, esp. 102-106. - But the royal knowledge of history too had a Carolingian origin; see Janet L. NELSON, History-Writing at the Courts of Louis the Pious and Charles the Bald. In: Historiographie im frühen Mittelalter, ed. by Anton SCHARER and Georg SCHEIBELREITER, Vienna/Munich 1994, 435-442.

their own kingdoms, for the purposes of both political intelligence and moral judgment.

But the existence and demands of the court also posed dangers, to kings as well as courtiers and clerics. Anti-curial satire such as that of Walter Map, and anti-curial moralizing such as that of the too much neglected first half of John of Salisbury's *Policraticus* both pointed to the unique vices that, as the sources often noted, *crept in* with the new courtly ideal[26]. Among these was *vana curiositas,* which appears as early as 1115-1120 in the *Vita posterior* of Ulrich of Zell in a specifically courtly context[27]. The most interesting instance of the type of the *rex curiosus,* however, occurs in the figure of Pharaoh in the *Morale Somnium Pharaonis* of John of Limoges, a Cistercian abbot of Zirc in Hungary from 1208 to 1218, dedicated to Theobald IV of Champagne, ostensibly an exchange of letters among Pharaoh, Joseph, and others (Gen 41), in which Pharaoh is identified by John as a *rex curiosus* and Egypt as a *typus cuiuslibet regni studiosi*[28]. Joseph's undertaking is to make the ruler a *rex rationabilis* who will be advised by courtiers possessing *intellectus,* and when Pharaoh's courtiers point out to Joseph that they have urged the king to study and withdraw from the cares of the court, Joseph denounces the *rex curiosus* who speculates and studies but does not attend to his kingly duties and cultivate the *virtutes civiles*[29]. There is indeed proper royal knowledge, but it is not the same kind of knowledge that can and should readily be acquired by others in royal service.

---

26 On criticism of both courts and the courtly idea, see C. St. JAEGER (note 24) esp. 54-66, 87-100, 152-194.

27 Discussed in C. St. JAEGER (note 24) 153-154.

28 The text is discussed in W. BERGES (note 24) 301-302, but most extensively by C. St. JAEGER (note 24) 87-95. It has been edited by Constantin HORVATH, Johannes Lemovicensis, Abbatis de Zirc 1208-1218, Opera Omnia, 3 vols., Vesprem 1932.

29 C. St. JAEGER (note 24) 92 suggests that here is the plot of *The Tempest,* although it is only part of the plot; the king is not in seclusion in order to study magic, but because he refuses to "drape royal purple over a rustic mind." He resembles rather more Cassiodorus's Theoderic, or, in a Shapespearean context, the case of Ferdinand, King of Navarre, in *Love's Labour's Lost* (I.i. 12-17), who proposes, with three companions, to make his court a *little academie, / Still and contemplative in living art.* Cited from Love's Labour's Lost, ed. by G. R. HIBBARD, Oxford 1990, 96. I am grateful to Barbara Traister for this reference.

Joseph's distinctions are both Ciceronian and Ambrosian, and they had other scriptural antecedents, particularly I Kings 3:5-12. There, God asks Solomon to ask of Him what he will. Solomon responds that he is ignorant of ruling and requests the skills that a ruler needs. God answers that because Solomon has not asked for a long life, riches, or the lives of his enemies, but rather for *sapientia ad discernendum iudicium*, God will give him a *cor sapiens et intelligens* to such a degree that this had been possessed by no one before Solomon and would be possessed by no one after him. In *Paradiso* XIII Thomas Aquinas explains this last point to the pilgrim Dante, but Thomas changes several details. Instead of not having asked for long life, riches, or the lives of his enemies, Solomon is now praised for not having asked,

> *to know the number of the mover spirits here above,*
> *nor if necesse with a contingent ever made a necesse;*
> *nor si est dare primum motum esse; nor if in a*
> *semicircle a triangle can be so constructed that it*
> *shall have no right angle.*
> (*Paradiso* 13:97-102)

Solomon's unique *regal prudenza* pertains properly, Thomas says, only to kings. No second *king* has ever arisen with such wisdom. The gifts Solomon does not ask for are perfectly appropriate for others, but not for kings. In fact, the answers to the questions that Aquinas says that Solomon did not ask are perfectly appropriate in the fields of theology, dialectic, physics, and geometry - but appropriate only for those whose proper business it is to investigate them at these levels[30].

---

30 Solomon had long held a reputation as a great magician himself, as the *Testamentum Salomonis* and Josephus both indicate. See A. MURRAY (note 24) 118-119. - Dante's description of what might be called Solomon's *opportuna studia* echoes his criticism of the philosophical opinion about nobility of Frederick II, in his capacity as emperor, in the *Convivio*. See E. KANTOROWICZ (note 3) 455-456. Dante may also have had Alfonso X in mind. Alfonso had been approached with the prospect of an alliance by Florence in his capacity as imperial candidate, Brunetto Latini being the ambassador. Alfonso did not accept the invitation, opening the way for Charles of Anjou. Dante might have considered Alfonso's studies an element in his failure to come to the aid of Florence. See Julia BOLTON HOLLOWAY, The Road through Roncesvalles: Alfonsine Formation of Brunetto Latini and Dante - Diplomacy and Literature. In: Emperor of Culture: Alfonso X the Learned of Castile and his Thirteenth-Century Renaissance, ed. by Robert I. BURNS, S.J., Philadelphia 1990, 109-

Whether Dante knew of the work of John of Limoges is impossible to determine, but the sentiments of the *Morale* and *Paradiso* XIII are virtually identical, particularly since Dante has substituted the study of the subjects in the *artes liberales* for the originally unasked-for gifts of III Kings. The *rex* becomes *curiosus* not because he pursues inherently forbidden subjects or trivial studies, or even natural philosophy, but because in pursuing them he engages in an activity improper for a king.

Between John of Limoges and Dante, of course, there appeared Frederick II, whose enemies certainly accused him of improper study, but whose court appears to be, if anything, simply the ideal court raised to an extraordinary degree. But there is some evidence, notably in the questions that Michael Scot once said that Frederick asked him, that sounds suspiciously like the kind of inquiry that Dante had prohibited in the case of kings[31]. And it brings Frederick into the orbit of yet another arrogant, inquiring king, Alexander the Great.

The figure of Alexander attracted many themes, from that of Jewish and Christian apocalyptic prophecy to hermetic denunciations of his limitless desire. Walter of Chatillon's *Alexandreis* offers a picture of Alexander's denunciation by the Scythians (who in the poem have replaced the earlier Indian gymnosophists, themselves thinly disguised Stoic critics) in VIII, 374-390. And in Book X the dialogue between *Natura* and Leviathan concerning

---

123. - Dante had other objections, of course, to different inappropriate royal activities, including preaching, especially on the part of Robert of Naples. See Darleen PRYDS, Rex Praedicans, PhD. Diss. University of Wisconsin 1994. I am grateful to Gregory Moule for this reference.

[31] See the discussion in Ernst H. KANTOROWICZ, Frederick the Second 1194-1250, trans. by E. O. LORIMER, New York 1931, rpt. New York 1957, 350-359, and more recently in David ABULAFIA, Frederick II: A Medieval Emperor, New York/Oxford 1988, 257-264. But not all commentators were critical of Frederick in this respect. Jean Dunbabin has cited an anonymous early fourteenth-century commentator on Aristotle's *Politics* to the effect that a king who is not a scholar is not a legitimate ruler, and cites Frederick II as an ideal: *Sicut apparet de Frederico, qui fuit non est multum diu, qui fuit optimus astrologus. Et nisi isti principes habeant speculativam cum practica, dico quod non sunt nobiliores aliis habentibus felicitatem speculativam.* Jean DUNBABIN, Aristotle in the Schools. In: Trends in Medieval Political Thought, ed. by Beryl SMALLEY, New York 1965, 65-85, at 68 n.13.

Alexander's limitless investigations elaborates on the theme[32]. In subsequent literature, Alexander sought the Earthly Paradise, devised a glass diving-bell in which to explore the bottom of the sea, and finally travelled into the heavens. Such royal enthusiasm is, of course, a romance trope, but it fits well with the kinds of royal curiosity that were not entirely unheard of between the late twelfth and the late thirteenth centuries.

Frederick II and the legendary Alexander were regarded as dangerous figures because their interest in learning was characterized as deriving from a fundamental arrogance that knew no moral limits. This moral perspective on the desire for learning had a Stoic origin, taken over by the Fathers, and transmitted initially through monastic criticism of certain kinds of monastic learning, particularly in the area of scriptural exegesis. Such contemporaries of Frederick as Louis IX, however, had also begun to surround themselves with specialists in a new kind of knowledge more suitable for kings. Louis IX, Berges points out, established a virtual "political academy" at his court and was succeeded in this by Philip the Fair and, after the problematic succession crisis after 1314, resumed by Charles V, under whom "legal learning, historiography, philosophical political theory, and not least the new thought on national economy came to his assistance."[33] "The courtly ideal of the *rex literatus*", says Berges, "appears in this regard as much less ethical than that of the *rex*

---

[32] WALTER OF CHATILLON, The Alexandreis, trans. by R. TELFRYN PRITCHARD, Toronto 1986. The standard surveys are G. CARY, The Medieval Alexander, Cambridge 1956 and David J. A. ROSS, Alexander Historiatus: A Guide to Medieval Illustrated Alexander-Literature, 1967, rpt. Hildesheim 1988. See also Hans HOLLANDER, Alexander: *Hybris* und *Curiositas*. In: Kontinuität und Transformation der Antike im Mittelalter, ed. by Willi ERZGRÄBER, Sigmaringen 1989, 65-79, and A. MURRAY (note 24) 119-121, in the context of the *Secretum Secretorum*. Most recently on the latter, see William EAMON, Science and the Secrets of Nature, Princeton 1993. There is an important discussion in W. BERGES (note 24) 108-113.

[33] W. BERGES (note 24) 69. There is a large literature. For the beginning of the process, see, e.g., Ernst KANTOROWICZ, Kingship under the Impact of Scientific Jurisprudence, rpt. in: IDEM, Selected Studies, Locust Valley, NY 1965, 151-166, and L. K. BORN (note 25). Cf. A. MURRAY (note 24) 121-124. Berges' discussion of the new thirteenth-century *Fürstenspiegel*, beginning with that of Gilbert of Tournai (150-159) and continuing into the fourteenth century remains the most detailed treatment. On the role of aristotelianism, see W. BERGES (note 24) 113-123, 189.

sapiens"[34]. The new aristotelian-educated ruler is one, "der vom Schreibtisch aus regiert"[35]. In the case of Charles V, one might add: "auch von der Bibliothek aus"[36].

The new ethical and intellectual demands upon rulers were further articulated by the early humanists. Leonardo Bruni's debates with Niccolo Niccoli and his letters to Humphrey, Duke of Gloucester, and to the Kings of Aragon and Castile endorse the study of Aristotle as essential to good and responsible governance[37]. Thus, one can trace the transformation of the courtly ideal through that of the aristotelian *rex sapiens*, through Bruni, Erasmus, and Rabelais' *Pantagruel* to the debate between Pole and Lupset and the concerns of Osorio over the kind of knowledge suitable to nobles and rulers - knowledge that cannot be acquired or enjoyed in seclusion and must serve the common good. It is a kind of knowledge that Frances Yates sees praised in the cases of civic-minded noblemen - although with a more substantial hint of its magical character - in George Chapman's prefatory letter to *The Shadow of Night*[38].

That is one line of approach to the case of Prospero. There is a second that is closely linked to it and converges with it in the particular figure of Prospero: the problem of magic. Antiquity had also left some legacies of the figure of the royal magician (as well as accounts of kings who had opposed or rejected

---

34 W. BERGES (note 24) 70.

35 W. BERGES (note 24) 70. Such practical learning also had its potential for royal interest in some forms of magic and astrology, against which Nicole Oresme repeatedly warned Charles V. The case is well argued and provided with extensive sources by S. M. BABBITT (note 17) esp. 6, and E. DENNERY, La librairie de Charles V, Paris 1968, xv-xxi, 5-6.

36 On the adventures of the royal library in France, see now Roger CHARTIER, Forms and Meanings: Texts, Performances, and Audiences from Codex to Computer, Philadelphia 1995, 25-42.

37 Readily available in The Humanism of Leonardo Bruni: Selected Texts, trans. and ed. by Gordon GRIFFITHS, James HANKINS, David THOMPSON (Medieval and Renaissance Texts and Studies 46), Binghamton 1987, 154-157, 166-168, 253-254. In general, see Eugene F. RICE, Jr., The Renaissance Idea of Wisdom, Cambridge, Mass. 1958.

38 F. YATES (note 6) 136. On the Renaissance version of the courtly aesthetic in Shakespeare, see Gary SCHMIDGALL, Shakespeare and the Courtly Aesthetic, Berkeley/Los Angeles 1981, 69-99. - There is an extensive discussion of the advantages of natural magic for rulers in William EAMON, Science and the Secrets of Nature: Books of Secrets in Medieval and Early Modern Culture, Princeton 1994, 194-233.

magic; e.g., Constantine's accusations against his rivals Maxentius and Licinius in 312 and 324 of using magic and magicians against him), but for Medieval and Renaissance Europe the most striking were the Magi and the figure of Antichrist[39]. The Magi were acknowledged to have been not only astrologers, but also sorcerers who used their arts to discover the Christ child, but then gave them up after they had found him. As Tertullian remarked in the *De praescriptione hereticorum,* (not speaking of the Magi), *cedat curiositas fidei.*

The kind of magic that Prospero has studied and now practices seems clearly to be a version of what Frances Yates has called "The Occult Philosophy" - a combination of hermetic Renaissance Platonism and Cabala that produced a theory of natural magic that circulated in the fifteenth and sixteenth centuries in the works of Pico and Ficino, Agrippa of Nettesheim, Dürer's *Melancholia,* and the idea of the Saturnine human type as potentially the most talented of learned, artistic, and contemplative figures[40]. Yates argues that this tradition, although savagely attacked in mid-century, revived and came down to the end of the century in such figures as Giordano Bruno and John Dee. According to its proponents, such magic might be considered good and beneficient if it drew upon natural forces and benevolent spirits, but it could be dangerous and impious if it drew upon improper traffic with evil spirits. The most vociferous opponents, of course, denied it any good character at all. It is in the good and beneficient activities in the lower realms of the art (storms, illusions, and misled sense impressions generally, as well as the use of an innocent spirit)

---

[39] On the Antichrist, one of the earliest associations with magic is in the text of the Latin Tiburtine Sibyl, in Bernard MCGINN, Visions of the End: Apocalyptic Traditions in the Middle Ages, New York 1979, 49, from Ernst SACKUR, Sibyllinische Texte und Forschungen. Pseudomethodius, Adso und die tiburtinische Sibylle, Halle 1898, 185-186. On Constantine, see Ramsay MACMULLEN, Constantine, New York 1969, 1971, 129-136, and EUSEBIUS, *Historia Ecclesiastica,* IX.9.3. One of the panegyrics in fact described the first encounter between a Christian ruler and his opponent as the triumph of *divina praecepta* over *superstitiosa maleficia.* E. GALLETIER, Panegyriques latines. 3 vols., Paris 1949-1955, Pan. IX.4.

[40] F. YATES (note 6) is her last account of the phenomenon. She traces this aspect of Shakespearean criticism on p.160, including reference to her own book, Shakespeare's Last Plays: A New Approach, London 1975. More recently, however, see William H. SHERMAN, John Dee: The Politics of Reading and Writing in the English Renaissance, Amherst 1995, which locates Dee and some aspects of magic rather differently.

that Prospero seems to operate. His art must be partly, at least, of the celestial degree, since it is superior to that of Sycorax and Setebos, which is then to be construed as the demonic side of the lowest level of magic.

Although Agrippa seems not to have allowed for a melancholia-inspired ruler, he did allow for melancholia-inspired artists, prophets, and inspired intellectuals who perceived the divine. But it was not impossible for such a royal magician to be crafted, either benevolently or maliciously. As Yates points out, Henri III of France was accused of being a magician by his enemies of the League, and Rudolf II was certainly thought to be one[41]. One might see in Prospero the opposite.

Prospero, a ruler who called his studies "liberal arts", may have come to this magic out of a course of literary-philosophical study in much the same way as Marlowe's Faustus, but without Mephistopheles, just as his interest in private study removes him from the civic magical imperialism of Guillaume Postel, the figures in Chapman's letter, and Elizabeth I, but also from the identification with Marlowe's Tamburlaine, an overweening, arrogant, and proud immoralist in the tradition of the criticism of Frederick II and the legendary Alexander. We do not have to go as far as Yates and identify Prospero literally with John Dee as Shakespeare's contribution to the Elizabethan revival that took place in early Stuart England to see Prospero as a figure that draws together and indeed concludes a number of themes of the sixteenth-century and the later Middle Ages.

As Barbara Traister has demonstrated, magicians of all kinds and ranks departed from the English stage quickly after the first quarter of the seventeenth century (although they returned in later opera - *The Magic Flute*, for instance, or Jules Massenet's *Esclarmonde*). So, it seems, did magician-rulers. Kings continued to require knowledge, and to have secrets (which, so the angel Raphael told Tobit and Tobias [Tobit 12:7], it was wise and proper to keep), but appropriate royal knowledge was not the knowledge provided in the

---

[41] Frances YATES, The French Academies of the Sixteenth Century, London 1947, 261-262.

recluse's library (whether with books of magic or not) or under the wrapping of a cloak of art. Francis Bacon and others had a more complex agenda for both royal knowledge and royal patronage[42].

They continued, of course to collect books, but fewer books on magic. And they collected other things, too, in cabinets of curiosities and proto-museums[43]. They collected practical and impractical information from questionaires, surveys, and travellers[44]. They went, in short, from the celestial science to the dismal ones, probably to everyone's ultimate benefit.

But what about the cloak, staff (which has just made its last circle), and books? The cloak must have been disposed of somehow (we are not told), and *I'll break my staff,/ Bury it certain fathoms in the earth,/ And deeper than did ever plummet*

---

[42] See the interesting discussion by James R. JACOB, "By an Orphean charm": science and the two cultures in seventeenth-century England. In: Politics and Culture in Early Modern Europe: Essays in Honor of H. G. Koenigsberger, Cambridge 1987, 231-249; Carlo GINZBURG, High and Low: The Theme of Forbidden Knowledge in the Sixteenth and Seventeenth Centuries. In: Past & Present 73 (1976) 28-41, rpt. in: IDEM, Myths, Emblems, Clues, trans. by John and Anne C. TEDESCHI, London/Sydney 1990, 60-76, 194-197. L. MARIN (note 8) 169-185. See also the sources cited in the next note.

[43] The most thorough assessment of cabinets of curiosities and the developments of early museums is the volume edited by Oliver IMPEY and Arthur MACGREGOR, The Origin of Museums: The Cabinet of Curiosities in Sixteenth- and Seventeenth-Century Europe, Oxford 1985. For a well-known English case, see Arthur MACGREGOR, Tradescant's Rarities: Essays on the Foundation of the Ashmolean Museum 1683. With a Catalogue of the Surviving Early Collections, Oxford 1983. Further, Horst BREDEKAMP, The Lure of the Antique and the Cult of the Machine: The 'Kunstkammer' and the Evolution of Nature, Art, and Technology, Princeton 1994; A. REGOND-BOHAT and A. LOECHEL, Les cabinets des curiosités au XVIe siècle. In: Jean CÉARD, et al., La curiosité à la Renaissance, Paris 1986, 65-70; Krzysztof POMIAN, Collectors and Curiosities: Paris and Venice, 1500-1800, Cambridge 1990, and Th. DACOSTA KAUFMANN (note 9), as well as IDEM, Court, Cloister and City: The Art and Culture of Central Europe, 1450-1800, London 1995.

[44] For one example of such a royal questionaire, see William A. CHRISTIAN, Jr., Local Religion in Sixteenth-Century Spain, Princeton 1981. On the *ars apodemica*, "the art of travel", see Justin STAGL, Die Apodemik oder 'Reisekunst' als Methodik der Sozialforschung vom Humanismus bis zur Aufklärung. In: Statistik und Staatsbeschreibung in der Neuzeit, vornehmlich im 16.-18. Jahrhundert, ed. by Mohammed RASSEM and Justin STAGL, Paderborn/Munich 1980, 131-202; IDEM, Ars Apodemica: Bildungsreise und Reisemethodik von 1500 bis 1600. In: Reisen und Reiseliteratur im Mittelalter und in der frühen Neuzeit, ed. by Xenja von ERTZDORFF and Dieter NEUKIRCH, Amsterdam/Atlanta 1992, 141-189; Wolfgang NEUBER, Fremde Welt im europäischen Horizont. Zur Topik der deutschen Amerika-Reiseberichte der frühen Neuzeit, Berlin 1991.

sound / I'll drown my book (V.i.54-57). Ariel does indeed *discase* Prospero of these, giving him the ruler's hat and rapier, *as I was sometime Milan* (V.i.86). But the books present a particular problem. Historically, books of magic could be buried, burnt, or drowned - or at the very least, forgotten and left to sit on the shelves of royal (or ducal or papal) libraries awaiting the tender mercies of later bibliographers and scholars. Caliban has suggested that Stephano and Trinculo seize and burn Prospero's magical books (III.2.87-95) - another of Caliban's many mistakes. But there were protocols for this, too, and Caliban did not know them. The treatment of *magici libri* became a troublesome subject almost as soon as the bibliographical genre itself came into existence, possibly during the fourth, certainly during the third century B.C.[45]. And books, as we know well, are difficult - both emotionally and physically - to get rid of. Magic books in any case posed a particular problem. Suetonius observed that Augustus had burned most of the books of the diviners[46]. Cassius Dio (75.13) tells that Septimius Severus buried all the magic books he could collect in the tomb of Alexander the Great. But buried magical books had a way of being found, and often were. Numa was said to have accidentally dug some up once. In the end, Prospero will drown his books, but others besides Augustus had considered the alternative of burning them. *The Apostolic History* of Abdias (a work well known in the sixteenth century - both Bosch and Bruegel had depicted the episode described here) rehearses the dilemma. James the Greater, having defeated the magician Hermogenes, gave the magician his staff to protect him from his former familiar demons and sent him to get rid of his *materia magica*. Hermogenes collected his books in a basket and prepared to burn them, but James prohibited this, *lest the smoke vex the unwary. Cast them into the sea.* And Hermogenes obeyed, undid his earlier magical deceptions, distributed his ill-gotten wealth in charity, grew in faith, and even worked miracles[47]. Yet James'

---

[45] On the genre, see Arthur DARBY NOCK, Paul and the Magus. In: IDEM, Essays on Religion in the Ancient World, ed. by Zeph STEWART. 2 vols., Cambridge, Mass. 1972, Vol. 2, 317-323; IDEM, Greeks and Magi, ibid., 515-519. See also W. H. SHERMAN (note 40).

[46] *Augustus* 31, trans. by J. C. ROLFE, Suetonius, Cambridge, Mass. 1951, 170. There is a brief discussion in V. I. J. FLINT (note 14) 13.

[47] M. R. JAMES, ed., The Apocryphal New Testament, Oxford 1924, 463. The *Apostolic History* was immensely popular, and in the mid-sixteenth century Pieter Bruegel depicted the encounter between St. James and Hermogenes.

counsel was not always followed. The Jewish magicians in *Acts* 19:19 burned magical books worth fifty thousand pieces of silver, and the unwary apparently were not vexed. Fortunately, the *Sefer ha-Razim* was not composed until the third or fourth century and was not at risk in the conflagration described in *Acts*[48]. Overall, drowning magical books might have seemed a pious alternative in the early seventeenth century - and drowning (or at least the danger of drowning) runs like a leitmotif through the entire play.

Was the *rex curiosus* ever more than a moral, political, or literary fancy? From time to time, and to some thinkers, including John of Limoges and Dante, he must have seemed so. And for a moment or two in the late sixteenth and early seventeenth centuries, he seemed so again, and with good reason. And kings, as the angel Raphael had warned, indeed did have secrets, the *arcana imperii*, or "mysteries of state" about which Ernst Kantorowicz has written[49]. And, also as Raphael warned, such mysteries were best kept secret - as Dr. John Cowell found out when an angry James VI and I charged him with searching into "the deepest mysteries that belong to the persons or state of King and Princes, who are Gods on earth"[50]. But, as Kantorowicz also showed, these "mysteries" were of a legal nature and pertained especially to the royal *dignitas*, which, among other things, never died.

Such mysteries were neither reclusive study nor magic, and they survived the *reges curiosi*, but not for long. Prospero, James, and Rudolf were succeeded by rulers who sometimes became - or fell under the influence of - "projectors", as a number of rulers and Goethe's later Faust did[51]. And then there came the new

---

[48] For the *Sefer ha-Razim*, see Judah GOLDIN, The Magic of Magic and Superstition. In: Aspects of Religious Propaganda in Judaism and Early Christianity, ed. by Elizabeth SCHUSSLER FIORENZE, Notre Dame 1976, 115-148.

[49] Ernst KANTOROWICZ, Mysteries of State: An Absolutist Concept and Its Late Medieval Origins. In: IDEM, Selected Studies, Locust Valley, N.Y. 1965, 381-398.

[50] Ibid., 382-383.

[51] See the discussion by Wilhelm HENNIS, Goethe, Goya and the Threat of Modernity. In: Times Literary Supplement 4780, November 11, 1994, 15-16. Ironically, the central figure in Hennis's essay is Prince Rupert (1619-1682), third son of the Elector Palatine Frederick V and Elizabeth Stuart, at whose marriage the second performance of *The Tempest* is often said to have taken place. - Maps, too, were forms of increasing a ruler's power. See the interesting

political magicians - rulers who worked a more dangerous magic directly into the very fabric of rulership - the magic of political propaganda and massive, deadly power ruthlessly used (and even these were followed in the later nineteenth century by a group which Lewis Namier once designated the "mountebank dictators")[52]. The former type was no longer a *rex curiosus*, or a "projector," but the manipulative despot with an elaborate apparatus of ceremony, myths of the state, and limitless force. One such also ended up on a remote Atlantic island - St. Helena - where he (and his court in exile and his captors) continued to surround himself with the imperial court etiquette and the magic of a stateless emperor[53]. But Napoleon never disposed of his equivalents of staff, cloak, and books (and only with great difficulty got rid of his anti-Gonzalo, General Gourgaud), never discased himself, never restored domestic and political peace and good rule, and never left St. Helena alive or wiser. For, unless the island and its magic were left, there remained only what Gourgaud repeated again and again in his diary: *I am oppressed with boredom ... Boredom ... Great boredom ... Terrible boredom*[54]. On the whole, Prospero had the better and kinder fortune.

---

discussion in Larry WOLFF, Inventing Eastern Europe: The Map of Civilization on the Mind of the Enlightenment, Stanford 1994.

[52] Lewis NAMIER, The First Mountebank Dictator. In: IDEM, Vanished Supremacies: Essays on European History 1812-1918 (The Collected Essays of Sir Lewis Namier 1), Freeport, N.Y. 1970, 54-64.

[53] See the meditation of Julia BLACKBURN, The Emperor's Last Island: A Journey to St. Helena, New York 1991.

[54] Lewis NAMIER, The End of Napoleon. In: IDEM: Vanished Supremacies (note 52) 1-8, at 7.

VI

ROI FAINÉANT : THE ORIGINS OF AN HISTORIANS' COMMONPLACE

" From the monarch, as from a never-failing spring, flows a stream of all that is good or evil over the whole nation. " Thomas More's observation on the role of kingship in the ideal commonwealth, from the first part of *Utopia*, reflects a widely-held medieval and renaissance attitude toward the nature of politics and social change.[1] From St. Augustine to Hobbes, most writers of history or political theory would have agreed that whatever forces or institutions effect profound changes in society, it is ultimately the character of the ruler which establishes or subverts the good state. Like their medieval predecessors, political theorists and historians of the sixteenth and seventeenth centuries were most frequently concerned with the ideals of justice and morality which they assumed to be prerequisites for all good governance. In their approach to the institution of kingship, therefore, they paid most attention to the " good or evil " for which, like More, they held the monarch responsible, and they treated individual rulers accordingly as either just kings or tyrants.[2]

Book II, Chapter iv, of Jean Bodin's *Les Six Livres de la Republique* contains one of the most elaborate analyses of the differences between

---

[1] St. Thomas More, *Utopia*, ed. Edward J. Surtz, S. J. (New Haven and London, 1964), 17. Cf. William Baldwin's first preface to *A Mirror for Magistrates:* " The goodness or badness of any realm lieth in the goodness or badness of its rulers.. for indeed the wealth and quiet of every common weal, the disorders and miseries of the same, come specially through them..." cited in E.M.W. Tillyard, *Shakespeare's History Plays* (rep. London, 1961), 83. The best general discussion of medieval and renaissance theories of kingship is that of E.H. Kantorowicz, *The King's Two Bodies* (Princeton, 1957).

[2] Although this study will concentrate on a concept of kingship most commonly treated by sixteenth- and seventeenth-century historians of medieval France, general contemporary political ideas played an important role in its genesis. General discussions of the distinctions between the just king and the tyrant in the period as well as of kingship more broadly treated may conveniently be found in the following works : A.J. and R.W. Carlyle, *A History of Medieval Political Theory in the West* (rep. N.Y., 1949), Vol. VI, 219-290, 329-462 ; J. W. Allen, *A History of Political Thought in the Sixteenth Century* (rep. N.Y., 1960) ; P. Mesnard, *L'Essor de la philosophie politique au XVIe siècle;* J.N. Figgis, *Political Thought from Gerson to Grotius: 1414-1625* (rep. N.Y., 1960) ; G. Weill, *Les théories sur le pouvoir royal en France pendant les guerres de religion* (Paris, 1891) : J.H.M. Salmon, *The French Religious Wars in Englisch Political Thought* (Oxford, 1959) ; Guenter Lewy, " Some Theology about Tyranny," in *The Renaissance Reconsidered: A Symposium*, Smith College Studies in History, Vol. XLIV (Northampton, Mass, 1964), 79-90 ; R. H. Murray, *The Political Consequences of the Reformation* (Boston, 1926).

the just king and the tyrant which the sixteenth century produced.[3] After describing the effects of beneficient, then of tyrannical rule, Bodin sets out in a long series of symmetrical pairs the opposing characteristics of each type and contrasts in a conventional manner the misery of the tyrant's life, death, and subsequent reputation with the corresponding felicity of those of the just king. Thus far, excepting the extensive scope and detail of his historical references and his careful attention to rhetorical structure, Bodin does not differ significantly from earlier writers on the same topic, most of whom regarded " civil " — or political — history chiefly in terms of royal governance. Their overriding interest in the abstract concepts of justice, salvation, public welfare, or the precepts of natural law inclined them to treat individual rulers in terms of idealized royal types, personifications of justice and morality on the one hand, or of sovereignty and public law on the other.

After describing these extreme types, however, Bodin goes on to note that such contrasts between idealized figures are easily seen, but that it is much more difficult to judge a prince who has in him something of both the *roy tres-juste* and the *tyran tres-meschant.* Circumstances sometimes cause a ruler to do things which seem tyrannical to some and praiseworthy to others. Since governments differ one from another according to the natures of different peoples and places, it is necessary to consider the acts of the prince with care and to avoid hastily labelling him a tyrant.

Il est bien vray que le moyen de vertu environné de plusieurs vices, comme la ligne droite entre un million de courbes, est difficile à trouver. [4]

To illustrate his point further, Bodin discusses the problem of necessary severity on the part of the just ruler and, for emphasis, contrasts some of the characteristics of the tyrant with those of the weak, overly-generous king who ruins his realm by allowing governance to pass into the hands of unworthy favorites, thus setting up, in fact, ten thousand tyrannies instead of one. For Bodin, excessive severity is required more often than not, and the ruler who is excessively weak, pusillanimous, incompetent, or generous may well be a greater disaster to the kingdom than one who appears to be a tyrant. [5]

---

[3] *Les Six Livres de la Republique* (Paris, 1583 : photo-rep. Aalen, 1961), 289-297. Cf. Book VI, iv, 961. Besides the works cited in the preceding note, see Beatrice REYNOLDS, *Proponents of Limited Monarchy in Sixteenth-Century France: François Hotman and Jean Bodin* (N.Y., 1931).

Republique, ed. cit., 297.

[5] *ibid.*, 295 : "Car telle simplicité sans prudence est tres dangereuse & pernicieuse en un Roy & beaucoup plus à craindre que la cruaté d'un Prince sévère, chagrin, revesche, avare & inaccessible. Et semble que nos peres anciens n'ont cit ce proverbe sans cause, De meschant homme, bon Roy... Par la souffrance & niaise simplicité d'un Prince trop bon, il advient que les flatteurs les corratiers, & plus meschants emportent les offices,

The question of royal severity had, of course, been a concern of earlier political theorists and historians. In the sixteenth century alone, both Machiavelli and More had argued for its necessity, Machiavelli's remarks on the " good and evil cruelty " of *The Prince* being quite similar to Bodin's own observations.[6] William Tyndale had given the distinction between the tyrant and the weak king dramatic expression in *The Obedience of a Christian Man:*

> Yea, and it is better to have a tyrant unto thy king: than a shadow; a passive king who does nought himself, but suffereth others to do with him what they will, and to lead him whither they list. For a tyrant, though he do wrong unto the good, yet he punisheth the evil, and maketh all men obey, neither suffering any man to poll but himself only. A king that is soft as silk and effeminate, that is to say turned into the nature of a woman — what with his own lusts, which are the longing of a woman with child, so that he cannot resist them, and with the wily tyranny of them that ever rule him — shall be much more grievous unto his realm than a right tyrant. [7]

Yet the distinction between the weak king and the tyrant usually remained on the periphery of early modern political thought. Like their predecessors, the Reformation political theorists generally upheld the doctrine of obedience to all rulers, but their attention was focused on the extreme ends of the political spectrum and not on the more frequent but less dramatic human mean. The figure of the weak king remained as it had in Bodin and Tyndale, rather an exemplary abstraction than a political problem. Although another side of the sixteenth-century political consciousness, the progressive awareness of the contrast between the individual humanity of the ruler and his function as the personification of the abstract ideals of justice, law, and sovereignty, is reflected in some political literature, it was to have its most profound treatment in the political and historical drama of Marlowe and Shakespeare rather than in " politick discourses " or " civil histories." [8]

---

les charges, les benefices, les dons, espuisans les finances d'un état : & par ce moyen le povre peuple est rongé jusqu'aux os, & cruellement asservi aux plus grands ; de sorte que pour un tyran il y en a dix mil..."

[6] MACHIAVELLI, *The Prince*, c. viii. The problem also appears in the contrast between the figures Basilius and Euarchus in Sidney's *Arcadia*. Cf. W.R. BRIGGS, " The Political Ideas of Sidney's *Arcadia*," *Studies in Philology* 28 (1931), 137-161; E.W. TALBERT, *The Problem of Order* (Chapel Hill, N.C., 1962), 89-120; Irving RIBNER, " Sidney's *Arcadia* and the Structure of *King Lear*," *Studia Neophilologica* 24 (1951/1952) 63-68.

[7] Cited in Irwing RIBNER, *The English History Play in the Age of Shakespeare* (2nd. ed. N.Y., 1965), 158. Cf. the *Vindiciae Contra Tyrannos*, ed. H.J. Laski (rep. Gloucester, Mass., 1963), 133-136, 183-213; Francis OAKLEY, *The Political Thought of Pierre d'Ailly: The Voluntarist Tradition* (New Haven-London, 1964), 211-230.

[8] For Shakespeare and Marlowe, see Ribner's study, cited in the preceding note. See also KANTOROWICZ, *The King's Two Bodies*, 24-41; M.M. Reese, *The Cease of Majesty* (London, 1961); Christopher MORRIS, " Shakespeare's Politics," *The Historical Journal* 8 (1965), 293-308.

Neither Bodin's observations on the complexity of political experience nor Shakespeare's portraits of tortured, all-too-human rulers appears to have had much influence on the concept of royal inadequacy, particularly as it came to be expressed by the term *roi fainéant* in the political and historiographical vocabularies of the seventeenth and eighteenth centuries. The term was to serve as a commonplace for the sort of royal inadequacy described in Bodin and Tyndale and as an approximate equivalent to another term which some medieval writers had coined to designate a similar phenomenon, the *rex inutilis.* [9] A brief outline of the origins and early development of the term *roi fainéant* may serve to illustrate some of the aspects of royal inadequacy treated by writers of the early modern period, since it is the one still most frequently used to label the medieval and later rulers who seem to conform most closely to Bodin's portrait of the incompetent prince.

Claude Fauchet, *Président à la cour des monnaies* and historiographer of France under Henry IV, appears to have been the first modern historian to have considered the origins of the term *roi fainéant.* The term itself made its first appearance in the fourteenth century in the *Grandes chroniques de France* as an attempt to translate the Latin *rex nihil faciens* of some eleventh-century chroniclers.[10] These writers had used it to describe the brief rule of a fictitious Louis, son of Carloman and grandson of Louis the Stammerer:

> Loys-Fai-noient... Sy fu ansi surnommé ou pour ce qu'il fit nule chose que l'on doite mettre en memoire ou pour ce que il traist une nonnain de l'abbaye de Chiele et l'epousa en mariage.[11]

They had also used it to designate Louis V, the last Carolingian ruler of France. The term does not appear to have been of wide currency in the later fourteenth and fifteenth centuries, but it became somewhat more popular in the vernacular histories of medieval France produced in the sixteenth century.[12] When Fauchet came to write his *Antiquitez et histoires Gauloises et Françoises* in 1599, in fact, it is evident that the term had come to mean not the brevity of these

---

[9] For the origins of the medieval term, see this writer's "*Rex inutilis:* Sancho II of Portugal and Thirteenth-Century Deposition Theory," *Studia Gratiana* 13 (1968), 1-50, part of a forthcoming book-length study of the medieval concept in law and literature.

[10] See F. Godefroy, *Dictionnaire de l'ancien langue française*, Vol. IX, *Complément* (Paris, 1938), 393. For the date of 1321, see Oscar Bloch, *Dictionnaire etymologique de la langue française*, Vol. II (Paris, 1932), 88.

[11] P. Paris, ed., *Les grandes chroniques de France*, Vol. III (Paris, 1837), 96-98. Cf. F. Lot, *Les derniers carolingiens* (Paris, 1891), 97 n.1.

[12] A brief account of the most important of these may be found in A. Tierry, "Notes sur quatorze historiens antérieurs a Mézeray," in his *Lettres sur l'histoire de France, dix ans d'études historiques* (Paris, 1866), 539-582. See also Nathan Edelman, *Attitudes of Seventeenth-Century France toward the Middle Ages* (N.Y., 1946), esp. 44-84; W.H. Evans, *L'historien Mézeray et son temps* (Paris, 1930); Donald Kelley, "*Fides Historiae:* Charles Dumoulin and the Gallican View of History," *Traditio* 22 (1966), 347-402.

kings' reigns, but the dissoluteness of their characters. Fauchet set himself two tasks: he provided good grounds for disproving the existence of the fictitious *Loys-Fai-noient*, and he attempted to give an accurate historical definition to the chroniclers' *rex nihil faciens, roi fainéant.*[13]

Noting that no Louis, son of Carloman, had appeared in the chronicles of Regino and others, Fauchet conjectured, rightly, that the ruler had been in fact only "*supposé*":

> Et pour ce ie croy que ce mot de faineant doit estre approprié à Louis le Begue, duquel quelque Chroniqueur Latin avoit dit, *Ludovicus nihil fecit*; comme fait ledit de Saint Aubin: pour *brevi et inglorio regno perfunctus est*, c'est-à-dire il regna peu de temps, et ne fit rien de remarque, que depuis un translateur ancien a tourné *fainéant*, au lieu qu'il devoit dire, *qui ne fait rien de memorable*. Et ceux qui depuis sont venus ont prit ce mot de fainéant en mauvais part: comme si les Latins eussent entendu *Nihili*. Car Odoran parlant de Louys quatriesme fils de Lothaire roy de France a dit: *Ludovicus nihil fecit*... c'est a dire, Louis qui ne fit rien, à cause de peu de temps qu'il vesquit: que ceux qui n'entendoient pas bien le Latin ont tourné fainéant.[14]

Although Fauchet's remarks on the subject are indicated by many seventeenth- and eighteenth-century dictionaries as authoritative,[15] his subtle distinction between the two meanings of *fainéant* does not seem to have influenced the subsequent history of the term during the next two centuries.

One reason for this must be sought in the very practice which inspired Fauchet to discuss the several meanings of *fainéant* in the first place. Sixteenth-century France had produced not only a revival of scholarly and antiquarian interest in her medieval past, but also a number of popular histories, particularly of early rulers, complete with portraits, elaborate genealogies, coins, medallions, coats of arms, and other — usually quite spurious — iconographic material.[16] General interest in the early history of France led both students and

---

[13] Ed. cited is that of Paris, 1610. See J.G. ESPINER-SCOTT, *Claude Fauchet, sa vie, son œuvre* (Paris, 1938) and *Documents concernant la vie et les œuvres de Claude Faichet* (Paris, 1938); *idem*, " Les théories de Claude Fauchet sur le pouvoir royale, " *Humanisme et Renaissance* 7 (1949), 233-238, esp. 234. For Fauchet's place in other historiographical problems, see Donald Kelley, " *De origine feudorum:* The Beginnings of an Historical Problem." *Speculum* 39 (1964), 207-228. Recent bibliographical studies of many of the writers mentioned here may be found in G. GRENTE, ed., *Dictionnaire des lettres françaises: le seizième siècle* (Paris, 1951) and A. CIORANESCU, *Bibliographie de la littérature française du seizième siècle* (Paris, 1959) and their companion volumes for the seventeenth century.

[14] FAUCHET, *Antiquitez*, fols, 396^r, 470^v. Cf. Fauchet's " Lettre de Claude Fauchet sur les successeurs de Charlemagne," in ESPINER-SCOTT, *Documents*, 198.

[15] Cf. Gilles MÉNAGE, *Les origines de la langue Française* (Paris, 1650), 308. For the *Dictionnaire des Théroux*, see below, n. 37.

[16] In general, see Nathan EDELMAN, *Attitudes of Seventeenth-Century France toward the Middle Ages* (N.Y., 1946). For the illustration of popular histories, see Jeanne DUPORTAL, *Etude sur les livres à figure édités en France de 1601 à 1660* (Paris, 1914), 73-95, 275-279; Robert BRUN, *Le livre illustré en France au XVIe siècle* (Paris, 1930). For an early eighteenth-century attitude toward this material, see below, n. 39.

popularizers to note in common certain features of medieval royalty. No less a scholar than Estienne Pasquier, for example, devoted a chapter of his *Les recherches de la France* to popular royal surnames, remarking that such titles were given for faults as well as virtues and citing Charles *le Simple* and Louis *le Fainéant* as examples. [17] A few years later, in his polemical *Franco-Gallia*, François Hotman attacked the laxity and incompetence of later Merovingian and later Carolingian rulers chiefly to strengthen his own thesis of the powers of the popular assemblies of this early period.[18]

Some historians, to be sure, regarded the meaning of the term in much the same manner as Fauchet. Nicholas Vignier, in his *Sommaire de l'histoire des Françoys*, published in 1579, sounds very much like Fauchet:

> ... Loys, qui le surnom Fait-neant a esté donné (ou pource qu'il dura peu, ou qu'en son regne il ne fait chose digne de memoire)...[19]

Jean du Tillet, whose *Recueil des Roys de France* appeared shortly after Fauchet's *Antiquitez*, echoes these remarks almost verbatim.[20] None of these works, however, achieved the popularity of Bernard de Girard, Seigneur du Haillan's *Histoire generale des Roys de France*, a work which was to remain the best-known history of medieval France until the appearance of that of Scipion Dupleix between 1621 and 1648.[21] Du Haillan's work appears to have been the first major history to link the terms *fainéant* and *néantise* to both the later Carolingians and the later Merovingians and to impart to it the pejorative tone to which Fauchet was to take such learned offense.[22] Although du Haillan barely avoided the attribution of the epithet *rois fainéants* to the most famous of its subsequent bearers, the Merovingian successors of Clovis II, his attacks on their persons and on their political incapacity linked them with his scorn for Louis V,

---

[17] The first edition appeared in Paris in 1560. I have used the edition of 1611, also of Paris. The discussion is Bk. IV, ch. xxi, p. 481.

[18] The relevant parts of *Franco-Gallia* are chs. xii-xiii. The work exists in numerous editions. For the author see now R.E. GIESEY, " When and Why Hotman Wrote the *Francogallia*," *Bibliothèque d'humanisme et de la Renaissance* 29 (1967), 581-611.

[19] N. VIGNIER *Sommaire de l'histoire des Françoys* (Paris, 1579), 166. Cf. p. 213 : " Odoramnus l'a (Louis V) surnommé Faitnéant : pour ce qu'il n'eut loisir de faire aucune chose memorable pour la briefeté de son regne."

[20] J. du TILLET, *Recueil des Roys de France, leurs couronne et maison* (Paris, 1602), 51-52, 191. For du Tillet, see Donald R. KELLEY, " Jean du Tillet, Archivist and Antiquary," *Journal of Modern History* 38 (1966), 337-354. This article, as does the same author's " *De Origine Feudorum...*" cited above, n.13, contributes much to our knowledge of sixteenth-century French historiography and the intellectual milieu of Fauchet, du Tillet, Pasquier, and others.

[21] For the importance of du Haillan, see EVANS, *L'historien Mézeray et son temps*, cited above, n. 12. The edition used for this study is that of Paris, 1616, Vol. I.

[22] Du HAILLAN, *Histoire générale des Roys de France*, ed. cit., 81, 88-89, 96-97, 110-112, 118-119.

> Louis Faineant... pource qu'il fut homme de peu de valeur, adonné à la pailliardise, oisiveté et vices... [23]

and for Charles *le Simple*, " *prince idiot.*" [24] Du Haillan also noted the other definition of *fainéant*, that of little achievement because of a short reign, but his heaviest emphasis always falls upon the personal degeneracy of these rulers, in this respect in a manner not very different from that of Hotman.[25]

One of the first instances of the application of the term *fainéant* to the later Merovingians was the series of *Les vrais Portraicts des Rois de France* published in 1634 by Jacques de Bie.[26] The second edition of this work, with the text expanded by short biographies of the rulers discussed, further emphasizes the *fainéantise* of the later Merovingians. De Bie's portraits might have acquired little historical significance, however, since the practice of illustrating histories of earlier rulers had become popular as early as 1522 and was to continue long after,[27] had not François de Mézeray used them and their inscriptions to illustrate his massive *Histoire de France*, which appeared in 1643 and 1646 and was to supplant the work of Dupleix in popularity until displaced in its turn by the history of Gabriel Daniel in 1715.[28] Mézeray, like Fauchet and others before him, used the most advanced historical techniques of his day, but his contempt for royal weakness far outweighed his sensitivity to semantics, and his comments on the last Merovingians ring with scorn :

> Nous avons assez donné à la mémoire de Clovis (II) d'avoir souffert une dizaine de ses successeurs, tous fainéants, hébetez, et plongés dans les ordures du vice... [29]
>
> ... et la fainéantise, desormais hérédetaire à cette première race, (est) cause qu'il ne se lit rien de memorable de son regne. [30]

---

[23] Du HAILLAN, *Histoire générale des Roys de France*, ed. cit. 251. Cf. 283f.

[24] *ibid.* 260-263.

[25] *ibid.* 284 : " Quelques uns l'ont appellé Fainéant pource qu'il n'eust aucun loisir de faire aucune chose memorable, pour la brieveté de son regne."

[26] For de Bie, see Duportal (above, n.16), 275-279 ; EVANS, *L'historien Mézeray*, 47-51. The biographies were added by H. de Coste, the epigrams beneath the portraits by Jean Baudoin.

[27] Between 1522 and 1668 there were at least eighteen popular histories printed with illustrations of individual rulers. Because these have not been available to me, I have been unable to check one interesting aspect of the development of the *roi fainéant:* a popular pictorial tradition reflecting the low esteem in which such rulers came to be held. A brief note is given in EDELMAN, *Attitudes of Seventeenth-century France toward the Middle Ages*, 88. De Bie's portraits do not appear to reflect a pictoral tradition of *rois fainéants*, although others certainly may. See below, n. 31.

[28] For DANIEL, see below, nn. 41f.

[29] François de MÉZERAY, *Histoire de France* (Paris, 1643), Vol. I, 142. Cf. 96-115 (Clovis II to Childeric III).

[30] *ibid.* 101.

The success of Mezeray's history and its portraits inspired Jacques Boulanger to reissue Jean de Serres ' *Inventaire de l'Histoire de France* in 1648 with a new series of portraits, this one including a "*promenade des Rois fainéants.*" [31] In 1668 Mezeray published his *Abregé chronologique ou extrait de l'histoire de France* and again gave the Merovingians short shrift:

> D'ailleurs il sembloit juste que la France apres tant d'idoles et de fainéans se donnast un roi effectif.[32]

Thus, in spite of Fauchet's careful etymological distinctions, the figure of the *roi fainéant* had begun to take shape in the historiography of seventeenth-century France.

Other usages of the word *fainéant* hastened the process. From Malherbe to Voltaire and after the term appears in literary satire in much the same sense as it had in Mézeray.[33] In Cotgrave's French-English *Dictionary* it is highly pejorative:

> An idle, drowsie, lither, slothful luske; a heartlesse loytrer, a lazy fellow; one that's without wit, without vertue, without spirit; a droane, a dullard, a housedove; also a lewd companion, a loose fellow.[34]

In 1683 John Bulkeel's translation of Mézeray appeared. Although Bulkeel translated *fainéans* (in the last citation from Mezeray above) as "shadows." he found it necessary when discussing Louis V to provide a gloss on Mézeray's epithet, "*Louis le fainéant*":

> Louis the lazy or Sloathful... (in margin, as gloss to Lazy:) Faineant, Lazy, Idle, Do-Nothing.[35]

Toward the end of the century Furetière's *Dictionnaire universel* defined *fainéant* as:

> Paresseux, oisif qui ne fait rien, ou fait peu de chose en comparaison de ce qu'il devroit faire, qui aime à ne pas travailler, ou qui ne veut rien faire. En une République bien policée on doit punir les *fainéans*. Il y a des Ordonnances contre les *fainéans* et vagabonds. Ce Conseiller a vendu sa charge, il veut vivre *fainéant*. Un *fainéant*, est proprement un homme ou sans vertu, ou sans cœur, ou sans esprit, ou sans adresse... L'inutilité fait regarder un homme comme un *fainéant* méprisable... Ce mot de *fainéant* s'est dit de certains Rois de France de la première Race, parce qu'ils ne se mêloient de rien, les

---

[31] Duportal, *Etude sur les livres à figures*, 277. I have not seen the work.

[32] Méseray, *Abregé chronologique ou extrait de l'histoire de France* (Paris, 1668), 138. Cf. 295-297.

[33] Godefroy's earliest references to the term *fainéant* after the fourteenth century are to the works of Malherbe, Boileau, and Voltaire. Cf. E. Littré, *Dictionnaire de la langue française*, Vol. II, D-H (Paris, 1885), 1597.

[34] Randle Cotgrave, *A French-English Dictionary*, with supplements by James Howell (London, 1650), *s.v. fainéant*.

[35] François de Mézeray, *A General Chronological History of France*, trans. John Bulkeel (London, 1683), 198. Cf. also 87, 153, 199.

maires du palais gouvernant les affaires de l'Etat selon leur caprice et selon leurs intérêts. On en compte XI dont le premier est Clovis II et le dernier Childeric, qui fut mis dans un couvent... [36]

Early in the eighteenth century, the *Dictionnaire des Théroux* elaborated Furetière's definition and finally established the meaning of the term in French, although ironically citing Fauchet as its authority :

> Paresseux, qui ne fait rien, ou qui ne veut rien faire. *Piger, deses, desidiosus...* Il y a eu des Rois de la première Race qu'on a appellés *Fainéans...* On trouve dans les anciens titres et dans les chroniques, *Ludovicus nihil faciens*, Louis le fainéant ; on écrivoit même autrefois *Futneant.* Aimoin moine de Fleury dans le second livre des miracles de Saint Benoit, *Augusto Karolo rebus humanis exempto, filius eius Ludovicus successit, qui nihil fecisse praenomen sortitus est, sive quod vix duobus annis regno potius nil strenue gessit, sive quod sanctimonialem quandam, sicuti a majoribus accepimus, Kale monasterio puellarum abstractum, conjugio copulans suo, peccatum quod nihil esse noscitur, perpetravit.*[37]

Thus *fainéant* evolved in the vocabularies of scholars, popularizers of history, and literary satirists.

Fauchet may have suspected that he was fighting a losing battle, and surely the depictions of the later Merovingians and later Carolingians in many medieval chronicles and legal texts indicated something of their future at the hands of Mézeray and his successors.[38] Even Mézeray, however, like Bodin and others, used the term not as an accurate means of historical description but as a commonplace of contemporary social opprobrium. Mézeray's history, like those of many of his predecessors, appealed to a wide public which was interested chiefly in the depiction of royal vices and virtues set against seventeenth-century standards of political and moral conduct. It appears to have been used in this sense, for example, to inculcate cautionary lessons into the young Louis XIV. The seventeenth century was willing to tolerate, within certain limits, depictions of royal inadequacy. These limits, however, were narrow. In his *Histoire de France*, published in 1715, Gabriel Daniel was to reduce Mézeray's invective against the last Merovingians to a few pages devoted to "*quatre ou cinq de ces Rois qu'on appelle Fainéants,*"[39] and to use them chiefly as illustrations of the basic political truths that :

> Outre la leçon si commune de l'inconstance et de la décadence des choses humaines qu'on peut apprendre par tout, on en trouve ici une importante qui regarde en particulier les Princes : c'est que l'oisiveté,

36 The edition cited here is that printed at La Haye, 1727, Vol. II, *s.v. fainéant.*

37 *Dictionnaire universel françois et latin... vulgairement appellé Dictionnaire des Théroux* (Paris, 1743), Vol. III, col. 29 *s.v. fainéant.*

38 One of the best known of these was the so-called chronicle of Aimoin of Fleury. The work served the compilers of the *Grandes chroniques de France* and was first printed separately in Paris in 1514. The most recent remarks on the work are those of J. F. Lemarignier, " Autour de la royauté française du XIe au XIIIe siècle," *Bibliothèque de l'école des chartes* 113 (1955), esp. pp. 25-36.

39 Gabriel Daniel, *Histoire de France* (Paris, 1729), Vol. I, xlv-xlvii.

l'inapplication, la lâcheté, l'amour du plaisir, et du repos, ne furent jamais les fruits et les avantages legitimes d'une Couronne ; qu'ils en ternissent toujours l'éclat, et que si les vertus opposées ne la soutiennent, elle n'est jamais hors de danger d'être ébranlée et de tomber.[40]

Daniel's history elaborated upon his earlier attacks on Mezeray's language and style. He did not object, however, to Mezeray's usage of *fainéant,* and he even used *Rois fainéants* in a manner which suggests that it had become by his day a common term. Even Pierre Bayle's *Dictionnaire,* although it did not use the term *fainéant,* observed, in the article on David, that the worst things which could be said against a ruler were that he was a tyrant or that he gave himself up to wicked counsel, one of the stock traits of the *roi fainéant* and a topic in political literature from the middle ages to the present.[41] By 1700 the figure of the *roi fainéant,* given up to vices or wicked counsel or both, dominated by unworthy favorites or a wicked queen, stripped of all power of governance, and defenceless against a righteous national church, an outraged aristocracy, or a heroic popular assembly, — in short, already a stock character out of the historian's repertory company — had entered the commonplace vocabulary of historians, poets, and social critics, where he has since remained.

Historical judgments often tell us more about the men who make them than about the things which are judged. The stylized, oversimplified, and essentially moral terms in which many such evaluations of rulers are couched pose a further danger for the later historian, since their comfortable vagueness lends them to other presuppositions about morals and politics than those in whose midst they were created. Historians, in fact, often reject the moral or political bias of their predecessors only to retain, in much of the casual terminology which that bias had helped to shape, many of the postulates of earlier historical thought. In a study of " Good Kings and Bad Kings in Medieval English History," V. H. Galbraith examined some of this bias as exemplified in medieval and Victorian attitudes toward several English rulers, particularly John and Edward I.[42] The reduction of medieval kings to the categories of " hero, saint, failure, and villain," understandable in terms of the monastic chronicler's willingness to disregard those elements of political experience which did not seem to contribute to the history of salvation — of which the abstract concept of the morality of the ruler was a constitutive

---

40 Gabriel DANIEL, *Histoire de France* (Paris, 1729), Vol. 1, 514.

41 *Dictionnaire historique et critique* (La Haye-Utrecht, 1740), Vol. II, p. 254. The relevance of the article to Bayle's view of kingship is discussed by Walter REX, " Bayle's Article on David," in his *Essays on Pierre Bayle and Religious Controversy* (The Hague, 1965), 197-255. On renaissance theories of counsel, see J.H. HEXTER, *More's " Utopia ": The Biography of an Idea* (Princeton, 1952), 99-157.

42 *History* 30 (1945), 119-132.

element — became especially misleading in view of the peculiarly moral cast of Victorian historical thought which echoed it.[43] The history of the term *roi fainéant*, long since extended beyond the figures of the hapless Merovingians, reflects a similar problem. The term is in fact no more valid an instrument of historical description than is the distinction between "good" and "bad" kings which Galbraith criticized.

The *roi fainéant*, far from being identical with the medieval *rex inutilis*, is a figment of seventeenth-century historical taste. In scholarship, it has become an easy substitute for exactness, in popular history a vague commonplace used to label any ruler whose reign appears to have been characterized chiefly by indolence, incompetence, pusillanimity, or subjection to the wills of others. It has been used to describe, besides the last Merovingians and last Carolingians, Philip I, Louis VI, Charles VI. and Henry III of France, Stephen, John, Henry III, and Henry VI of England, and even the figure of Arthur in some courtly romances. Whatever traits — if any — these rulers shared are hardly clarified by calling them, one and all, *rois fainéants*. When a single category of kingship, itself originally a product of a far later period than that to which historians usually apply it, becomes so comprehensive as to include all these kings, its accuracy and usefullness necessarily diminish. The commonplace vocabulary is convenient for the historian to use, but it is hardly very informative. The frequency with which it appears, however, should recall Bodin's observation that extreme political types are easily identified, but that any deviation from these remains to be judged on its own merits, and, one might add, not against a standard designed to satisfy the consumers of popular medieval history in seventeenth-century France.

[43] GALBRAITH's criticisms are repeated and elaborated in his *An Introduction to the Study of History* (London, 1964), 3-21.

VII

REX INUTILIS: SANCHO II OF PORTUGAL AND THIRTEENTH-CENTURY DEPOSITION THEORY

SUMMARY: Medieval deposition theory usually concentrated on the figures of the *rex iustus* and the *tyrannus*. From the twelfth century on, however, other political categories began to emerge, including that of the *rex inutilis*, the useless or inadequate ruler. The contributions of the canonists from Huguccio to Johannes Andreae were instrumental in shaping this concept, and Innocent IV's action against Sancho II of Portugal in 1245 represented the culmination of this line of canonist thought. Innocent's solution to the problem of the *rex inutilis*, assigning a *curator* to govern Portugal while allowing the king to retain the royal *dignitas*, did not constitute a practical method for checking inept governance, although it had legitimate antecedents in canonist thought. Sancho's case, moreover, did not correspond at all points with the figure of the *rex inutilis* as worked out in canonist political theory. Although Innocent's solution was partially successful in Portugal, the procedure which he outlined was never to become an independent approach in later deposition proceedings [*E. M. P.*].

The universal character of the medieval Canon law often gave great legal significance to events which would not normally have exerted any appreciable influence upon the course of European history. In 1202, for example, the request of Count William of Montpellier that Innocent III legitimize the Count's natural children elicited the decretal *Per venerabilem,* which not only disposed (unfavorably) of the Count's request but also laid down a series of observations on the relation between *sacerdotium* and *regnum* which remained " to the time of Hostiensis... the focus of the freshest canonist thinking about the principles of the relations of the two powers" (1). In 1220 Honorius III found cause to complain of certain privileges granted by Andrew II of Hungary which the pope considered injurious to the *honor coronae*. Honorius' opinion, given in the decretal *Intellecto*, summed up a century of juristic theories concerning the inalienability of political authority and remained the starting-point for future discussions of this increasingly important aspect of legal theory (2). In these and other incidents legal problems which might have remained isolated were worked into the articulation of a coherent structure of ecclesiastical jurisprudence having consequences not only within the papal administration of the *respublica christiana* but also within the increasingly more sophisticated public law of the territorial monarchies.

Another such case arose in Portugal in the second quarter of the thirteenth century. On July 24, 1245 Innocent IV issued the decretal *Grandi*, by which he deprived Sancho II of the governance of Portugal and appointed Sancho's brother Afonso, Count of Boulogne, guardian or *curator* of the realm. Afonso arrived in Portugal early in 1246 at the head of a crusading army, took Lisbon, and proceeded to enforce the terms of *Grandi* in the face of armed resistance on the part of his brother. Although Sancho had the support of some of the Portuguese nobility as well as that of Ferdinand III of Castille and his son Alfonso, he was driven from his kingdom and forced to seek refuge in Toledo, where he died in 1248. Upon Sancho's death Afonso of Boulogne ascended the Portuguese throne as Afonso III (3).

---

(1) J. A. Watt, *The Theory of Papal Monarchy in the Thirteenth Century: The Contribution of the Canonists*, in: *Traditio* 20 (1964), 179-318 at 214-216. Also published separately, New York and London, 1965.

(2) The fullest discussion of *Intellecto* is that of P. Riesenberg, *The Inalienability of Sovereignty in Medieval Political Thought*, N.Y., 1956; cf. Gaines Post, *Studies in Medieval Legal Thought*, Princeton, 1964, 415-433; H. Hoffmann, *Die Unveräusserlichkeit der Kronrechte im Mittealter*, in: *Deutsches Archiv* 20 (1964), 389-474.

(3) *Dat. Lugd.* IX *Kal. Aug. A.* III (1245). *Corpus Iuris Canonici*, ed. E. Friedberg, Leipzig, 1879-1881, Vol. II, cols. 971-974: *Liber Sextus* 1.8.2 *de supplenda negligentia praelatorum.* E. Berger, *Les Régistres d'Innocent IV*, Rome, 1884-1921, no. 1389. O. Raynaldi, *Annales Ecclesiastici*, Colonia Agrippina, 1664f., Vol. XXI, *ad an.* 1245, no. 68. Mansi, Vol. XXIII, cols. 652-653. Portuguese text in: D. A. Caetano da Sousa, *Provas da historia genealogica da casa real portuguesa*, rep. Coimbra, 1946, Vol. I, 57-61; F. A. Brandão, *Monarchia Lusitana*, Lisbon, 1632, Vol. IV, *Escritura* xxiii (= *Cronicas de D. Sancho II e D. Afonso III*, Porto, 1946, 358-361). The following abbreviations will be used throughout: P. Pres-

Sancho's case has not attracted the attention of many historians of thirteenth-century political theory (4). Some of this neglect may be explained by the peripheral status of Portugal in the wider world of European political affairs, by the overshadowing of Sancho's case by the more spectacular deposition of Frederick II which had occurred a week earlier, and by the turbulent political conditions in England, Italy and the Empire. However, Sancho's difficulties with his own nobles and prelates, the role of *Grandi* in papal political thought, and the subsequent interest which the decretal and its glosses generated in the territorial monarchies during the fourteenth and fifteenth centuries give the episode some importance for the historian of constitutionalism and public

---

SUTTI, *Regesta Honorii Papae III*, Rome, 1895 = PRESSUTTI; L. AUVRAY, *Régistres de Grégoire IX*, Paris, 1890-1910 = AUVRAY; E. BERGER, *Les Régistres d'Innocent IV*, Rome, 1884-1921 = BERGER; all papal register citations cited by document number. VISCONDE DA SANTAREM and REBELLO DA SILVA, *Quadro elementar das relações politicas e diplomaticas de Portugal com as diversas potencias do mondo*, Lisbon, 1842ff, Vol. IX = *QE*, followed by page no. J. ABRANCHES, *Fontes do direito ecclesiastico portuguez*, Coimbra, 1895 = ABRANCHES, followed by document no. The standard abbreviations for the *Corpus Iuris Canonici* and the *Corpus Iuris Civilis* will be used. For additional abbreviations see below, n. 18.

An earlier version of this study was included in the writer's doctoral dissertation, *Rex inutilis: Aspects of Royal Inadequacy in Medieval Law and Literature*, 751-1400, Yale University Unpub. Diss., 1967. I wish to thank Professors Robert S. Lopez, Stephan Kuttner, W. H. Dunham, Jr., and Harold Johnson for their advice and ungrudging assistance on difficult points. Professor Robert Benson of Wesleyan University and Rev. John F. Kenney of St. John's Seminary have been kind enough to discuss a number of points with me, as have Mr. Richard Hoffmann and Mr. Robert Somerville of Yale University.

(4) The only extensive discussions in recent years have been those of J. A. CANTINI, *De autonomia judicis saecularis et de Romani Pontificis plenitudine potestatis in temporalibus secundum Innocentium IV*, in: *Salesianum* 23 (1961), 407-480; G. CASPARY, *The Deposition of Richard II and the Canon Law*, in: *Proceedings of the Second International Congress of Medieval Canon Law* (*Monumenta Iuris Canonici, Subsidia*, Vol. I), Rome, 1966, 189-201. Brief notice is taken in P. RIESENBERG, *The Inalienability of Sovereignty*, 168-169; L. BUISSON, *Potestas und Caritas. Die päpstliche Gewalt im Spätmittelalter*, Cologne, 1958, 288-289; A. D. DE SOUSA COSTA, *As Concordatas portuguesas*, Braga, 1966, 11-15. After this study had been completed I discovered another work which deals with similar materials: JAMES M. MULDOON, *The Medieval Origins of the State: The Contributions of the Canonists from Gratian to Hostiensis*, Cornell University Unpub. Diss., 1965, esp. pp. 146-148, 171-173. I am grateful to Professor Muldoon for permission to read his work and for several discussions concerning this topic and to Professors Caspary and Kuttner for permission to read 'The Deposition of Richard II' in proof. Professor Caspary has been kind enough to discuss several points with me in correspondence.

law, particularly in so far as his work involves a study of changing concepts of kingship during the later middle ages (5).

I

Innocent addressed *Grandi* to:

> *Baronibus communitatibus, consiliis tam civitatum quam castrorum et aliorum locorum, ac universis militibus et populis per regnum Portugalliae constitutis* (6).

The *arenga* consists of a series of observations on the aims and responsibilities of Christian kingdoms, the benefit to Christendom when these aims are fulfilled, and its grief when they are rent by discords, allow the ardor of devotion to cool, neglect justice, and permit evil to flourish. When these kingdoms are deflected from their proper courses it is the duty of the pope to see to their reform, just as it is his duty to maintain good kingdoms in a state of prosperity (7).

The *narratio* summarizes the events in Portugal's recent history which have led to the issuing of the decretal. Sancho, led on by wicked counsel, had violated many ecclesiastical liberties, made numerous oppressions and exactions of churches and monasteries, and had permitted his officials to do the same. Certain prelates of the kingdom had appealed to Innocent's predecessors, and Gregory IX, after many admonitions, interdicts, and sentences of excommunication, had finally forced Sancho to promise to restore their original liberties and goods to those churches and monasteries whose rights he had violated. Sancho, however, not only neglected to keep his promise but increased his oppres-

---

(5) Two recent papers which survey the importance of studies on the medieval Canon law are A. STICKLER, *Die Bedeutung der klassischen Kanonistik für die Geschichtswissenschaft des Mittelalters*, in: *Resumés des communications*, *XIe Congrès International des Sciences Historiques*, *Stockholm*, 1960, Uppsala, 1960, 98-100, and B. TIERNEY, *Medieval Canon Law and Western Constitutionalism*, in: *Catholic Historical Review* 52 (1966), 1-17.

(6) The text of *Grandi* here cited is that of FRIEDBERG, Vol. II, cols. 971-974.

(7) 'Exultamus in Domino gaudio, quum christianae professionis regna sic salubri diriguntur statu... Vehementi autem dolore turbamur si quando regna ipsa... scinduntur discordiis, circa fidei cultum remisso devotionis ardore tepescunt, iustitiam negligunt, et in se ipsis permittunt illicita perpetrari... Nos convenit, ut christianorum regna quae in statu sunt prospero, incommutabiliter in illo regantur, et quae periculoso ruere dignoscuntur, reformatione laudabili reparentur'.

sions of the churches. Not only ecclesiastical but lay goods and rights were violated. Because of the king's negligence criminals of all kinds were free to do as they liked without fear of punishment. Others were free to contract marriages within the prohibited degrees, to steal the goods of churches, and to create clear dangers to the faith, thus leading their own souls and the souls of others into the danger of heresy (8).

The cause of this disorder was the king's own negligence (*negligentia*), his idleness (*desidia*), his acquiescence in wicked counsel, and his pusillanimity. He neither defended nor in any way cared for those things which had been placed in his charge against the incursions of the Saracens. Because of royal indifference many individuals, clerical and lay, had again appealed, this time to Innocent, to correct the evils of the realm. The pope had attempted unsuccessfully to force Sancho to act in two previous letters. From day to day the evils of the kingdom grew worse on account of Sancho's negligence and idleness. Innocent, therefore, wishing to relieve the kingdom from its adversities (in part at least because Portugal was a financial tributary of the papacy) decided to take the following steps. The Count of Boulogne, who would by law of the kingdom succeed to the throne if Sancho should die without heirs, is to assume the *cura et administratio generalis et libera* of the kingdom, as much for the welfare (*utilitas*) of the king himself as for that of the realm. Innocent adds the reserva-

(8) ' Ceterum castra, villas, possessiones et alia iura regalia, idem rex propter ipsius desidiam, suique cordis imbecillitatem deperire permittens, ac passim et illicite malignorum acquiescens consiliis... Terras insuper et alia christianorum bona in confinio Saracenorum posita non defendens, ea infidelibus devastanda, seu etiam occupanda ex animi pusillanimitate relinquit. Et licet a supradictis praelatis, ut ad corrigenda praemissa, pluraque alia nefanda, quorum seriosa narratio fastidium generaret, ardenter, ut tenetur, assurgeret, monitus fuit diligenter, idem tamen, eorum monitionibus obauditis, id efficere non curavit; propter quod nos episcoporum, abbatum, priorum et aliorum tam religiosorum, quam saecularium regni eiusdem conquestionibus et clamosis insinuationibus excitati, regem ipsum per nostras litteras ut praemissa corrigeret rogandum duximus attente... '. Cf. the remarks of Innocent's biographer, Nicholas da Curbio, *Vita Innocenti Papae IV*, in E. BALUZE, *Miscellanea Historia*, Lucca, 1761, Vol. I, 194-206 at c. 20: ' Rex Portugalliae Sancius, qui erat circa regni sui regimen multiplici negligentia et ignavia iam defectus, propter quod pupillo non iudicabat causa viduae ad ipsum non ingrediens deperiebat, Ecclesie destruebantur et monasteria, ipsum regnum et multipliciter quassabatur, meritis ipsius accusatis et examinatus in ipso consilio ad petitionem et instantiam praelatorum ipsius regni... '. For the question of conciliar deposition, see below, n. 57.

tion that he does not intend by this action to deprive Sancho (or such legitimate issue as he may have) of the kingship (*regnum adimere*) that is, of the royal dignity, but only of the administration, the governance, of the realm so that the kingdom may be saved by the providence of Afonso from the danger of desstruction (9).

The emphasis of Innocent's thought in *Grandi* falls heavily upon Sancho's inadequacy and upon the evil advantage which others have been able to take of the king's negligence and ineptitude and not on the criminal character of the king himself, as had been, for example, the case in the deposition of Frederick II (10). Sancho was not in Innocent's eyes a *rex iniquus* or *tyrannus,* a criminal ruler, but a *rex inutilis,* an inadequate one. Innocent's action against Sancho was determined by the direction of canonists' speculation on the nature of kingship and on the problem of royal inadequacy. Canonist's theories had been based in turn upon the general development of medieval political thought from the fourth to the twelfth centuries.

During this period kingship had been the chief means by which increasingly articulate theories of justice, law and polity took shape out of the amorphous tribal collectives of post-Roman Europe. Throughout its early history the institution was shaped by such diverse influences as Old Testament political ideas, Roman legal thought, patristic interpretations of Scripture, and Celtic and Germanic custom. Political discussions from the eighth century on often appeared to weld these elements into a homo-

---

(9) ' Grandi non immerito... Mandamus, quatenus dilectum filium nobilem virum comitem Boloniensem, praefati regis Portugalliae fratrem, de devotione, probitate ac circumspectione multipliciter commendatum, qui eidem regi, si absque legitimo decederet filio, iure regni succederet, quique examinatae dilectionis affectu, quo vos et praedictum regnum prosequitur, magnanimitate ac potentia sibi plurimum suffragantibus, regnum ipsum maturius reformaturus firma credulitate speratur, praesertim quum ad curam et administrationem generalem et liberam regni eiusdem, tam pro saepe dicti regis quam ipsius regni utilitate... Per hoc non intendimus memorato regi vel ipsius legitimo filio, si quem habuerit, praedictum regnum adimere; sed potius sibi et eidem regno destructioni exposito, ac vobis ipsis in vita ipsius regis per sollicitudinem et providentiam comitis consulere supra dicti '.

(10) Innocent's decretal *Ad apostolice* of 17 July, 1245 is in the *Liber Sextus* of Boniface VIII, 2. 14. 2. There is a useful condensation in G. PILATI, *Chiesa e stato nei primi quindici secoli*, Rome, 1961, 235: ' Et ut ad praesens de ceteris eius sceleribus taceamus, quattuor gravissima commisit: Deiuravit... pacem violavit... perpetravit sacrilegum... capi faciens cardinales... de heresi quoque... suspectus habetur (facta criminosa declarantur)... '.

geneous structure of political ideas strengthened by the formation of a vocabulary of ecclesiastically-inspired political categories based chiefly upon patristic interpretations of Scripture and surviving ideas of Roman law. Yet the homogeneity of early medieval political theory was at best forced. Ideas of kingship centered chiefly upon the moral character of the *rex iustus,* the just king, and the *tyrannus,* the tyrant. The just ruler followed the political-moral precepts laid down in patristic and later ecclesiastical writings. The *tyrannus* opposed his own will to that of the divine source of his authority (11).

In practice, of course, medieval kings often faced problems far which they found little practical guidance in ecclesiastical political thought. The clear dividing-line which existed in terms of morality often was of little use when applied to the practical difficulties of governance. Few kings, judged by this latter scale, were completely just; few, on the other hand, were totally depraved. As aspects of kingship became more sharply delineated during the ninth century and after, other categories of kingship began to appear in political literature. In the twelfth and thirteenth centuries there emerged the paradoxical figure of the *tyrannus utilis,* the efficient tyrant — Roger II of Sicily (12). At the same time a complementary category, that of the *rex inutilis,* the useless king, began to engage the attention of jurists. During the twelfth century, as Dr. Wieruszowski points out, " under the impact of new ideas infiltrating the area of political thought from more realistic quarters, the dividing line between *rex iustus* and

---

(11) The literature on medieval notions of tyranny is voluminous. Some of the most useful works are: W. PARSONS, *The Medieval Theory of the Tyrant,* in: 4 *Review of Politics* (1942), 129-143; F. KERN, *Gottesgnadentum und Widerstandsrecht im Früheren Mittelalter,* 2nd. ed. by R. BUCHNER, Münster, 1954, 334-338. This appendix is not in the English version of the work: S. B. CHRIMES, trans. *Kingship and Law in the Middle Ages,* Oxford, 1939; A. J. and R. L. CARLYLE, *A History of Medieval Political Theory in the West,* Vol. I, 172-173, 221-222, 228-234, 250-2; Vol. III, 38, 52-72, 73, 112-146; C. H. MCILWAIN, *The Growth of Political Thought in the West,* New York, 11th printing, 1959, 285ff; J. SPÖRL, *Gedanken zum Widerstandsrecht und Tyrannenmord im Mittelalter,* in: *Widerstandsrecht und Grenzen der Staatsgewalt,* ed. B. PFISTER and G. HILDMANN, Berlin, 1956, 11-32 with good bibliography of recent studies.

(12) See HELENE WIERUSZOWSKI, *Roger II of Sicily, Rex-Tyrannus, in Medieval Political Thought,* in: *Speculum* 38 (1963), 46-78. For the same king more recently, Cf. R. ELZE, *Zum Königtum Rogers II. von Sizilien,* in: *Festschrift Percy Ernst Schramm,* Wiesbaden, 1964, Vol. I, 102-116.

tyrannus begins to fade away" (13). The patristic and Carolingian notion of kingship as an office, a *ministerium* within the church — what Ladner has called the "functional" theory of kingship — gradually gave way to the idea of kingship as an office which functioned primarily for the public welfare, the *publica utilitas* of the kingdom (14). The king became less the *minister Dei* than the *minister utilitatis publicae* (15). Parallel changes occurred also in the related concepts of *dignitas, maiestas, status,* crown, community, and public law (16). *Grandi* and *Ad apostolice,* the decretal which pronounced the deposition of Frederick II, represented the ultimate conclusions reached by thirteenth-century canonists on the subject of rulers who, through criminal acts or negligence, became unfit to rule over Christian subjects. When the fourteenth century witnessed what Kern called "the substitution of a constitutional for an ecclesiastical procedure" in deposition proceedings against legitimate rulers, contemporary lawyers and propagandists were often to turn for guidance to the principles summed up in the work of Innocent IV and other thirteenth-century glossators of the Canon law (17).

The charges listed in *Grandi* constitute a reliable, if strongly biased approach to the study of Sancho's reign, since they are based upon the most copious source of evidence for the period, the large body of papal correspondence dealing with the realm between 1223 and 1245 (18). Although the papal correspondence

---

(13) WIERUSZOWSKI, p. 78.

(14) G. B. LADNER, *Aspects of Medieval Thought on Church and State*, in: *Review of Politics* 9 (1947), 403-422, and IDEM, *The Concepts of Ecclesia and Christianitas and their Relation to the Idea of Papal Plenitudo Potestatis from Gregory VII to Boniface VIII*, in: *Miscellanea Historiae Pontificiae* 18, Rome, 1954, 49-78.

(15) See, e.g., ERNA BUSCHMANN, *Ministerium Dei — idoneitas. Um ihre Deutung aus den mittelalterlichen Fürstenspiegeln*, in: *Historisches Jahrbuch* 82 (1962), 70-102. The polar terms *idoneus* and *indignus* which medieval writers used most frequently possessed chiefly moral implications which comprehended the more specifically political categories of the *tyrannus* and the *rex inutilis*.

(16) For discussions of much recent scholarship on these terms, see GAINES POST, *Studies in Medieval Legal Thought: Public Law and the State*, 1100-1322, Princeton, 1964; ERNST KANTOROWICZ, *The King's Two Bodies*, Princeton, 1957. Some contrary views may be found in WALTER ULLMANN, *Principles of Government and Politics in the Middle Ages*, N.Y., 1966.

(17) See, esp. G. CASPARY, *The Deposition of Richard II and the Canon Law, passim.* The citation from KERN is from S. B. CHRIMES, trans., *Kingship and Law in the Middle Ages* Oxford, 1939, p. 126.

(18) I have traced one hundred ninety-eight papal letters for Portugal during the pe-

provides a distinctly onesided view of Portuguese history during the first half of the thirteenth century, it does provide an adequate background for a study of Innocent's action and its immediate political and legal consequences.

From 1185 to 1245 Portugal was the scene of a struggle between the monarchy and the lay and clerical magnates not unlike similar conflicts in other contemporary kingdoms (19). The king and his advisors attempted continually to strengthen the financial and judicial powers of the monarchy, and the magnates struggled to preserve intact their established rights and immunities. The political conclusion of this conflict was the deposition of Sancho, although the reigns of Sancho I (1185-1211) Afonso II (1211-1223) and Sancho II (1223-1245-48) all reflect parallel political disputes. In terms of the specific quarrel between king and clergy, Afonso III (1245-48-1279) later encountered difficulties similar to those of the brother whom he had helped to remove. The problems which lay at the heart of Portuguese political difficulties in Sancho's reign were not then entirely new to Portugal, nor can they safely be attributed exclusively to Sancho's personal inepti-

---

riod 1223-1245, of which at least one-third deal with the relations between Sancho and the Portuguese higher clergy. The chief locations of these documents are listed above, n. 3. The best history of the period is that of A. HERCULANO, *Historia de Portugal*, 8 vols., 9th ed. Lisbon, 1916-17, esp. Vols. IV and V (hereafter HERCULANO IV or V). There exists an unacknowledged English translation of parts of HERCULANO's history in E. MCMURDO, *History of Portugal*, 2 vols., London, 1888, but this work lacks HERCULANO's apparatus and often omits important passages without notice. There are no contemporary chronicles. Later chronicles are RUY DE PINA, *Cronica do... D. Sancho II*, Lisbon, 1728; *Cronicas dos sete primeiros Reis de Portugal*, ed. C. DE SILVA TAROUCA in: *Fontes narrativas da historia portuguesa*, No. 1, Vol. I, Lisbon, 1952, 211-246; A. DE MAGELHAES BASTO, *Cronica de cinco Reis de Portugal*, Vol. I, Porto, 1945. For a general discussion of the chronicle sources, see MAGELHAES BASTO, *Estudios. Cronistas e cronicas antigas, Fernão Lopes e a ' Cronica de* 1419 ', Coimbra, 1959. No recent history supersedes that of HERCULANO. Sancho's reign is discussed in H. V. LIVERMORE, *A New History of Portugal*, Cambridge, 1966, 74-80, (hereafter cited as LIVERMORE). The best study of the ecclesiastical problems of the reign is that of A. E. REUTER, *Königtum und Episkopat in Portugal im 13. Jahrhundert*, in: *Abhandlungen zur mittleren und neueren Geschichte*, Heft 69, Berlin-Grünewald, 1928 (hereafter cited as REUTER). For the earlier period, see C. ERDMANN, *Das Papsttum und Portugal im ersten Jahrhundert der portugiesischen Geschichte*, *Abh. Akad. preuss.*, Berlin, 1928. Cf. MIGUEL DE OLIVEIRA, *Historia ecclesiastica de Portugal*, Lisbon, 1940, 89-96. The best guide to the history and literature of medieval Portugal is now A. H. DE OLIVIERA MARQUES, *Guia do estudante de historia medieval portuguesa*, Lisbon, 1964.

(19) A good brief account is to be found in LIVERMORE, pp. 67-80.

tude. Several characteristics of Portuguese kingship, of the juridical position of the magnates, and of the political problems of the latter part of Sancho's reign all served to aggravate the conditions which had developed in the twelfth century and culminated in *Grandi*.

The king of Portugal was the hereditary ruler of a territory which had declared itself an independent kingdom in 1139 (20). In 1143 Afonso Henriques had declared his realm to be a financial tributary of the papacy, but papal recognition of Portuguese autonomy did not come about till 1179 (21). The kings of Portugal were not anointed, nor were they crowned in a liturgical ceremony (22). In the eyes of the papacy, the clergy, and Por-

(20) For early Portuguese kingship, see H. DE GAMA BARROS, *História da administração publica em Portugal nos seculos XII a XV*, 2nd. ed. by T. DE SOUSA SOARES, Lisbon, 1945-54, Vol. I, 149-372, Vol. III, 304-320. Cf. A. CAETANO DO AMARAL, *Para a historia da legislação e costumes de Portugal*, ed. M. LOPES DE ALMEIDA, Porto, 1945, Vol. III, 297, 315-320, 394.

(21) The earliest papal communications with Portugal are discussed and printed in C. ERDMANN, *Papsturkunden in Portugal*, *Abh. Ges. Wiss. Göttingen*, Neue Folge, Bd. 20.3, Berlin, 1927. Afonso Henriques had originally offered the pope a yearly tribute of four ounces of gold. There exists a falsified bull of Innocent II which confirms the gift (ERDMANN, *Papsturkunden*, no. 32, pp. 19-23). In 1179 the king changed the tribute to one hundred ounces yearly in addition to a lump payment of one thousand pieces immediately (ERDMANN, *Papsturkunden*, no. 81, pp. 254-255). Portugal's financial obligations to the papacy, noted by Innocent IV in *Grandi*, are the subject of numerous papal letters of the late twelfth and early thirteenth centuries. In 1190 Clement III reminded Sancho I of the tribute which the king had evidently neglected to pay (ERDMANN, no. 124, pp. 342-343; *QE* 25-26). In 1198 Innocent III wrote to Sancho I citing earlier papal letters of Lucius II, Clement III, and Alexander III in the decretal *Serenitatem regiam* (*QE* 29-30; POTTHAST, 103; cf. A. LUCHAIRE, *Les royautés vassalles au saint siège*, Vol. V of his *Innocent III*, Paris, 1908, 8-10). Later in the same year Innocent III wrote again (*In eminenti sedis*, *QE* 31; POTTHAST, 447), and again in 1209 (*QE* 35). The problem is the subject of two letters of 1212 (POTTHAST, 4432; *QE* 72). In 1218 Honorius III mentions the annual tribute as being two marks of gold (*QE* 72; POTTHAST, 5663). All questions concerning payment appear to have been settled during the reign of Afonso II. For the general aspects of the tribute, see W. E. LUNT, *Papal Revenues of the Middle Ages*, in: *Columbia Records of Civilization: Sources and Studies*, No. XIX, 2 vols., N. Y., 1934, Vol. I, 57-64. See also D. MAURICIO, *Portugal e o censo a Santa Se*, in: *Broteria* 21, 98-107.

(22) Not until 1428 did Portuguese kings receive papal permission to be anointed. The bull of Martin IV is discussed by GAMA BARROS, Vol. III, p. 312, n. 2. The study of P. MEREA (*A aclamação dos nossos reis*, in: *Revista dos Centenarios*, no. 16, Lisbon, 1940) noted by SOUSA SOARES, has been revised and expanded with a useful bibliography under the title, *Sobre a aclamação dos nossos reis*, in: *Revista Portuguesa de Historia* 10 (1962), 411-417. However, after the pontificate of Gregory VII, coronation and anointing appear to have had much more ef-

tuguese laymen, the king's chief role was that of a crusading warrior whose primary duty was to drive the Moors from the Iberian peninsula. Many subsequent conflicts between Sancho and his clergy hinge upon this conception of the kingship. Later accusations of inefficient generalship directed at Sancho carried more weight in Portugal than they might have elsewhere. For the king of Portugal crusading was a *raison d'etre;* failure there meant ultimate failure as a Christian ruler (23).

The apparent unity of purpose which the crusading ideal gave to the kingdom did not contribute greatly toward the unification of dissident political elements into a whole. Although the amount of royally-owned territory and royally-controlled justice was greater in Portugal than in any kingdom north of the Pyreness, the extent of land and judicial power outside the king's hands was considerable. The king could demand such tribute as the *colheita* (free maintenance during his visits to most castles and towns), monopolize coinage, and command extraordinary services and restrictions of local privileges for the purpose of the crusade. His power was, however, continually weakened by the magnates' vigorous efforts to maintain their own established rights and their equally vigorous resistance to the royal *inquirições*, inquiries into the origins and legitimacy of many titles, land rights, and jurisdictional preserves (24).

The clergy derived its great strength from its extensive territorial and jurisdictional rights and from its position as director of the spiritual life of a crusading kingdom (25). It constituted far more a political than a moral opposition to the king. It had exercised its strength in earlier conflicts with Sancho I and Afonso

---

fect in the eyes of subjects than in those of the church. See E. KANTOROWICZ, *The King's Two Bodies*, 318-328, and B. C. KEENEY, *The Medieval Idea of the State: The Great Cause*, 1291-2, in: *University of Toronto Law Journal* 8 (1949:50), 48-71.

(23) As late as the fifteenth century, kings of Portugal cited their military successes as their chief attributes. See F. M. ROGERS, ed. and trans., *The Obedience of a King of Portugal* (Minneapolis, 1958), a letter from King John II to Innocent VIII.

(24) The royal actions against the clerical and lay magnates consisted chiefly of *inquirições*, investigations into the legality of claimed rights and immunities similar to the English *Quo Warranto* proceedings. For the nobles, see GAMA BARROS, Vol. III, 341-496; for the clergy, *ibid.*, 13-289 and REUTER, *passim.*

(25) GAMA BARROS III, 13-289.

II from which it had emerged victorious (26). The brevity of these reigns, the pattern of misfortunes associated with each of their ends, the fact of Sancho's minority in 1223, and the precedent of crippling concessions which both of his immediate predecessors had made to the clergy constituted severe handicaps to successful rule at the outset of Sancho's majority (27).

Portugal also suffered from the extent of allodial lands entirely outside the royal control in the hands of the powerful nobility. The king, strengthened by none of the ties of feudal land tenure, was forced to depend almost entirely on the good will and personal loyalty of the *ricos homens* with whom he filled the offices of court (28). The role played by this powerful nobility during the reign of Afonso II and the minority of Sancho II is indicative of the extent to which the king's freedom of action was limited, not by constitutionalist theories of kingship *sub lege*, but by the actual resources of power outside royal control.

Sancho's reign has had two distinct schools of interpreters. Most of the papal correspondence, documents from the reign of Afonso III, and some modern historians put the case for the legitimacy of the deposition in the strongest possible terms. For these, " Sancho ruled badly in every conceivable way... (He) neglected the welfare of his subjects; clerics, widows, and children went unprotected... Churches, monasteries, and the nation's defences fell into disuse and ruin... (Sancho) presented an extreme case, in the sense that his ineptitude for rule was so acute " (29). On the other hand, other contemporary sources and other later historians suggest that Sancho was the unwitting victim of clerical avarice and papal political ambitions. Herculano, the greatest historian of medieval Portugal, is chief among the latter. Finally,

---

(26) See, for some general remarks, REUTER, pp. 8-20. For the disputes of 1211 see the papal letters *Graves oppressiones* (*QE* 26-37 and POTTHAST, 4001) and *Si diligenter* (*QE* 39 and POTTHAST 4187). For a recent study, see A. D. DE SOUSA COSTA, *Mestre Silvestre e Mestre Vicente, juristas das contendas entre D. Afonso II e suas irmas*, in: *Itinerarium* 9 (1963), 249-311.

(27) HERCULANO, IV, 161-180; REUTER, 16-24. A letter issued by Honorius III (PRESSUTTI, 5135) takes Sancho and the kingdom under the protection of the Holy See. Two other letters of the same date (October 22, 1224; PRESUTTI, 5136, 5137) announce the appointment of friar Gonsaldo as Apostolic Nuncio to Portugal during Sancho's minority and notify others in Portugal of the papal action.

(28) Discussed briefly in LIVERMORE, 67-69.

(29) P. RIESENBERG, *The Inalienability of Sovereignty*, 168-169.

there is a body of literature, chiefly of the genre known as the *cantigas de escarnho* (satirical broadsides somewhat resembling the Provençal *sirventes*) which frequently evinces great sympathy for Sancho's cause (30).

Neither of these positions seems now to be entirely tenable. Sancho's opposition cast its charges into a recognizable rhetoric of malfeasance whose terms had been shaped by jurists, chroniclers, and publicists between the ninth and the thirteenth centuries and which would remain in use till the end of the middle ages. His supporters, notably Herculano, tend to read back a distinct anticlericalism into the contemporary sources and to ignore the real problems of public law inherent in the two sets of conflicting claims. Sancho was certainly guilty of unwise and imprudent political behavior and of characteristic royal high-handedness, but he was far from being on the one hand the inept cipher described in the papal correspondence or on the other the heroic victim of papal visions of world monarchy (31).

The first of *Grandi*'s charges, that Sancho had violated legitimate ecclesiastical liberties, set the dominant tone for the papal correspondence throughout the king's reign and illuminates what was perhaps the chief cause of Sancho's troubles. At the very outset of his reign Sancho had been forced to make immense financial reparations to Estevam Soares, Archbishop of Braga, in order to lift the interdict placed upon the kingdom during his father's lifetime and to be able to bury his father in consecrated ground (32). The cause of the interdict and of Afonso II's ex-

---

(30) Cf. Carolina Michaelis de Vasconcellos, *Em volta de Sancho II*, in: *Lusitania* 2 (1924), 7-25. There is a new edition of these *cantigas* by M. Rodrigues Lapa, *Cantigas, d'escarnho e de mal dizer: dos cancioneiros medievais galego-portugueses*, Coimbra, 1965. Brief notice of this literary support is taken by A. J. Saraiva, *Historia de cultura em Portugal*, Lisbon, 1950, Vol. I, 310-312 and A. E. Beau, *Die Entwicklung des portugiesischen Nationalbewusstseins*, Hamburg, 1945, 41-42.

(31) The terminology of medieval political opprobrium consisted chiefly of maxims and moral categories which pertained primarily to the typical ruler rather than to the individual man. Sancho, by becoming, for a time at least, a *tyrannus* (see next note) inherited many of the characteristics of the *tyrannus*. For the use of these political clichés in panegyric, see, e.g., A. Kühne, *Das Herrscherideal des Mittelalters und Kaiser Friedrich I.*, in: *Leipziger Studien auf dem Gebiet der Geschichte*, Vol. V. 2 (Leipzig, 1898), 4-44.

(32) Sancho's character undergoes several distinct changes in the papal correspondence between Honorius III and Innocent IV. The letters of Honorius often picture the king as an active oppressor of the church (cf. Pressutti, 4683). In 1222 Honorius had written to Afon-

communication had been, characteristically, an earlier dispute between the old king and the archbishop concerning royal encroachments upon the financial and jurisdictional preserves of the higher clergy (33). The *Concordata* of 1223, the instrument of Sancho's agreement with Soares, resembles the acts of the Cortes of 1211, which had consisted chiefly of similar concessions which Afonso II had made to the clergy at the outset of his own reign (34).

Between 1223 and 1228 and again between 1232 and 1240 Portugal witnessed periods of growing antagonism between king and clergy interrupted briefly by successful military campaigns against the Arabs and concluded by temporary reconciliations between political opponents whose underlying enmity only left the way open for further conflicts. After 1240 Sancho's failure to continue his crusading efforts and his increasingly intransigent attitude toward the claims of the higher clergy and the nobility gave his opponents no alternative that they could perceive other than that which resulted in a joint effort to bring about his downfall. Between 1241 and 1245 the efforts of most of the Portuguese higher clergy and of a large part of the nobility were directed to this end. The appearance of Afonso of Boulogne as a likely candidate for the Portuguese throne and the far-reaching concerns of Innocent IV for the political stability of Christendom resulted in the promulgation of *Grandi* and in the three years of intermittent warfare required to enforce its terms upon the kingdom.

The first of these periods of heightened antagonism may be said to begin with the reconciliation and concessions of 1223. Sancho's difficulty in observing these terms is reflected in the papal registers dealing with this period. The registers indicate a large number of complaints on the part of the clergy against the exac-

---

so II threatening him with outright deposition: " Alioquin nos non solum praedictas sententiae faciemus frequentius publicari... verum etiam crescente contumacia tua severius contra te... procedemus, terram tuam exponendo regibus et principibus occupandam... ' (POTTHAST 6860; *QE* 82). For the early thirteenth-century context of such papal threats, see O. HAGENEDER, *Das päpstliche Recht der Fürstenabsetzung*, in: *Archivum Historiae Pontificiae* 1 (1963), 53-95 at 71. Gregory IX deals far more with the depredations of the royal officials than with the criminal character of the king himself.

(33) REUTER, 11-20; HERCULANO IV, 1-160.

(34) The *Concordata* of 1223 is printed in GABRIEL PEREIRA DE CASTRO, *De Manu Regia*, a work which I have been unable to consult. See also *QE* 89-93; HERCULANO IV, 162-167; REUTER 23.

tions of royal officials (35), on the part of the monastic orders against the exactions of the secular clergy (36), and on the part of the bishops of Lisbon and Oporto against the exactions of the king (37). These complaints indicate not only the absence of a centralized judicial authority, but the presence of numerous local centers af power, each armed with rights and immunities and bent on serving its own interests, often in the name, but in the name only, of serving the king. The crusading campaign of 1226 did not lessen the antagonism appreciably, and in 1228 the complaints and cross-complaints had become so widespread that Gregory IX sent Jean d'Abbeville to Portugal as papal legate with authority to listen to all complaints and to work out a solution to Portugal's difficulties. The legate's efforts at mediation and ecclesiastical re-organization appear to have been, for a time, at least, successful (38). The *Cortes* of 1228 proclaimed a new crusading campaign, inaugurated a resettlement program in the newly-rehabilitated see of Idanha-Guarda, and witnessed another temporary reconciliation between king and clergy.

The second period, although it in a sense duplicates the events

---

(35) See Presutti, 4664, 4665, 4672, 4674, 4678; Auvray, 71; *QE* 94, 100-101. Most of these complaints concern royal judges claiming jurisdiction in ecclesiastical territories, diocesan clerics who leave their benefices in order to serve the king, and royal officials' (*praetores, alvaziles, et maiordomos ac alios regis Portugalensis satellites*) exactions of goods and money.

(36) The question of the rivalry among secular clergy, the religious orders, and the military orders is extremely involved. Sancho favored the military orders, giving them immense grants of land and jurisdiction, and invited a number of religious orders into the kingdom. These groups generally supported him, and the role of the secular clergy as middlemen between papal financial claims and the kings served to alienate them further from royal favor. Herculano and Almeida (*Historia de la Igreja em Portugal*, Coimbra, 1910-1922, Vol. I) cite an otherwise unknown papal letter of 17 Dec., 1226 (Almeida, *Igreja*, 393) reflecting some of this rivalry. Other documents are: Abranches, 74, 77, 79, 80; *QE* 101, 101-102, 102 (Auvray, 169); Abranches, 84, 86, 88, 89, 95 (*QE* 9, 105), 91, 92.

(37) Presutti, 4664, 4665, 4666, 4667, 4672, 4673, 4679, 4683, 4684, 6141 (*QE* 94), 6188 (*QE* 95-97; Raynaldi, *ad. an.* 1227, no. 10; Potthast, 7656), 6187 (*QE* 97-98); Auvray, 70 (*QE* 99-100). The lack of a centralized administration reflects Portugal's separation of centers of real power. The wealth and power of the king could not make headway against the entrenched liberties of the clergy and the nobles, although elsewhere, e.g., England and France, such centralization had begun much earlier.

(38) Cf. the letter of Gregory IX of 13 July, 1232 (Auvray, 829) concerning the legate's suspension of 1,786 clerics of illegitimate birth from their benefices. For the mission generally, see Reuter, 27-29, Herculano IV, 190-205; Almeida, 397-398.

of the first, is characterized by a greater intensity on the part of each side and by the rise of new clerical opponents of the king. Pedro Salvadores succeded Martinho Rodrigues in the see of Oporto, and Silvestre Godinho, who had succeeded Estevam Soares in the archiepiscopal see of Braga in 1228, began to complain of royal activities even more vociferously than had his predecessor. Johannes Falbertus (João Rolis) succeeded Sueiro Gomes in the Lisbon episcopate. The election of Johannes illustrates both the character of Sancho's new opponents and the extreme seriousness of the steps which both sides began to take. In 1234 Sueiro of Lisbon died. His successor, D. Paio, lived only a few months and was in turn succeeded by Johannes, papal physician, dean of the Lisbon cathedral chapter, and a strong supporter of clerical privileges. Johannes' rival in the episcopal election, Sancho Gomes, obtained royal support and urged the king to prevent Johannes from entering his new office (39). On one occasion, the royal forces, commanded by Ferdinand of Serpa, the king's brother, pursued Johannes' friends into a church. When his own soldiers refused to violate their sanctuary, Ferdinand turned a troop of Moslem mercenaries after his quarry. The mercenaries killed Johannes' friends, destroyed his goods, and desecrated the church into which they had fled. This royal offense, coupled with another quarrel between Sancho himself and Pedro Salvadores more than outweighed Sancho's crusading successes in 1228 and 1232. The punishment levelled against Ferdinand of Serpa and Sancho and their humble acceptance of it indicates both the psychological and juridical disadvantage at which they stood (40).

By 1240, Sancho and Ferdinand of Serpa had again made peace with the pope and the Portuguese prelates, although Ferdinand's acceptance of an unusually harsh penance appears to have alienated the brothers permanently (41). The interdict and

---

(39) For Silvestre, see the studies of Sousa Costa (above, n. 26) and I. da Rosa Pereira, *Silvestre Godinho, um canonista portugues*, extract from *Lumen* (1962). For the dispute, see Reuter, 32-33; Herculano IV, 274-286; Auvray, 1525, 1664, 1669, 1670, 2019 (= Potthast 9495), 2388-2390, 2476, 4976-4977, 4994-4995, 4997, 5002-5003, 5005-5011, 5316 (*QE* 135-8); *QE* 123-124.

(40) Herculano IV, 345-347; Reuter, 29-32, 34.

(41) Ferdinand's oath is in Auvray, 4996. For the new truce, Reuter, 34-36; Auvray,

excommunications were lifted, and a new crusading effort was planned. This settlement, however, was to be no longer-lasting than the others. The crusade failed to materialize, and Sancho, unwisely antagonizing his clerical opponents, married Mecia Lopes de Haro, daughter of the Lord of Biscay. The clergy considered this marriage a direct affront, since Sancho and Mecia Lopes were consanguineous within the fourth degree. Besides the ecclesiastical difficulties which the marriage presented, there arose a number of political problems centered on the marriage, and one may see the years between 1241 and 1245 as the period in which political and ecclesiastical opposition to Sancho began to coalesce. The marriage was the first, but not the only step in the process (42).

The clergy were not the only ones in Portugal who concerned themselves with Sancho's marriage. The king's brother, Afonso of Boulogne (43), who, according to Herculano, had harbored at his court those Portuguese nobles who fled from Sancho's disfavor, appears from this period on to have worked actively with the Portuguese clergy for the removal of Sancho. Whether Afonso was, as Herculano claims, a permanent center of political opposition to his brother since his marriage to the heiress of Boulogne in 1238, is not entirely demonstrable. However, Afonso is designated as the major complainant in Innocent IV's decretal annulling the marriage in February, 1245 (44). The cause for Afonso's role in the actions against Sancho after 1241 may well have been his concern that the marriage, valid or not, might produce an heir whose claims to succeed Sancho would, according to Portuguese custom, be considerably stronger than his own (45).

5210 (= *QE* 140-141; ABRANCHES 111), 5367 (= *QE* 141; *Monarchia Lusitana* IV, fol. 144; POTTHAST 10989; ABRANCHES 112).

(42) For Mecia Lopes, see HERCULANO V, 12-13, 281-288. Her depiction in the sources is far closer to that of the characteristic wicked queen than to an individual description. Cf. JOHANNES MARIANA, *De rebus Hispaniae*, Mainz, 1519, 545-546.

(43) Afonso, apparently by the patronage of Blanche of Castille, had married the heiress of Boulogne in 1238. REUTER, 36-38.

(44) The decree of invalidation is *Sua nobis dilectus filius* of 12 February, 1245 (BERGER, 995; *QE* 144).

(45) For the terms of succession, see GAMA BARROS III, p. 297. In his commentary on *Grandi* Innocent IV was to note briefly this aspect of the case (*Apparatus super libros Decretalium*, Venice, 1481, fol. 45r *ad v. regni*): "*Speciale est in regno quam reges non possunt privare nec dum filios nec fratres vel alios consanguineos ex stirpe paterna descendentes a regno sola voluntate*". For the general development of juridical thought in Portugal, see M. J. DE AL-

Moreover, the connections between Afonso of Boulogne and Innocent IV on the one hand and Afonso and Blanche of Castille and Louis IX of France on the other, although never thoroughly traced, may have given Afonso support as great as that offered by the Portuguese nobility and clergy (46).

Sancho's failure to carry out his crusading plans also counted heavily against him. Indeed, his earlier military successes had stood him in good stead with Rome and had on occasion served as a buffer between his own high-handedness and the clerical wrath which had plagued him since his succession (47). Some of the narrative sources and some of the papal correspondence strongly imply a progressive mental and physical dilapidation on the part of the king, partly from the supposed magical powers of his new wife (48). Apocryphal as these suggestions probably are, they provide an imaginative dimension to the very real political problems which the king was unable to solve. The figures of evil queens and wicked counsellors are familiar motifs in medieval and renaissance political rhetoric, but the political difficulties which they always imply are real enough. However technically inaccurate these charges were, they were a characteristic response to what thirteenth-century men considered bad governance.

After 1241 ecclesiastical and political opposition to Sancho began to coalesce. Afonso's opposition to the marriage, the articulate hostility of a new generation of clerical opponents (and perhaps their greater legal skill), and the failure of Sancho's later advisors to measure up to the diplomatic and legal ability of the earlier great chancellors Mestre Julião and Mestre Vicente (49), all contributed to a unified opposition which made it even less likely

---

MEIDA COSTA, *Para a historia da cultura juridica medieva em Portugal*, in: *Boletim de Faculdade de Direito* 25, Coimbra, 1960, 253-276.

(46) The subject has never been thoroughly studied. See E. BERGER, *Saint Louis et Innocent IV*, Paris, 1893, p. 150.

(47) Sancho's campaigns are discussed briefly in C. SELVAGEM, *Portugal militar*, Lisbon, 1931, 86-90. For papal defense of Sancho see, e.g., the bulls of October, 1232 (AUVRAY, 926) and, more important, of August, 1234 (*QE* 121; ABRANCHES, 105).

(48) Cf. above, n. 42.

(49) The careers of these two great chancellors remain to be studied in full. See the remarks of POST, *Studies in Medieval Legal Thought*, p. 485 and SOUSA COSTA, above, n. 26. For Mestre Vicente, see now S. KUTTNER, *Emendationes et notae variae: I: " Wo war Vincentius Hispanus Bischof?"* in: *Traditio* 22 (1966), 471-474.

that the king might reach a political settlement on terms less disasterous than those of 1223 or 1228. Moreover, in 1241 another event took place which probably hastened Sancho's downfall. Frederick II intercepted a papal fleet off Pisa and scattered the prelates who were proceeding to Rome for general council. Among those who escaped Frederick and fled to Rome were some of Sancho's most persistent opponents. The prolonged stay of these prelates in Rome suggests to Herculano that this was the period in which the plans for the deposition were laid, and that from the autumn of 1241 on, Sancho's removal was a question of direct concern to the prelates, to Afonso and his French supporters, and to the pope himself (50).

The coincidence of a concerted opposition after 1241 and a simultaneous decline of Sancho's personal and political powers constitutes a neat, but hardly verifiable picture. The official descriptions of Sancho's ineptitude and lethargy are belied by his earlier crusading victories, by the vigor with which he pursued his exactions, and by his effective resistance so Afonso between 1245 and 1247. These descriptions, however, did reveal one important fact: in not having pursued the crusade, Sancho abandoned the one course of action which might have saved him. With support for his crusade gone, Sancho forfeited his strongest claim, not only to a status higher than that of his clergy, but to any right to rule at all. Sancho's political bad judgement, his inability to control large influential segments of the nobility and the clergy, and his inability to hold his own in the battle of charges and countercharges reflected in the papal correspondence resulted in the portrait drawn in the *narratio* of *Grandi*. In general, that portrait was the result of a political breakdown within the kingdom not unlike those which took place in other contemporary realms. But unlike some wiser and more fortunate rulers, Sancho was able to profit neither from the scientific jurisprudence of recent legal scholarship nor from the factionalism within the ranks of the nobility.

Between 1241 and 1245 Sancho remained militarily, but not politically, inactive. He continued his attempts to control clerical jurisdiction and to arrogate to himself more and more governmental power. With the accession of Innocent IV, however,

(50) A letter from the prelates to Gregory IX is in *QE* 141-142. See also REUTER, 34-36.

Sancho's opposition found a willing pope. Between February and July of 1245 four papal letters were issued for Portugal, each of which constituted one step in the process of removing Sancho from the throne. The first of these, the letter of anullment, mentions Afonso of Boulogne as complainant and declares the marriage invalid.

The second, dated March 20, is the decretal *Inter alia,* directly addressed to Sancho, which describes the state of Portugal in terms which were to be echoed almost verbatim in *Grandi* (51). The letter further states that if Sancho's outrages continue, they will put the well-being of both the kingdom and the soul of the king in great danger (52). Before allowing this to happen, says In-

---

(51) The full text is given only in Raynaldi (above, n. 3), *ad annum* 1245, no. 6 (Vol. 21, Tome II, pp. 318-319). *Dat. Lugduni* XIII *kal. ap. ann.* II, *Illustri Regi Portugalliae... Inter alia desiderabilia.* See above, nn. 6, 7: " Inter alia desiderabilia cordis nostri salutem fidelium, quorum regimini, licet immeriti, Deo praesumus disponente, principaliter affectantes grandi gaudio exultamus in Domino, cum ea nobis de ipsis fidelibus referuntur, per quae suarum profectus provenire dignoscitur animarum; et vehementi dolore turbamur, si nos illa de eis audire contingat, quae ipsis et aliis pravo exemplo salutis afferunt detrimentum: unde tanto laetitia majori replebimur, si cultui virtutum insistens studeas te ante oculos reddere divinae maiestatis acceptum, quanto plures ex hoc et a malo retrahere et ad exercitium bonitatis inducere comprobaris. Sane non sine gravi turbatione mentis audivimus, quod post clamores et querelas multiplices praelatorum et aliorum regni Portugalliae contra te super conculatione libertatis ecclesiasticae, aliisque oppressionibus ecclesiarum eiusdem regni depositas, et admonitiones frequentes tibi propter hoc a Rom. pontificibus nostris praedecessoribus; et provisiones super iis a felicis recordationis Gregorio Papa praedecessore nostro inter te et quosdam ex praelatis ipsis, ac promissiones a te in hac parte super articulis certis factas; tu circa malefactorum ipsus regni audaciam reprimendam sic negligens inveniris... '.

(52) The letter ends: ' Caeterum castra, villas, possessiones et alia iura regalia deperire permittens personarum tam ecclesiasticarum, quam saecularium, nobilium et ignobilium, occisiones nefarias, dum religioni non parcitur, nec sexui, vel aetati; rapinas, incestus, raptusque monialium et saeclarium mulierum; rusticorum et clericorum, ad negotiatorum tormenta gravia, quae ipsis a nonnullis regni praefati pro extorquenda ab ipsis pecunia infliguntur; ecclesiarum et coemeteriorum violationes et incendia, fractiones treugarum, et alia enormia, quae a tibi subjectis libere committuntur, scienter toleras: quin potius tot tantisque malis, dum ea praeteris impunita, consentire videris, et pandis aditum ad pejora. Terras insuper et alia Christianorum bona in confinio Sarracenorum posita non defendens, ea infidelibus occupanda relinquis. Et licet a supradictis praelatis, ut ad corrigenda praemissa pluraque alia nefanda, quorum coenosa narratio fastidium generaret, ardenter, ut teneris assurgeres, monitus fueris diligenter; tu tamen eorum monitionibus obauditis, id hactenus officere neglixisti. Nos igitur eidem regno super tam miserabili statu paterno condolentes affectu, et cupientes ipsum a tot respirare angustiis, totque oppresionibus relevari; serenitatem regiam monemus, rogamus, et hortamur attente in remissionem tibi peccaminum iniungentes, quatenus prudenter considerans, quod si omnipotens Dominus tuam super iis negli-

nocent, he will take steps to correct them. He appoints the bishops of Oporto and Coimbra and the Dominican prior to urge Sancho to make the necessary reforms and to report to the pope at the Council of Lyons if the king should prove intractable. The brief period between the promulgation of *Inter alia* and that of *Grandi* leads Herculano and others to conclude that the former was simply a technical ultimatum which the pope knew perfectly well Sancho could not carry out (53). Innocent, says Herculano, issued *Inter alia* simply in order to add a necessary charge of contumacy to the final decree of deposition.

The third document, the decretal *Cum zelo fidei*, was addressed to the Count of Boulogne and granted to him and his soldiers the customary crusading indulgences for his forthcoming campaign against the Moors (54). Herculano regards this document to be one further example of papal duplicity, a political move disguised as a crusading privilege (55). The final document is *Grandi*. As noted above, Sancho did not carry out Innocent's instructions, and the pope, considering the merits of Afonso, transferred to him the care of the realm, yet allowed Sancho to retain the *regnum*, or *dignitas*. In September, 1245, Afonso went to Paris, where he concluded a formal agreement with the Portuguese clergy similar to those of 1211, 1223, and 1228 (56), by

---

gentiam ad tempus forte sustineat, postremo tamen si in te, ac tuis contemnas errata corrigere, illam et hic impunitam non deseret et in futuro nihilominus ulciscetur gravius; sic ad corrigenda praemissa solerter et ferventer exurgas, ut culpas subditorum tuas per reprobabilem patientiam non efficias: sed in te ac ipsis proberis odire malitiam et diligere bonitatem; et de persona tua grata de caetero auctore Domino audiamus. Quod si forte, quod non credimus, fueris circa haec corrigenda remissus, nequaquam tolerare sedes Apostolica poterit, quin super iis ad salutem tuam dictique regni commode remedium adhibeat opportunum: et nihilominus venerabilibus fratribus nostris Portugallensi et Coimbriensi episcopis, ac dilecto filio priori fratrum Praedicatorum Coimbriensium litteris nostris iniungimus ut te ad id monentes attente, et efficaciter intendentes, qualiter super hoc faciendum duxeris, et de ipsorum circa te in hac parte processu, nos in concilio a nobis proximo celebrando certificare procurent'.

(53) HERCULANO V, 19-53.

(54) HERCULANO V, 30-46. The letter is POTTHAST, 11625; *QE* 146-147; *Monarchia Lusitana* IV, fol. 156[v]; ABRANCHES, 121. Cf. the earlier crusading privilege, *Terra sancta Christi dispersa* of January, 1245 (*QE* 143; ABRANCHES, 120; cf. POTTHAST, 11491, 11516, 11517).

(55) HERCULANO V, 30-46.

(56) For the agreement at Paris, see HERCULANO V, 49-60; *QE* 153-157; *Monarchia Lusitana* IV, fol. 278 (= *Cronicas de D. Sancho II*, 363-364); RUY DE PINA, *Cronica do... D. Sancho II*, 7-9; A. CAETANO DA SOUSA, *Provas* (above, n. 3), I, doc. no. 26; A. H. DE SOUSA

now almost a necessity for a new Portuguese ruler. Although Sancho and his allies put up a spirited resistance to Afonso's forces, the king had no choice by 1247 but to withdraw from the kingdom,

> *omni spe depulsus regni obtinendi, Toleti consenuit, viventi vectigalia Regis (Ferdinand III) liberalitate donata* (57).

Until his death, Sancho continued to use the title, *Dei gratia Rex Portugalliae;* at the same time, Afonso referred to his own capacity in official documents as that of *curator, governador,* or *visitator* of Portugal (58).

COSTA, *As concordatas portuguesas*, Braga, 1966, 15; *Cronicas dos sete primeiros reis de Portugal*, 218-222; LIVERMORE, 78-79.

(57) MARIANA, *De rebus Hispaniae*, 546. For RUY DE PINA, Sancho was 'a disgraced king... in life and death an example of human infelicity'. In 1735 Caetano da Sousa had Sancho neatly deposed 'by the three estates of the realm *com injuria de magestade*', *Historia genealogica da casa Real portuguesa*, rep. Coimbra, 1946, Vol. I, p. 100. Many scholars, including MANSI, long thought that *Grandi* and *Ad apostolice* had both been pronounced during the Council of Lyon. In MANSI, Vol. XXIII, *Grandi* is in fact printed among the *additiones* to the Council. The question of conciliar deposition had apparently been bruited about long before Mansi, however, since Johannes Andreae took note of it in his *Apparatus* to the *Liber Sextus* (*ad* 2.14.2 *Ad apostolice*): 'Et sine sententia vel licentia consilii, sententia papae sufficeret imperatorem, et quemcumque alium. 15.6.3 *alius*, ibi non dicitur quod in concilio facta fuerit depositio: enim ipse habet plenitudinem potestatis'. The deposition of Frederick II took place at the first and third sessions of the Council. See HEFELE-LECLERQ, *Histoire des conciles*, Vol. V, Paris, 1913, 1633-79 and P. POUZET, *Le Pape Innocent IV à Lyon — le Concile de* 1245, in: *Revue de l'histoire de l'église de France* 15 (1929), 281-318. For Innocent's views of his own authority, see M. PACAUT, *L'Autorité pontificale selon Innocent IV*, in: *Le moyen âge* 66 (1960), 85-120 and the recent studies of J. A. WATT, *The Theory of Papal Monarchy in the Thirteenth Century* (above, n. 1), and *Medieval Deposition Theory: A Neglected Canonist Consultatio from the First Council of Lyons*, in: *Studies in Church History*, Vol. II, G. J. Cuming, ed. London, 1965, 197-214. The case of Sancho, however, was not part of the council's business in any case. See S. KUTTNER, *Die Konstitutionen des ersten allgemeinen Konzils von Lyon*, in: *Studia et documenta historiae et iuris* 6, Rome, 1940, 70-131. KUTTNER's distinction between the conciliar and non-conciliar legislation of Innocent contradicts the brilliant, but quite false picture drawn by HERCULANO (V, p. 46) of Innocent haughtily waving *Grandi* and *Ad apostolice* under the noses of the assembled prelates and peremptorily including them as conciliar canons. For further Innocentian legislation, see P.-J. KESSLER, *Die Novellengesetzgebung Innocent IV.*, in: *Zeitschrift der Savigny-Stiftung für Rechtsgeschichte, Kanonistische Abteilung* 31 (1942), 142-320; 32 (1943), 300-383; 33 (1944), 56-128. For further comments, cf. WALTER ULLMANN, *Medieval Papalism*, London, 1949, 201-207.

(58) E.g., in both of Sancho's wills. In the first, written early in 1245, he disposes of the kingdom; in the second, written in 1248, he does not. His title is the same, however, in both. These wills may be found in *Monarchia Lusitana* IV, foi. 278 (= *Cronicas*, pp. 363-

II

The issues at hand in the case of Sancho and Innocent's disposal of them sharply illustrate some of the difficulties of public law in the early thirteenth century. Innocent's concern, as he himself notes, is for the *utilitas* of the king and kingdom, for the *necessitas* of the kingdom, and for its *status*, not merely spiritually, but in a distinct temporal sense as well. The solutions which the pope proposed for Portugal's difficulties reveal certain conceptions of kingship and papal jurisdiction, and analysis of which may serve to shed some light on Innocent's view of the character of the temporal state and its relation to papal *plenitudo potestatis*.

At first glance, Sancho's difficulties with his clergy and nobles do not appear to differ significantly from those of other contemporary and near-contemporary rulers such as John of England, Frederick II, Otto IV, and Sancho's own father, Afonso II. All of these rulers were excommunicated, and all were deposed or threatened with deposition by Innocent III, Honorius III, Gregory IX, or Innocent IV. It is not unlikely that Sancho's offenses, seens exclusively in the light of the papal correspondence of the early part of his reign, might have merited for him the fate of Frederick II. Yet Innocent IV went to great pains to point out that Sancho was not technically deposed (59). Innocent's decision, as the remainder of this study will show, was consistent with some earlier canonist political thought, although in practice it was to invoke principles which were to prove unworkable. The practical political difficulties involved in separating the *administratio* of a kingdom from the royal *dignitas* were effectively to prevent such an approach from evolving into a successful theory of kingship. The military defeat of Sancho in 1247 marked a limited success for Innocent's principles, but the course of action suggested by *Grandi* could never become, given thirteenth-

---

365) and in Caetano da Sousa, *Provas*, Vol. I, nos. 24-25. For Afonso's titles, see Gama Barros (above, n. 20), Vol. III, 316 and Almeida, *Historia de Portugal*, Coimbra, 1910, Vol. I, 452-456.

(59) Most Portuguese historians do not hesitate to refer to Innocent's action as a deposition. Given the political conditions of Portugal in 1245, however, Afonso of Boulogne certainly appeared to consider Sancho deposed *de facto*, if not *de iure*.

century ideas of monarchy, a generally accepted alternative to deposition (60).

Innocent outlined his own view of papal authority in cases of negligent kingship in his remarks on his own decretal *Ad apostolice,* the instrument of the deposition of Frederick II, which Innocent as a canonist glossed among the decretals in the *Liber Extra* of Gregory IX. In his *Apparatus* Innocent asks:

> *But what if another king is negligent, or another prince who has no superior? We say then that (the pope) succeeds to his jurisdiction, not because (that king) holds his kingdom from (the pope), but because of the plenitude of power which (the pope) has because he is the vicar of Christ* (61).

The problem of royal negligence here allows Innocent to outline concisely the distinction between legal-political superiority and judicial *plenitudo potestatis.* The pope may act, not because he is the legal superior, the ultimate monarch or lord of negligent rulers, but because he is empowered by virtue of his vicariate of Christ to act extraordinarily, as Maitland once remarked, as " an omnicompetent court of first instance for the whole of Christendom " (62).

In the late twelfth and early thirteenth centuries canonists began to give considerable attention to the different occasions upon which these extraordinary papal judicial powers might be used. They compiled lists of these instances which grew in length and complexity as scholarship and speculation on the Canon law became more comprehensive and papal decretals began to incor-

---

(60) Both the English barons' declaration of 1308 and *Grandi* represent essentially abstract conclusions concerning the character of royal authority. Although such terms as *administratio*, *regnum*, *corone*, and *person* were capable of being the subjects of abstract political discussion during the period, their meaning was never sufficiently defined to enable them to stand as concrete political realities. For the text of the Barons' declaration, see H. G. Richardson and G. O. Sayles, *The Governance of Medieval England*, Edinburgh, 1963, 466-469.

(61) Ed. cit. above, n. 45, *X.* 2.2.9 *ad v. vacante.* Cf. Watt, *Theory of Papal Monarchy*, pp. 275-276.

(62) *William of Drogheda and the Universal Ordinary*, in Maitland's *Roman Canon Law and the Church of England*, London, 1898, 100-131. The most recent discussion of the problems of *plenitudo potestatis* is that of J. A. Watt, *The Use of the Term Plenitudo potestatis by Hostiensis*, in: *Proceedings of the Second International Congress of Medieval Canon Law* (cited above, n. 4), 161-188.

porate the results of earlier canonist thought. Among the starting-points of such speculation was Innocent III's decretal *Per venerabilem,* briefly noted above (63). Papal intervention in the affairs of temporal rulers was, however, similar to the more strictly ecclesiastical question of the rights of ecclesiastical judges to intervene in lay judicial affairs. The occasions on which such intervention was permissible comprehend the specific political occasions described by Innocent III, Tancred, Hostensis, and others. In the middle of the thirteenth century Goffredo da Trani provided a particularly comprehensive list in his *Apparatus* to the *Liber Extra* of Gregory IX:

> *There are, however, certain causes in which jurisdiction belongs to the ecclesiastical judge... such as causes between servants or farmers of the church... causes of penitents... causes of wretched persons... causes concerning the feudal rights of the church... causes of travellers or pilgrims... causes concerning the theft of ecclesiastical property... causes concerning spiritual affairs or things connected to spiritual affairs... causes in which the secular judge is negligent... causes in which the secular judge is suspect... or during a vacancy in the empire... or because of the temporal jurisdiction which the Church possesses in temporal affairs or because of custom... also in causes concerning doweries... or in causes involving ecclesiastical crimes* (64).

To be sure, other Innocentian decretals further developed the judicial role of the papacy in temporal affairs. The most influential of these was probably *Novit* (X. 2, 1, 13), which laid down the famous principle of papal intervention *ratione peccati* (65). In a sense, the decretal activity of Innocent III constitutes the framework which supported the attempts of thirteenth-century canonists to describe the function of the papacy in precise legal terminology, to complete the development of the idea of *christianitas* in its politico-legal aspects.

---

(63) Above, p. 255-56. See also Watt, *Theory of Papal Monarchy*, 211-236, and B. Tierney, *Tria quippe distinguit iudicia... A Note on Innocent III's Decretal Per venerabilem*, in: *Speculum* 37 (1962), 48-59.

(64) Gottofredus de Trano, *Apparatus super titulis Decretalium*, Venice, 1491, fol. 28v. For discussions of other similar lists, see Watt, *Theories of Papal Monarchy*, p. 290; Tierney, *Tria quippe...* pp. 52-53; W. Ullmann, *Medieval Papalism*, London, 1949, 102-109.

(65) Cf. Watt, *Theories of Papal Monarchy*, 218-219, 296-300.

Whithin this characteristic of legal thought the case of Sancho illustrates a number of justifiable grounds for papal intervention. Sancho had created *causae miserabilium personarum.* He and his officials had also been *raptores rerum ecclesiae* and were doubtless *suspecti* as judges. Sancho himself was a *judex negligens,* and his case technically was disposed of during a vacancy of the Empire. In one sense Portugal was a *feudum ecclesiae,* and there may even have been some question of ecclesiastical jurisdiction in Portuguese temporal affairs, since the Canon law had been publicly declared legally binding on all subjects of the king of Portugal at the *Cortes* of 1211 (66). More important, however, was the general canonist theory that the papal authority to depose or otherwise correct temporal rulers extended not only to those incorrigibly guilty of *quodlibet peccatum,* but to those who were *minus utilis* as well (67).

Since the pontificate of Gregory VII the papal authority to depose temporal rulers had been the starting-point for discussions of the most pressing questions concerning the relations between *sacerdotium* and *imperium.* Gregory himself, not only in the case of Henry IV but in his references to other deposition proceedings, had made the issue a critical one in the publicistic and canonical literature of the late eleventh and early twelfth centuries (68). Although Gregory's contribution of texts to the *Decretum* was small and did not include the deposition proceedings against Henry IV, one citation of his which found its way into Gratian's collection was to constitute a primary text for subsequent canonist

---

(66) Reuter, 11-13.

(67) Cf. Johannes Teutonicus, *Glo. Ord.* D. 40 c. 6 *Si papa, ad vv. a fide devius:* ' Sed pro quo peccato potest Imperator deponi? Pro quolibet: si est incorrigibilis unde deponitur, si est minus utilis, ut 15 q. 6 alius '.

(68) For the literature, see C. Mirbt, *Die Publizistik im Zeitalter Gregors VII.*, Leipzig, 1894, 328-458; H.-X. Arquillière, *Saint Grégoire VII*, Paris, 1934, 201-288; more recently, K. J. Leyser, *The Polemics of the Papal Revolution*, in B. Smalley, ed., *Trends in Medieval Political Thought*, N.Y., 1965, 42-64. For Gregory's own views, see G. Herzfeld, *Papst Gregors VII. Begriff der bösen Obrigkeit*, Diss., Greifswald, 1914, esp. pp. 63-68. The writer is presently at work on a book-length study of the problem of royal inadequacy between the eighth and the fourteenth centuries, part of which will discuss the Gregorian approach. Two recent studies by K. F. Morrison have contributed greatly to aspects of this discussion: introduction to K. F. Morrison and T. E. Mommsen, *Imperial Lives and Letters of the Eleventh Century*, New York and London, 1962, and *Canossa, A Revision*, in: *Traditio* 18 (1962), 121-148.

discussions of deposition theory (69). In his letter of 1081 to Hermann of Metz, Gregory had cited the case of Pope Zacharias, Pippin, and Childeric III, the last Merovingian king of the Franks, as an example of papal power to absolve subjects from oaths of fealty to unworthy rulers (70). Gregory used the episode also to show that the pope could excommunicate even kings when they transgressed divine law. The text, cited hereafter from its opening words as *Alius item,* is as follows:

> *Another Roman pontiff deposed a king of the Franks, not so much because of his evil deeds as because he was not equal to so great an office, and set in his place Pippin, father of Charles the Great, releasing all the Franks from the oath of fealty which they had sworn to (the king)* (71).

Gregory's casual citation was probably not intended to bear upon the deposition, but upon the excommunication of Henry. Moreover, the phrase *tantae potestati non erat utilis* does not appear to have pertained so much to the *publica utilitas* of the *regnum Francorum* (the meaning of which, in 1081, was certainly not the same as it would be after 1200) as to the personal character of the king (72). Gregory's view was probably not far from that of the ninth-century writer who had the deposing pope remark of Childeric: *Nec sibi nec aliis utilis est* (73).

---

(69) In Gratian's *Decretum* Gregory's text is C. 15 q. 6 c. 3. For the early canonical collections, see P. FOURNIER and G. LEBRAS, *Histoire des collections canoniques en occident depuis les fausses décrétales jusqu'au Décret de Gratien*, Vol. II, Paris, 1932; for the transmission from Gregory to Gratian see FRIEDBERG, *Corpus Iuris Canonici*, Vol. I, cols. 755-756. Cf. W. ULLMANN, *The Growth of Papal Government in the Middle Ages*, 2nd. ed. London, 1962, 359-381.

(70) The letter is in E. CASPAR, ed., *Gregorii VII registrum*, *MGH*, *Epistolae selectae* II, VIII, 21, pp. 544-563. See K. G. HUGELMANN, *Die deutsche Königswahl im Corpus Iuris Canonici*, Bresslau, 1909, 30-41, 106-109.

(71) Gregory VII, Reg. VIII, 21: 'Alius item Romanus pontifex regem Francorum non tam pro suis iniquitatibus quam pro eo, quod tantae potestati non erat utilis, a regno deposuit et Pippinum Caroli Magni imperatoris patrem in eius loco substituit omnesque Francigenas a iuramento fidelitatis, quam illi fecerant, absolvit'. Gratian mistakenly attributed this text to Pope Gelasius I.

(72) For a contrary view, see W. ULLMANN, *The Growth of Papal Government in the Middle Ages*, pp. 286-288.

(73) *Erchanberti Breviarium*, ed. G. H. PERTZ, *MGH*, *Scriptores*, Vol. II, p. 328. See also H. LÖWE in: WATTENBACH-LEVISON-LÖWE, *Deutschlands Geschichtsquellen im Mittelalter, Vorzeit und Karolinger*, Heft 3, Weimar, 1957, 349-350.

The case of Pope Zacharias and Childeric had briefly occupied the attention of Carolingian chroniclers, although some had suggested that the Frankish magnates and Pippin, not Zacharias, had actually deposed the king (74). Other ninth and tenth-century depositions occurred against rulers whose cases appear to have been somewhat analogous to that of Childeric (75). By and large, however, the figure of the *rex inutilis* was omitted from such discussions of kingship as were written during the ninth, tenth, and early eleventh centuries (76). Gregory's citation of the case, his restriction of deposing power to the pope alone, and the wide circulation of his correspondence contributed to the background of the text in Gratian's collection (77).

Like other " political " texts in the *Decretum, Alius item* furnished the canonists with opportunities to discuss points of law not all of which were concerned with the relations between *sacerdotium* and *imperium* (78). Some canonists, for example, gave their attention chiefly to the general question of oaths and the difference between oaths to individuals and oaths to *dignitates* or offices (79). Those who considered the political aspects of the text restricted their concerns either to the deposing authority itself, i.e., the question of whether pope or magnates really depose

---

(74) The best recent discussions of these sources are those of H. Büttner, *Aus den Anfängen des abendländischen Staatsgedankens. Die Königserhebung Pippins*, in: *Historisches Jahrbuch* 71 (1951), 77-99 and R. Buchner, *Das merovingische Königtum*, in: Theodor Mayer, ed., *Das Königtum. Seine geistigen und rechtlichen Grundlagen*, Mainauvorträge 1954 (*Vorträge und Forschungen*, Vol. III, Lindau-Konstanz, 1956, rep. 1965), 143-154 (Büttner's study also included in this collection, pp. 155-168).

(75) E.g., Pippin of Aquitaine, Louis the Pious, Charles the Fat.

(76) For the crisis of kingship at the end of the Carolingian period, see, e.g., L. Boehm, *Rechtsformen und Rechtstitel der burgundischen Königserhebungen im 9. Jahrhundert. Zur Krise der karolingischen Dynastie*, in: *Historisches Jahrbuch* 80 (1960).

(77) For the impact of the text, see Ullmann, *Papal Government*, 262-310; Watt, *Medieval Deposition Theory* (above, n. 57); Caspary, *The Deposition of Richard II;* Watt, *The Theory of Papal Monarchy*, 190-211.

(78) The principles of interpretation are described by A. M. Stickler, *Sacerdotium et regnum nei decretisti e primi decretalisti. Considerazione metodologiche di ricerca e testi*, in: *Salesianum* 15 (1957), 575-612.

(79) E.g., Rufinus, *Summa Decretorum*, ed. H. Singer (Paderborn, 1902, rep. 1963), ad. C. 15 q. 6 c. 3: ' His sciendum est quod iuramenta fidelitatis fiunt aliquando intuitu personarum, aliquando dumtaxat intuitu dignitatum '. Stephen of Tournai, Simon of Bisignano, Johannes Faventinus, and Huguccio were among those who also considered this aspect of the text.

an unsuitable ruler (80), or to the nature of the offense and the penalty invoived, i.e., whether incorrigible uselessness was to be considered the legal equivalent of tyranny and treated by outright deposition, or as a different offense entirely meriting a different treatment. Others added to these considerations such topics as defense of the *patria*, the individual moral character of rulers, and later, the relationship between the personal weakness of the individual ruler and the *status regis* (81). Still others drew parallels between the uselessness of a temporal ruler and that of prelates. Thus a brief text such as *Alius item* might serve as a point of departure for the consideration of many legal problems not all of which shed light upon the specific canonist concept of the *rex inutilis*.

Many of these approaches to the text influenced others, and each new opinion often influenced subsequent opinion. In regard to the question of the deposing authority, the earliest decretists generally upheld Gregory VII's own view that deposition lay with the pope alone (82). Others later revived, whether consciously or not, the older Carolingian idea of deposition by magnates and approval alone by the pope (83). In spite of the changes in relations between *sacerdotium* and *imperium* from the mid-twelfth to the mid-thirteenth centuries, the political implications of he-

---

(80) See J. JUNCKER, *Die Summa des Simon von Bisignano und seine Glossen*, in: *Zeitschrift der Savigny-Stiftung für Rechtsgeschichte. Kanonistische Abteilung*, 15 (1926), 326-500. Simon's gloss C. 15 q. 6 c. 3 *ad v. deposuit* reads: ' Id est deponentibus consensit, vel subditos ab eius fidelitate absolvit, quod per consequentiam fuit eum deponere, infra 32 q. 5 Preceptum, supra 1 q. 4 Quia '. For a fuller discussion of the niceties of canonist deposition theory, see the studies of J. A. WATT cited above and those of O. HAGENEDER, *Das päpstliche Recht der Fürstenabsetzung*, in: *Archivum Historiae Pontificiae* 1 (1963), 53-95 and *Exkommunication und Thronfolgeverlust bei Innocenz III.*, in: *Römische Historische Mitteilungen* 2 (1957-58), 9-50.

(81) See the remarks of GAINES POST, *Studies in Medieval Legal Thought*, 264, 435-452, 368-404.

(82) On early decretist scholarship in general, see S. KUTTNER, *Bernardus Compostellanus Antiquus: A Study in the Glossators of the Canon Law*, in: *Traditio* 1 (1943), esp. 279-292. Among the decretists who held for deposition by the pope may be included Rolandus, Rufinus, and the authors of the *Summa Coloniensis* and the *Summa Reginensis*.

(83) Among these were Stephen of Tournai, Huguccio, Alanus, and the author of the *Glossa Palatina*. But see A. M. STICKLER, *Alanus Anglicus als Verteidiger des monarchischen Papsttums*, in: *Salesianum* 21 (1959), 366-368; S. MOCHI ONORY, *Le fonti canonistiche dell'idea moderna dello stato*, Milan, 1951, 156ff; G. CATALANO, *Impero, regni e sacerdozio nel pensiero di Uguccio da Pisa*, in: *Rivista di Storia del Diritto Italiano* 30 (1957), 93-139.

resy after 1190, and the development of nearly *de facto* sovereignty after 1200, these two views were both vigorously maintained to the fourteenth century (84).

In regard to the question concerning the nature of royal *inutilitas,* we may note still another instance of divided canonist opinion. Some canonists argued for the " Gregorian " solution, i.e., that the *rex inutilis* should be deposed, just as should a *tyrannus* (85). Others, however, probably beginning with Huguccio of Pisa, maintained that uselessness was a different kind of offense and should be treated differently. To be sure, they admitted that Childeric had been *inutilis* and that he had been deposed. However, they redefined the Gregorian use of the term *non erat utilis* so that Childeric's uselessness constituted, in effect, an *iniquitas.* Childeric had been, according to Johannes Teutonicus, the author of the ordinary gloss to the *Decretum,*

> *non... inutilis id est insufficiens, sed dissolutus... cum mulieribus et effeminatus* (86).

This variety of approaches to the Gregorian text may be found not only in glosses to *Alius item,* but in glosses to other texts in the *Decretum,* in *Notabilia, Casus, Quaestiones,* and *Summae:* in all the literary forms which canonists used during the twelfth and thirteenth centuries.

Johannes' distinction between, as it were, two distinct kinds of royal *inutilitas,* of which one meant that the ruler was *insuffi-*

---

(84) See CASPARY, *The Deposition of Richard II.* A mid-thirteenth century example of the continuation of earlier views is that of Henricus Merseburgensis (Yale Law Library MS 1 fol. 81v — I am grateful to Dr. Peter Landau of the University of Bonn for this reference, as well as for advice and information on numerous other points): ' Item notandum quod quandocumque aliquis secularis princeps fuerit inutilis, dissolutus et negligens in heresi extirpanda, vel alia iusticia observanda, non solum potest ab ecclesia excommunicari set etiam deponi, unde Zacharias papa deposuit Lodovicum regem francorum et praedecessorem pippini patris Karoli '. The confusion here concerning the predecessor of Pippin is characteristic of some canonists' concern, or lack of it, for historical circumstances. In the case of Henricus, the source of the error may have been Tancred. See GAINES POST, *Some Unpublished Glosses on the Translatio imperii and the Two Swords,* in: *Archiv für katholisches Kirchenrecht* 117 (1937), at 408-409. See below, n. 94.

(85) See the many texts cited by A. M. STICKLER, *Imperator vicarius Papae. Die Lehren des französisch-deutschen Dekretistenschule des 12. und beginnenden 13. Jahrhunderts über die Beziehungen zwischen Papst und Kaiser,* in: *Mitteilungen des Instituts für österreichische Geschichtsforschung* 62 (1954).

(86) Johannes Teutonicus, *Glo. Ord.* C. 15 q. 6 c. 3 *ad v. deposuit.*

ciens and the other that he was *dissolutus* or *effeminatus*, was derived also from Huguccio. Huguccio was faced with a legal paradox when he came to comment on *Alius item*. On the one hand, the text made it perfectly clear that the pope deposed Childeric III because Childeric had been *inutilis*. On the other, Huguccio knew that prelates who were considered *inutiles* were definitely not to be deposed, but given a coadjutor, as indicated by a number of texts in the first *quaestio* of *Causa* VII (87). Like many other canonists, Huguccio considered temporal rulers as, in a sense, " equiparated " with higher prelates, not so much on theological as on procedural grounds. Indeed, the formula *prelatus vel princeps* was a canonical commonplace which arose, I suspect, not from the ecclesiological disputes of the eleventh and twelfth centuries, but from the lawyers' habit of finding analogies among all ranks of human society for purely juristic purposes (88). Although Huguccio's and Johannes Teutonicus' remarks hardly squared with the intentions of Gregory VII, or, for that matter, of Zacharias, their approach to the implications of political ineptitude reflects to a large extent the scientific character of twelfth-century canonical jurisprudence (89).

Childeric, Huguccio notes, lived dissolutely, was effeminate, and neglected his duties. Charles, the father of Pippin, observed this and made it known to the pope, who in turn gave his permission that Childeric should be deposed and someone else elected in his place (90). Huguccio further notes that Childeric was not

---

(87) See below, nn. 105-118. In addition to these texts, cf. C. 7 q. 1 c. 1 *Scripsit;* C. 7 q. 1 c. 4 *Pontifices;* C. 7 q. 1 c. 6 *Sicut.*

(88) Cf. Johannes Andreae, *Glo. Ord. VI.* 2.14.2 *Ad apostolice*, *ad v. deiuravit:* 'Periurium crimen ecclesiasticum est. supra de iu. novit supra de eo lib. de foro competenti c. ult. Et gravissimum crimen in quolibet; praesertim in *prelato vel principe;* cum eorum facta trahantur ab aliis in exemplum supra de voto. magnae. et ideo gravius punitur. 11 q. 3 praecipue. Additio dicit Inno. quod *praelati et principis* verbum debet esse firmissimum, etiam sine iuramento '.

(89) Recent discussions of some aspects of the scientific jurisprudence of the twelfth century upon contemporary and later ideas of kingship and governance may be found in the studies of Ernst Kantorowicz, *The King's Two Bodies*, Princeton, 1957, and *Kingship under the Impact of Scientific Jurisprudence*, in: M. Clagett, et. al., *Twelfth-Century Europe and the Foundations of Modern Society*, Madison, Wisc., 1961, 89-111.

(90) *Summa*, C. 15 q. 6 c. 3 *ad v. in istum* (cited here from Mochi Onory, *Le fonte canonistiche del'idea moderna dello stato*, Milan, 1951, 156f): ' Nota papa sententiam non intulit, set de eius consensu et voluntate fuit depositus et eiectus, ut enim legitur in ystoria Fran-

simply inadequate to administer the kingdom, in which case he would have to have been given a coadjutor, but because he

effeminatus et otio torpens cum mulieribus dissolute vivebat (91),

an opinion which directly inspired the neat, but perplexing distinction of Johannes, mentioned above. As Professor Post has noted, " we must not worry about the historical accuracy of this version of the story " (92). In fact, of course, Charles Martel had died before Childeric ever ascended the Frankish throne, and the canonists' scornful remarks concerning that king's dissolute life contrast sharply with Einhard's portrait of the impoverished ruler who lived on a small manor with a few aged servants and was drawn to the Marchfield in an oxcart, *rustico more agente* (93).

The source for Huguccio's knowledge of the Childeric episode may have been Stephen of Tournai, who appears to have been the earliest canonist to describe Childeric as a drunkard and lecher. Stephen's source remains obscure, since he refers only vaguely to an unspecified *liber historiae Francorum* (94). Stephen's story,

---

corum, iste rex effeminatus et otio torpens cum mulieribus dissolute vivebat, quod videns quidam princeps militie eius, id est Carolus, pater Pippini, pape totum significavit, et tunc dedit ei et aliis licentiam ut illum eiecerent et alium eligerent; quo eiecto alium scilicet Pippinum filium Caroli, qui postea fuit pater Magni Caroli, regem fecerunt '.

(91) See text cited in preceding note.

(92) *Studies in Medieval Legal Thought*, p. 439. It would be useful, however, to investigate the historical sources used by some canonists for their compilations of *Casus*, summaries of the historical aspects of each text in the *Decretum*. See following note.

(93) *Vita Caroli Magni*, c. 1. The character of the deposing action taken against Childeric III in 751 is still the subject of some controversy. A recent survey of the problems is that of J. M. Wallace-Hadrill, *The Long-Haired Kings and Other Studies in Frankish History*, N.Y., 1962, 231-248.

(94) See Post, *Studies in Medieval Legal Thought*, pp. 438-440. Post cites also the near-contemporary *Summa ' Elegantius in iure divino '* and the slightly later *Summa* of Johannes Faventinus to the same effect. The question of the *historia Francorum* cited by Stephen (J. F. v. Schulte, ed., *Die Summa des Stephanus Tornacensis über das Decretum Gratiani*, Giessen, 1891, *ad* C. 15 q. 6 c. 3) and others has not been resolved. No contemporary sources for the deposition suggest that Childeric had been given over to spectacularly riotous or dissolute living. Among twelfth-century accounts, that of Godfrey of Viterbo seems characteristic (*Pantheon*, *PL* 198, cols. 923-926): ' Hildericus... ignavus rex... Stabat enim in rege sola nominis umbra, in Pippino vero potestas et dignitas efficaciter apparebat. Erat tunc Hildericus rex ignavus et inutilis, ex antiquorum regum Francorum genealogia, qui reges a Mirovaeo, filio Clodii, omnes Mirovaei fuerant appellati, qui etiam inane regis nomen habebant... umbra fuit, non rex... Rex quasi funesta '. The *Pantheon* also edited by

such as it was, accounted for the deposition of Childeric, at least in the eyes of Huguccio. By virtually ignoring the syntactic opposition of *non tam pro suis iniquitatibus quam pro eo, quod... non erat utilis*, in Gregory's text, Huguccio explained the deposition as a result, in fact, of acts on Childeric's part which strongly resembled, if they were not precisely called, *iniquitates*. This left Huguccio with some observations to make concerning the other meaning of *inutilis*, that is *insufficiens*. In his comment, he says,

> *his duabus de causis depositus fuit, unde non est questio quare illi non datus fuit coadiutor tunc enim illud locum habet cum quis innocens invenitur insufficiens administrationi, ut VII q.* 1 (*c.* 14) *Quamvis,* (*c.* 17) *petisti,* (*c.* 18) *quia, et VIII q.* 1 (*c.* 1) *Si Petrus* (95).

Huguccio here cites other Canon law texts to support his thesis that a king who is not adequate to administer his kingdom should not be deposed but ought to be given a coadjutor. All these texts concern, however, not temporal rulers, but incapacitated or inept prelates. Huguccio's bringing together of these texts constitutes the single most important canonist contribution to the theory of the *rex inutilis*. The highly developed ecclesiastical laws concerning the *prelatus inutilis* were to sharpen considerably ecclesiastical and secular views of the inadequate ruler.

The canonical texts which Huguccio brought to bear on the Gregorian *rex inutilis* reveal a series of remarkably clear ideas on the nature of the episcopal office, the distinction between office

---

G. Waitz, *MGH*, *Scriptores* XXII, pp. 21-93. It may be noted here that the eighteenth-century *Dictionnaire de Théroux*, following the sixteenth-century royal historiographer Claude Fauchet, cited the *Miracula Sancti Benedicti* and its author Aimoin (Cf. Wattenbach-Levison-Löwe, Heft 3, p. 348A for the chronicler) as a source for the etymology of the expression '*roi fainéant*' *à propos* Childeric. The chronicle which went under Aimoin's name was in fact a compilation chiefly of the late eleventh century. See J.-F. Lemarignier, *Autour de la royauté française du IXe au XIIIe siècle*, in: *Bibliothèque de l'école des chartes* 113 (1955), esp. pp. 25-36. The chronicle appears to have been a major source for twelfth-century chroniclers dealing with the Merovingian and Carolingian periods. Its composite character and wide circulation suggests that perhaps a variant of one of its sections contained the version of the Childeric story known to Stephen of Tournai and passed on by him to Huguccio and others. It must be noted, however, that the known versions of Aimoin's chronicle all contain the 'standard' version of the Childeric deposition given by Einhard. The writer is now completing a study of the origins of the term '*roi fainéant*'.

(95) *Summa*, Admont, Stiftsbibliothek MS 7, fol. 268r.

and incumbent, and, more important for our present purpose, the clear distinction between episcopal office as *administratio* and episcopal office as *dignitas* (96). These aspects of office were not exclusively, of course, the discovery of the twelfth-century canonists. As early as the fourth century there had occurred " the gradual disaggregation of the corporate ministry in a face-to-face fellowship. Thereupon the various orders of the clergy came to be thought of as the ecclesiastical counterpart of the succession of offices or the *cursus honorum* through which a magistrate normally advanced in the service of the state " (97). The influence of the administrative structure of the Roman state extended to clerical costume, regalia, ordination, and to the devotional formulas of public and private documents. Although not all prelates approved the use of *famosum typum saeculi,* as one ecclesiastical council described temporal elements, Roman administration, Roman diplomatic, and Roman legal ideas contributed significantly to the constitutional structure of the fourth, fifth, and sixth-century Church (98). During the pontificate of Gregory I many of these early changes became incorporated into the systematic directions which the papacy issued to the far-flung churches under its care. From Gregory's own register many of these ideas made their way into the work of Gratian (99).

---

(96) The early history of this distinction has not been fully worked out. For ecclesiastical concepts of office, see D. E. HEINTSCHEL, *The Medieval Concept of an Ecclesiastical Office*, in: *Catholic University of America Canon Law Studies*, No. 363, Washington, 1956 an extract from which may be found in *The Jurist* 16 (1956), 1-24. See also M. D. CHENU, *Officium: théologiens et canonistes*, in: *Etudes d'histoire du droit canonique dediées à Gabriel Le Bras*, Paris, 1965, Vol. II, 835-839; RIESENBERG, *The Inalienability of Sovereignty*, *passim*. The forthcoming study of the powers of bishops-elect by Professor Benson should also be noted.

(97) G. H. WILLIAMS, *The Ministry of the Ante-Nicene Church*, in: *The Ministry in Historical Perspectives*, N.Y., 1956, 27-59 at 29.

(98) Besides the work of KANTOROWICZ, see THEODOR KLAUSER, *Der Ursprung der bischöflichen Insignien und Ehrenrechte*, Bonner akademische Reden, I, Krefeld, 1949; P. E. SCHRAMM, *Sacerdotium und Regnum im Austausch ihrer Vorrechte. Eine Skizze zur Entwicklung zur Beleuchtung des " Dictatus Papae " Gregors VII.*, in: *Studi Gregoriani* 2 (1947), 403-457.

(99) Two recent studies on the influence of Gregory I on the medieval episcopate are: H. HURTEN, *Gregor der Grosse und der mittelalterliche Episkopat*, in: *Zeitschrift für Kirchengeschichte* 73 (1963), 16-41 and J. GAUDEMET, *Patristique et pastorale: la contribution de Grégoire le Grand au " Miroir de l'Évêque " dans le Décret de Gratien*, in: *Etudes... Le Bras* (cited above, n. 96), Vol. I, 129ff.

Gregory's concern was not exclusively for the spiritual suitability or adequacy of prelates. He remarked, in a text which also found its way into the *Decretum* (D. 39 c. 1 *Petrus*):

> *Notis, quia hoc temporis talis in regiminis debet arce constitui, qui non solum de salute animarum, verum etiam de extrinseca subiectorum utilitate, et cautela sciat esse sollicitus.*

In a *dictum* preceding this text, Gratian remarks of prelates that *saecularium negotiorum oportet eos habere solertiam.* The *Glossa Ordinaria* later notes (*ad v. solertiam*): *id est industriam, et solicitudinem... solicitus in arte et utilis,* and Gratian's own rubric notes that *Saecularium negotiorum imperiti non sunt in episcopos ordinandi* (100). The complex character of a bishop's duties kept both spiritual and temporal qualifications to the forefront of papal concern and constituted the background for papal legislation in regard to episcopal deviations from the norm, both criminal and accidental.

The question of criminal deviation need not concern us long. The question of accidental deviation, however, bears directly upon later ideas of the *rex inutilis.* In his *Summa* to *Causa* VII, Rufinus notes two kinds of episcopal *inutilitas* which probably form the basis for Huguccio's later distinction:

> *Duo sunt que episcopos tanquam inutiles pontificatu ipsis adhuc viventibus privant, scil. pravitas criminis et debilitas corporis. In superioribus igitur causis egit de criminum pravitate, accusatione et condempnatione; nunc incipit agere de corporis debilitate, quo modo ea impeditus episcopus episcopatui possit supersedere et alium substituere* (101).

Further, in his *Summa* to the first *quaestio* of C. 7, Rufinus lists seven causes which may authorize the removal of a bishop:

> (*Episcopus*) *Removetur autem pro his septem causis: pro crimine, pro egritudine, pro senectute, pro vaga animi levitate, pro utilitate, pro necessitate, pro humilitate ... pro egritudine, ut quando subvertente infirmitate ecclesiae suae inu-*

---

(100) The secular efficacy of bishops is a strong theme in the *Decretum*, especially in D. 38 and D. 39. The injunctions of St. Paul and others against the dangers of *negotia secularia* (2 *Tim.* 2, 4) were usually restricted to monks and canons regular.

(101) Ed. H. SINGER (Paderborn, 1902, rep. 1963), p. 285. This distinction probably influenced Huguccio's approach to C. 15 q. 6 c. 3.

> *tilis redditur; pro senectute, cum antiquatus viribus in solicitudine gregis tepidus efficitur* (102).

Of these seven, only the second and third concern this study (103). *Aegritudo* and *senectus* are quite distinct from iniquities on the one hand, and administrative decisions and personal morality on the other. Although they may lead to harmful consequences in both body politic and body ecclesiastic, they are normally not sins nor crimes in themselves, but accidents (104). The juridical problems which arose from the actions of irresponsible officials were complex and presented knotty problems not only to early popes, but so later canonists and political theorists.

Some of these solutions are reflected in the texts which Huguccio used to clarify one meaning of the term *inutilis* in *Alius item*. The first text, *Quamvis* (C. VII q. 1 c. 14), consists of part of a letter sent by Gregory I to Bishop Etherius of Lyon discussing the procedure so be followed in the case of an insane prelate. In such cases, Gregory says, it should be determined whether the condition is permanent or temporary. If it is permanent, the chapter should elect a *coadiutor* who will administer the affairs of the diocese until the death or resignation of the incumbent, when he himself will be consecrated bishop (105). If the condition is temporary, or if the bishop has lucid intervals, he should be asked to resign voluntarily. If he does so, another bishop is to be elected immediately. If he refuses to do so, a *coadiutor* is to be elected who will administer the affairs of the diocese during

---

(102) *Ibid.*, p. 286.

(103) The first, *pro crimine*, roughly equates the bishop to the *tyrannus*. The fourth, *pro vaga animi levitate*, derives from the vocabulary of the vices and virtues. The fifth and sixth, *pro utilitate* and *pro necessitate*, refer respectively to administrative transfers and to the exigencies of social or political disorder. The seventh, *pro humilitate*, refers to the prelate's retirement to the monastic life or to his becoming a penitent.

(104) They are opposed, e.g., to the vices, particularly *acedia*, which had become more explicitly delineated during the twelfth century. See S. WENZEL, *Acedia*, 700-1200, in: *Traditio* 22 (1966), 73-102.

(105) See, e.g., the *Summa Parisiensis*, ed. T. P. McLAUGHLIN, Toronto, 1952, p. 135: ' Hic agitur de quodam qui mente alienatus erat ex infirmitate et dicitur quod si quando rediret in sanam mentem et voluerit abrenuntiare, alius loco suo poterit promoveri et ei assignabitur redditus. Si vero numquam redit ad sanam mentem, nec abrenuntiare poterit, et idcirco non destituetur ab episcopatu, sed eo manente ecclesiae illius episcopo, alius in subsidiarium ibi ordinabitur qui post mortem eius sit episcopus '.

the bishop's terms of insanity (106). Gregory further notes the difference between criminal offenses and those resulting from a condition over which the offender has no control (107). A number of preceding *capitula* in the same *quaestio* deal with this and related problems (108). A *dictum* of Gratian to C. 7 q. 1. c. 11 neatly sums up the canonical procedure:

> *Ecce his auctoritatibus patenter ostenditur quod episcopo vivente alius superordinari non potest, nec etiam pro eius aegritudine. Sed illud Gregorii intelligendum est, quando ille, qui aegrotat alium sibi substitui non rogat.*

The chief ecclesiastical concern in the question of shared jurisdiction was the canonical impossibility of two bishops occupying a single see. This concern led directly to an analysis of episcopal office, an attempt to distinguish those aspects which pertained to *administratio* and could be delegated from those which pertained to *dignitas* and could not (109).

In the course of that analysis, the popes and canonists developed the idea of an episcopal *curator, coadiutor,* or *dispensator* of suitable character who could administer the affairs of the see, because, as the glossators said, *inutilitas praelati non debet redundare in damnum ecclesiae* (110). The prototype of the eccle-

---

(106) See preceding note.

(107) See *Gregorii Papae Registrum Epistolarum*, edd. P. Ewald and L. Hartmann, *MGH*, *Epistolarum*, I, *partes* 1-3 (Berlin, 1887-1889): III, 24; XIII, 8; XI, 29.

(108) See above, n. 87.

(109) See, e.g., the *Glossa Ordinaria* to C. 7 q. 1 c. 1 *Scripsit*, *ad. v. curam omnem:* ' Idest res administrare, sed quae spectant ad pontificale officium, vicini episcopi supplebunt... Et est hic arg. quod coadiutor et administratores vel visitatores debeant habere liberam et generalem administrationem '. The things which the coadiutor could not do were chiefly consecrations and the imposing of orders. Cf. the *Summa Parisiensis*, p. 133: ' Si enim episcopus non possit administrare... vicini episcopi erunt sibi subsidio in consecrationibus et ordinibus '.

(110) See the *Glossa Ordinaria* to C. 16 q. 6 c. 6 *Si fortassis, ad v. non inutilis:* ' Propter hoc quod praelatus inutilis factus, quasi diceret, inutilitas praelati non debet redundare, etc. '. The rubric in Gratian reads: ' Inutilis sacerdos ecclesiam suam dignitate non privat '. For a brief discussion of some of these texts, see W. Ullmann, *Nos si aliquid incompetenter... (Some Observations on the Register Fragments of Leo IV in the Collectio Britannica)*, in: *Ephemerides Iuris Canonici*, An. IX, nos. 3-4 (1953), 279-287. Ullmann's doubts concerning the authenticity of the sentiments expressed in Leo IV's letters are perhaps well taken, but the problem of the *papa inutilis*, particularly as it concerns such a pope as Celestine V, remains to be studied. The *Glossa Ordinaria* to C. 16 q. 6 c. 2 *Placuit, ad v. causae* reads: ' Quantum ad possessorium iudicium etiam quia puniri debet in litis aestimatione si habet propria ad

siastical *curator* was the Roman law *curator* who, like the *tutor, rector,* and *procurator,* performed functions in private law which were normally the exclusive right of the person in whose stead he was acting. Roman law had worked out an elaborate system of regulating the activities, rights, and duties of those who, like Labeo's " madmen, children, and cities ", were unable to act in their own interest (111). Gregory's text, in fact, seems remarkably similar to a rescript of Justinian of the year 535 (*Code* 5. 70. 6), a resemblance perhaps noted by Innocent IV in his *Apparatus* to *Grandi,* but apparently not by many others (112). The *casus* to Justinian's text in the *Code* remarks:

> *Cum quis furiosus est, aut perpetuo, aut ad tempus, primo casu curator administrare debet continue: nec eius cura finitur. Si autem dilucida habeat intervalla, an interim debeat cessare cura? Dicitur quod certum est, constitutum; sed in dilucido intervallo haereditatem adire, vel contrahere potest sine auctoritate curatoris.*

Other passages in the *Institutes, Digest,* and *Code* deal at length with the legal status of curators and with the rights of their charges (113). All of these constituted a convenient guide to Gregory I

---

similitudinem eius quod de tutore dicitur, C. de admi. tut. non ignotum (= *Code* 5.37.19) et C. unde vi meminerint (= *Code* 8.4.6), ut sicut factum tutoris non redundat in pupilli damnum: ita nec hoc delictum personae redundabit in damnum ecclesiae '. Thus the *regula* from Justinian's *Code* was applied to the delicts of the ecclesiastical *persona,* as in the ordinary gloss to the *Decretum,* C. 16 q. 6 c. 2 *ad v. non inutilis:* ' Propter hoc quod praelatus inutilis factus est, quasi diceret, inutilitas praelati non debet redundare in damnum ecclesiae '. The principles of the Roman law for tutors gave juristic precision to a problem, aspects of which had threatened the Church first in the Donatist controversies and later in the Investiture Contest dispute concerning reordinations. In short, a theological development concerning the character of sacraments found juristic expression in the norms of Roman law and was transformed into a legal maxim. For some of the theological aspects of the development, see N. M. Haring, *The Augustinian Axiom: Nulli sacramento injuria facienda est,* in: *Medieval Studies* 16 (1954), 87-117.

(111) Cited by Kantorowicz, *The King's Two Bodies,* p. 374. Cf. Riesenberg, *The Inalienability of Sovereignty,* p. 59f.

(112) The standard work on the uses of Roman law in the early middle ages is that of M. Conrat, *Geschichte der Quellen und Literatur des römischen Rechts* (Leipzig, 1891, rep. Aalen, 1963). Conrat does not cite Gregory I's use of the Justinian text.

(113) For the rights of the insane in Roman law, see Carl Saas, *Die Behandlung der Geisteskranken im römischen Recht,* Zürich, 1911. For the Canon law, S. Kuttner, *Kanonistische Schuldlehre von Gratian bis auf die Dekretalen Gregors IX., Studi e Testi* 64, Città del Vaticano, 1935, 85-109, also R. C. Pickett, *Mental Affliction and Church Law,* Ottowa, 1952,

and his successors. If the private rights of Roman citizens were protected to such a degree, how much more should those of prelates, who belonged to an *ordo* and possessed a *dignitas* and fulfilled an *officium* infinitely higher than those of Roman laymen, be protected? Gregory's text formed the groundwork for the subsequent texts which Huguccio cited (114).

The second of these texts, *Petisti* (C. 7, q. 1, c. 17), applied the Gregorian principle to the case of the *episcopus senex*. Boniface, Archbishop of Mainz, had written to Pope Zacharias asking to be allowed to select a *coadiutor* because of his age and illness. The rubric in Gratian notes that the text illustrates the rule that coadjutors ought to be assigned to those *senectute gravatis* (115). The third text, *Quia* (C. 7, q. 1, c. 18), describes yet another condition which is the legal equivalent of *aegritudo* and *senectus*, that of *simplicitas*. Johannes, Bishop of Narnia (now Narni), asked Pope Pelagius for a *coadiutor* on the grounds that he himself was the least suitable person for directing the administration of his see and for maintaining ecclesiastical discipline. He asked that a *presbyter* should be given him, *ut ea, quae sunt necessaria, competenti disponente sollicitudine fiant, nihil indecens fieri, vel inutile permittatur* (116). The *Summa Parisiensis* comments:

> *Iste multum erat simplex ut nesciret disponere saecularibus. Non tamen removetur, sed ei in subsidium adhibetur pres-*

1-70; G. Oesterle, *Amentia*, in: *Ephemerides Iuris Canonici* 11 (1955), 284-309, esp. 308-309.

(114) See the studies cited above, n. 99.

(115) C. 7 q. 1 c. 17: ' Senectute gravato, coadiutor est dandus, qui morienti succedat '. For a more striking example, cf. *Liber Extra*, 1.9.1 *Litteras tuas*, a letter from Alexander III to the Bishop of Lund, who had requested replacement because of his advancing age: ' Si tuam aut senectutem aut insufficientiam forte considerans... (the bishop should not resign because it would be better to have the church under his well-known name — *si commissa tibi ecclesia sub umbra tui nominis gubernetur* — than under that of an unknown person — *quam si alteri novae incognitaeque personae gubernanda in tanto discrimine commitatur* — finally describing the *vigor devotionis* of the old bishop as being unaffected by his *corpore senescente*).

(116) C. 7 q. 1 c. 18, *Casus:* ' Iohannes episcopus Narniensis ecclesiae adeo simplex erat, quod res ecclesiae ministrante nesciebat '. For a distinction between two kinds of *simplicitas* recognized in Canon law, see, e.g., the ordinary gloss to D. 39 c. 1 *Petrus, ad vv. Petrus... simplex est:* ' Quaedam est simplicitas quae est contraria dolo. et illa est bona, ut 16 q. 1 *si cupis.* Sed hic vocat simplicitatem negligentiam sive stultitiam, ut 36 dist. in princ. illa enim impedit promovendum, ut hic et arg. 74 dist. *episcoporum.* sed promotum non deiicit, sed datur ei coadiutor, ut 7 q. 1 *quia frater.* et 12 q. 2 *vobis* '.

> *byter nomine Constituto ad ordinationem patrimonii, i.e., possessionis ecclesiae* (117).

All three of these cases fall under the general ruling expressed in the rubric to *Quia: Non successor, sed coadiutor viventi episcopo datur.*

The last text which Huguccio noted was C. 8, q. 1, c. 1 *Si Petrus.* This text, Gratian's *dictum* to which contains the only reference to papal *plenitudo potestatis* in the *Decretum,* describes the obscure pattern of papal succession among the three immediate successors of St. Peter: Linus, Cletus, and Clement. The text (from a letter of Pope John III) notes that although Peter constituted Linus and Cletus his *adiutores,* he did not transfer to them his *potestas pontificii, aut solvendi aut ligandi,* but gave this to St. Clement. Linus and Cletus *ministrabant exteriora;* St. Peter *verbo et orationi insistebat.* This distinction between two aspects of office, the (in this case) *potestas* and the *administratio,* occurs in a number of other texts in the *Decretum,* the glosses to which often draw parallels between these aspects of ecclesiastical office and similar aspects of temporal offices (118).

The canonical texts here cited by Huguccio all deal with the general principle that a living bishop could not be removed on grounds of inadequacy, but had to be given a *coadiutor.* Inadequacy, or *inutilitas,* consisted of *aegritudo* (*furor, amentia*), *senectus,* or *simplicitas.* The canonical procedure for handling these cases derived from the Roman law concerning insane citizens; the protection which the law afforded was carried over into Canon law and strengthened because of the difference in *ordo, dignitas* and *officium* between a bishop or higher prelate and an ordinary Roman citizen. Canon law, as well as Roman, recognized the legal consequences of insanity, not only in the cases of prelates, but in the cases of lesser clerics and laymen as well (119). The

---

(117) Ed. cit. above n. 105, p. 136.

(118) Cf. esp. D. 22 c. 1 *Omnes sive.* The *Summa 'Antiquitate et tempore'* notes, *ad vv. terreni simul et celestis:* 'Sed animadvertendum est, quod ius aliud est auctoritatis, aliud administrationis. Et quidem ius auctoritatis est ut in episcopo ad cuius ius omnes res ecclesiastice spectare dicuntur, quia eius auctoritate omnia disponuntur. Ius administrationis sicut in yconomo. Iste enim habet ius amministrandi sed auctoritate caret imperandi'. Cited by Stickler, *Imperator Vicarius Papae,* (cited above, n. 85), p. 9 n. 21. Cf. pp. 201-202n, 203.

(119) See the study of W. Ullmann, cited above, n. 110, and *idem, Medieval Views*

relationship between the Roman law procedure relating to insanity and the Canon law procedure relating to inadequacy, or *inutilitas,* may account in part for the frequent conjuncture of accusations of insanity and ineptitude in later ecclesiastical and political literature dealing with the *rex inutilis.*

The distinction between the spheres of authority of incumbent and *coadiutor* was drawn, of course, in other areas of the law besides the ones described above. In the Canon law, perhaps the most noteworthy discussion occurs in the glossators' remarks on D. 21 c. 7 *Nunc autem,* which describes action taken by two Roman emperors reigning simultaneously. The text itself has attracted more attention because it dealt with the trial of a pope. However, in the *Glossa Ordinaria* to the *Decretum,* Johannes Teutonicus remarked (*ad v. Diocletiani*):

> *Nota simul duos fuisse Imperatores. Dic, quod erant duae personae, sed tamen erant loco unius. Sed contra, 7 q.* 1 *in apibus. S e d f o r t e u n u s h a b u i t d i g n i t a t e m : a l t e r a d m i n i s t r a t i o n e m* (spacing mine) (120).

Johannes rejected the first explanation, that two persons simply occupied one office, because he was, of course, familiar with the famous canonical text *In apibus* (C. 7, q. 1, c. 41):

> *In apibus princeps unus est; grues unam sequuntur ordine litterato; imperator unus, iudex unus provinciae. Roma condita duos fratres simul habere reges non potuit et parricidio dedicatur. In Rebeccae utero Esau et Jacob bella gesserunt: singuli ecclesiarum episcopi, singuli archipresbyteri, singuli archidiaconi, et omnis ordo ecclesiasticus suis rectoribus nititur.*

These words of St. Jerome became one of the bases of theories of ecclesiastical administration. Only one incumbent could enjoy a given *dignitas.* The increased legal sophistication of churchmen, however, avoided the full consequences of this theory by

---

Concerning Papal Abdication, in: *Irish Ecclesiastical Record* 71 (1949), 125-133. The character of papal authority in regard to councils and individual ineptitude or heresy has been discussed in numerous studies by BRIAN TIERNEY, M. J. WILKS, ULLMANN, LECLERQ and others.

(120) Johannes' attitude toward the imperial office is here determined solely by his familiarity with ecclesiastical office.

reserving a single *dignitas* but considering the *administratio* as distinctly separate from it. Later, of course, the question of delegated authority was to cause even more complicated divisions of power than this (121). In the course of the twelfth and thirteenth centuries questions of *libera administratio, libera potestas,* and *plena potestas* made the powers of such individuals as the *curator* and the *legatus* extremely complex. The legal actions involving delegated authority in both spiritual and temporal spheres increased in scope and frequency and had to be dealt with not only by Canon lawyers, but by those responsible for royal minorities (122), by those who served in representative assemblies, and generally by anyone who acted in the king's stead.

Canonists thus recognized the divisibility of both spiritual and temporal offices, and they used the distinction between *administratio* and *dignitas* to describe a procedure to be followed in the cases of *episcopi inutiles.* The *coadiutor* could administer all those affairs of a see which did not concern the bishop's own *ordo* and *dignitas.* For those duties which the *coadiutor* could not perform, e.g., ordination, other bishops from nearby sees were to be called in. By the late twelfth century, then, ecclesiastical theories concerning episcopal inadequacy had been systematically and articulately described and defined in papal letters, conciliar canons, and in the apparatus of legal thought which constituted the framework for the academic study of the *Decretum.*

Huguccio's contribution to the concept of the *rex inutilis* in Canon law reflects both the broadened scope of legal thought in the late twelfth century and the increasingly abstract conceptions of *regnum, praelatio,* and *episcopatum* applied to kingdoms or ecclesiastical units as administrative or corporate entities. The welfare, or *utilitas,* of these entities became in legal thought the object of royal or episcopal activities. Although Huguccio's conclusions in regard to the two types of royal *inutilitas* were not adopted by all subsequent canonists, they were influential upon Johannes Teutonnicus and contributed substantially toward his

(121) For the development of representative assemblies, see POST, *Medieval Legal Thought*, 61-240.

(122) For the question of royal minorities in France, see F. OLIVIER-MARTIN, *Les régences et la majorité des rois sous les Capétiens et les premiers Valois*, Paris, 1931. For England, see JOAN KENNEDY, *The King's Nonage*, Yale University Unpub. Diss., 1956.

Apparatus, which became the ordinary gloss to the *Decretum* and marked the end of one stage of canonist scholarship. Johannes' work remained the standard commentary to which the decretalists would later turn and helped to direct Innocent IV's approach to the question of Sancho II and his legal status. Up to Huguccio's own day, *Alius item* had served as an illustration of the papal right to depose not only tyrannical, but incompetent rulers; Huguccio had opened up a new line of thought, a line not consistent with contemporary political practice, but in keeping with other canonist ideas about the nature of governance and other aspects of kingship. Between 1190 and 1243, however, this approach existed solely in theory. It remained for Innocent IV to test Huguccio's alternative, and he did so in the case of Sancho, brought before him in 1243 by the *clamores multiplices praelatorum et aliorum regni Portugalie* (123).

III

During the second half of the thirteenth century the response to *Grandi* contributed further to the clarification of ideas of public law and kingship. The canonists, including Innocent himself, generally approved of the action taken, although at least one of them appears to have maintained that Innocent should have deposed Sancho outright (124). Contemporary political response, however, appears to have been just as uniformly unfavorable. Both Alfonso of Castille and Frederick II took the occasion provided by the publication of *Grandi* to criticize papal conduct severely (125). As late as the sixteenth century, in fact, no less a political thinker than Jean Bodin was to remark some of the political problems which the decretal raised (126).

Although Innocent failed to include *Grandi* in his own first

---

(123) See above, nn. 51-52. The phrase is from Innocent's decretal *Inter alia*.

(124) Bernardus Compostellanus Junior. See RIESENBERG, *The Inalienability of Sovereignty*, 168-169. I have not been able to consult Bernardus' comments directly.

(125) See below, nn. 138-141.

(126) JEAN BODIN, *De Republica Libri Sex Latine* (I cite the ed. of Frankfurt, 1641), I, pp. 187-188. BODIN may have gotten his information from MARIANA, but the case of Sancho had also been discussed briefly by Baldus (*Repertorium in omnia Consiliorum*, Venice, 1580, Vol. I), *Consilia* I, cons. 271, no. 3, fol. 81v.

two collections of his decretals, he did include it in the so-called *Collectio* III, a list of incipits indicating those of his decretals which he wished included in an official lawbook (127), and he commented in his discussions of some of his decretals in his *Apparatus* to the *Liber Extra.* In 1298 *Grandi* was included in Boniface VIII's official collection, the *Liber Sextus,* under the title *De supplenda negligentia praelatorum* (*VI.* 1.8.2). Partly as a result of its delayed appearance in Innocent's collections, *Grandi* was often omitted in early canonists' discussions of Innocent's decretal production (128). However, in the ordinary gloss of Johannes Andreae to the *Liber Sextus* and in his *Novella,* the decretal became something of an influential canonical text (129).

Innocent himself discussed several aspects of the decretal in his *Apparatus:* the law of succession in Portugal, the *libera administratio* of the curator, the *utilitas regis et regni,* and the role of the pope when there exists no *iudex superior* from whom justice may be obtained. Of these four topics, the third is most important for this study:

> *Nota causas iustas dandi curatorem regibus... si nesciunt suum regnum defendere vel in eo iustitiam et pacem servare maxime religiosis personis locis et pauperibus. Et etiam quod plus est si nesciunt perdita recuperare. Et idem quod diximus in regibus servandum est in ducibus comitibus et aliis qui habent iurisdictionem super alios. Aliis autem privatis non datur curator nisi sint furiosi vel prodigi. C. de cur. fur* (130).

Innocent's repetition of *nesciunt* suggests strongly the ruler's

---

(127) The literary history of Innocent's decretal collections has been traced by SCHULTE, *Die Dekretalen zwischen den Decretales Gregorii IX* und *Liber VI Bonifacii VIII*, in: *S. B. Wien* 55 (1867) and IDEM, *Beiträge zur Literatur über die Dekretalen Gregors IX., Innocenz IV., Gregors X.*, in: *S. B. Wien* 68 (1871). More recently, S. KUTTNER, *Decretalistica*, in: *Zeitschrift der Savigny-Stiftung für Rechtsgeschichte, Kanonistische Abteilung* 26 (1937), 471-489, and P.-J. KESSLER, cited above, n. 57.

(128) KESSLER, following KUTTNER, held that Innocent had withheld *Grandi* (*Collectio* III, c. 7) and *Ad apostolice* (*Collectio* III, c. 23) from his earlier collections precisely because of their powerful political implications. He also cites (*ZfRG, K.A.* 31 (1942), 25n) the subsequent use made of *Ad apostolice* (*Grandi* also appears to have been used) in the deposition of Adolf of Nassau in 1298. See also CASPARY, *The Deposition of Richard II*, *passim.*

(129) *Novella in Sextum*, Venice, 1499, rep. Graz, 1963, 75-76.

(130) *Apparatus* X. 1.10 *Grandi, ad v. utilitate.*

own incompetence, his lack of what the Carolingians had been among the first to call the *scientia regnandi.* Further, Innocent purposely draws a parallel between *nescire* and *furiosus vel prodigus* (*esse*) in the Roman law concerning the assigning of curators. A ruler who lacks the *scientia* to govern properly merits the same treatment as a citizen who is unable to govern his own private affairs.

Nor was Innocent capricious, as Herculano and others have sometimes suggested. In his *Apparatus* to *Ad apostolice,* Innocent noted the problems involved in taking public action against rulers:

> *Est enim memorandum de hac sententia depositionis que non debet ferri nisi urgente multa necessitate et multis causis et criminibus et infamiis manifestis contra imperatorem clamantibus* (131).

In other part of his commentary on the same decretal, he remarks at greater length:

> *Bene facit papa quod non solum multa crimina sed etiam multa genera peccatorum subiecit sententiae depositionis imperatoris. Magna enim causa subesse debet depositioni imperatoris. Non est simile eius ad depositionem clericorum, qui pro quolibet peccato deponi possunt... Imperatores et alii principes deponi non possunt absque magnis et multis periculis et periculum est causa quare aliquid detrahitur rigori.*

Fully aware of the implications of papal deposition, not only in the immediate political and social circumstances surrounding the act, but in the history of canonist commentary as well, Innocent refrained from deposing Sancho outright precisely because his case did not appear at all points to be identical to that of Frederick II. Yet the *publica utilitas* of Portugal was doubtless in great danger, at least according to Innocent's sources of information. The previous history of relations in Portugal between *regnum* and *sacerdotium,* the threats of Honorius III and Gregory IX, and the articulate complaints of influential Portuguese clergy contributed toward forcing Innocent's hand. Between the *rex iustus* and the *tyrannus,* there emerged the *rex inu-*

(131) *Apparatus* X. 2.14 *Ad apostolice, ad v. sempiternam.*

tilis, guilty of no sin except ignorance and inadequacy, for whom a new course of action had to be instituted. Innocent found his grounds for that action in the history of the *praelatus inutilis*, in Huguccio's remarks on *Alius item*, and in Roman private law (132).

Innocent's point of view was taken up and expanded in Johannes Andreae's ordinary gloss to the *Liber Sextus*. In his comment on *Ad apostolice*, Johannes notes:

> (VI 2.14.2, ad v. privamus) *Propter crimina ergo deponit Papa Imperatorem, ut hic. Idem cum est inutilis* 15. *q.* 6 *alius et dat coadiutores ipsis male administrantibus supra, eodem lib. de sup. negl. prael. grandi. Per negligentiam ipsorum iurisdictionem assumit, supra de foro competente licet. Compellit ipsos iustitiam facere,* 23 *q.* 5 *administratores, et ius canonicum etiam debitus casibus observare, supra, eodem lib. de foro competenti, c.* 2 *de iureiurando licet, infra de sent. excom. decernimus. Unum enim opportet esse principatum ad quem omnes recurrant,* 7 *q.* 1 *in apibus, qui fil. sint. legi. per venerabilem.*

Johannes here makes the distinction between a ruler's crimes (*propter crimina*) and his ' uselessness ' (*cum est inutilis*) and appears to add a third category (*male administrantes*). His remarks on the first two categories reflect the older canonist response to the deposition of Childeric III because '*tantae potestati non erat utilis*'. In this case, one should consider *inutilis* to mean not *insufficiens*, but something close to criminal negligence, as it had for Huguccio and Johannes Teutonicus earlier.

Watt has said, in regard to Innocent IV's remarks on the decretal *Licet* of Innocent III:

> *If, then, there is no other superior to whom recourse might be had in this crisis, the pope would act as that superior in an act of prerogative power held in virtue of his* plenitudo potestatis *as vicar of Christ. He would supply this deficiency, just as he would any other defect of law if for lack of a higher authority justice would be denied anyone or peace endangered* (133).

---

(132) *Ibid. ad v. gravissima.*

(133) *Theory of Papal Monarchy*, p. 276. Cf. CANTINI (cited above, n. 4), p. 479.

No pope, however, may act *motu proprio* in such cases; an appeal to him must be made. Innocent's own remarks reveal his awareness of the implications of papal *plenitudo potestatis* when it is used in cases such as those of Frederick II and Sancho II. Johannes Andreae repeated Innocent's remarks concerning the gravity of deposition in his own *Apparatus:*

> (Apparatus *VI* 1.8.2, ad v. gravissima) *bene dixit: quia maxima causa subesse debuit imperatoris depositioni. Nec est similis depositioni clericorum, qui pro quolibet peccato deponi possunt, 81 dist. c.* 1.

The pope's authority to act and the nature of the action which he took ought not to be considered separately. Innocent IV was well aware of the separate areas of jurisdiction of spiritual and temporal judges, and his meticulous legal reasoning in the cases of Sancho and Frederick reveals the solicitude, if not the political sophistication, of the greatest of the medieval lawyer-popes.

When Johannes Andreae came to comment on *Grandi* proper he had a less substantial history of canonist commentary on the decretal than had Johannes Teutonicus, for example, on *Alius item.* Nevertheless, his work had substantially the same effect. In a *notabile* to *Grandi* he sums up the general significance of the text:

> *Nota primo principalem effectum huius cap. videlicet quod si ille qui praeest alicui communitati sit negligens et remissus, potest suus superior sibi dare coadiutorem qui in iure vocatur curator. Nota ulterius conditiones requisitas in coadiutore, et in illo, qui praeest alicui communitati: quia debet esse devotus erga Deum, circumspectus, plenus oculis, et bonus mundanus... sed glossa ista debet intellegi, quod adiutor istius regis successisset in regnum, si rex ipse nullos habuisset filios.*

Sancho, Johannes goes on to note, '*dissipator erat et negligens*'. The Count of Boulogne, on the other hand, was '*devotus, circumspectus, magnanimus et potens*' (134).

Guillelmus Durantis and Guido de Baysio (*Archidiaconus*)

---

(134) Qualities which were, in many respects, identical to those attributed to or desired of ecclesiastical curators.

both had some observations to make concerning *Grandi* and its implications. Although Durantis considers *Alius item* an instance of deposition by the pope alone on account of the ruler's iniquities, he notes that *Grandi* has become the standard treatment for *reges inutiles:*

> *Deponit* (*Papa*) *imperatorem propter ipsius iniquitates, ut ext. de re iud. lib.* 6 (= *VI* 2.14.2 Ad apostolice), *et etiam reges* 15. *q.* 6 *alius, et dat eis curatores ubi ipsi sunt inutiles ad regendum: et extr. de sup. neg. prel. grandi lib.* 6 (= *VI* 1.8.2) (135).

In Durantis' view, *Ad apostolice* and *Alius item* are parallel texts which concern respectively the deposition of emperors and kings, both for iniquities or crimes. *Grandi*, however, is the standard approach for kings who are inadequate (= *inutiles*) to rule. *Inutilitas* is not, as it had been for Rufinus, Tancred, Alanus, and others, a sufficient cause for judicial deposition.

The most significant dissenting voice among the canonists appears to have been that of Bernardus Compostellanus *junior* (136). Without, however, entirely disagreeing with Innocent's action, Bernardus maintained that he should have deposed Sancho outright, that is, removed the *dignitas* (= *regnum*) as well as the *administratio* from the incompetent king. Thus Bernardus' view seems to be quite close to that of Gregory VII and an influential group of late twelfth and early thirteenth-century canonists, and it may have suggested to Johannes Andreae the distinction between the *rex inutilis* and the bad administrator. Bernardus Raymundus, the author of an early *Apparatus* to the *Liber Sextus*, agrees with the assigning of a *curator*, '*ubi rex superiorem non habens negligens est et remissus*' (137).

Besides his commentaries as a canonist, Innocent IV found other opportunities to discuss *Grandi* and its implications. Alfonso of Castille, an ally of Sancho who had been given territories and incomes in Portugal, wrote several letters to Innocent complaining of the Count of Boulogne's mishandling of his com-

---

(135) Guillelmus Durantis, *Speculum Iudiciale*, I *De Legato*, 17.

(136) See above, n. 124. Also G. Barraclough, *Bernardus Compostellanus junior*, in: *English Historical Review* 49 (1934), 487-494.

(137) University of Pennsylvania MS Lat. 114, fol. 20v.

mission. The damage caused by the Count's activities, Alfonso claimed, was greater by far than that which he had been called in to correct (138). Alfonso's repeated complaints resulted in several further letters from the pope, including one to the Count of Boulogne in which Innocent expounded at greater length on the duties of curators (139). More serious, however, was the opposition of Frederick II. Frederick's letters following his deposition are remarkable documents in which the emperor used all the political pressure he could bring to bear on his fellow rulers in order to sway royal and aristocratic opinion away from the papal cause (140). To the king of Castille, Frederick used the case of Sancho to illustrate the danger to other kingdoms of Innocent's greed for power:

> *Vos tamen, quorum in hoc non minus vestra causa quam nostra nunc agitur... Verum cum istae Romanae Sedis antistites ab ea forsitan devians pietate, quam praedicat quocunque; modo poterit (licet contra nos suum posse non valeat) tam in Imperio quam in regnis nostram nitatur offendere majestatem, motus nostros arcere non possumus, quin causam nostram et aliorum injuriam viriliter tueamur. Requirimus igitur, et adfectionem vestram rogamus attente, quatenus diligentius advertentes, qualiter summus pontifex suis viribus qui nihil habere debet, cum gladio non contentus, in alienam messem falcem praesumptuosus immittit: et ut non longe petatur a nobis exemplum: qualiter in regno Portugalliae honoris sibi usurpavit dignitatem, curas vestras et animos excitet* (141).

Neither Alfonso's nor Frederick's protests, however, effected any change in Innocent's legal arrangements. Frederick lent Sancho no assistance, and Alfonso, engaged upon his father's

---

(138) For the correspondence, see Berger, 1932, 8027; Potthast, 12177, 12512, 12513; *QE* 163-164, 181; Herculano V, 66-68. For the Castillian point of view, see A. Ballesteros-Beretta, *Alfonso X El Sabio*, Madrid, 1963, 74-77.

(139) See preceding note.

(140) *Petrus de Vineis Epistolae*, ed. S. Schard, Basel, 1566, esp. I, 2 and I, 21 (pp. 99, 152-172).

(141) *Ibid.*, I, 16, pp. 133-136. See also F. Graefe, *Die Publizistik in der letzten Epoche Kaiser Friedrichs II.*, Heidelberg, 1909, 288 n. 70.

crusade, could not swing the military balance in Sancho's favor with the aid he did send.

In 1245, the public law of the *respublica christiana* was strengthened by the addition of a legal process for cases of royal inadequacy. The figure of the *rex inutilis,* familiar in practice, if not always in theory, from 751 on, became the object of a legal definition made, not by those who suffered from the consequences of inept rule, but by one who felt himself entrusted with the duty to remedy all defects of law by virtue of an authority which men had come to regard as being judicial as well as theological. If the writings of Huguccio and others created a juristic contingency existing only in theory, Innocent IV gave full legal meaning to that contingency by his action against Sancho II.

Innocent, however, solved only the judicial, not the political problems connected with the *rex inutilis.* History, seen under the aspect of law, must also take into account the men who effect (and are affected by) changes in that law. The elaborate legal scholarship contained in *Grandi,* in Innocent's *Apparatus* to *Grandi,* in his letters to Alfonso of Castille, and in his other political decretals fell on unsophisticated political ground in the kingdom of Portugal. *Grandi,* indeed, contained the results of the most articulate legal tradition which Europe had seen since the age of Justinian, but few territorial monarchies were capable, in 1245, of profiting fully from that tradition. The reign of Afonso III reveals how little *Grandi* contributed toward solving the real problems of Portugal (142).

A little-known episode from the end of Sancho's reign may illustrate these problems as effectively as any document discussed thus far.

> *When Sancho II departed from Castille, he left behind as* alcaide *of Coimbra a certain Martim de Freitas. The Count of Boulogne laid heavy siege to the castle, but neither his promises nor his power were able to reduce the people within, who, in spite of great hardships, resisted for a long time until news was brought to them of Sancho's death at Toledo. The faithful* alcaide *asked for and received security from*

(142) For Afonso's reign, see HERCULANO V and LIVERMORE, 80-84.

Afonso of Boulogne and passed through the ring of besiegers. He directed his way to the ancient capital of Spain and ordered that Sancho's tomb be opened, that he might see with his own eyes that the king truly was dead. Having assured himself that the sad event had indeed taken place, he placed in the hands of the dead king the keys of the castle whose care had been entrusted to him. Then, taking the keys again, he returned to Portugal and gave them to Afonso, opening the gates of the city to the besieging army. The prince, struck with admiration at such loyalty, asked Martim to retain the office of alcaide. *The knight, however, far from accepting, cursed any of his descendants who might ever presume to receive from any king the castle which had once been in his charge* (143).

Mariana remarks: '*Viri fidem atque constantiam omnibus seculis praedicandam. Lusitani generis et sanguinis propriam laudandam*' (144).

The legal authority of the Count of Boulogne and the personal fidelity of Martim de Freitas illustrate the two political poles which many kingdoms had to reconcile in the twelfth and thirteenth centuries: that of impersonal public law and that of private fidelity. Each of these repeatedly articulated its own claims, sometimes in legal decisions, sometimes in heroic gesture. The legal history of the *rex inutilis* is inextricably bound up with a series of specific local problems like those of Portugal. It must be considered at least as much in terms of them as in terms of the general history of law. 1245 did not see the final date in the process of reconciliation, but neither did it quite see, as Herculano claimed, '*Uma grande obra de trevas, de corrupção, e de hypocrisia*' (145).

---

(143) This version may be found in HERCULANO V, 73-74. Cf. MARIANA, *De rebus Hispaniae*, pp. 546-547.

(144) MARIANA, p. 547.

(145) HERCULANO V, p. 36.

VIII

Non legitur in historia francorum: Stephen of Tournai, the Last Merovingians, and the Capetian Dynasty

I

The most widely known and cited doctrine of royal incapacity in medieval Europe was shaped by popes and canon lawyers from the pontificate of Gregory VII to that of Innocent IV.[1] In his letter of 1076 to Bishop Hermann of Metz on the subject of the papal right to depose unsuitable rulers and to absolve subjects from their oaths of allegiance to such rulers, Gregory VII cited the precedent of Pope Zacharias in 751, who, Gregory said, "deposed a king of the Franks and released all his subjects from their oath of allegiance." Five years later, in another letter to Hermann, Gregory expanded the reference:

> Another Roman pontiff deposed a king of the Franks not so much on account of his evil deeds as because he was not equal to so great an office, and set in his place Pepin, father of the emperor Charles the Great, releasing all the Franks from the oath of fidelity which they had sworn to him.[2]

This expanded reference, consistent with the historical sources which Gregory is most likely to have had at his disposal, appears to have been phrased purely for rhetorical emphasis; if a pope could depose a ruler even

---

1 The subject is extensively considered in Edward Peters, *Rex inutilis: Sancho II of Portugal and Thirteenth-Century Deposition Theory*, SG 14 (1967), 253-306, and idem, *The Shadow King: Rex Inutilis in Medieval Law and Literature*, New Haven 1970; Linda Fowler, *Innocent Uselessness in Civilian and Canonist Thought*, ZRG Kan. Abt. 58 (1972), 107-165. An early version of this paper was presented to the Medieval and Renaissance Conference at New College, University of South Florida, Sarasota, in 1986. I am grateful to Patrick Geary, Thomas G. Waldman, Gabrielle Spiegel, and Kimberly LoPrete for their considerable assistance and advice.

2 Erich Caspar, *Das Register Gregors VII.*, Berlin 1920-1923, 4.2, 293-7; 8.21 (MGH Epp. sel. 2). Some of the historical arguments used in the Investiture conflict have been considered by Jürgen Ziese, *Historische Beweisführung in Streitschriften des Investiturstreits*, Munich 1972 (Münchener Beiträge zur Mediävistik und Renaissance-Forschung 8). On the literature of the conflict generally, see I. S. Robinson, *Authority and Resistance in the Investiture Contest: The Polemical Literature of the Late Eleventh Century*, Manchester-New York 1978.

though the ruler had not committed evil deeds, how much more was the pope entitled to depose an actively evil ruler, i.e. Henry IV?

The excerpt from Gregory's second letter, cited above, was included by Ivo of Chartres in his *Panormia* and was taken up from Ivo into the *Concordia discordantium canonum* of Master Gratian, where, as 15.6.3 *Alius item*, it became the starting point for all later canonist and other discussions of the problem of the *rex inutilis*.[3]

From the late eighth century to the early twelfth, chroniclers discussing the revolution in Frankish royal history that had occurred in 751 followed a line of interpretation that had originated in the work of early Carolingian propagandists and was best known and most commonly represented in Einhard's *Vita Karoli Magni* and the Royal Frankish Annals.[4] This line of interpretation and characterization of the last Merovingians was contained in a tradition of literary self-justification on the part of the Carolingians, according to which they defined a set of criteria for legitimate Christian rulership, declared these criteria to have been conspicuously absent from the last Merovingians,

---

3 Ivo of Chartres, *Panormia*, Book 5, c. 109 (PL 161.1235-1236). The text and its citation by Gratian were unusual, in that there were relatively few Gregorian texts included in the *Decretum*: see, most recently, Horst Fuhrmann, *Papst Gregor VII und das Kirchenrecht. Zum Problem des Dictatus Papae*, in: *Studi Gregoriani* 13, Roma 1989, 123-150, at 126, n.9, and James A. Brundage, *Sexuality, Marriage, and the Reform of Christian Society in the Thought of Gregory VII*, in: *Studi Gregoriani* 14, Roma 1990, 69-73.

4 For a general survey, see F. L. Ganshof, *L'historiographie dans la monarchie franque*, in: *La Storiografia Altomedioevale, Spoleto Settimane 1970*, Spoleto 1973, 2.631-685 (Settimane Alto Medioevo 17). There is a useful discussion of Carolingian concepts of *vigor regis* in Helmut Beumann, *Die Historiographie des Mittelalters als Quelle für die Ideengeschichte des Königtums*, in: H. Beumann, *Wissenschaft vom Mittelalter. Ausgewählte Aufsätze*, Cologne-Vienna 1972, 201-240, at 229-230. Beumann cites parallel ideas in the work of Widukind of Corvey and Richer. There is an extensive discussion of Merovingian uses of the key terms *utilis*, *utilitas*, in Franz Irsigler, *Untersuchungen zur Geschichte des fränkischen Adels*, Bonn 1969, Ch. 3 (Rheinisches Archiv 70), English trans. by Timothy Reuter, *The Medieval Nobility*, Amsterdam-New York 1978, 105-136. Irsigler's texts emphasize that *utilitas* and *utilis* meant not only 'suitability' in a general or modern sense, but those distinctive royal qualities that included *virilitas*, *felicitas*, *virtus* and *strenuitas*. See also Michael H. Hoeflich, *The Concept of Utilitas Populi in Early Ecclesiastical Law and Government*, ZRG Kan. Abt. 66 (1981), 36-74. For the use of the term in early devotional formulas, see K. Schmitz, *Ursprung und Geschichte der Devotionsformeln bis zu ihrer Aufnahme in die fränkische Königsurkunde*, in: U. Stutz (Hg.), Kirchenrechtliche Abhandlungen, Heft 81 (1913), 102, 117, 139.

and asserted that the criteria were present only in themselves. Among the qualities of a legitimate ruler according to the Carolingian sources were those of actively governing the Frankish kingdom, protecting the Church, and vigorously (and successfully) protecting the kingdom from its enemies.

The first chapter of Einhard's *Vita Karoli Magni* sums up the Carolingian definition of the last Merovingians in this context:

> "Gens Merovingorum, de qua Franci reges sibi creare soliti erant, usque in Hildericum regem, qui iussu Stephani [*sic*] Romani pontificis depositus ac detonsus atque in monasterium trusus est, durasse putatur."

The royal line, Einhard goes on to say, had for a long time lacked *vigor* and possessed only the empty name of king. *Et opes et potentia regni* were in the hands of the mayor of the palace and had been for a long time. The last Merovingian kings had to be content, *regio nomine*, *crine profuso*, *barba sumissa*, *ad speciem dominantis effingeret*. They met legates from various parts of the realm in a purely ceremonial setting, travelled to the palace and the Frankish assemblies in an ox cart, *rustico more agente*, ineffective and useless as rulers of a vigorous Christian people. Einhard's version echoes and is echoed by other Carolingian versions of the events of 751, from the eighth-century Royal Frankish Annals through the annals of Lorsch and Fulda, and the *Breviarium Erchanberti*, all of which give the same picture.[5] The deposition of Childeric III became part of a seamless Carolingian web of political history and theory, one that embraced the anointing of Pepin by St. Boniface, the *consultum* of Zacharias, and the admirably routinized formula of the *Clausula de unctione Pippini*:

---

5 Einhard, *Vita Karoli Magni*, c.1. General discussion in Peters, *The Shadow King*, 47-57, and the recent works cited in the next note. For a non-Carolingian view of late Merovingian history, see Richard Gerberding, *The Rise of the Carolingians and the Liber Historiae Francorum*, Oxford 1987. Einhard began his *Vita Karoli* with a general characterization of the last century or so of Merovingian kingship. It is possible that later readers may have attributed to Childeric III some of the attributes of his predecessors, e.g., Childeric II. See J. M. Wallace-Hadrill, *The Fourth Book of the Chronicle of Fredegar with its continuations*, London 1960, 81: "Erat enim ipse Childericus rex levis atque citatus nimis... gentem invicem Francorum in sedicionem mittens in scandalum ac derisum, donec odium non modicum inter ipsos usque ad scandalum et ruinam." The reference is to Childeric II.

> Pepin was a pious king, raised to the throne by the *authority* and *order* of Pope Zacharias, by *anointing* with holy chrism at the hands of the... bishops, and by the *election* of the Franks.[6]

The large scholarly literature on the events of 751 and their subsequent Carolingian *interpretatio* has long since shattered the smooth picture painted by Einhard and others, although the 'official' Carolingian version survived to dominate later Carolingian historiography, and it was the only one available to Gregory VII, Ivo, Gratian, and the earliest canonist commentators on *Alius item.*[7]

Indeed, no historical or legal source before the early twelfth century offered a different reading from this one. From the later Carolingian annals through Flodoard, Radulphus Glaber, and Richer, to Adhemar of Chabannes and later writers, the Carolingian portrait of the last Merovingian kings of the Franks was repeated with strikingly little variation.[8] For Adhemar, these kings were merely *insipientes viri*; for Hugh of Fleury, the Annalista Saxo, Sigebert of Gembloux, to Hugh of Flavigny and Ekkehard of Aura, brief references to the events of 751 usually consisted of a mere paraphrase of the

---

6 In: G.Waitz, W.Wattenbach u.a. (Hgg.), *Supplementa,* 1 sqq (MGH SS 15, 1). The text's disputed value as an eye-witness account has recently been reasserted by Rosamund McKitterick, *The Frankish Kingdoms under the Carolingians, 751-987*, London-New York 1983, 48-49 and by Werner Affeldt, *Untersuchungen zur Königserhebung Pippins. Das Papsttum und die Begründung des karolingischen Königtums im Jahre 751*, FMSt 14 (1980), 95-187, at 103-109. Among the items of a large recent literature, see especially Adolf Grauert, *Noch einmal Einhard und die letzten Merowinger*, in: Lutz Fenske et al. (Hgg.), *Institutionen, Kultur und Gesellschaft im Mittelalter. FS Josef Fleckenstein zu seinem 65. Geburtstag*, Sigmaringen 1984, 59-72; Konrad Bund, *Thronsturz und Herrscherabsetzung im Frühmittelalter*, Bonn 1979, 367-384; Karl Brunner, *Oppositionelle Gruppen in dem Karolingerreich*, Vienna 1979.

7 There is a good survey in Edmond-René Labande, *L'historiographie de la France de l'ouest aux Xe et XIe siècles*, in: *La Storiografia Altomedioevale* (see note 4), 2.751-791.

8 For Adhemar, see Labande, *L'historiographie de la France*, 782-788; Adhemar, *Historiarum Libri III*, in: G.Pertz u.a. (Hgg.), *Annales, chronica et historiae aevi Carolini et Saxonici*, 106-148, 114 (MGH SS 4); Hugh of Fleury, *Historia Ecclesiastica*, in: G.Pertz u.a. (Hgg.), *Chronica et annales aevi Salici*, 349-364, 358 (MGH SS 9); Annalista Saxo, in: G.Pertz u.a. (Hgg.), *Annales, chronica et historiae aevi Carolini et Saxonici*, 550-777, 555 (MGH SS 6); Sigebert of Gembloux, in: G.Pertz u.a. (Hgg.), *Chronica et annales aevi Salici*, 300-374, 353 (MGH SS 6); Hugh of Flavigny, in: G.Pertz u.a. (Hgg.), *Chronica et gesta aevi Salici*, 288-502, 340 (MGH SS 8); Ekkehard of Aura, in: G.Pertz u.a. (Hgg.), *Chronica et annales aevi Salici*, 17-32, 26 (MGH SS 6).

original Carolingian sources. This, then, is the historiographical tradition within which Gregory VII wrote and the context of understanding concerning the deposition of *reges inutiles* that governed the interpretation of the text by Ivo, Gratian, and the first commentaries on the *Decretum*.

In 1159-1169, Stephen of Tournai composed his *Summa* to the *Decretum* of Gratian, and in it he added a significantly different version of the story of Childeric III, Pepin, and Zacharias to the *casus* of 15.6.3 *Alius item*:

> "Legitur in historia Francorum quia Carolus Tudites qui sic a tundendo, id est percutiendo et subigendo hostes dictus est quem et adhuc Francigene in eadem significatione vulgariter Carolum Martellum vocant cum esset senescalcus sive princeps militie cuiusdam regis Francorum, qui mollis et effeminatus in ocio vivebat, hostes regni debellauerit eosque subiugaverit. Unde et idem Carolus remissam ignauiam regis attendens, domino apostolico scripsit, rogans, ut ei rescriberet quis dignior esset corona regni: aut qui deliciis et ocio torpebat in thalamo cum mulieribus dissolute vivens aut qui in armis et castris sudabat pro regno cum hostibus assidue pugnans. Cumque rescripsisset ei Papa quia regno dignior esset, qui pro regno pugnaret et hostes reprimeret, noluit se coronare. Set Pininum [sic] filium suum, qui postea Caroli Magni pater fuit, regem fecit eumque, qui regno inutilis erat, eiecit. Nota ut quidam aiunt interesse, an aliquis faciat fidelitatem alicui intuitu persone vel intuitu dignitatis ipsius persone. Si intuitu persone quis faciat fidelitatem alicui, dicunt quia numquam ab apostolico vel ab alio poterit absolui a sacramento fidelitatis. Si vero intuitu dignitatis quis faciat fidelitatem alicui, amissa dignitate absoluetur a sacramento fidelitatis; verbi gratia: aliquis factus est episcopus, multi faciunt ei fidelitatem ratione episcopalis dignitatis, eo deposito ab episcopali dignitate, absoluuntur a fidelitatis sacramento qui ei tenebantur; michi videtur quia ab omni sacramento causa cognita potest apostolicus absoluere."[9]

---

9 Herbert Kalb, *Studien zur Summa Stephans von Tournai. Ein Beitrag zur kanonistischen Wissenschaftsgeschichte des späten 12. Jahrhunderts*, Innsbruck 1983, 90-91. Kalb's study is the most recent and fullest examination of Stephen's politcal thought and contains a full bibliography. Schulte did not print the *casus* in his own edition of Stephen's *Summa*: J. F. von Schulte, *Die Summa des Stephanus Tornacensis über das Decretum Gratiani*, Gießen 1891; rpt. Aalen 1965. See Kalb's comment on 91, n. 49. Kalb persuasively dates the *Summa* to between 1166 and 1169 (*Studien zur Summa Stephans von Tournai*, 108-112) as opposed to Schulte's date of 1159-1160. Although my argument need not necessarily fail if the later date is preferred, a time of composition before the birth in 1165 - or at least the adolescence - of Philip Augustus would suit it better. The somewhat unusual designation of Charles Martel as *Carolus Tudites* echoes earlier usages in *Francia*, notably that of Hugh of Fleury. The word appears to have entered Carolingian Latin via Paul the Deacon. See K. O. Müller (Ed.), *Sexti*

In Stephen's *casus* a very different picture of the last Merovingian emerges, one for which the best known historical sources did not provide, but also one which, when taken up by later canonists - Johannes Faventinus, the author of the *Summa 'Elegantius in iure divino'*, and Huguccio of Pisa, permitted canonists to identify two distinct kinds of royal incapacity. Huguccio, the principal formulator of the new doctrine, argued that there could be, on the one hand, "innocent uselessness", for which the proper remedy was for the pope to appoint a *curator* who would possess the *administratio* of the kingdom, while the now powerless, but innocent king would retain the *dignitas regis*. Huguccio here, as *Linda Fowler* has conclusively shown, based his idea of innocent uselessness upon the canon law governing situations of episcopal incapacity, which stated that an incapacitated or otherwise incapable prelate should be assigned a coadjutor, while the prelate himself retained the episcopal *dignitas*.[10]

On the other hand, Huguccio argued, there was also a kind of incapacity which was not innocent, but sinful, consisting of a vicious character flaw and behavior which not only prevented the king from ruling vigorously, but also distracted his energies and focused them upon improper objects of royal activity. The penalty for the latter was outright deposition and the release of subjects from oaths of faith that they had sworn to him. Huguccio was helped in making his distinction between innocent and culpable incapacity by two elements in *Alius item*: Gregory VII's assertion that Zacharias had deposed Childeric III outright, and Stephen of Tournai's depiction of Childeric as a soft, unmilitary, and lazy womanizer, a characterization that transformed innocent uselessness into culpable uselessness.

That Zacharias had indeed deposed Childeric without appointing a *curator* and thereby preserving the king's *dignitas* was clearly evident from the Carolingian and post-Carolingian sources. It is safe to say that the distinction

---

Pompei Festi de verborum significatione quae supersunt cum Pauli epitome, Leipzig 1839; rpt. Hildesheim-New York 1975, 353: "Tudites mallei a tundendo dicti."

10 The discussion here cannot take full account of the richness of Fowler' s research in *Innocent Uselessness*. Her study fully traces the sources of Huguccio's and later doctrines in the problems concerning coadiutors for bishops, abbots, and archdeacons, precedents from the Roman laws concerning insane magistrates, theories of surrogate service in many offices, and the distinction between realms inherited and realms to whose rule candidates were elected. For Johannes Faventinus, see Herbert Kalb, *Das Recht der Herrscherabsetzung bei Johannes Faventinus*, ZRG Kan. Abt. 78 (1992), 159-182.

that so engaged Huguccio had not occurred either to Zacharias or to Gregory VII, or indeed to Gratian. By the mid twelfth century, however, the analogy between kings and bishops had become common - it appears in the commentaries of both Rufinus and Stephen - and the episcopal model offered a useful distinction which Huguccio was quick to grasp. It explained the outright deposition of Childeric III and laid the groundwork for another kind of case, one involving innocent uselessness, which Innocent IV was to invoke in the case of Sancho II of Portugal in 1245.

Stephen's *casus* was important because Stephen was the first ultramontane commentator on Gratian and presumably knew the Frankish subject-matter in 15.6.3 better than the Bolognese school. Where did Stephen find his portrait of the king, who *deliciis et ocio torpebat in thalamo cum mulieribus dissolute vivens*? Several decades ago, Gaines Post noted Stephen's text in the context of a study of the medieval royal responsibility to defend the state from its enemies, and he pointed out the historical novelties in Stephen's version as well.[11] In 1968 I suggested that Stephen might have had access to a late eleventh- or early twelfth-century revision of Frankish history which contained the version of the events of 751 that he used, although none of the known chronicles contained that version. My source for that suggestion was the sixteenth-century royal historiographer Claude Fauchet, citing the work of the late eleventh-century chronicler and compiler Aimoin of Fleury as the original source.[12]

As long as the events of 751 remained within the confines of an enduring Carolingian historiographical tradition, there was neither a need nor an opportunity for a different version of the story to emerge. But in the historiography of the tenth century, when the Carolingian dynasty was being replaced in *Francia occidentalis* and *Francia orientalis*, when even Carolingian historiography was not always readily available, and when strenuous kingship and lordship were once again at a premium, the case of the last Merovingians, as

---

11 Gaines Post, *Studies in medieval Legal Thought: Public Law and the State 1100-1332*, Princeton 1964, 439.

12 Peters, *The Shadow King* (see note 1), 123-124. In 1972 Linda Fowler, *Innocent Uselessness* (see note 1), 159, suggested that a version of the deposition of the Byzantine emperor Justin II may have been known to Stephen and that Stephen may have transferred it to the case of Childeric III. I agree with Fowler that the source of the episode was not Childeric III in known or unknown chronicle sources, but argue below for a different source. For Fauchet and other sixteenth- and seventeenth-century French historians, see below, n. 52.

well as the new cases of the last Carolingians, began to be considered differently. Richer, who did not alter the traditional Carolingian version of the events of 751, in his depiction of Louis V seems to echo it:

> "Ludovicus vero, quia morum informatorum non habebat, utpote adolescens levium rerum vanitatibus insistebat. Habitum patriae gentis pro peregrinis penitus deposuerat. Itaque in miserandam fortunam res penitus dilapsa est, ut et moribus degener et regnandi impotentia inglorius esset, et qui paulo ante rex genere, fama atque copiis potens, nunc erumnosis et inops, rei familiaris simul et militaris calamitate squaleret."[13]

Louis V added an unseemly *levitas* and questionable moral standards to the powerlessness and poverty that characterized the type of the conventional Merovingian *rex inutilis* in early Carolingian sources.

Thus, the second dynasty of the Franks had come to an end in conditions of royal penury and impotence similar to those that had long characterized the first dynasty, but with other distinctive features as well. In fact, the chroniclers of the tenth century were the first to formulate the doctrine of the *trois races royales*, the three *generaciones* who ruled *Francia latina*. As Bernd Schneidmüller has indicated, the historians of western *Francia* had to account for another dynastic change as well as to separate the rulers of western *Francia* from those of eastern *Francia*, to 'forget', as it were, the line of East Frankish kings after 888.[14]

---

13 Richer, *Histoire de France*, ed. Robert Latouche, Paris 1937, 2.95, 120.

14 On the uses of Carolingian tradition in the historiography of the tenth century, see Bernd Schneidmüller, *Karolingische Tradition und frühes französisches Königtum*, Wiesbaden 1979; see also Schneidmüller, *Nomen Patriae. Die Entstehung Frankreichs in der politisch-geographischen Terminologie (10.-13. Jahrhundert)*, Sigmaringen 1987 (Nationes 7). On Richer and the end of the Carolingian dynasty in *Francia*, see *Karolingische Tradition*, 57-58. The problem of dynastic consciousness and the transition from one dynasty to another has been studied in great detail by Andrew W. Lewis, *Royal Succession in Capetian France: Studies on Familial Order and the State*, Cambridge, Mass. 1981. On the 'national' sense of the chroniclers, see Joachim Ehlers, *Karolingische Tradition und frühes Nationalbewußtsein in Frankreich*, Francia 4 (1976), 213-235, and Edward Peters, *'The Infancy of Celebrated Nations': Folk, Kingdom, and State in the Middle Ages*, in: E. Peters (Ed.), *Folk Life in the Middle Ages*, Special Issue, *Medieval Perspectives* III, No. 2, 1988, 18-37. For some of the background to tenth-and eleventh-century chroniclers' views of royal power, see Janet L. Nelson, *Kingship, Law and Liturgy in the Political Thought of Hincmar of Rheims*, EHR 92 (1977), 241-279, rpt. in Nelson, *Politics and Ritual in Early Medieval Europe*, London-Ronceverte 1986, 133-171.

As Schneidmüller points out, it is the *regnum* and its history that begins to determine the representation of the history of individual kings and dynasties in their writings. By the year 1000 the failure of royal dynasties had twice caused dynasties to be replaced in West *Francia*, and the device of royal incompetence had become an explanatory mechanism for both revolutions, thanks to the Carolingians' original depiction of their own immediate predecessors and the resemblance of the chroniclers' depictions of the last Carolingians to them.

Once freed from their Carolingian historiographical confines, the last Merovingians, as, indeed, many other episodes and figures of Frankish history, were treated in the enlarged concerns of new kinds of historical literature. In the tenth and eleventh centuries, as western Europeans grew more distant in time from the already legendary and by then barely comprehensible activities of the early Carolingians, the earlier history of Europe acquired a new shape. The new European historiography had to serve other purposes besides dynastic praise of the Carolingians and to inform a public with different interests and purposes whose demands on historiography were not necessarily those of the Frankish chroniclers and their audiences of the eighth and ninth centuries.[15]

Among the new accounts of Merovingian history, all, as we have seen, preserved the Carolingian version of the deposition of Childeric III, the version known to Gregory VII, Ivo, Gratian, and most of the early commentators on the *Decretum*. Some of these, however, offered a somewhat wider scope for the kind of alternative version given by Stephen of Tournai. By the late eleventh century the composite chronicle of Aimoin of Fleury with its continuations was frequently used as a base text for contemporary histories, as was the later history of Hugh of Fleury.[16] These generally served as satis-

---

15 The process is considered in the work of Schneidmüller and Ehlers cited above, and in that of Bautier, Lemarignier, Werner, Spiegel, and others cited below. For a similar change et a later period, see Gabrielle M. Spiegel, *Pseudo-Turpin, the crisis of the aristocracy and the beginnings of vernacular historiography in France*, JMH 12 (1986), 207-223.

16 The general field is sketched out well in Roger D. Ray, *Medieval historiography through the Twelfth Century: Problems and Progress of Research*, Viator 5 (1974), 33-59. On the histories of Aimoin and Hugh, as well as the *Historia francorum senonensis* and other historical texts discussed here, see Robert-Henri Bautier, *L'historiographie en France aux Xe et XIe siècles*, in: *La Storiografia Altomedioevale*, 2.793-850 (on Aimoin and Fleury 833-835), and, more recently, Bautier, *La place de l'abbaye de Fleury-sur-Loire dans l'historiographie française du IXe au XIIe siècle*, in: René Louis

factory accounts of Frankish history down to the late seventh century, replacing Gregory of Tours, Fredegar's continuators, the *Liber historiae francorum*, and the Royal Frankish Annals. The rhetorical presentation of Aimoin and his continuators appears to have satisfied eleventh-century readers more readily than had the older works of Gregory and others, often attributing to figures in the remote past traits of character and motivation compatible with eleventh-century psychology and values - in much the same way as did the historical *chansons de geste* and some of the early romances."[17]

The texts of Aimoin served the new historiography adequately, and for a century they could be filled out and extended by interpolations and continuations. *Jean-Francois Lemarignier* has commented on just such a *liber historiae francorum*.[18] Paris, BN Ms. lat. 12711 contains the *historia* of Aimoin

---

(Ed.), *Etudes Ligeriennes d'histoire et d'archéologie médiévales*, Auxerre 1975, 25-33, a study that contains an important critique of another substantial work, that of Alexandre Vidier, *L'historiographie à Saint-Benôit-sur-Loire et les miracles de Saint Benôit*, Paris 1965. Further, Karl Ferdinand Werner, *Die literarischen Vorbilder des Aimoin von Fleury*, in: *Medium Aevum. FS Walter Bulst*, Heidelberg 1960, 69-103. Aimoin's own text extended only to 653, and a number of continuations were added in various manuscripts by various writers. Thus, not Aimoin himself, but an *additio* dealing with the mid-eighth century would have contained the version of the deposition of Childeric III and the succession of Pepin that might have been known to Stephen of Tournai. See also Vidier, *L'historiographie à Saint-Benôit-sur-Loire*, 71-75; Bernd Schneidmüller, *Ein Geschichtskompendium des frühen 13. Jahrhunderts aus Saint-Denis (Vat. Reg. 550) als Vorläufer der Grandes Chroniques*, QF 67 (1987), 447-461, discussing the work of Christiane Le Stum, *L'Historia francorum d'Aimoin de Fleury. Etude et édition critique*, BEC 134 (1976), 466. See also the discussion of Paris, BN Ms. lat. 12771 below. An interesting recent study is that of Nico Lettinck, *Comment les historiens de la première moitié du XIIe siècle jugeaient-ils leur temps?*, Journal des Savants (1984), 51-77.

17 E.g. the case of Dagobert. See Laurent Theis, *Dagobert, Saint-Denis et la royauté française au moyen-âge*, in: B. Guenée (Ed.), *Le métier d'historien au moyen-âge*, Paris 1977, 19-30, and Christoph Wehrli, *Mittelalterliche Überlieferungen von Dagobert*, Bd.1, Bern-Frankfurt 1982; for Charles Martel, see Ulrich Nonn, *Das Bild Karl Martells in den lateinischen Quellen vornehmlich des 8. und 9. Jahrhunderts*, Frühmittelalterliche Studien 4 (1970), 70- 137, and in general, Stephen G. Nichols, Jr., *Romanesque Signs: Early medieval Narrative and Iconography*, New Haven 1983.

18 Jean-François Lemarignier, *Autour de la royauté française du IXe au XIIIe siècle*, BEC 113 (1955), 5-36. Paris, BN Ms. lat. 12711 had earlier been described in some detail by Siméon Luce, *La continuation d'Aimoin et le manuscrit latin 12711 de la Bibliothèque Nationale*, in: *Notices et Documents publiés pour la Société de l'histoire de France*, Paris 1884, 57-70. The relevant text reads (Paris, BN Ms. lat. 12711, f.98r-v):"Burchardus [wurze]burgensis episcopus et Fulradus capellanus missi sunt Romam ad Zachariam papam ut consulerent pontifice de causa regum qui illo tempore fuerunt in

down to Dagobert and Clovis II, an anonymous continuation carrying Frankish history down to the death of Louis the Pious, and two interpolations dealing with the monastery of Saint-Germain-des-Prés. Besides Aimoin's text, the compiler also drew upon the *Liber historiae francorum*, the second continuation of Fredegar, and the *Historia francorum senonensis* - the same sources that had provided Adhemar of Chabannes with his own version of Frankish history a few decades earlier. The new *liber historiae francorum*, Lemarignier states, had to come from Saint-Pierre-le-vif at Sens via Saint-Germain-des-Prés between 1015 and 1025. Such works as this and others like it constitute the background to the emergence of a 'national' royal historiography which was taken up (slowly and hesitantly, as Gabrielle Spiegel has pointed out) from the 1120s on, in the *Gesta gentis francorum* and in the *Nova gesta francorum*, and later in the chronicle sequence of Saint-Denis and still later in the vernacular *Grandes Chroniques de France*.[19] It is in these texts that we must look for the version of the events of 751 as told by Stephen of Tournai, since only here could Stephen have learned of an alternative version.[20]

Stephen, of course, became Stephen 'of Tournai' when he became its bishop in 1192. But he was raised in Orléans, became a canon regular at the Victorine house of St. Euverte in Orléans (where he composed his *Summa*),

---

Francia, qui nomen tantam regis sed nullam potestatem regiam habebant. Per quos predictus pontifex mandavit melius esse illum vocari regem apud quem summa potestas consisteret. D[einceps?] auctoritate sua iussit Pippinum rege instituti. Hoc anno secundum Romani pontificis sanctionem Pippinus rex Francorum appellatus est et ad huius dignitatem [f.98v] honoris unctus sacra unctione manu sancte memorie Bonifacii archiepiscopi et martyris et more Francorum elevatus in solium regni Suessionis civitate. Hildericus vero qui falso regis nomine fungebatur tonso capita in monasterium missus est." The transcription is that of Gabrielle Spiegel with several readings of my own. The manuscript has been persuasively dated to the late eleventh century by Jean Derens, *Gislemar, historien de Saint-Germain des Prés*, Journal des Savants (1972), 228-232. I am grateful to Carlrichard Brühl for this reference.

19 Gabrielle M. Spiegel, *The Chronicle Tradition of St. Denis: A Survey*, Brookline, Massachusetts-Leiden 1978.

20 Another ms. may also be cited: Paris, BN Ms. lat. 12710. It has been described in considerable detail by Jules Lair, *Mémoire sur deux Chroniques latines composées au XIIe siècle à l'abbaye de Saint-Denis*, BEC 35 (1874), 543- 580. Both this and BN Ms. lat. 12711 have been discussed by Vidier, *L'historiographie à Saint-Benôit-sur-Loire*, 80-81. Vidier (81) states, a propos BN Ms. lat. 12711, that there is, "dans l'ouvrage des traces d'une origine orléanaise certaine." Other mss. are discussed in Schneidmüller, *Ein Geschichtskompendium*.

studied at Bologna, and was later abbot at Ste. Geneviève in Paris.[21] One of the most learned masters of the twelfth century, Stephen came from a place well within the orbit of Sens-Fleury-Paris, particularly in the early Capetian period. It is not at all unlikely that Stephen's knowledge of early Frankish history derived from a work similar to that contained in BN Ms. lat. 12711 (particularly since Vidier has identified it with Orléans). On the other hand, it is also possible, although considerably less likely, that his knowledge of Frankish history was essentially regional and that it may have drawn upon materials that did not succeed in making their way into the more widely known traditions of Frankish history that came to dominate Latin historiography in the twelfth century and vernacular French historiography in the thirteenth.[22] Stephen was not a purely localized scholar, however, and it seems unlikely that he would have relied upon a purely local and fugitive account of late Merovingian history in preference to the better-known chronicle accounts considered here.

Moreover, not only did Stephen cite a version of the deposition of Childeric III that is unknown in all of the *libri historiae francorum*, but he cited a version that possessed several distinctive features: the description of Childeric III as a womanizer; the identification of Charles Martel as the engineer of the deposition; the failure to name the pope whom Charles consulted, the error in the name of Pepin, and the omission of the name of the king who was deposed. Moreover, he discussed briefly the appellation *Tudites* as a synonym for *Martellus*. These features constitute the parameters of Stephen's source, since they are distinctive and for the most part do not occur elsewhere, although errors in the name of the deposing pope of 751 do occur in a number of

---

21 Stephen's life and thought have most recently been considered by Herbert Kalb, *Studien zur Summa Stephans von Tournai* (see note 9). See also Stephen Ferruolo, *The Origins of the University*, Stanford 1985, 269-277.

22 The earliest vernacular history of France has been discussed by P. Botineau, *L'histoire de France en français de Charlemagne à Philippe-Auguste. La compilation du ms. 624 du fonds de la Reine à la Bibliothèque Vaticane*, Romania 90 (1969), 79-99. As Botineau points out, the ms. begins with Einhard's *Vita Karoli Magni*, although an earlier section of the ms. once existed that probably dealt with late Merovingian history. It is clear that the author had available to him not only the *Historia regum francorum monasterii Sancti Dionysii*, but also a number of other texts, including a continuation of Aimoin. Another version of the vernacular history has been discussed by Ronald N. Walpole, *La traduction du Pseudo-Turpin du manuscrit Vatican Regina 624*, Romania 99 (1978), 484-514, based on ms. 869 (522) of the library of the Musée Condé at Chantilly.

sources, including Einhard, who mistook Stephen II for Zacharias. Such features ought at least to narrow the search for Stephen's source, since they are numerous and uncommon. Indeed, one of them, the discussion of *Carolus Tudites*, occurs only in the *Miracula Sancti Benedicti* of Fleury, although the rest of the *Miracula* version accords with the standard Carolingian account.[23] The *Miracula* follows the error of Einhard in identifying Stephen II as the pope who gave permission for Pepin to replace Childeric III, *inertissimus rex*, although not at the request of Charles Martel.

The accounts of both Gregory of Tours and Fredegar ended before the mid-eighth century. The continuations of Fredegar are various and often sketchy. The Royal Frankish Annals and the *Liber historiae francorum* had provided Einhard with his own version of the events of 751, but later writers who rewrote Gregory and Fredegar had a wide variety of sources to make use of between the late seventh and the late eighth century.[24] Even Aimoin's rewriting of Gregory and Fredegar leaves off at 653, leaving almost as much opportunity for discovery and invention on the part of Aimoin's continuators as that of Fredegar's. In addition, several historiographical traditions began to be taken up in collections of saints' lives and collections of miracle stories, detatched from the formal chronicle tradition. From the early eleventh century on, all of these traditions might mingle unexpectedly and not always in historical accounts proper, particularly in places in which local traditions, shrines, or textual communities might have survived independently of the main Carolingian chronicle tradition.

The continuations of Aimoin in BN Ms. lat. 12711, for example, contain interpolations dealing with the affairs of Saint-Germain; manuscripts from Saint-Denis contain much uniquely dionysian history and other material; still other manuscripts contain materials of local interest in Sens, Fleury, and Orléans. Such different conditions left room for a number of different versions of many of the events of Frankish history between 650 and 800, particularly those produced after the turn of the millennium. What is surprising, however is the relatively limited number of substantially different variants of the story and other Carolingian events that do appear. The Carolingian version

23 E. de Certain (Ed.), *Les miracles de Saint Benôit*, Paris 1858, 1.xiv, 36-37. For a discussion of the work, see Vidier, *L'historiographie à Saint-Benôit-sur-Loire*, 152-180; Benedicta Ward, *Miracles and the Medieval Mind*, Philadelphia 1982, 46-56.

24 In addition to the works cited above, see also Carl-Richard Brühl, *Deutschland-Frankreich. Die Geburt zweier Völker*, Cologne-Vienna 1990, 83-180.

swept all before it until the early eleventh century, when a few variants appeared in the continuations of Aimoin, but the Carolingian version again asserted itself, modified, largely from Aimoin and his continuators, into the history of the *regnum Franciae* in the early twelfth century and dominated that history, in both Latin and vernacular versions, afterward.

These aspects of the historiographical circumstances of western *Francia* in the eleventh and early twelfth centuries lay out the necessary conditions under which a search for Stephen of Tournai's source must be conducted. Although I have conducted such a search, I have not found a chronicle or non-chronicle source for Stephen's version of the character of Childeric III, nor have I found a source that carries the traces of the other distinctive features of Stephen's version. Such a source, if it ever existed, would have had to have been extremely localized in the region of Orléans and virtually non-circulating elsewhere, since none of the many manuscript and printed versions of late Merovingian history refer to it at all. Thus, Stephen's casual observation, *legitur in historia francorum*, cannot refer to any *liber historiae francorum* that influenced the development of the Latin historiography of *Francia* from the mid-twelfth century on.

The preceding consideration of the distinctive features of Stephen of Tournai's account of the character and deposition of Childeric III and the historiographical circumstances in which he would have been likely to encounter them raise the question of whether Stephen 'read' his account in any *historia francorum* at all. *Linda Fowler*, noting some of the features discussed above, raised this same question. Perhaps an examination of some of the most distinctive elements in Stephen's version outside the context of late Merovingian history may suggest an alternative answer.

The most distinctive feature of Stephen's account is his introduction of the element of sexual misconduct - or what he perceived to have been sexual misconduct - on Childeric's part. From the eleventh century, the question of sexual behavior loomed large in ecclesiastical reform circles, in terms of both clergy and laity, especially lay rulers. As *James Brundage* has shown, accounts of crusade history placed great emphasis upon crusader sinfulness as an explanation for the failures of crusades after 1099.[25] Among the most

---

[25] James A. Brundage, *Prostitution, Miscegenation and Sexual Purity in the First Crusade*, in: Peter W. Edbury (Ed.), *Crusade and Settlement: Papers... Presented to R. C. Smail*, Cardiff 1985, 57- 65; cf. Brundage, *Law, Sex, and Christian Society in Medieval Europe*, Chicago 1987, esp. 179-187, and Brundage, *Sexuality, Marriage, and the*

prominent of crusader sins, perhaps not surprisingly in the monastic milieu of much crusade historiography, were those of sexual incontinence and adultery. Again and again, the sexual offences of crusaders are cited as a principal explanation of the failure of crusading movements. In describing the causes of the failure of the crusade of 1101, for example, Geoffroi de Breuil states that:

> Duke William of Aquitaine went with many others to Jerusalem, but nevertheless he contributed nothing to the Christian cause. He was, indeed, a fervent womanizer and for that reason he showed himself to be inconstant in what he did.[26]

Sexual sin, particularly improper sexual attention to women, was a popular device in twelfth-century historiography to account for political and military failure, particularly when those to whom it was attributed were not otherwise known to be wicked, proud, or violent. Contemporary discussions of clerical sexuality, particularly in the context of clerical marriage and concubinage, formed the background of this concern. It was precisely in the context of Charles Martel's military successes that Stephen of Tournai describes Childeric's military diffidence and libidinousness.

The chroniclers of the last Carolingians had linked royal ineffectiveness to royal libidinousness. The *Grandes Chroniques de France* mentioned a "Loys-Fai-noient... sy fu ansi surnomme ou pour ce qu'il fit nule chose que l'on doive mettre en memoire *ou pour ce que il traist une nonnain de l'abbaye de Chiele et l'epousa en mariage*," which Fauchet asserted derived from tenth- and eleventh- century chroniclers. Richer's characterization of Louis V as having poor moral standards may also refer to such illicit sexual activity - or at least could be read as such.[27]

Reform of Christian Society (cited above, n. 3). Several of the sources for the *mutatio regni* from the Carolingians to the Capetians also cite the alleged marriage of Charles of Lorraine to a low-born woman (Aimoinus Floriacensis, De regibus francorum, in: A.Pertz u.a. (Hgg.), *Chronica et annales aevi Salici*, 374-376, 375 (MGH SS 9)). See also J. M. van Winter, *Uxorem de militari ordine sibi imparem*, in: *Miscellanea Mediaevalia in memoriam Jan Frederick Niermeyer*, Groningen 1967, 116.

26 Cited in Jonathan Riley-Smith, *The First Crusade and the Idea of Crusading*, Philadelphia 1986, 133-134, from Geoffroi de Breuil, *Chronica*, M. Bouquet et al. (Edd.), *Recueil des historiens des Gaules et de la France*, 12.430.

27 There is a brief discussion of this text and its sources in Peters, *The Shadow King* (see note 1), 5-6.

Given the descriptions of some of the last Carolingians, particularly their sexual misconduct in addition to their ineffectiveness, the repetition of similar accusations in accounts of the early Capetians, as well as the scandalized reports concerning the presence of women on the Second Crusade, the motif of sexual misconduct was firmly linked to military and political failure.

Moreover, the sexual misconduct of rulers had a scriptural history as well, whose focus was the sin of Solomon, defined by St. Augustine, according to the mid-eleventh-century *De tribus quaestionibus* of Odorannus of Sens, as:

> "Salomon... vir tante sapientie, numquit nam credendum est quod in simulacrorum cultu credidit esse aliquit utilitas? Non, sed mulierum amori ad hoc malum trahenti resistere non valuit, faciens quod sciebat non esse faciendum, ne suis quibus deperibat atque defluebat delicias contristaret."[28]

The *peccatum Salomonis* considered by Odorannus and Augustine before him was described in 3 Kings 11: 1-13:

> King Solomon, however, was a lover of foreign women, and besides Pharaoh's daughter, he married many women... from the nations with whom the Lord had forbidden the Israelites to intermarry, "because", he said, "they will entice you to serve their gods." But Solomon was devoted to them and loved them dearly .... The Lord therefore said to Solomon. "Because you have done this and have not kept my covenant and my statutes as I commanded you, I will tear the kingdom from you and give it to your servant. Nevertheless, for the sake of your father David I will not do this in your day; I will tear it out of your son's hand. Even so not the whole kingdom; I will leave him one tribe for the sake of my servant David and for the sake of Jerusalem my chosen city.

The Frankish kingdom in 751 had indeed been torn from the hands of a king and given to a 'servant', and it had been taken - as the sources implied - from the former royal dynasty by the earthly representative of God. Here, a dynastic change occurred because of forbidden womanizing and the consequences to the kingdom which it entailed. 3 Kings 11: 1-13 was not a text

[28] Odorannus of Sens, *Opera Omnia*, edd., Robert-Henri Bautier et Monique Gilles, Paris 1972, 134. Odorannus is citing Augustine, *De genesi ad litteram* 11.59. The loss of rulership in Israel as the result of failing to keep divine laws is also reflected in the prophecy of Samuel to Saul (1 Samuel [1 Kings] 15:23-29).

with an extensive history of exegesis. Augustine had cited it in the *De genesi ad litteram*, and Bede had commented upon it allegorically several times. Hrabanus Maurus mentioned it briefly, identifying the *mulieres* of Solomon with the *ecclesiae electae ex gentibus*, and these with heretical movements, and Odorannus cited it, as we have seen, in his *De tribus questionibus*. These verses were not glossed in the *glossa ordinaria*, nor are they mentioned by the victorines or Rupert of Deutz.[29]

The similarity of the sin of Solomon to Stephen's account of Childeric III does not, of course, do any more than suggest that he or his source might have found in 3 Kings the portrait of a ruler whose kingdom was taken by God from his *stirps* and himself and given to a servant as a punishment for the sin of sexual misconduct, an offense that was particularly resonant in the eleventh and twelfth centuries. The question of idolatry, of course, would not have applied here, but that of the *divisio regni* would certainly have been on the minds of twelfth-century churchmen in the *regnum Franciae*. Indeed, the motif of kings either distracted by wicked consorts or engaging in extra-marital sexual activities to the detriment of their rule and the welfare of their kingdoms was something of a topos in Carolingian and post-Carolingian Europe.[30]

If the sin of Solomon and the eleventh- and twelfth-century concern with royal and noble sexual practices may be said to constitute some of the intellectual background for Stephen's description of Childeric III, more immediate was the case of the Capetian dynasty from the reign of Philip I (1060-1108) to Stephen's own time of writing in the 1160s. Philip's opposition to the Gregorian reform movement elicited a stinging letter in 1074 from Gregory

---

29 Bede, *In proverbia Salomonis allegoriae interpretationes*, PL 91.1065-1066; Hrabanus Maurus, *Commentaria in Libros IV Regum*, 3, c.11, PL 109.198-199. On some 'political' uses of exegesis in the eleventh century, see I. S. Robinson, *The Bible in the Investiture Contest: The South German Gregorian Circle*, in: Katherine Walsh and Diana Wood (Edd.), *The Bible in the Medieval World: Essays in Memory of Beryl Smalley*, Oxford 1985, 61-84 (Studies in Church History, Subsidia 4).

30 There is a brief discussion in Peters, *The Shadow King* (see note 1), 103. The work of Mars, of course, was usually thought to be vitiated by the temptations of Venus. For an early example, see Janet L. Nelson, *Queens as Jezebels: Brunhild and Balthild in Merovingian History*, rpt. in: Nelson, *Politics and Ritual in Early Medieval Europe*, London-Ronceverte 1986, 1-48; see also Pauline Stafford, *Queens, Concubines and Dowagers: The King's Wife in the Early Middle Ages*, Atlanta-London 1983. For other early medieval criticisms of libidinous rulers, see Bund, *Thronsturz und Herrscherabsetzung*, 637, 780nn.

VII addressed to the archbishops of Reims, Sens, and Bourges, and to the bishops of Chartres and other dioceses, condemning both Philip's tyranny and his negligence and laxity of rule.[31] Later in the same year Gregory wrote to William of Poitou condemning Philip in even stronger terms.[32] In 1092 Philip carried off Bertrada of Montfort, wife of Fulk le Rechin, Count of Anjou, and in 1092-1093 he persecuted the diocese of Chartres for Bishop Ivo's opposition to his marriage to Bertrada.[33] Excommunicated at the Council of Clermont in 1095, in spite of the fact that he was supported by most of the French bishops, Philip did not improve his relations with the papacy until 1104, culminating in the agreements for accepting ecclesiastical reform in France in 1107.[34]

Philip's reign, characterized in the correspondence of Gregory VII as both tyrannical and negligent, was characterized by later chroniclers chiefly in terms of the king's inactivity, caused by his lust for Bertrada of Montfort. In the early 1140s, when Suger of Saint-Denis wrote the life of Philip's son Louis VI, the *Vita Ludovici Grossi*, Suger mentioned nothing at all of Philip's rapacity and tyranny, even terming the king *rex magnificus* on one occasion.[35] On Philip's conduct after 1092, Suger focused on the king's inability

---

[31] E.Caspar, *Das Register Gregors VII* (see note 2), 2,5.129-133. There is a brief discussion in Elizabeth Hallam, *Capetian France, 987-1328*, London-New York 1980, 75-78, 105-108. The fullest account is still the work of Augustin Fliche, *Le règne de Philippe Ier, Roi de France (1060-1108)*, Paris 1912.

[32] E.Caspar, *Das Register Gregors VII* (see note 2), 2,18.150-151.

[33] On the marriage of Philip and Bertrada, see Georges Duby, *Le chevalier, la femme et le prêtre. Le mariage dans la France féodale*, Paris 1981, 7-26; Eng. trans. by Barbara Bray, *The Knight, the Lady, and the Priest: The Making of Modern Marriage in Medieval France*, New York 1983, 3-21. Ivo of Chartres' views on marriage are considered in Brigitte Basdevant-Gaudemet, *Le mariage d'après la correspondance d'Yves de Chartres*, RHD 61 (1983), 195-215. Gregory VII himself had called Philip 'useless': E.Caspar, *Das Register Gregors VII*, 2.5 (see note 31), and Rudolf Schieffer, *Gregor VII und die Könige Europas*, in: *Studi Gregoriani* 13 (see note 3), 188-211, at 195, 207, and Jean Gaudemet, *Grégoire VII et la France*, in: *La Riforma Gregoriana e l'Europa*, 1.213-240. In 1106 Hugh of Cluny invited Philip to leave the kingship and enter Cluny as a monk: H. E. J. Cowdrey, *Two Studies in Cluniac History 1049-1106*, in: *Studi Gregoriani* 11, Roma 1978, 153-155.

[34] See Uta-Renate Blumenthal, *The Investiture Controversy: Church and Monarchy from the Ninth to the Twelfth Century*, Philadelphia 1988, 159-167.

[35] Suger of St. Denis, *Vie de Louis VI le Gros*, ed. and trans. Henri Waquet, Paris 1929, c.1, 4. Most recently on Suger and the *Vita Ludovici*, see John F. Benton, *Introduction: Suger's Life and Personality*, and the other studies in: Paula Lieber Gerson (Ed.), *Abbot Suger and Saint-Denis*, New York 1985, 3-15.

to control other violent people rather than on the king's own violence. After the king's abduction of Bertrada, Suger remarks:

> "Deinceps, in diem proficiente filio, pater eius rex Phillipus in diem deficiebat; neque enim post superductam Andegavensem comitissam quicquam regia majestate dignum agebat, sed rapte conjugis raptus concupiscentia, voluptati sue satisfacere operam dabat. Unde nec reipublice providebat nec proceri et elegantis corporis sanitati, plus equo remissus, parcebat. Hoc unum supererat quod timore et amore successoris filii regni status vigebat. Cumque fere sexagenarius esset, regem exuens, apud Mildunum castrum super fluvium Sequane, presente domino Ludovico, extremum clausit diem."[36]

Moreover, it is against this background of royal indifference and negligence that Suger sets off the piety and youthful valor of the young Louis VI. Unable to engage in the customary youthful recreations of the hunt and other appropriate juvenile activities, Suger's Louis was immediately plunged into the adult wars for the defense of the realm that occupy the first few chapters of Suger's *Vita*. Louis, the *inluster et animosus regni paterni defensor*, could respond at once to claims for justice that had been made one hundred times to his father without response.[37]

In c. 13, summing up the career of Philip just before describing his death, Suger states that after 1092 the king concentrated upon nothing but the satisfaction of his fleshly desires, "did nothing worthy of the royal dignity", "made no provisions for the needs of the kingdom," nor even for those of his own body. Without his vigorous and pious son, Philip would have lost the kingdom, Suger observes, either to William II of England (which would have been *nec fas, nec naturale*), or to some other invader.[38] Suger's judgement of Philip was echoed by Ordericus Vitalis and by other twelfth-century and later historians.[39] It may have seemed much more likely to Suger and other

---

[36] *Vie de Louis VI le Gros*, c. 13 (Ed. Waquet 80-82). Suger says something similar about William II of England, c.1.

[37] *Vie de Louis VI le Gros*, c.1 (Ed. Waquet 6, 10).

[38] *Vie de Louis VI le Gros*, c.1 (Ed. Waquet 10).

[39] *The Ecclesiastical History of Ordericus Vitalis*, ed. and trans. Marjorie Chibnall, Vol. 5, Oxford 1975, 10, 5, 214: "Philippus enim rex piger et corpulentis belloque incongruus erat." Cf. 218 on the defence of the villages around Chaumont by the French in 1098: "sine rege legitimoque ductore". On Philip's conduct after the abduction of Bertrada of Montfort, 9.2, 10: "a fedo reatu resipiscere noluit, sed senio et aegritudine tabidus in adulterio stercore flebiter computruit". On the views of William of Malmes-

contemporary chroniclers than it has often seemed to later historians that the Capetian dynasty might have been perilously close to extinction during Philip's reign and that Philip's conduct, at least as depicted by Suger, Orderic, and others, seemed strikingly similar to that of the last Merovingians and the last Carolingians, with the explicit sexual dimension now obviously present.

Dynastic awareness on the part of the Capetian family and its clerical clients seems to have been particularly acute in the late eleventh and early twelfth centuries. Sometime before 1050 a monk at Saint-Valéry described a prophecy made by his saint to Hugh Capet, that Hugh's dynasty would last for seven generations, a prophecy repeated, but now attributed to Saint Riquier, shortly before 1088.[40] Depending upon how one calculates the number of Capetian generations, the seventh generation would be represented by Louis VII, who at the time of Stephen's writing the *Summa*, was still without male issue. Philip Augustus was not born until 1165 - and then was called *Dieudonné*.

By 1160, the connection between inert, negligent kingship and sexual profligacy had been explicitly and repeatedly made in a number of different circumstances, but chiefly in terms of the failure of dynasties and the division of kingdoms, first the Merovingian, and then the Carolingian. The case of Philip I and the prophecy of seven generations of Capetian rulers fit such a typology nicely. If the Carolingians and the recent Capetian king had behaved in such a way as to link negligence and sexual profligacy, had not the last Merovingians done this as well? It was Philip's good fortune, or perhaps, in Suger's terms, blessing from God, to have had the valorous and pious son that the last Merovingians and last Carolingians had lacked, and it was certainly a sign of God's favor toward the *regnum Franciae*. But that son had unnaturally lost a childhood and had been forced even to take up arms as a child. Louis VI had indeed preserved the kingdom, and he preserved the dynasty by producing Louis VII. But Louis VI had also married (as Charles of Lorraine was said to have done) a woman from a castellan family which was beneath the royal dignity - the reason the marriage was dissolved in

---

bury and other chroniclers through the mid-twelfth century, see Duby, *The Knight, the Lady, and the Priest* (see note 33), 14-15. Duby indicates that the case remained well known during the twelfth century throughout most of France and England.

40 The prophecy is discussed in Lewis, *Royal Succession in Capetian France*, 36, 50, 106 (the prophecy appears to have been widely known), 110-111.

1107 - and his first son by the second marriage, Philip, although annointed in 1129, died in 1131. Louis VII himself had had a troubled marital life, clouded by scandal and separation from Eleanor of Aquitaine - indeed, Louis VII had been married three times and, before 1165, had yet had no legitimate male heir. Failing a male heir, there were those outside the Capetian dynasty who could make strong claims to the French throne.

Legitur in historia francorum? My search for a chronicle or other narrative source for Stephen of Tournai's version of the deposition of Childeric III has found none, and it has also raised the question of whether, given the parameters of the source, one ever existed. The version Stephen gives left no traces in later twelfth- and thirteenth-century historiography. But it did echo a scriptural topos, one known in eleventh- and twelfth-century *Francia*, and it did fit the model of the fall of dynasties and the division of kingdoms that had become widely known in the same period and was certainly a distinct possibility between the reign of Philip I and the birth of Philip Augustus in 1165, perhaps even later.

After the various continuations of Aimoin, and largely building upon his work, the writing of history in *Francia* became predominantly that of the Saint-Denis historians, who, looking back from the dynastic security of the reign of Philip Augustus and his successors through the thirteenth century, did not need to worry about royal negligence and only intermittently about royal sexual misconduct. They merely amended the original Carolingian history of the *gens Francorum* to correct for the *troisième race royale*, whose cause and whose *regnum* their work served.

II

The 'importance' of both 'innocent' and 'culpable' uselessness that had influenced narrative historiography, if not canon law, before Stephen's *casus* to 15.6.3 did not influence Huguccio's distinction between the two, nor does it seem to have occupied later canonists. Huguccio's distinction enabled royal uselessness to be considered in terms of the ecclesiastical idoneity which Innocent III and subsequent popes used as a standard of judging both ecclesiastical and secular office. Innocent IV's deposition of Sancho II of Portugal in 1245 became the new standard illustrating 'innocent' uselessness, and, as *Gerard Caspary* and others have shown, this case influenced later cases of both papal and local deposition of a number of later European rulers, whether innocent or criminal: Adolf of Nassau, Edward II of England, Richard II of England, and Wenceslaus IV of Bohemia and the Empire, as well as the case of the abdication in 1294 of Pope Celestine V.[41]

Another case, that of Henry II of Cyprus, has generally gone unnoticed, although its date, 1306, and its duration and notoriety, 1306-1310, gave it a significance that may well have influenced the proceedings against Edward II, Richard II, and Wenceslaus IV.[42] As had occurred in the case of Sancho II, Amaury of Lusignan, the king's brother and heir presumptive, claimed the titles of *gubernator et rector* of the kingdom because of the king's 'illness' and general incapacity:

> "the king had failed to provide for the security and well-being of the kingdom; despite the advice of his vassals he had done nothing to avert the

---

41 G. Caspary, *The Deposition of Richard II and the Canon Law*, in: *Proceedings 2CongMCL Boston 1963*, Città del Vaticano 1965, 189-201 (MIC, C, 1); Peters, *The Shadow King* (see note 1), 116-169, 210-245; William Huse Dunham, Jr. and Charles T. Wood, *The Right to Rule in England: Depositions and the Kingdom's Authority, 1327-1485*, AHR 81 (1976), 738-761; Charles T. Wood, *Joan of Arc and Richard III: Sex, Saints, and Government in the Middle Ages*, New York 1988, 93-116, 152-174; Natalie Fryde, *The Tyranny and Fall of Edward II. 1321-1326*, Cambridge 1979; Edward Peters, *Vox populi, vox Dei*, in: Edward B. King and Susan J. Ridyard (Edd.), *Law in medieval Life and Thought*, 1990, 91-120, at 110-116 (Sewanee Medieval Studies 5); Helmut G. Walther, *Der gelehrte Jurist als politischer Ratgeber: Die Kölner Universität und die Absetzung König Wenzels 1400*, in: *Miscellanea Mediaevalia* 20, Berlin-New York 1989, 467-487. I am grateful to Professor Walther for this reference. For Celestine V, see Martin Bertram, *Die Abdankung Papst Cölestins V (1294) und die Kanonisten*, ZRG Kan. Abt. 87 (1970), 1-101; Peter Herde, *Cölestin V. (1294) (Peter von Morrone). Der Engelpapst*, Stuttgart 1981, 143-160 (Päpste und Papsttum 16); John R. Eastman, *Papal Abdication in Later Medieval Thought*, Lewiston 1990; Tilmann Schmidt, *Der Bonifaz-Prozess. Verfahren der Papstanklage in der Zeit Bonifaz' VIII und Clemens' V*, Cologne-Vienna 1989, 40. It is striking that, given the canonists' and others' insistence on royal *inutilitas* in terms of deposition or suspension from *administratio*, that there is very little about royal *utilitas* in the coronation *ordines*. The only *ordo* that seems to mention the term specifically is the twelfth-century *ordo* from Burgundy: "Cum necessitas exposcit, ut populus eligat sibi regem, virum utilem providere debet et sapientem ac timentem Deum et qui odiat avaritiam nec diligat munera..." The *ordo* has been edited by Reinhard Elze, *Königskrönung und Ritterweihe. Der Burgundische Ordo für die Weihe und Krönung des Königs und der Königin*, in: *FS Josef Fleckenstein* (see note 6), 327-342, at 333. I am grateful to Richard Jackson for this reference.

42 The case is described at length in Peter W. Edbury, *The Kingdom of Cyprus and the Crusades 1191-1374*, Cambridge 1991, 100-140. Edbury cites the extant scholarly bibliography.

> danger posed by the Genoese; nor had he taken action to counter the sultan's threatened naval attack or send aid to the kingdom of Armenia which had suffered much in recent years at the hands of the Muslims; he was accused of inaction in the face of hostile shipping, of allowing Cyprus to become increasingly isolated both diplomatically and militarily, and of failing to arrange food supplies at a time of famine, even when foreign corn had been on offer; everyone was concerned with the absence of military preparedness; what was more, with delays of up to twenty years, there was no justice to be had so that heirs were disinherited and the clergy and the Military Orders were denied redress for injuries they had suffered."[43]

The deposition of Henry II on grounds of uselessness was intended to be permanent. Henry was kept initially under house arrest, although he retained the oaths of homage and fealty of his principal liegemen, until terms could be decided upon, and the next several years saw sympathy veering back and forth between Henry and Amaury, Henry's brief exile to Armenia, extensive papal and other efforts to reconcile the brothers, and Henry's final return to rule in Cyprus after Amaury's death in 1310.

Henry's partially successful and politically embarrassing resistance to his brother's actions, the residual support that a living king generated, and the drawn-out activities of the papal curia in attempting to decide the rightness of the case offered no clear-cut appeal to the idea of the *rex inutilis* as an independent rationale for deposition - such a single charge might, as the case of Henry II illustrates, leave too much leeway for opposition to the new government to form around the still-living former king, since the person of the king preserved too much royal *dignitas* and majesty for a charge of *inutilitas* to be universally accepted. Later royal depositions undertaken by local rivals tended to include incapacity, but only as one among a number of stiffer charges, including that of tyranny, perhaps mindful of the unsatisfactory results of the case of Henry II.

The twelfth century saw other manifestations of royal incapacity as well, particularly the case of the prince who failed to prosecute heresy in his territory. In this instance, too, yet another attribute was added to the *interpretatio* of the hapless Childeric III. The thirteenth-century canonist Henricus Merseburgensis misidentified Childeric as Ludovicus, *inutilis dissolutus et*

---

[43] Edbury, *The Kingdom of Cyprus*, 114.

negligens in heresi extirpanda.[44] As had been the case with sexual sin, the failure to prosecute heresy was read back by later commentators onto the figure of the original *rex inutilis*.

Such a failure had not been a significant topic of discussion before the Investiture Conflict, nor had it developed in canonist usage until the late twelfth century, and then in the wake of ecclesiastical consideration of the deposition of heretical prelates.[45] The obligation of temporal rulers to turn their powers against heresy was acknowledged by the Third Lateran Council of 1179. The decretal of Lucius III, *Ad abolendam*, of 1184 was the next decisive attempt to systematize the duties of lay rulers in regard to heterodoxy.[46] At about the same time Raymond V of Toulouse discovered that a lay ruler's failure to prosecute heresy in his dominions might constitute an advantage for his internal enemies who could attack his lordship on that ground. The possible personal heretical beliefs of lay rulers aside, the active protection that they might afford heretics in their dominions or the flourishing of heresy because of their indifference or incapacity to deal with it became points considered especially by Innocent III, beginning with the decretal *Vergentis in senium* of 1199. Here, Innocent began his attack not only on heretics, but on their supporters, defenders, associates, and upon rulers who permitted their activities to continue untroubled by the just discipline of temporal authorities, likening heresy to treason and thereby opening the prosecution of heresy to the same broad spectrum that treason prosecution offered in Roman law.[47] These steps justified Innocent's rationale for the confiscation of the lands of

---

44 Yale Law Library MS no. 1, fol. 81v. Printed in Peters, *The Shadow King* (see note 1), 121, n.3, from the transcription of Peter Landau.

45 Titus Lenherr, *Die Exkommunikations- und Depositionsgewalt der Häretiker bei Gratian und den Dekretisten bis zur Glossa ordinaria des Johannes Teutonicus*, St. Ottilien 1987 (MThSt III, 42); Lothar Kolmer, *Ad capiendas vulpes. Die Ketzerbekämpfung in Südfrankreich in der ersten Hälfte des 13. Jahrhunderts und die Ausbildung des Inquisitionsverfahrens*, Bonn 1982 (Pariser Historische Studien 19).

46 Kolmer, *Ad capiendas vulpes* (see note 45), 29, n., 21.

47 Othmar Hageneder, *Studien zur Dekretale 'Vergentis' (X. V, 7. 10). Ein Beitrag zur Häretikergesetzgebung Innozenz' III.*, ZRG Kan. Abt. 49 (1963), 138-173; in general, see Walter L. Wakefield, *Heresy, Crusade and Inquisition in Southern France, 1100-1250*, Berkeley and Los Angeles 1974; Richard M. Fraher, *Conviction According to Conscience: The Medieval Jurists' Debate Concerning Judicial Discretion and the Law of Proof*, Law and History Review 7 (1989), 23-88; idem, *Preventing Crime in the High Middle Ages: The Medieval Lawyers' Search for Deterrence*, in: James Ross Sweeney and Stanley Chodorow (Edd.), *Popes, Teachers, and Canon Law in the Middle Ages FS Brian Tierney*, Ithaca 1989, 212-233.

those lords who protected heretics in 1204, his excommunication of Raymond VI of Toulouse in 1207, and the launching of the crusade in 1208. By the end of the first quarter of the thirteenth century, as Henricus Merseburgensis' text indicates, the failure to prosecute heresy had added one more category of royal *inutilitas* to those of inactivity and sexual misconduct.

A final category appears, neither in canon law nor narrative historiography - and it was one never attributed to the last Merovingian king - but in several exegetical and literary works of the thirteenth and early fourteenth centuries: that of the *rex curiosus*. During the twelfth and thirteenth centuries, scriptural models of good and bad rulers and courtiers were frequently invoked by moralists. Among the most popular of such models was the figure of Joseph in Egypt, and among the most interesting texts concerning the role of Joseph in thirteenth-century cases was the treatise by John of Limoges, abbot of the Cistercian monastery in Zirc, Hungary, from 1208 to 1218, the *Morale somnium Pharaonis*.[48] In this work dedicated to Count Theobald IV of Champagne, John commented upon Pharaoh's efforts to have his dream explained, and in *Ep.* 18 Joseph denounces Pharaoh as a *rex curiosus*, given over to random and undisciplined *curiositas* about inappropriate subjects and neglecting the proper knowledge suitable to a king.

The theme did not belong to John of Limoges alone. In Paradiso xiii, Dante has Thomas Aquinas praise Solomon's request to God for knowledge,

> that would serve his royal task - and not to know the number of the angels on high, or, if combined with a contingent, *necesse* ever can produce *necesse*, or *si est dare primum motum esse*, or if, within a semicircle, one can draw a triangle with one right angle.[49]

Royal prudence in attaining knowledge was a concern of both John of Limoges and Dante. And although there may have been a number of rulers -

---

48 I have not been able to consult the text of John of Limoges directly, but there is an extensive discussion of it in C. Stephen Jaeger, *The origins of Courtliness: Civilizing Trends and the Formation of Courtly Ideals, 939-1210*, Philadelphia 1985, 87-95. The text is in: Constantin Horvath (Ed.), *Johannes Lemovicensis, abbatis de Zirc 1208-1218 opera omnia*, 3 vols., Vesprem 1932. The question of proper and improper royal learning, however, had a long history; cf. Bede, *Super parabolas Salomonis allegorica expositio*, 1.4, PL 91.956: "declinat ad dexteram, qui vult plus sapere quam oportet sapere", and J. M. Wallace-Hadrill, *The Via Regia of the Carolingian Age*, in: Beryl Smalley (Ed.), *Trends in medieval Political Thought*, New York 1965, 22-41.

49 Dante, *Paradiso*, trans. Allen Mandelbaum, New York 1986, XIII, 96-102.

Frederick II, for example - who indulged in unkingly quests for learning, the charge seems never to have been made against any reigning king as a constitutional ground for deposition. It remained for Shakespeare to create Prospero, and for sixteenth- and seventeenth-century rulers to develop increasingly respectable cabinets of curiosities.[50]

Childeric III, the prototype of all later *reges inutiles*, managed to avoid at least this last charge of *curiositas*. But his career was not finished with the charge of failing to extirpate heresy. Among the most violently anti-papal-and indeed anti-prelatal-tracts of the Reformation in England were Robert Barnes' *A supplycacion unto the most gracyous prynce H. the viij.* of 1534, and his *Vitae Romanorum Pontificum* of 1535, the latter also dedicated to Henry VIII. Among the many instances of the horrendous aggrandizement of papal power that Barnes cites is the episode of Zacharias, Childeric III, and Pepin.[51] Zacharias had deposed Childeric, says Barnes, on the grounds that Childeric had once been a monk, and Barnes points out that the clergy say that Childeric was deposed because he was living in lechery (a point surely not lost on Henry VIII), although clergy do not always choose to prosecute lecherous or adulterous rulers, and this is a secret doctrine of the Roman church.

Thus, Stephen of Tournai's *casus* of the case of Childeric III and Huguccio's elaboration of it survived in the religious polemic of the sixteenth century. It was taken up by French historians of the seventeenth century and transformed into the type of the *roi fainéant*, a figure that hardly does justice to the intricate and adventurous legal thought that had produced it, from the Carolingian publicists to the canon lawyers of the twelfth and thirteenth centuries.[52]

---

50 See Oliver Impey and Arthur MacGregor (Edd.), *The Origins of Museums: The Cabinet of Curiosities in Sixteenth- and Seventeenth-Century Europe*, Oxford 1985.

51 Rainer Pineas, *Robert Barnes's Polemical Use of History*, Bibliothèque d'humanisme et Renaissance 26 (1964), 55-69. The case is also mentioned by William Tyndale; see Pineas, *William Tyndale's Use of History as a Weapon of Religious Controversy*, Harvard Theological Review 55 (1962), 121-141.

52 Edward Peters, *Roi fainéant: The Origins of an Historians' Commonplace*, Bibliothèque d'humanisme et Renaissance 30 (1968), 537-547; idem, *The Shadow King* (see note 1), 1-13.

IX

Henry II of Cyprus, *Rex inutilis*: A Footnote to *Decameron* 1.9

The ninth story of the first day, the shortest in Boccaccio's *Decameron,* tells of *una gentil donna di Guascogna,* a gentlewoman of Gascony, who stops off at Cyprus on her return from a pilgrimage to the Holy Land. Assaulted and humiliated by a group of ruffians, the woman proposes to seek justice from the king of Cyprus but is told that the king is too weak and pusillanimous either to correct wrongs done to others or to avenge insults to himself. Indeed, when people in the kingdom are angry about anything, they freely insult the king with impunity. The gentlewoman, despairing of justice but now bent on revenge, goes to the king and asks him to explain to her how he is able to bear his great shame, since she would like to learn how to bear her own. Her words sting the king, and, like one roused from a sleep, he avenges the injury to the woman and goes on to become the scourge of all those who have shamed him and dishonored his crown.[1]

The elements of the story were not original with Boccaccio. A shorter and far less ornate version is found in the late-thirteenth-century *Il Novellino,* and the story may have existed in a source common to both the author of *Il Novellino* and Boccaccio.[2] Nor was Boccaccio the last to tell it; it was retold by Sercambi (who substituted a king of Portugal for the king of Cyprus—a point to which I

An earlier version of this essay was delivered in March 1996 at the New College Conference on Medieval and Renaissance Studies at the University of South Florida, Sarasota. I am grateful to Lee Daniel Snyder for his hospitality on this and other occasions and to the members of the audience who commented on the paper, as well as to two very helpful anonymous readers for *Speculum.* I am also grateful to my colleague Victoria Kirkham for her generous reading of a later draft of the article and several useful bibliographical suggestions, as well as to Elissa Weaver, and especially to Pier Massimo Forni, who permitted me to read his unpublished *lectura* of *Decameron* 1.9, from which I have benefited greatly. The article is dedicated to Gerard E. Caspary, who long ago put me on to the trail that has led to Henry II of Cyprus. See below, n. 33.

[1] Giovanni Boccaccio, *Il Decamerone,* in *Tutte le opere di Giovanni Boccaccio,* ed. Vittore Branca (Milan, 1976), 4: *Giornata prima, novella nove,* pp. 81–82.

[2] *Il Novellino,* ed. Cesare Segre, in *La prosa del duecento,* ed. Cesare Segre and Mario Marti (Milan and Naples, 1959), no. 51, p. 839. The more recent edition by Sebastiano Lo Nigro (Turin, 1968), pp. 137–38, interpolates material from Boccaccio into the original *Novellino* story without sufficient warrant. The *Novellino* version is brief enough to be cited in full here (my translation): "There was a Gascon woman (*una guasca*) in Cyprus to whom one day was done a deed of such villany and shame that she could not suffer it. She moved herself and went to the king of Cyprus and said, 'Sire, to you have been done already ten thousand affronts and to me but one; you who have sustained so many, please teach me how to sustain mine.' The king was ashamed and began to avenge his affronts and ceased to tolerate them." On the two versions, see Alfonso Paolella, *Retorica e racconto: Argomentazione e finzione nel "Novellino"* (Naples, 1987), pp. 110–12, and in general on the difference between the earlier and later styles of narrative, see Erich Auerbach, *Mimesis,* trans. Willard R. Trask (Princeton, N.J., 1953), pp. 203–31, and Luigi Russo, *Letture critiche del Decameron* (Rome and Bari, 1973), pp. 133–35.

will return) later in the fourteenth century, by Sansovino in the early seventeenth, and by others later.[3]

But the tales of the *Decameron* are never merely versions of earlier stories that in their turn are retold by others. The stories themselves are landmarks in the history of narrative art in vernacular prose. Each story must also be cross-located in the context of its day, its narrator, its relation to the macro-text of the entire work, and its role in illustrating the themes that Boccaccio weaves through many of his stories, as well as in the frame narrative, in this case the moral rebuke of a superior by an inferior which is accepted by the offending superior and thus legitimated.

In the case of the story of the king of Cyprus, Boccaccio has also made a number of significant changes from his original. There is nothing necessarily Cyprus-specific about the *Novellino* version; its exemplary character could be as easily served by any offended woman speaking about the same subject to any king in any country or century. Boccaccio makes the story much more Cyprus-specific by identifying the king as "the first king of Cyprus after the conquest of the Holy Land by Godfrey of Bouillon," thus locating the exchange more precisely in both place and time. The plain *una guasca* of the *Novellino* has become *una gentil donna di Guascogna,* thus elevating the social rank of the king's critic to one that is more suitable for gaining access to and criticizing a king face to face. She has also become a *pellegrina,* a pilgrim, adding yet another status change to the *Novellino* version, one that makes the insults she suffers even more legally grievous, since they violate the protected legal status of a pilgrim. The original and vague "indignity" has been transformed into a vicious physical assault by wicked people; that is, the gentlewoman-pilgrim has been raped.

Boccaccio also introduces an unnamed third character, who performs the function of informing the woman of the king's pusillanimity and of the extent to which it has affected the entire kingdom. The information she receives causes the woman to lose all hope of obtaining justice and inspires her with the idea of alleviating her own grief by tormenting the king to his face. She does so in an elaborate, syntactically complex speech that elegantly performs the service, advertised in the prologue to the story by the narrator, Elissa, of showing how "a single word, uttered by chance rather than *ex proposito,* has managed to bring about a positive change in a person previously unaffected by reproaches and punishments." As both Luigi Russo and Mario Baratto put it, the woman becomes "an artist of revenge."[4] She also becomes inadvertently an artist of moral and political regeneration.

Finally, the king's transformation, described by the common medieval trope of a noble or royal character change for the better as waking from political or moral

[3] Giovanni Sercambi, *Il Novelliere,* ed. Lucian Rossi (Rome, 1974), *Exemplo* lii, pp. 305–7. For later retellings, see A. C. Lee, *The Decameron: Its Sources and Analogues* (1909; repr. New York, 1972), p. 24, and for Boccaccio's immediate successors in the genre, Christopher Nissen, *The Ethics of Retribution in the "Decameron" and the Late Medieval Italian Novella* (Lewiston, N.Y.; Queenston, Ont.; and Lampeter, Wales, 1993), pp. 75–122.

[4] Russo, *Letture critiche del Decameron,* p. 134; Mario Baratto, *Realtà e stile nel "Decameron"* (Vicenza, 1970), pp. 37–40.

somnambulism, is sharply contrasted to his former state of pusillanimity, as he harshly avenges the injuries done to the woman (not noted in the *Novellino* version) and relentlessly prosecutes everyone who discredits the honor of his crown (also not noted in the *Novellino* version but appropriate for Boccaccio, who had long studied law and knew the implications of the phrase). These reforms also presumably affected the historical kingdom of Cyprus, at least in the narrative, since Boccaccio has firmly located the story there.

The story is perfectly appropriate to the theme of the first day, which is in a number of ways recapitulated on the sixth and tenth days, and to the narrator, Elissa, recently and persuasively identified by Michael Paden as the unnamed *ghibellina* of 10.7 and 10.8.[5] Ghibellines made high claims for noble status and royal legitimacy, but they also had particularly high expectations of moral and ethical standards for kings and aristocrats, as Elissa's other stories, especially those of the Count of Antwerp (2.8) and Guido Cavalcanti (6.9) nicely illustrate. The story at 1.9 fits with other "historical" tales throughout the work, and it also bears a number of Boccaccian themes, a point that scholars have widely noted.[6]

In Boccaccio's hands the story is both an elaborated exemplum, as Sercambi called it in his own later version, and a *fabula ornata,* not only enriched by Boccaccio's narrative art, but naturalistically located in a particular reign in a particular kingdom. Accurate historical references are neither, of course, extraneous to fictional narrative, nor do they necessarily serve a further purpose than that of attaching a particular story to an especially renowned historical figure in order to make it more memorable, morally trustworthy, or authoritative. Boccaccio himself offers some very peculiar English, French, Brabantine, and Scottish "history" in the stories of the Count of Antwerp (2.8) and of Alessandro, the financial agent who marries the daughter of the king of England and later becomes king of Scotland (2.3). Still other stories are attached to named and unnamed rulers of Sicily, Naples, Aragon, France, and Babylon. Boccaccio's history is usually ethical rather than exact, and there is normally no reason why it should not be so.

Moreover, Boccaccio may also here be drawing on what may be termed "the matter of Cyprus," that is, a general impression of the island kingdom and its culture that was widely held by writers and drawn upon when needed, a subject that belongs also to the general technique of characterizing "national" groups and their lands (or, as Paul Meyvaert has recently termed one of its aspects, "voicing national antipathy") that occupied the attention and interest of many kinds of writers from the eleventh century on.[7] Thus it also applies to other literary locations as well as to Cyprus. David Wallace has recently treated Chaucer's "Flaundres" in this way, although Chaucer is far more detailed about Flanders and Lombardy, since he had traveled to both places and knew Flanders intimately, than

[5] Michael Paden, "Elissa: La ghibellina del Decameron," *Studi sul Boccaccio* 21 (1993), 139–50.

[6] E.g., Russo, *Letture critiche del Decameron;* Baratto, *Realtà e stile nel "Decameron";* Thomas M. Greene, "Forms of Accommodation in the *Decameron,*" *Italica* 45 (1968), 297–313.

[7] Paul Meyvaert, " 'Rainaldus est malus scriptor Francigenus'—Voicing National Antipathy in the Middle Ages," *Speculum* 66 (1991), 743–63, with a useful literature cited, particularly Ludwig Schmugge, "Über 'nationale' Vorurteile im Mittelalter," *Deutsches Achiv für Erforschung des Mittelalters* 38 (1982), 439–59.

Boccaccio is about Cyprus, which he never visited.[8] The rich markets of Cyprus attract ambitious foreign merchants (4.4). Cypriot merchants are immensely prosperous and generous (2.7), and it is not implausible that the traveling Saladin and his Saracen nobles pass themselves off successfully in Pavia as Cypriot merchants (10.9). But elsewhere in Cyprus, and especially in its higher social ranks, there is not always such gentleness and good manners. Another king of Cyprus (2.7) has failed to reward the faithful and diligent service of Antigono as he should, and he, too, needs to be prodded by an inferior into performing a good deed. The son of a Cypriot aristocrat refuses to be educated and remains a rustic buffoon until his love for a noble woman reverses his disposition (5.1). Nor is the "matter of Cyprus" a uniquely Boccaccian trope. Benvenuto da Imola, commenting on Dante's observations about a later king of Cyprus and its people (*Paradiso* 19.145–48), observed, not excluding the merchants, that they "exceeded all other kings and peoples of Christian kingdoms in their superfluity of luxury, gluttony, softness, and in all kinds of voluptuousness." Later writers expressed similar sentiments.[9] Thus, in addition to Boccaccio's ethical use of history, the "matter of Cyprus" may also account sufficiently for both the original location of the story and Boccaccio's making it even more Cyprus-specific.

Boccaccio's invitation to historical Cyprus in 1.9 may also have other resonances. Boccaccio had interesting personal connections with the Lusignan dynasty that ruled Cyprus from 1192 to 1473.[10] It is possible plausibly to identify the king in the story, and it is also possible to point out a more recent case of royal pusillanimity in Cyprus with which Boccaccio was certainly familiar and which he may also have addressed in 1.9. Finally, the exemplum of royal ineptitude in 1.9 also echoes the recent elaboration of the canon law and later, generally European constitutional doctrine of the useless king, the *rex inutilis.* These aspects of the world in and out of the story invite some further consideration of the gentlewoman from Gascony and the pusillanimous king.

Both Boccaccio's commentators and those of the *Novellino* tale uniformly identify the king of Cyprus in both stories as Guy of Lusignan, a historical figure about whom several other uncomplimentary stories circulated from the late twelfth century on.[11] But Boccaccio's and others' identification of Guy as "the first king of Cyprus after the conquest of the Holy Land by Godfrey of Bouillon" is not immediately obvious. Legally, Cyprus had been part of the Byzantine Empire and

[8] David Wallace, "In Flaundres," forthcoming in *Studies in the Age of Chaucer* 19 (1997).

[9] Benvenuto de Rambaldis da Imola, *Comentum super Dantis Aldighierii Comoediam,* ed. W. W. Vernon and J. P. Lacaita (Florence, 1887), 5:252. On Dante's view, see below, p. 770. Some later expressions of the same idea are collected in R. M. Dawkins's notes to Leontios Makhairas, *Recital concerning the Sweet Land of Cyprus entitled "Chronicle,"* ed. and trans. R. M. Dawkins, 2 vols. (Oxford, 1932), 2:82.

[10] Vittore Branca, *Giovanni Boccaccio, profilo biografico* (Florence, 1977), pp. 24, 83, 157. The work has been translated into English as *Boccaccio: The Man and His Work,* trans. Richard Morges (New York, 1986), pp. 88, 109, 160–62.

[11] E.g., Branca's notes to *Decameron* 1.9, p. 1038, note to p. 81: "La sua [Guy's] incapacità e la sua debolezza furono famose. . . ." Most commentators repeat variations of Branca's remark, including Natalino Sapegno, Charles Singleton, Alfonso Paolella, Luigi Russo, and Mario Baratto. The identification appears to have been made by Boccaccio's earliest readers.

ruled by the emperors until a renegade governor, Isaac Comnenus, proclaimed himself emperor in 1184 and retained control of the island until its conquest by Richard I of England in 1191.[12] Although Richard claimed possession of Cyprus by right of conquest, he did not bother to claim to be its king, and he sold it, first to the Knights Templar, who held it in 1191–92 but found themselves unable to rule it and returned it to Richard. Richard then sold it in 1192 to Guy of Lusignan, his former protégé in the Latin Kingdom of Jerusalem, for the sum of 100,000 bezants.[13] Guy ruled as lord of Cyprus, *Cypri dominus,* until his death in 1194, when he was succeeded by his brother, Aimery. Aimery (1194–1205) became the first king of Cyprus when he installed a Latin ecclesiastical hierarchy on the island, professed himself a vassal of the emperor Henry VI, and received a royal crown from Henry, part of Henry's growing ambitions in the eastern Mediterranean, as was Henry's simultaneous creation of the kingdom of Cilician (Lesser) Armenia. At first glance, the identity of Boccaccio's king of Cyprus may seem far from clear and hardly specific to Guy of Lusignan. But the number of candidates can be easily reduced. Isaac Comnenus is consistently represented in the sources as a savage tyrant who imprisons and mistreats even shipwrecked and storm-driven visitors, once threatening Richard's sister and his then-fiancée Berengaria of Navarre, who were driven by a storm into the harbor at Limassol on May 1, 1191. Richard, too, must be excluded for obvious reasons; nothing in the record or literature about him fits Boccaccio's king. So, too, must Aimery, technically the first king of Cyprus after the capture of Jerusalem in 1099, since no source says anything remotely uncomplimentary about him. Guy, on the other hand, is in fact the most likely candidate, but for reasons that originally had nothing to do with Cyprus.

Guy's reputation was developed and set out in an extensive and vituperative literature long before he ever set foot on Cyprus. He had been invited to the Kingdom of Jerusalem from the family estates in Poitou by his brother Aimery, at the time constable of the Latin Kingdom. Guy came to Outremer as the bridegroom of Sybilla, daughter of King Amaury II and sister and apparent successor of the childless Baldwin IV of Jerusalem. Through his marriage and the influence of his brother, Guy joined the circle around Sybilla's mother, the dowager queen Agnes of Courtenay, which represented the interests of relatively new arrivals in the kingdom and was opposed by the supporters of Sybilla's half sister Isabella, representing the older nobility of the kingdom, including the historian William of Tyre. Guy's quick rise to prominence and prospects made him powerful and ar-

[12] The best recent history is that of Peter W. Edbury, *The Kingdom of Cyprus and the Crusades, 1191–1374* (Cambridge, Eng., 1991), with a full literature cited, and, more briefly, Peter W. Edbury, "The Latin East, 1291–1669," in *The Oxford Ilustrated History of the Crusades,* ed. Jonathan Riley-Smith (Oxford and New York, 1995), pp. 294–325. See also Jean Richard, "The Institutions of the Kingdom of Cyprus," in *A History of the Crusades,* 6: *The Impact of the Crusades on Europe,* ed. Harry W. Hazard and Norman P. Zacour (Madison, Wis., 1989), pp. 150–174, and idem, "Le droit et les institutions franques dans le royaume de Chypre," repr. in Jean Richard, *Croisés, missionaires et voyageurs* (London, 1983).

[13] John Gillingham, *Richard the Lionheart* (London, 1978), pp. 163–68; James A. Brundage, "Richard the Lion-Heart and Byzantium," repr. in James A. Brundage, *The Crusades, Holy War and Canon Law* (Aldershot, Eng., and Brookfield, Vt., 1991). See also Ambroise, *The Crusade of Richard Lion-Heart,* trans. Merton Jerome Hubert (New York, 1941), pp. 74–108.

ticulate enemies. He was named *bailli* of the kingdom in 1183, but baronial opposition and his loss of the favor of Baldwin IV cost him the office later in the same year.[14] At the death of Baldwin in 1186, however, Guy was crowned king of Jerusalem by right of his wife. The reign was marked by the disaster at Hattin in 1187, the conflicting politics of the Third Crusade, Guy's own capture and imprisonment by Saladin, and continuing intense baronial opposition, which crystallized after Sybilla's (and her and Guy's two daughters') death in 1190, when Guy's title was challenged by the opposing party, led now by the anti-king Conrad of Montferrat. The two disputants did not reach an agreement until 1191, which gave Guy the crown of Jerusalem, but only for life. Guy retained the title, "in sancta civitate Iherusalem Latinorum rex VIII," until his death on Cyprus in 1194.[15] In 1191 Guy purchased Cyprus from Richard I, and, although he was not technically the king *of* Cyprus, he was still king of Jerusalem and thus a king *in* Cyprus, all contemporary and later sources designating him in both Jerusalem and Cyprus as "li rois Guis." Elissa's error (or Boccaccio's) had more than adequate precedent. Subsequent rulers of the Lusignan dynasty of Cyprus also seem to have counted their ancestor Guy as king.

The opposition to Guy of Lusignan in the Kingdom of Jerusalem took literary as well as political form, most strikingly in the *Historia rerum in partibus transmarinis* of William of Tyre and in the continuation of William's account in the vernacular and more widely accessible *Chronique* of Ernoul.[16] William consistently disparaged Guy, as he did most of the circle around Agnes of Courtenay, in Guy's case because William considered him to be unequal to the high positions he had acquired, lacking sufficient rank and reputation to be an effective leader and a poor choice as consort of Sybilla. Ernoul painted an even darker picture. R. C. Smail has said of his chronicle that (in writing about Guy of Lusignan, among others), "the author displays skills which might be the envy of a modern journalist, especially those of ridicule and caricature."[17] In Ernoul's narrative Guy takes bad counsel, is cowardly, is powerless against Saladin, and is personally responsible for the loss of the kingdom. He begs Richard pitifully for Cyprus, for he is a king

[14] There is a large literature. See Jonathan Riley-Smith, *The Feudal Nobility and the Latin Kingdom of Jerusalem* (London and Hamden, Conn., 1973), pp. 104–22, 153–54; Marshall W. Baldwin, *Raymond III of Tripolis and the Fall of Jerusalem (1140–1187)* (Princeton, N.J., 1936), pp. 35–45; and idem, "The Decline and Fall of Jerusalem, 1174–1189," in *A History of the Crusades,* 1: *The First Hundred Years,* ed. Marshall W. Baldwin (Madison, Wis., 1969), pp. 590–621. On William of Tyre, see Peter W. Edbury and John Gordon Rowe, *William of Tyre, Historian of the Latin East* (Cambridge, Eng., 1988).

[15] On the title, see Edbury, *The Kingdom of Cyprus and the Crusades,* p. 32, n. 15.

[16] The best study is that of R. C. Smail, "The Predicaments of Guy of Lusignan, 1183–1187," in *Outremer: Studies in the History of the Crusading Kingdom of Jerusalem Presented to Joshua Prawer,* ed. B. Z. Kedar, H. E. Mayer, and R. C. Smail (Jerusalem, 1982), pp. 159–76. On Ernoul, see Margaret Ruth Morgan, *The Chronicle of Ernoul and the Continuations of William of Tyre* (Oxford, 1973), and idem, *La continuation de Guillaume de Tyr (1184–1197)* (Paris, 1982), esp. pp. 136–39.

[17] Smail, "The Predicaments of Guy of Lusignan," p. 163. On the beginnings of vernacular prose historiography, see Gabrielle M. Spiegel, *Romancing the Past: The Rise of Vernacular Prose Historiography in Thirteenth-Century France* (Berkeley, Los Angeles, and London, 1993). Although Spiegel does not discuss Ernoul, Smail's brief discussion of his literary technique is consistent with Spiegel's observations on historiography in late-twelfth- and thirteenth-century France and Flanders.

without a land, disinherited and poor.[18] There is certainly ample material in the work of William of Tyre and especially Ernoul to characterize Guy as the inert king of Cyprus in *Novellino* 51 and *Decameron* 1.9.

Boccaccio was well connected to the Lusignan dynasty of Cyprus, both from his early years at the court of Naples and in his later relationships with Hugh IV of Cyprus (1325–59), who solicited and to whom was dedicated the *Genealogia deorum*, and with the circle around Hugh's son and successor Peter I (1359–67).[19] In his treatment of the king's change of heart and character in *Decameron* 1.9 Boccaccio may have extended a graceful courtesy to his royal Lusignan friends, ameliorating some of the rumors of *debolezza* that still clung to the memory of their ancestor Guy.

On the other hand, the Boccaccio version may also echo a more recent instance of royal pusillanimity in Cyprus, a case that had occurred just before Boccaccio's birth (a favorite chronological setting for many of the stories) and was well known, especially at the court of Naples and in the classrooms of canon law in which Boccaccio spent much of his youth. It is the case of Henry II of Cyprus, *rex inutilis*.

Henry II succeeded his brother John as king of Cyprus in 1285 and was crowned king of Jerusalem at Tyre in August of the same year.[20] The beginning of the reign was largely concerned with efforts to restore the city of Acre to the Lusignan dynasty, but these came to nothing when the city fell to the Mamluks in 1291. Henry then turned his attention to Cyprus, although he kept up his attempts to regain at least part of the Holy Land in conjunction with the king of Cilician Armenia and the Mongol Ilkhan of Persia.

After 1291 Cyprus was both an anxious and a distressed kingdom. Refugees from the Muslim conquests greatly burdened its local resources, as did the arrival of Templars and Hospitallers, both orders establishing headquarters on Cyprus after 1291 and developing strained relations with the king.[21] Henry's reign was also troubled by the Genoese, whose war with Venice and resentment over trading privileges in Cyprus granted to Pisa and Barcelona had soured relations with Henry. The Genoese threatened a trade boycott and even an invasion of Cyprus. But the most significant opposition to the king came from his own family, particularly his brother Amaury, and several members of the powerful and rival family of the Ibelins. Sometime early in 1306 Henry also fell ill, although the nature of the illness is not known. Possibly it was a recurence of his childhood epilepsy.[22]

On April 26, 1306, Henry's brother Amaury declared the king to be incapacitated by illness and therefore unfit to rule. Amaury assumed the title "gubernator

[18] Morgan, *La continuation de Guillaume de Tyr*, pp. 136–39.

[19] Above, n. 10.

[20] On the reign, see especially Edbury, *The Kingdom of Cyprus and the Crusades*, pp. 101–40; Norman Housley, *The Later Crusades, 1274–1580* (Oxford, 1992), pp. 125–91; Harry Luke, "The Kingdom of Cyprus, 1291–1369," in *A History of the Crusades*, 3: *The Fourteenth and Fifteenth Centuries*, ed. Harry W. Hazard (Madison, Wis., 1975), pp. 340–60. On Henry's place in contemporary crusade movements, see Sylvia Schein *"Fideles crucis": The Papacy, the West and the Recovery of the Holy Land, 1274–1314* (Oxford, 1991), pp. 154–56, 181–218.

[21] On Henry and the military orders, see Schein, *"Fideles crucis,"* pp. 153–55.

[22] The late-fifteenth-century chronicle of Leontios Makhairas (cited above, n. 9), based on earlier sources, both denies and affirms the seriousness of the king's illness.

et rector" of the kingdom. The majority of Henry's vassals supported Amaury, and the seizure of power was achieved with little violence and with none to the king himself. Amaury retained power until his murder in 1310, when Henry resumed the governance of Cyprus.

Besides the king's illness, Amaury and his supporters alleged the king's reliance on inappropriate counselors; his refusal to listen to proper advice on how to deal with the Genoese, who had publicly defied the king and the kingdom; his inability to provide for the defense of the kingdom against both the Genoese and the sultan of Egypt; his failure to cooperate with his allies in Armenia and Persia; and his failure to provide adequate aid for Cilician Amenia. He also failed to see to the food supply and to military preparedness generally, and he had shamefully allowed justice to fail.[23]

The case became widely known. Not only did both Amaury and Henry send delegations to Pope Clement V at Poitiers, but the documents they brought eventually reached Avignon (whence they did not return to Rome until 1671), and news of Henry's case reached Dante, who castigated Henry in *Paradiso* 19.145–48 as "the beast of Nicosia and Famagosta" and included him in the list of evil rulers condemned by the eagle.[24] It is safe to assume that the events of 1306–10 were well known in Naples and elsewhere in Europe, since Cyprus featured prominently in most of the many proposals for a new crusade that circulated throughout Europe in the early fourteenth century.[25]

The charges against Henry II were in fact those of a textbook case of the *rex inutilis,* the useless king, as that category of constitutional law had been established by Innocent IV's decretal *Grandi* in 1245, in the ordinary gloss to *Grandi* by Johannes Andreae in Boniface VIII's *Liber sextus,* in glosses by other commen-

[23] Near-contemporary accounts in *Les gestes des Chyprois,* ed. Charles Kohler, Recueil des Historiens des Croisades, Documents Arméniens, 2 (Paris, 1906), pp. 651–872, at pp. 857–62. Two documents in Old French were published by Louis de Mas Latrie, "Texte officiel de l'allocution addressée par les barons de Chypre au roi Henri II pour lui notifier de sa dechéance," *Revue des questions historiques* 53 (1888), 524–41, repr. in *Chroniques d'Amadi et de Strambaldi,* ed. René de Mas Latrie (Paris, 1891), pp. 242–48. The documents were brought to Clement V at Poitiers in 1307–8, either by the party representing Amaury or that representing Henry II, since both men had appealed to the pope. In 1908 Charles Kohler published a Latin version of the charter announcing the election of Amaury as regent of Cyprus. See Charles Kohler, "Documents chypriotes du début du XIVe siècle," *Revue de l'Orient latin* 11 (1908), 440–52, and Kohler's edition of *Les gestes des Chyprois,* pp. 858–62.

[24] The rulers condemned in *Paradiso* 19.112–48 are a mixed group, comprising both negligent and rapacious rulers, having in common the disruption they cause to the empire and to Christian society generally. Dante took a much harsher view of Henry II than that of even Amaury and his supporters. On Dante's treatment of other negligent rulers, see Edward Peters, "I principi negligenti di Dante e le concezioni medioevali del *Rex inutilis,*" *Rivista storica italiana* 80 (1968), 741–58. As noted above, the case was well known to Benvenuto da Imola and other fourteenth-century commentators on Dante.

[25] Discussions among the papacy and the rulers of France, Naples, and Aragon concerning a new crusade sometimes included the possibility of the displacement of the Lusignan dynasty from Cyprus and the substitution of a more crusade-minded dynasty. Sometimes these discussions were carried on as if Cyprus were completely rulerless. See the discussions in Norman Housley, *The Avignon Papacy and the Crusades, 1305–1378* (Oxford, 1986); Michael Wilks, *The Problem of Sovereignty in the Later Middle Ages: The Papal Monarchy with Augustinus Triumphus and the Publicists* (Cambridge, Eng., 1963), p. 429, n. 1; and Schein, "*Fideles crucis.*"

tators (including Innocent himself), and in the case of the deposition of the emperor Adolph of Nassau in 1298.[26] In the last instance it is clear that the electors who deposed Adolph of Nassau cited *Grandi* and its commentators, often verbatim, but it is also true that they acted independently of the pope, a problem that they were forced to defend against the opposition of Boniface VIII.[27] Henry II of Cyprus had been no *tyrannus,* as the companion doctrine of bad rulership would otherwise have required for deposition, a doctrine spelled out in the decretal announcing the deposition of Frederick II, *Ad apostolice sedis,* issued by Innocent IV in 1245, but rather a *rex inutilis,* now the other formalized type of the bad ruler.[28]

Grandi had dealt with the case of Sancho II of Portugal, removed from the governance of his kingdom, but not from the royal *dignitas,* by his brother Afonso in 1245. Afonso became king upon the death of the childless Sancho in exile at Toledo in 1248 and retained the royal title and the governance of Portugal until his own death. Innocent IV had based his decision in *Grandi* on the text *Alius item,* found in *Causa* 15, *quaestio* 6, *canon* 3 of Gratian's *Decretum.*[29] *Alius item* was a passage from a letter of Gregory VII describing the alleged papal deposition of the last Merovingian king of the Franks on the grounds of ineptitude in 751, cited by Gregory to emphasize his own authority to depose the emperor Henry IV, who, according to Gregory, had committed far more serious offenses than

[26] On the case of Sancho II of Portugal, which elicited *Grandi,* see Edward Peters, "*Rex inutilis:* Sancho II of Portugal and Thirteenth-Century Deposition Theory," *Studia Gratiana* 14 (1967), 253–305, and idem, *The Shadow King: "Rex inutilis" in Medieval Law and Literature, 751–1327* (New Haven, Conn., and London, 1970); Linda Fowler, "Innocent Uselessness in Civilian and Canonist Thought," *Zeitschrift der Savigny-Stiftung für Rechtsgeschichte,* Kanonistische Abteilung 58 (1972), 101–61; Helmut G. Walther, "Depositions of Rulers in the Later Middle Ages: On Theory of the 'Useless Ruler' and Its Practical Utilization," in *As relacões de poder no pensamento da baixa idade média: Homenagem a João Morais Barbosa* (Lisbon, 1994), pp. 157–68, expanded with fuller documentation in Walther, "Das Problem des untauglichen Herrschers in der Theorie und Praxis des europäischen Spätmittelalters," *Zeitschrift für historische Forschung* 23 (1996), 1–28. I am grateful to Helmut Walther for copies of these articles and for several conversations and correspondence on the topic of the useless ruler.

Other categories of royal "uselessness" that did not apply to either Sancho II or Henry II but that were invoked against other rulers include womanizing: Edward Peters, "*Non legitur in historia francorum:* Stephen of Tournai, the Last Merovingians, and the Capetian Dynasty," in *Proceedings of the IX International Congress of Medieval Canon Law,* ed. Peter Landau (Vatican City, 1997), pp. 1053–78 (cf. *Decameron* 1.5); excessive study and withdrawal from governance: Edward Peters, "*Rex curiosus:* A Preface to Prospero," *Majestas* 4 (1996), 61–84; failing to prosecute heresy: Othmar Hageneder, "Die Häresie des Ungehorsams und das Entstehung des hierokratischen Papsttums," *Römische historische Mitteilungen* 20 (1978), 30–47, and the studies in the volume *Die Anfänge der Inquisition im Mittelalter,* ed. Peter Segl (Cologne, Weimar, and Vienna, 1993).

Sercambi (above, n. 3) may have echoed the case of Sancho II when he substituted a king of Portugal for the king of Cyprus in his *Il Novelliere, Exemplo* lii. Given Sercambi's informed devotional outlook, the identification is certainly possible.

[27] On Adolph of Nassau, see Walther, "Das Problem des untauglichen Herrschers," pp. 10–13.

[28] Friedrich Kempf, "Die Absetzung Friedrichs II. im Lichte der Kanonistik," in *Probleme um Friedrich II.,* ed. Josef Fleckenstein, Vorträge und Forschungen 16 (Sigmaringen, 1974), pp. 345–60; Anthony Black, *Political Thought in Europe, 1250–1450* (Cambridge, Eng., 1992), pp. 24–25, 140–52.

[29] On Gratian and methods of citation in canon law, see James A. Brundage, *Medieval Canon Law* (London and New York, 1995), pp. 44–69, 190–205.

ineptitude.[30] Since the appearance of the *Decretum,* commentators had drawn parallels between incompetent kings and incompetent prelates as well as enumerating the rights of the pope to intervene generally in temporal affairs under specific circumstances. The ordinary gloss to the *Decretum* succinctly summed up the consequences: "For what sin can an emperor be deposed? For any sin: if he is incorrigible he may be deposed, and if he is less than useful, as in 15 q. 6 *alius.*"[31] Incorrigibility is a feature of both the king in *Decameron* 1.9 and canonist justifications for deposition.

The case of Sancho II of Portugal had given Innocent IV the opportunity to deal, not with an emperor, but with the ruler of a hereditary monarchy, a different kind of case altogether. The ruler of a hereditary monarchy was not to be deposed outright, Innocent stated, but to retain the royal *dignitas* and have a *curator* appointed to wield the *administratio* of the kingdom, ideally with the right to succeed to the *dignitas* upon the death of the incapacitated king. Innocent's model here was the appointment of curators for ailing or senile prelates, now adapted for monarchies and the empire with considerable attention paid to the difference between hereditary and elective office. Later commentators allowed more readily for abdication and outright deposition in cases of royal uselessness, as the later cases of Edward II of England in 1327 and Richard II of England in 1399 show.[32] It is arguable that the case of Henry II of Cyprus may have influenced this later development of Innocent IV's doctrine.[33] In the case of Portugal, as in that of Cyprus in 1306, a vigorous and competent royal brother was on hand to be made *curator,* or *rector,* of the kingdom. Like Sancho II, Henry II was unmarried at the time and hence childless, and Amaury could also be expected to succeed to the royal *dignitas,* as Afonso of Portugal had done.

Although Innocent IV did not include *Grandi* and *Ad apostolice sedis* in his first two collections of his own decretals, possibly because of their strong political

[30] On the episode, see Peters, *The Shadow King,* pp. 30–80.

[31] Johannes Teutonicus, ordinary gloss to *Decretum,* D. 40, c. 6 *Si papa,* ad vv. *a fide devius,* cited and discussed in Peters, *The Shadow King,* p. 159.

[32] On abdication, chiefly discussed by canonists in terms of prelates and the papacy, see Peters, *The Shadow King,* pp. 217–32; Peter Herde, *Cölestin V. (1294): (Peter vom Morrone), der Engelpapst,* Päpste und Papsttum 16 (Stuttgart, 1991), pp. 84–160; and John R. Eastman, *Papal Abdication in Later Medieval Thought* (Lewiston, N.Y., 1990).

[33] Some years ago, Gerard E. Caspary suggested to me in correspondence that there should have been another case in the history of the *rex inutilis* between that of Adolph of Nassau in 1298 and that of Edward II of England in 1327. Aside from the difference in the procedures against an emperor and a hereditary monarch, Edward's case displayed other features not accounted for by the case of Sancho II, including the king's abdication as well as deposition and his subsequent murder. I propose to argue in a later study that the case of Henry II is indeed Caspary's missing case. See Gerard E. Caspary, "The Deposition of Richard II and the Canon Law," in *Proceedings of the Second International Congress of Medieval Canon Law,* ed. Stephan Kuttner and J. Joseph Ryan (Rome, 1966), pp. 189–201; Charles T. Wood, "Personality, Politics, and Constitutional Progress: The Lesson of Edward II," *Studia Gratiana* 15 (= *Post Scripta: Essays on Medieval Law and the Emergence of the European State in Honor of Gaines Post*) (1972), 519–36; idem, with William Huse Dunham, Jr., "The Right to Rule in England: Depositions and the Kingdom's Authority, 1327–1485," *American Historical Review* 81 (1976), 738–61; idem, "Celestine V, Boniface VIII and the Authority of Parliament," *Journal of Medieval History* 8 (1982), 45–62, repr. in Charles T. Wood, *Joan of Arc and Richard III: Sex, Saints, and Government in the Middle Ages* (New York and Oxford, 1988), pp. 100–116.

implications, he did include them in his third collection, and he commented on *Grandi* in his discussions of some of his own decretals in his *apparatus* to the *Liber extra* of Gregory IX, which he wrote in his private capacity as a canon lawyer. In 1298 *Grandi* was included in the official *Liber sextus* of Boniface VIII under the title *De supplenda negligentia prelatorum* (VI 1.8.2). The discussion of *Grandi* in Innocent's *apparatus* dealt with the law of succession in Portugal, the full powers of *administratio* on the part of the curator, the idea of the *utilitas* of both king and kingdom, and the authority of the pope when there exists no superior from whom justice may be obtained. Innocent's discussion of *utilitas* is relevant here: "Note the proper reasons for giving a curator to kings . . . if they do not know how to defend their kingdom or to preserve justice and peace in them, especially in the cases of religious persons and places and in the cases of the poor. And further, which is even greater, if they do not know how to recover [territories and rights that have been] lost. And what we have said concerning kings is to serve also in the cases of dukes, counts, and others who have jurisdiction over others. In other instances of private people, however, they are not to be given curators unless they are insane or prodigal."[34] In Innocent's view the differences between hereditary monarchy and empire, between public and private persons, must be observed, and *Grandi* was his solution to some of the most important of those differences. Innocent's emphasis on *nesciunt* suggests the ruler's lack of the *scientia regnandi,* and he draws a parallel between the public figure who is incompetent and the private person who is mad or prodigal. Innocent also warned against the precipitate use of his doctrine: "And it should be remembered concerning this sentence of deposition that it must not be used without there being much urgent necessity and many offenses and crimes and manifestations of infamy making a clamor against the emperor."[35] The warning was also intended for those who would depose kings.

Johannes Andreae's ordinary gloss to *Grandi* in the *Liber sextus* summed up the Innocentian doctrine: "The pope may depose the emperor on account of crimes . . . and when he is useless (*inutilis*) . . . and may appoint curators to those who administer badly. . . . He assumes their jurisdiction because they are negligent. . . . He compels them to do justice."[36] The pope must not act *motu proprio* in such cases, since an appeal must be made to him, and there must be evidence of the *clamor* and notoriety of the case and the consequent harm done to people and kingdom. Sancho of Portugal, Johannes Andreae goes on to say, was "dissipated and negligent," while Afonso was "devout, circumspect, magnanimous, and powerful."[37] In Portugal's case in 1245, as in that of Cyprus sixty-one years later, a vigorous and competent royal brother was indeed on hand to become the appropriate *curator* or *rector* of the kingdom and the successor to the throne.

But textbook case though that of Cyprus may have appeared, it lacked several of the crucial textbook elements: Amaury and his supporters had acted on their

[34] Innocent IV, *Apparatus super libros Decretalium* (Venice, 1481), ad X 1.10.1 *Grandi,* ad v. *utilitate.*

[35] Ibid., ad X 2.14.2 *Ad apostolice,* ad v. *sempiternam.*

[36] *Liber sextus decretalium* (Venice, 1595), ad VI 2.14.2, ad v. *privamus,* p. 258.

[37] Ibid., ad VI 1.8.2, *casus,* p. 138.

own, without papal permission, as had the electors who deposed Adolph of Nassau in 1298, and when Amaury turned to Clement V in 1307, he found that Henry, too, had sent an appeal against the usurpation. In 1308 the pope appointed commissioners to investigate the case, and they were active in 1310, but their report, if it was ever made, had not been found.

Henry did more than appeal to the pope. His initial dealings with the new regime focused necessarily on his own financial needs, but Henry refused to recognize Amaury as governor of the kingdom, and he retained the homage of his liege subjects. He moved to his estate at Strovolos and remained there until early 1307, when, fearing arrest by Amaury, Henry moved to his fortified palace in Nicosia. Henry also recovered from illness in 1307. Early in 1308, however, Amaury's pressure worked, and Henry agreed, apparently privately, to Amaury's lifetime governorship of the kingdom, although the duress under which Henry appears to have acted alienated a number of Amaury's supporters. The events of 1307–8 also allowed Cyprus time to reconsider the rule of Amaury, and time worked in Henry's favor. Fearing the growth of support for Henry, in 1309 Amaury demanded a public legitimation of his rule from Henry, and negotiations continued even after Amaury sent Henry as a prisoner to Cilician Armenia in February 1310. When Amaury was murdered as the result of a private dispute in June 1310, Henry began negotiations to be released from Armenian captivity, and he returned to Cyprus in August, resumed his rule, and reigned until his death in 1324, when he was suceeded by his nephew Hugh IV (not the son of Amaury, but of another brother, Guy, who had predeceased Henry). Hugh IV later became the patron of Boccaccio.

Like all good textbook cases, that of Henry II of Cyprus taught important lessons to those willing to learn, but not always the lessons that the creators of the textbook had intended. Although the right conditions had indeed prevailed in Cyprus—the inherited monarchy problem dealt with by the presence of a competent brother and likely successor, the royal *dignitas* preserved in the living king, and the original *gravamina* persuasive in the light of *Grandi* and its commentaries, if not entirely conclusive—in other respects the classical doctrine had proved capable of raising as many political problems as it had purported to solve. Amaury had not been as strong as Afonso of Portugal, and his initial support had weakened. The living king, retaining the oaths of loyalty given by his subjects, remained on the scene far too long and was removed to Armenia far too late, thus remaining a potential center of resistance. There had been no initial appeal to the pope and no final papal decision confirming the legitimacy of Amaury's coup, as there had been when Innocent IV issued *Grandi* for Portugal.

The initial statements made by Amaury and the barons strongly suggest that they had had the advice of a skilled canonist in drawing up their justifications for removing Henry, but they encountered a number of difficulties that canon law had not foreseen. One was that a living king who refused to abdicate, possessing the royal *dignitas* even if stripped of *administratio,* remained a threat and a potential embarrassment, especially if, unlike Sancho II of Portugal, he remained on the scene, however rusticated. The second was that accusations of royal incapacity depended crucially on the passage of time: if the king recovered from his illness or claimed persuasively that he was once again capable of resuming his royal duties, the position of the *gubernator et rector,* or indeed of any regent or curator however designated, became tenuous. Such proved to be the case in France in the later fourteenth and fifteenth centuries during the intermittent bouts of insanity and lucidity that marked the reign of Charles VI.[38]

What does the case of Henry II of Cyprus have to do with *Decameron* 1.9, if anything? Hugh IV had been raised by the childless Henry II and probably designated by him as his successor. By rehabilitating the reputation of one king of Cyprus, Guy of Lusignan, did not Boccaccio also rehabilitate that of a second and more recent king who had been accused of many of the same faults? And had not that king, too, resumed the responsible governance of his kingdom? Henry's later reign was marked by the increasing prosperity of Cyprus, and Henry no longer had Amaury, the Ibelins, or the Templars to worry about.[39] The kings of Cyprus did not have the best of presses in the medieval world, even though Aquinas had dedicated a treatise on kingship to Hugh II (1253–67), probably because their limited military resources and their complex relationship to the Kingdom of Jerusalem and the crusading movement generally in a difficult period did not permit them to please everyone, including their own most powerful and ambitious subjects. Later in the fourteenth century Peter I, the successor of Hugh IV, acquired a great reputation, one that apparently endured for some time.[40] But Henry II had run afoul, not only of ambitious subjects, but of ambitious subjects armed with the new and apparently tailor-made doctrines of canon law. *Dominus Johannes Boccaccius* knew a great deal of canon law himself, and on occasion practiced it and other laws, even as he made fun of lawyers and judges in the *Decameron.*[41] All the more reason gracefully to introduce the *gentil donna di Guascogna*—described, after all, by Elissa, "la ghibellina"—to stir the king into resuming his rightful role and restoring the proper dignity of the crown. And why not please a friend and patron at the same time?

[38] Françoise Autrand, *Charles VI: La folie du roi* (Paris, 1986).

[39] On the place of Cyprus in the downfall of the Templars, see Malcolm Barber, *The Trial of the Templars* (Cambridge, Eng., 1978), pp. 216–20; and Schein, *"Fideles crucis,"* pp. 240–46.

[40] John L. La Monte, "The 'Roy de Chippre' in François Villon's 'Ballade des seigneurs des temps jadis,' " *Romanic Review* 23 (1932), 49–53.

[41] Pier Giorgio Ricci, "Notizie e documenti per la biografia del Boccaccio, 5. *Dominus Johannes Boccaccius,*" *Studi sul Boccaccio* 6 (1971), 1–10. On the criticism, see Giuseppe Mazzotta, *The World at Play in Boccaccio's Decameron* (Princeton, N.J., 1986), pp. 213–40. On another instance of Boccaccio's use of his legal knowledge in the Decameron (6.7), see Kenneth Pennington, "A Note to *Decameron* 6.7: The Wit of Madonna Filippa," *Speculum* 52 (1977), 902–5.

X

THE FAILURE OF CHURCH AND EMPIRE: *PARADISO*, 30

THE thirtieth canto of Dante's *Paradiso* occupies an important place both in its own *cantica* and in the *Commedia* as a whole. It describes the final stage in the transformation of the pilgrim's vision and is the last canto in which Dante and Beatrice are together. It concludes with Beatrice's final words to Dante. On the scale of the entire vision, it is the point toward which Dante had started with Vergil when they began their journey out of the dark wood, and thus it stands as a representation of ultimate justice and order against the error of the *selva oscura* and the evil of the anti-city of Dis. The final twenty-five lines of the canto, however, may be said to possess an importance which extends even beyond the limits of the *Commedia.* They contain Dante's final political testament and thus complete the complex development of his thought on politics which first found expression in the *De vulgari eloquentia* and the *Convivio* and whose presence pervades not only the philosophical works and the letters, but the great poem of justice itself.[1]

Vergil had prophesied at the beginning of the *Inferno* that Dante might come to Paradise at the end of his journey but that Vergil himself could not guide him there:

> Ché quello Imperador che la sú regna,
> Perch'io fu ribellante a la sua legge
> Non vuol che'n sua città per me si vegna.
> In tutte parti impera, e quivi regge;
> quivi è la sua città e l'alto seggio:
> O felice colui cu'ivi elegge !
> (Inf., i, 123-128)

[1] Studies on Dante's political thought abound. A useful starting-point is provided in U. Parricchi, *Dante* (Rome, 1965), 273-291. In the same volume, see particularly P. Brezzi, "Il pensiero politico di Dante". Among other recent studies those especially valuable in preparing this article were, Ernst Kantorowicz, *The King's Two Bodies* (Princeton, 1957), 451-495 and A. P. d'Entrèves, *Dante as a Political Thinker* (Oxford, 1952).

Reprinted from *Medieval Studies* 34 (1972), 326–335, by permission of the publisher.

At the end of *Paradiso* xxx Vergil's prophecy is fulfilled. Dante stands within the city of the celestial rose, his pilgrimage behind him, engrossed in the contemplation of Beatrice's heavenly *città* just as he had once stood paralyzed by fear before the walls of the *citta dolente*. Immediately before she leaves him, Beatrice indicates to Dante a particular seat within the rose. It is the throne of the emperor Henry VII and is the subject of the last major reference to earthly life in the poem:

Nel giallo de la rosa sempiterna, —
  Che si dilata ed ingrada e redole
  Odor di lode al Sol che sempre verna, —
Qual è colui che tace e dicer vuole,
  Mi trasse Beatrice, e disse: 'Mira
  Quanto è 'l convento de le bianche stole!
Vedi nostra città quant' ella gira!
  Vedi li nostri scanni sì ripieni
  Che poca gente più ci si disira!
E 'n quel gran seggio a che tu li occhi tieni
  Per la corona che già v'è su posta,
  Prima che tu a queste nozze ceni
Sederà l'alma (che fia giù agosta)
  De l'alto Arrigo, ch'a drizzare Italia
  Verrà in prima che ella sia disposta.
La cieca cupidigia che vi ammalia
  Simili fatti v'ha al fantolino
  Che muor per fame e caccia via la balia.
E fia prefetto nel foro divino
  Allora tal che, palese e coverto,
  Non anderà con lui per un cammino.
Ma poco poi sarà da Dio sofferto
  Nel santo offizio: ch' el sarà detruso
  La dove simon Mago è per suo merto,
E farà quel d'Alagna intrar più giuso'.
(Par. xxx, 124-148)

Dante, pilgrim and prophet throughout his journey, here witnesses the resolution of one of the major themes of the poem, the conflict between papacy and empire which has prevented the establishment of the *vera città* on earth and is the result of the greater opposition between justice and greed which is the root of all earthly social and individual disorder.[2]

Beatrice's speech clearly falls into two symmetrical parts. Not only does she fulfill Vergil's earlier promise, but she also echoes Vergil's imperial

[2] The most comprehensive study of Dante's theory of justice is still that of A. H. Gilbert, *Dante's Conception of Justice* (rep. N. Y., 1965), See also E. Gilson, *Dante and Philosophy* (N. Y., 1949). 175-224, 277-281. For Dante as prophet, see G. R. Sarolli, "Dante, *Scriba Dei*". *Convivium*, 4-6 (1963), 385-422, 513-544, 641-671.

imagery which she transforms from an imaginative contrast between the Roman Empire of Augustus and the heavenly 'empire' of God into a deliberate philosophical contrast between the form of justice which pervades the *civitas Dei* and the injustice which has perverted human society on earth. Her first words carefully direct Dante's vision into the city of the rose to the throne of Henry VII. She then briefly describes the imperial mission and its failure. The second part of the speech consists of an analysis of the causes of the failure of empire and indictment of those whose greed had contributed to it. The brief reference to the life and death of Henry,

Ch' a drizzare Italia
Verrà in prima che ella sia disposta,

occupies the center of her discourse, referring back to the *alma agosta* and forward to the *prefetto nel foro divino*, who occupies the same prominence in the second half of the speech as does the *alma agosta* in the first. Not only are the roles of Henry VII and Clement V thus the immediate subjects of their respective halves of Beatrice's discourse, but the greater opposition of Heaven and Hell is invoked in its opening and closing lines. The *convento de le bianche stole* stands in symmetrical opposition to *La dove Simon Mago è*, the *Civitas Dei* to *Malebolge*. Within a few lines, Beatrice's speech moves from the highest part of Paradise to the depths of Hell by her citation of the paired issues of Henry's salvation and Clement's damnation in symmetrical halves of the discourse.[3]

Her opening words are joyous, echoing precisely that elation which Dante himself had experienced as soon as his vision had been transformed by the river of grace:

Poi, come gente stata sotto larve,
  Che pare altro che prima, se si sveste,
  La sembianze non sua in che disparve.
Così mi si cambiaro in maggior feste
  Li fiori e le faville, sì ch'io vidi
  Ambo le corti del ciel manifeste.
O isplendor di Dio, per cu'io vidi
  L'alto trionfo del regno verace,
  Dammi virtù a dir com' io lo vidi.
(Par. xxx, 91-99)

[3] On Dante's use of paired symbols of justice, see E. von Richthofen. "The Twins of Latona and Other Symetrical Symbols for Justice in Dante". in S. B. Chandler and J. A. Molinaro, *The World of Dante* (Toronto, 1966), 117-127. The author does not consider the emperor-pope opposition in *Paradiso* xxx. For the following discussion, see Joseph A. Mazzeo, *Mediaeval Cultural Tradition in Dante's "Comedy"* (Ithaca, N. Y.), 91-132.

The repetition of *mira* and *vedi* by Beatrice both echoes Dante's own response to his transformed means of perception and urges him to *see* now what she had promised him earlier:

> Qui vedrai l'una e l'altra milizia
> Di Paradiso, e l'una in quelli aspetti
> Che tu vedrai a l'ultima giustizia.
> (Par. xxx, 43-45)

Beatrice's exhortation, however, also serves to direct Dante's vision to one specific aspect of the rose — and that, from the next three *canti*, certainly not its most prominent — the *gran seggio* of the emperor Henry. These lines not only continue the earlier theme of the pilgrim's new vision, but in the process of narrowing Dante's attention from the general *convento* to the particular *seggio* through *città* and *scanni* invokes through systemmatic description another theme, that of the celestial rose as the *civitas Dei*, a city set off not only against the dark wood and *malebolge*, but against Florence itself in the next canto:

> Io, che al divino dal' umano,
> A l'eterno dal tempo era venuto,
> E di Firenze in popol giusto e sano,
> Di che stupor dovea esser compiuto!
> (*Par.* xxxi, 37-40)

Beatrice not only echoes Vergil's earlier description of the heavenly *città* and Dante's earlier *regno verace*, but by her selection of the throne of Henry VII as Dante's first point of concentration purposely emphasizes the political dimension of the Augustinian image — not, to be sure, its primary meaning for Augustine, but nevertheless a popular one in later medieval political thought. The whole scene, moreover, is dramatically constructed in such a way that the essential character of the rose is not altered and that Dante's complete vision of it is merely delayed in order to treat a problem which for the poet had to be resolved in the court of Heaven.

That the final word about earthly political disorder should be uttered in the celestial *civitas* is not surprising. Dante's views on the ordering of society transcended, as did those of other political thinkers, the temporal character of political institutions. That vision, in the *Commedia*, is an integral part of a broader concept of justice, and it is in terms of the relationship between divine justice and the earthly empire that the episode in *Paradiso* xxx must be considered. Dante, it may be remembered, lived in a period in which both civic and imperial political ideas were in a rapid process of change. The most striking example had been the reception of Aristotelian political thought from the mid-thirteenth century on, but the problems arising from the deposition of Adolf of Nassau, the abdication of Celestine V, the quarrel between Boniface VIII and Philip the Fair, and the imperial advent into Italy, all occuring between 1294 and 1313, constituted practical occasions for intensive revisions in political thought.[4] Dante's own concept of the *civitas*, moreover, like that of Remigio de Girolami and others, shows many of the traits which he was later to apply to the *imperium*.[5] As d'Entrèves notes,

> The word *città* is a keyword in the Comedy. There is not only the opposition between the City of the Damned and the Heavenly City. The word is used to denote the fundamental and 'typical' form of human association. Retracing the growth and development of man. Marco Lombardo, in the sixteenth canto of *Purgatorio*, indicates the setting up of the *vera città* as the primary imperative, even though of the true city men discern only the tower.[6]

Città, *regno*, and *imperio* are all strikingly analogous in Dante's thought, the *città* assuring the individual's need for justice in the same manner as the empire assured mankind's need. If Dante's *civitas Dei* is different from that of Augustine, the extent of that difference must be sought both in the poet's dramatic requirement for a scene of ultimate resolution of the political theme and in the new values professed by secular society and political organization in the thirteenth century, particularly in terms of Dante's subtle adaptation of those values in forming his theory of empire.

If mankind had failed, in Dante's view, to construct or find the *vera città*, that failure in no way diminished the power or the validity of the ideal. Yet in d'Entrèves' stimulating discussion of the role of the *civitas* in Dante's thought, the celestial rose is described only as a city "in the metaphorical sense, and *città* (in *Paradiso* xxx) is certainly more reminiscent of the Augustinian *civitas* than of the Aristotelian *polis*".[7] Grandgent suggests that "it may be that a sight of the Roman Coliseum influenced his conception of the great amphitheater of Paradise".[8] It may be suggested that, in view of Beatrice's choice of emphasis and the specific contrast between *Firenze* and a *popol giusto e sano* (Par. xxxi) neither of these views accurately describes the function of the city of the rose in the last lines of *Paradiso* xxx. The regalia of the emperor and the *città* itself belong to the same order of existence,

[4] A recent survey of historical studies dealing with the period of Dante's lifetime is that of Nicolai Rubinstein. "Studies on the Political History of the Age of Dante". *Atti del congresso internazionale di studi danteschi* (Florence, 1965), 225-247.

[5] For Remigio, see L. Minio-Paluello, "Remigio Girolami's *De Bono Communi*". *Italian Studies*, 11 (1956), 56-71 and C. T. Davis, *Dante and the Idea of Rome* (Oxford, 1957).

[6] *Dante as a Political Thinker*, 11.

[7] *Ibid.*, 19, n. 1.

[8] C. H. Grandgent, ed., *La Divina Commedia di Dante Alighieri* (Boston, 1933), 946, n. 1. This is the text of the *Commedia* used in the preparation of this article.

an order which Dante was able to perceive only *after* his illumination earlier in the canto and one more 'real' than the earlier manifestations of Paradise which belonged to an order of perception inferior to that which Dante achieved in *Paradiso* xxx. If, as Silverstein has shown, the throne and crown represent the absolute regalia of justice, the *città* must belong to the same order.[9] It is the perfected state of Marco Lombardo's *vera città* in which the two roads meet in *un cammino*, as they had long ago under the aegis of Rome:

> Soleva Roma, Che il buon mondo feo
> Due soli aver, che l'una e l'altra strada
> Facean vedere, e del mondo e di Deo.
> (*Purg*. xvi. 106-108)

Like many contemporary Italian cities, the rose-city is under the particular influence of the Virgin. Like them, its essence is a great meeting-place. Rather than a metaphorical city, modelled on a sight of the Roman Coliseum, Dante's celestial *civitas* is,, at least for a moment, a genuine *civitas Dei*, fulfilling Vergil's imperial imagery and resolving an imperial theme. Although its origins go back to Augustinian theology, it would hardly seem metaphorical to a people familiar with the vast frescoes on "Buon governo", such as those of Lorenzetti at Siena with their rows of enthroned figures or those which would be executed by Andrea da Firenze in the Spanish Chapel of Santa Maria Novella in the third quarter of the fourteenth century.[10]

The most immediately striking difference between the *civitas Dei* and the earthly empire, however, is the curious place given to the emperor in the former. The *alma agosta* of Henry VII, although it occupies briefly the center of Dante's interest, does not occupy a conspicuous place in the rose, as the reader learns in the following *canti*. His role on earth — to guide men to salvation by administering justice — no longer remains to be fulfilled. His soul, like Dante's ('*prima che tu a queste nozze ceni/Sederà l'alma de l'alto Arrigo...*'), is one of many which compose the *popol giusto e sano*. The throne and crown of the emperor are an indication of his former existence. In *Paradiso* xxx he is now a member of the *città* mentioned by Vergil in Inferno, i. The place of Henry VII in the celestial city echoes the theolo-

[9] See below, n. 14.

[10] On the *città* in Dante's thought, see d'Entrèves, *Dante as a Political Thinker*, 1-25. On the public architecture of the period, see Helène Wieruszowski, "Art and the Commune in the Time of Dante", *Speculum*, 19 (1944), 14-33, with bibliographical notes. See also Wolfgang Braunfels, *Mittelalterliche Stadtbaukunst in der Toskana* (Berlin, 1953), 189-208; Millard Meiss, *Painting in Florence and Siena after the Black Death* (rep. N. Y., 1964), 94-104.

gical language which Dante had used toward him in the seventh letter, yet reflects also his role as only a single member of the celestial *popolo.* Before discussing the possible significance of Henry's position in the rose, it may be useful to consider the imperial iconography and its role in the passage under discussion.

In his study of the throne and crown in *Paradiso* xxx, Theodore Silverstein has drawn several striking analogies between the place of Henry VII and earlier representations of the celestial disposition of just kings.[11] His conclusion, that the throne is not, as Grandgent had suggested, "a symbol of mundane sovereignty in Pardise", but a representation of the throne of justice which had long been a commonplace in visionary and political literature, is perfectly consistent with Dante's own theories of the role of imperial power on earth in the fulfillment of divine justice. Yet one may argue that the poet transformed this tradition too, just as he had others. First, the throne of the emperor Henry is not the center of the rose as had been some of the representations discussed by Silverstein. Second, the crown which Dante and Beatrice see above the throne is probably not, as Silverstein suggested, the crown of compassion, but the *corona gloriae et iustitiae* mentioned in imperial coronation *ordines* from the tenth century on.[12] Both throne and crown are the absolute regalia of justice, symbolically linked to — but only approximated by — earthly representations. Throne, crown, city — all transcend their earthly manifestations and complete them. They belong, in fact, to a higher order of existence connected to earthly institutions and earthly justice by the dual nature of the anointed emperor.[13] The order to which they belong was familiar to Dante's contemporaries as was the order to which belonged the frescoes of good government and

[11] "The Throne of the Emperor Henry in Dante's Paradise and the Medieval Conception of Christian Kingshi", *Harvard Theological Review*, 32 (1939), 115-129.

[12] On the general significance of the crown in medieval political iconography see P. E. Schramm, *Herrschaftszeichen und Staatssymbolik*, 2 (Stuttgart, 1954). A more recent study with bibliography is that of H. Hoffmann. "Die Krone im hochmittelalterlichen Staatsdenken," *Festschrift fur Harald Keller* (Darmstadt, 1963), 71-85. An early coronation *ordo* may be found in C. Vogel and R. Elze, *Le pontifical romano-germanique du dixième siècle*, I (Città del Vaticano: Studi e Testi 226, 1963), 264: '*Accipe signum gloriae in nomine patris et filii et spiritus sancti, ut, spreto antiquo hoste spretisque contagiis omnium vitiorum, sic iudicium et iustitiam diligas et misericorditer vivas, ut ab ipso domino nostro Iesu Christo in consortio sanctorum aeterni regni coronam percipias...*'. See also R. Elze, *Ordines coronationis imperialis: Die Ordines fur die Weihe des Kaisers und der Kaiserin*, Monumenta Germaniae Historica, Fontes iuris germaniae antiqui in usum scholarum, 9 (Hannover, 1960); C. A. Bouman, *Sacring and Crowning: The Development of the Latin Ritual for the Anointing of Kings and the Coronation of an Emperor before the Eleventh Century* (Groningen-Djakarta, 1957); Kantorowicz, *The King's Two Bodies*, 336-382, 482-483.

[13] *The King's Two Bodies*, 494-495.

had its origins in the history of Christian political thought and in the development of liturgical ceremony and pictorial symbolism.

The opposition between justice and greed, which Christian thinkers had long since adapted from the Stoic strain in Roman historiography and moral philosophy and more recently from the reception of Aristotle's *Ethics* and *Politics*, governs the syntactical divisions of Beatrice's discourse. *La cieca cupidigia* — the metaphor of blindness, traditionally associated with injustice, here made stronger in contrast to the light and vision imagery of the passage — has caused not only the failure of Henry of Luxemburg, but of human society and Dante's ideal of empire. There is a tone of disillusion in the *Paradiso* as well as in the later *Letters* when the topic of empire appears. It may be noted that Dante is pointedly silent in the *Commedia* about political events and prospects later than 1314. Even the *Letter to the Italian Cardinals* emphasizes the need for elemental reform of the church and sustains no hope of yet another imperial renewal.[14] Dante scholars have often tentatively described the changing stages of the poet's political ideas, yet few have paid attention to the stage reached in the passage under discussion. The events of *Paradiso* xxx constitute the final stage: Dante's earlier enthusiasm for the imperial cause and his hopes that it might triumph had been based, as parts of the *Commedia* and the *Letters* suggest, on an overestimation of the readiness of Italy, the church, and, by inference, of human society as a whole to achieve *humana civilitas*. In his final citation of the imperial mission, Dante revives yet another image, that of unreasonable childhood, which he had once applied not to the great emperors, but to the earliest kings of Rome, teachers and guardians of an unready people:

> Che se consideriamo li sette regi che prima la governaro, cioè Romolo, Numa, Tullo, Anco e li re Tarquini, che furono quasi baiuli e tutori de la sua puerizia...[15]

Clement V embodies not only the church, but Italy as well — in fact all of those,

> Simili fatti v'ha al fantolino
> Che muor per fame e caccia via la balia.

Childhood is always a period of unreason in the Commedia. Dante's earlier view of Henry VII as a new David, Aeneas, and Augustus, i.e., one who might create a new empire, appears to have changed into that of Henry as a ruler who comes to an unready people, willful, malicious, unreasonable, closer to the *adolescentia* of the early Romans, yet unlike even

[14] In P. Toynbee, ed., *Dantis Alagherii Epistolae*, 2nd ed. (Oxford, 1966), 121-147, esp. 137-142.
[15] *Il Convivio*, ed., G. Busnelli and G. Vandelli (Florence, 1937), Vol, II, IV, pp. 48-50.

them, possessed in certainty of no such glorious future. The theme is not original with Dante: it appears in literature dealing with the fall of the Britons, in the letters of Frederick II, and as late as the sixteenth century in a funeral exequy of Edward VI of England.[16] Yet it is a difficult admission for the prophet of empire to make, even in the *Civitas Dei*.

Henry VII and Clement V do not confront each other personally. Neither, in fact, is present, even though Henry's absence and the few remaining empty seats which Beatrice indicates would suggest that it is not literally the *ultima giustizia* which Dante sees. Beatrice's discourse, however, allows Dante the prophet to witness not only one more disposition of souls but also the disposition of the two powers which might have been the highest manifestations of justice on earth. Up to this point the political themes in the *Paradiso*, from the heaven of Mercury to the Eagle, prepare the traveller for the final confrontation of the forces which contended for power over man. Ironically, it is the spiritual power which causes the failure of the temporal, the more important of the two. Not inadvertently did Dante contrast the *alma agosta* with the *prefetto* Clement V. The Aristotelian-Thomistic view of political life with which Dante was certainly in sympathy had given a new vigor and a new direction to the old Carolingian idea of kingship as a *ministerium*. Dante, however, unlike most other political thinkers of the period, considered the ruler not only the *minister utilitatis publicae*, but the *minister omnium*. Clement's thwarting of the imperial ministry could not be tolerated by God much longer, but it had done damage enough: it had caused the empire to fail. It is fitting that Dante's final view of political failure should be embodied by the throne and crown of Henry VII and not by any heroic emperor of the past. If he had earlier urged ecclesiastical reform on the Italian Cardinals, it was doubtless because without it no empire could succeed and because imperial failure meant the failure of justice.

Thus Augustine's image of the city of God became briefly, in the last lines of *Paradiso* xxx, something different from its theological essence. In the remaining *canti* it becomes the city of the Virgin, its inhabitants the whole body of the saved, its rationale the direct perception of divine love through justice. For a moment, however, Dante had purposely altered its initial appearance in order to permit Henry VII, who was neither to find nor establish justice on earth, to find it as a member of the *corpus mysticum* of the *civitas Dei*. Dante, no longer the prophet of an imperial triumph but of

[16] See, e.g., Robert Hanning, *The Vision of History in Early Britain* (N. Y. 1966); *Petri de Vineis Epistolae*, ed. S. Schardius (Basel, 1566), I, 7, pp. 14-15; William Baldwin, *Beware the Cat and the Funerals of King Edward VI*, ed. William P. Holden (New London, Conn. 1963), 65-83.

ecclesiastical and imperial failure, translated the empire out of the world in which he had seen it inevitably fail into a city in which it inevitably triumphed. Henry VII had been the anointed, the *regulator*, the *minister* of justice. Whatever failure he encountered on earth — and which, without reform of the church, any imperial ideal would also encounter — it was justice itself which allowed Dante to represent him by the throne and crown in the heart of the golden city.

XI

I PRINCIPI NEGLIGENTI DI DANTE E LE CONCEZIONI MEDIOEVALI DEL *REX INUTILIS*

Le anime di Giustiniano e di Romeo nel sesto canto del *Paradiso* rappresentano una categoria di reggitori temporali che dallo zelo per la giustizia civile e per l'« *onore e fama* » del buon governo sono distolti dagli scopi propriamente spirituali e meritano perciò, in Paradiso, un posto più basso di quelli assegnati ad altri tipi di reggitore giusto. Tuttavia Dante, il cui zelo per la giustizia civile permea la *Commedia*, riconosce che tale colpa ebbe sempre come fine il bene degli stati che questi uomini ressero. Sebbene non possa trovarsi d'accordo con Remigio de' Girolami ed altri nel giudicare che il bene della società può, in casi di necessità, avere la precedenza sulla salvezza della propria anima, egli tiene ben fermo che anche lo zelo eccessivo per la giustizia temporale, per quanto possa essere spiritualmente pericoloso, merita un posto in Paradiso [1]. A quei reggitori invece che trascurano sia i doveri spirituali che quelli temporali Dante riserva una sorte diversa. Nel canto settimo del *Purgatorio* sono rappresentate le anime dei prìncipi che sono stati negligenti sia negli affari spirituali sia in quelli temporali. Il sesto ed il settimo canto del *Purgatorio* in effetti costituiscono un ampio e serrato commento politico in cui la figura dominante è quella del poeta provenzale Sordello ed il tono prevalente è quello dell'invettiva scurrile contro quei vizi che impediscono ai prìncipi deboli di governare in modo giusto.

La maggior parte degli studi delle teorie politiche di Dante si occu-

[1] Remigio e Dante sono stati studiati da CHARLES T. DAVIS, « Remigio de' Girolami and Dante: A Comparison of their Conceptions of Peace », « Studi Danteschi », 36 (1959), 105-136. V. anche L. MINIO-PALUELLO, « Remigio Girolami's *De bono communi* », « Italian Studies », 11 (1956), 56-71; ERNST KANTOROWICZ, *The King's Two Bodies*, Princeton, 1957, 478-479. Per Remigio e Agostino Trionfo, v. M. J. WILKS, *The Problems of Sovereignty in the Later Middle Ages*, Combridge, 1963, 26-28.

pano principalmente dei grandi temi trattati nel *De Monarchia*, nelle *Epistolae* e nella *Commedia*. Il conflitto tra papato ed impero, il posto dell'impero nell'ordine mondiale, le pretese monarchiche di Bonifacio VIII, il tradimento di Clemente V, la donazione costantiniana, la rapacità dei re di Francia occupano il primo piano di chi ha discusso la visione politica del poeta [2]. Le figure che compaiono nel settimo canto del *Purgatorio* tuttavia non rientrano facilmente nelle categorie eticamente polarizzate dei buoni e dei cattivi reggitori, i quali occupano una gran parte dell'attenzione (e dell'invettiva) di Dante nel resto della *Commedia*. Questi reggitori non sono buoni né completamente cattivi: sono dei negligenti, degli incapaci, dei codardi. Si avvicinano alla figura del *rex inutilis*, molto di più che non a quelle tradizionali del *rex iustus* e del *tyrannus*.

Il re inutile, il reggitore legittimo del tutto incapace a governare, era un tipo politico sviluppatosi nell'immaginazione popolare e nel pensiero giuridico tra l'ottavo ed il tredicesimo secolo. La visita nella valle dei prìncipi fornì così a Dante l'opportunità di trattare un tema politico dibattuto meno frequentemente di quelli che era abituato ad affrontare, un tema le cui radici si estendono nel regno della teoria giuridica e politica ufficiale ed insieme nel vocabolario più allusivo e meno rigorosamente strutturato della satira politica popolare.

Nel settimo canto del *Purgatorio* Sordello conduce Dante e Virgilio ad una vicina valletta dove essi devono passare la notte prima di salire verso i più alti luoghi del Purgatorio. I prìncipi che occupano questa valle erano stati, fa notare Sordello, negligenti nelle loro vite, sia per quanto riguarda la propria salvezza che il benessere dei regni affidati alla loro cura. Con la sua abituale scrupolosità letteraria e con forte senso dell'ironia Dante fa di Sordello, su un'opera del quale modellò il settimo canto del *Purgatorio*, la guida ed il narratore delle storie dei prìncipi negligenti. Nello stesso tempo tuttavia Dante ampia notevolmente il tema dell'incapacità regia, che Sordello aveva evocato nella sua poesia.

Nel suo *planh* in memoria di Blacatz, Sordello aveva pianto la morte del suo signore ed amico ed aveva osservato che la morte di Blacatz aveva privato il mondo della virtù a tal punto che l'unico rimedio per gli « sco-

[2] Il punto di partenza migliore per svolgere ricerche sul pensiero politico di Dante è ora U. PARRICCHI, *Dante*, Roma, 1965, 273-291. Nello stesso volume v. anche P. BREZZI, « Il pensiero politico di Dante », 149-158. Un esame recente degli studi di questo periodo è quello di NICOLAI RUBINSTEIN, « Studies on the Political History of the Age of Dante », *Atti del congresso internazionale di studi danteschi*, Firenze, 1965, 225-247; anche H. GRUNDMANN, et al., *Dante und die Mächtigen seiner Zeit*, Monaco, 1960.

rati » baroni che allora governavano sarebbe stato quello di mangiare il cuore del cavaliere morto per riguadagnare il coraggio e l'abilità che avevano perduto [3]. Tuttavia il *planh* servì a Sordello principalmente come cornice alla sua invettiva contro i reggitori della sua epoca. Sono tutti incapaci, Federico II, Luigi IX, Enrico III di Inghilterra ed i re di Castiglia, di Aragona e di Navarra. Sebbene Sordello stia compiendo qui quella che un commentatore ha definito recentemente la sua « funzione civile e politica », i suoi prìncipi incapaci ben difficilmente rientrano nei concetti del tredicesimo secolo del regnare in modo negligente [4]. L'unica caratteristica che questi reggitori hanno in comune è quella di essere stati tutti privati di terre che essi rivendicavano come proprie secondo il diritto. Senza dubbio la perdita di territorio era una delle caratteristiche del *rex inutilis*, come avrebbe poi chiarito un commento di Innocenzo IV sul caso di Sancio II del Portogallo [5]. Agli occhi degli uomini del tredicesimo secolo tuttavia Luigi IX e Federico II incarnavano i tipi del *rex iustus* o del *tyrannus* piuttosto che quello del principe incapace.

Nella sua rielaborazione della poesia di Sordello, Dante, d'altra parte, ci descrive una serie di reggitori sulla cui negligenza ed incapacità l'accordo era di gran lunga più generale. Al posto dei prìncipi le cui caratteristiche erano in contrasto con le accuse di incapacità mosse loro da Sordello, Dante descrive una serie di prìncipi che, collettivamente ed individualmente, avevano effettivamente mostrato quei tratti che nel tredicesimo secolo si era soliti vedere associati comunemente con l'incapacità reale.

Tutti i prìncipi negligenti possono essere definiti con le parole con cui Dante caratterizza Rodolfo di Asburgo, il primo del gruppo: « fa sembianti / D'aver negletto ciò che far dovea... ». Sebbene la negligenza dei doveri civili fosse generalmente la caratteristica forse più essenziale del *rex inutilis*, i doveri dell'imperatore erano stati formulati con maggior precisione da Innocenzo III e dai canonisti del tredicesimo secolo, con l'includere nella categoria della negligenza criminale il mancato perse-

[3] Il testo è in C. DE LOLLIS, *Vita e poesia di Sordello di Goito*, Halle, 1896, 153-156. V. C. M. BOWRA, « Dante and Sordello », in *In General and In Particular* New York, 1964.

[4] A. SERONI, « *Purgatorio*, Canto VII », « Studi Danteschi », 33 (1955), 187-205 ed in particolare 204.

[5] Innocenzo IV, *Apparatus super libros Decretalium*, Venezia, 1481, fol. 45r (*ad* VI 1,8.2 *Grandi* = X.1.10 *da supplenda negligentia prelatorum, ad v. utilitatem*): « Nota causas iusta dandi curatorem regibus... si nesciunt perdita recuperare ». V. sotto, n. 17.

guimento degli eretici e la mancata protezione della chiesa [6]. Per Dante tuttavia la negligenza di Rodolfo stava nel suo ignorare l'Italia:

> Rodolfo imperador fu, che potea
> Sanar le piaghe c'hanno Italia morta
> Sì che tardi per altro si ricrea.

In questo modo Dante stabilì un parallelo fra la negligenza dell'imperatore nei riguardi dell'Italia e la mancanza di interesse di qualsiasi reggitore temporale per i bisogni della sua *patria,* una mancanza che aveva già ricevuto un'attenzione notevole da parte dei giuristi e pubblicisti del dodicesimo e tredicesimo secolo e che nell'*Utopia* di Thomas More avrebbe poi suscitato reazioni altrettanto forti quanto nelle satire, nelle cronache e nella letteratura giuridica degli inizi del medioevo.

Gli altri prìncipi nella valle appaiono inabili sia per quanto concerne le loro mancanze personali e politiche sia per la loro incapacità a generare degni successori. In effetti quel che Dante ci dice di Ottakar di Boemia, il quale

> ne le fasce
> Fu meglio assai che Vincislao suo figlio
> Barbuto, cui lussuria e ozio pasce,

restò vero, per tutti i reggitori di questo canto, ad eccezione di Enrico III. Tali perversioni della relazione tra padre e figlio aggiungono una dimensione umana alle conseguenze politiche del governo negligente [7]. Ottakar stesso, che aveva protestato contro l'elezione di Rodolfo al trono imperiale (anche se per ragioni differenti da quelle di Dante), avrebbe poi prodotto una linea di successori contro i quali si sarebbero poi levate le stesse accuse, da Venceslao III nel 1305 a Venceslao IV nel 1400. Anche i tratti dell'indolenza e della voluttuosità, così pronunciati nel figlio di Ottakar Venceslao, erano comunemente associati con il principe incapace. Come

[6] Il miglior studio recente è quello di J. A. WATT, « The Theory of Papal Monarchy in the Thirteenth Century », « Traditio », 20 (1964), 179-319, pubblicato poi saeparatamente, N.Y. e Londra, 1965.

[7] Su altri aspetti della relazione tra padri e figli in Dante, v. WILKS, *The Problem of Sovereignty,* 145 sgg. Occorre naturalmente tener presente la perorazione di Dante al figlio di Rodolfo, « Alberto tedesco », *Purgatorio* vi, 97-151. Per i Capetingi, v. il discorso di Ugo Capeto, *Purg.* xx, e P. RAJNA, « Ugo Ciapetta nella *Divina Commedia* », « Studi Danteschi », 37 (1960), 5-20.

notò Benvenuto da Imola nel suo *Commentum* alla frase « *lussuria e ozio pasce* »,

> Quae duo vitia sunt valde detestabilia
> in uno vulgare nedum in rege; nam
> otiositas et voluptas arma sunt hostis
> antiqui, ad miseras animas captivandas[8].

L'attribuzione di tali vizi a tutti i reggitori non idonei, ma specialmente agli incapaci, diventò un argomento di uso comune nelle opere dei cronisti, giuristi e pubblicisti dall'ottavo secolo in poi. Il vocabolario politico di questi scrittori fu formato tanto da quello che sapevano o pensavano sul regno come istituzione politica quanto da quello che pensavano degli uomini in quanto individui mossi nelle loro azioni da Dio o da Satana, da impulsi di virtù e di vizi, dall'equilibrio o dallo squilibrio dei loro umori o dal capriccio della fortuna.

Alano di Lilla, per esempio, nella sua *Summa de arte praedicatoria* diede lo schema di un sermone *contra acediam*, un vizio la cui storia è connessa con molti aspetti della psicologia ed anche della teologia morale del medioevo[9]. Tra gli *exempla* si rifece ai re dell'Antico Testamento Davide e Salomone, mettendo in contrasto il Davide che combatte i nemici di Dio con il Davide che trascura i suoi doveri a palazzo, vittima della « lussuria e ozio » di Dante. Il re medievale veniva considerato particolarmente soggetto all'acedia e le osservazioni di Alano su Davide, Sansone e Salomone erano certamente qualcosa di più che un semplice riferimento simbolico ai reggitori del periodo medievale. In conseguenza di tali vizi essi si abbandonavano a delitti anche peggiori. L'omileta, pur non essendo principalmente un pensatore politico, poteva ciò non di meno tracciare severe analogie politiche per illustrare le difficoltà cui la fragilità umana è esposta. I suoi lettori a loro volta non potevano ragionevolmente dimenticare la propria esperienza politica nell'interpretare il contenuto spirituale e psicologico del trattato di Alano. Le relazioni semantiche tra i

[8] Benevenuti Rambaldis de Imola, *Commentum super Dantis Aldigherij comoedian*, a cura di G. W. Vernon, Firenze, 1887, vol. III, pp. 209-210 *ad vv.* « *cui... lussuria et ozio pasce* ».

[9] *Patrologia Latina*, vol. 210, coll. 125-128. La storia dell'*acedia* è stata tracciata recentemente da Siegfried Wenzel, *The Sin of Sloth: Acedia in Medieval Thought and Literature*, Chapel Hill, N.C., 1967. V. anche P. Michaud-Quentin, « La classification des puissances de l'ame au XIIe siècle », « Revue du moyen age latin », 5 (1949), 15-34.

termini *otiositas, negligentia, tepiditas, ignavia* e *imbecillitas* possono essere ricavate non soltanto dalla loro frequenza nelle discussioni dell'*acedia*, ma dal loro uso nelle cronache e nei trattati pubblicistici e dalla loro applicazione al tipo del *rex inutilis*. Dalla figura di Childerico III, l'ultimo re merovingio dei Franchi, a quella di Edoardo II d'Inghilterra nel 1327, il principe negligente o comunque incapace appare perseguitato dai suoi vizi nei racconti popolari, nelle leggende ed anche nella cronaca e nel *consilium*.

La negligenza, l'inabilità a generare un successore capace e il soggiacere alle conseguenze di vizi come l'*acedia* costituiscono caratteristiche del *rex inutilis*. Una quarta è l'incompetenza militare o codardia [10]. Filippo III di Francia, oltre a generare un figlio indegno, « il mal di Francia », Filippo IV, fuggì anche dal campo di battaglia: « Morì fuggiendo e disfiorando il giglio ». L'incapacità del reggitore medievale a combattere ed a morire per la *patria*, come ribadiscono sia i cronisti che i giuristi, era un segno ben definito di inidoneità a regnare. Questo difetto, legato alla perdita di territori suoi secondo il diritto, costituì forse la caratteristica più comunemente attribuita al reggitore inutile.

L'ultimo di questi reggitori, Enrico III d'Inghilterra, è un tipo diverso di principe negligente. La sua vita non è condannata severamente ed egli fu l'unico del gruppo che generò un figlio capace di succedergli. Dante tuttavia era senza dubbio a conoscenza delle difficoltà politiche causate dalla minore età di Enrico e dalla Guerra dei Baroni ed i suoi accenni alla « semplice vita » del re intendono probabilmente riferirsi alla sua *simplicitas mentis,* difetto particolarmente pericoloso non solo per i prìncipi, ma anche per i prelati, come è evidente in parecchi brani del *Decretum* di Graziano e nei commenti dei canonisti [11].

[10] Eccellenti studi sono quelli recenti di E. Kantorowicz, *The King's Two Bodies*, 232-272, e Gaines Post, *Studies in Medieval Legal Thought: Public Law and the State* Princeton, 1964, 434-481.

[11] V. anche, per es., *Decretum Gratiani: Corpus iuris canonici*, a cura di E. Friedberg, Leipzig, 1879-1881, vol. I (ma occorre anche usare una precedente edizione con la glossa ordinaria), C. 7 q.l. c. 18 *Quia*, con i commenti nel *casus* e nella glossa ordinaria. L'associazione della semplicità di mente nei prelati e nei principi sembra essere stata introdotta da Uguccione da Pisa nella sua *Summa* a C. 15 q. 6 c. 3 *Alius item* (Admont, Stiftsbibliothek MS 7, fol. 263r *ad v. inutilis*): « His duabus de causis depositus fuit, unde non est questio quare illi non datus fuit coadiutor tunc enim illud locum habet cum quis innocens invenitur insufficiens administrationi, ut VII q. 1 (c. 14) *Quamvis*, (c. 17) *Petisti*, (c. 18) *Quia*, et VIII p. 1 (c. 1) *Si Petrus* ». L'ho esaminato nello studio citato più sotto, n. 17.

Pertanto polemiche personali e la perdita giuridica delle loro qualità sono riservati ai prìncipi negligenti nel settimo canto del *Purgatorio*. Come per i discendenti di Ugo Capeto nel ventesimo canto del *Purgatorio*, le loro debolezze personali di uomini spesso oscurano o addirittura prendono il posto dei loro errori politici di reggitori. Dante non fu certamente l'unico scrittore politico che si trovò di fronte all'alternativa di condannare i vizi personali dei singoli reggitori oppure la loro conformità, dimostrata un po' forzatamente, secondo la retorica, ad un tipo politico mal visto. Mentre le teorie giuridiche e politiche ufficiali, il trattato pubblicistico e la *quaestio* filosofica spesso tendevano a dare al pensiero politico l'aria di una remota ed oscura sottodisciplina della teologia o del diritto canonico, l'invettiva letteraria e la satira parevano spesso ridurlo ad una serie di argomenti *ad hominem*. Quello del prìncipe impotente o comunque incapace fu un problema particolarmente difficile per i teorici della politica proprio perché non riguardava l'alternativa familiare tra usi giusti e usi ingiusti del potere politico, ma la più imbarazzante questione dell'assenza o della diminuzione di tale potere. Questo problema poneva interrogativi sulla natura della relazione tra la persona e l'ufficio ai quali le formule politiche non erano sempre in grado di fornire una risposta; ed inoltre batteva in breccia le opinioni più comunemente accettate rivelandone l'inadeguatezza nella formula di princìpi astratti che derivavano dall'esperienza e dalla necessità politica piuttosto che dalla teoria ecclesiastica. Così nel *Purgatorio*, i re medievali che si avvicinavano di più al modello stabilito nella tipologia politica del *rex inutilis* rimanevano problematici, né lodati né biasimati. Se non venivano condannati insieme al tiranno, neanche erano chiamati a dividere gli onori tributati al re giusto. Un breve esame delle categorie del pensiero politico medievale espresso nella letteratura politica ufficiale ed in quella popolare servirà a spiegare meglio la considerazione di Dante dei prìncipi negligenti e a fornire in qualche misura la storia di tale figura nella tipologia politica medievale.

* * *

Il potere, nelle strutture politiche della cristianità medievale, non era distribuito uniformemente attraverso un sistema amministrativo, giudiziario ed economico ben organizzato e strettamente regolato e tale da soddisfare le esigenze della società come un tutto e da assicurare le libertà personali degli individui. Più spesso, prima del dodicesimo secolo, era il diritto personale dei singoli reggitori che lo doveva sostenere con la forza. In mano ai re esso divenne la *vis et voluntas* e l'*ira et malevolentia regis* dei giuristi. Il re persino al tempo del *Decretum* di Graziano era precisamente uno che poteva costringere e finanche uccidere mantenendosi nella legalità. La distinzione tracciata da Isidoro di Siviglia tra la spirituale *doctrina sermonis* e la temporale *disciplina terroris*, le ingiunzioni di San Gerolamo ai re affinché proteggessero gli impotenti e le minacce di Papa Giovanni VIII ai re che non usano la forza, costituiscono tutti insieme lo « Specchio per i Prìncipi » nella prima importante compilazione del periodo classico del diritto canonico [12]. Persino il passo del *Decretum* sul regnare che è il più frequentemente citato, un passo di una lettera di Gregorio VII ad Ermanno di Metz, tratta delle difficoltà che nascono dal fatto che un re manchi di potere [13]. Quei pensatori ecclesiastici cercavano di incivilire l'istituzione del regno in una cornice giuridica ed in una concezione ecclesiastica della società umana. Ma finivano col fornire, fondamenti più o meno elevati alla forza politica. La giustificazione del potere individuale divenne così uno dei primi temi del pensiero politico medievale più antico e questa necessità può spiegare l'accento posto sulla distinzione tra il re giusto ed il tiranno, tipica già nella patristica e tra i Carolingi.

Tra il dodicesimo ed il quindicesimo secolo tuttavia sorsero in effetti governi creati da re e da consiglieri che si resero ben conto dell'utilità della distribuzione del potere tra le persone dei giudici e degli amministratori reali, particolarmente quando sembrò che tal metodo sollevasse il singolo suddito dalle pretese spesso arbitrarie e sempre incombenti del suo signore. Il carattere distributivo del potere politico nella posteriore storia medievale non fu certo identico a quello dei primi tipi di potere individuale. Il suo scopo principale non fu di riconoscere democraticamente i diritti dei sudditi minori, ma di mettere in evidenza le loro funzioni in quanto sudditi *reali*, imbrigliando così le pretese dei sudditi maggiori, i baroni ed i vescovi dei regni feudali. È quindi difficile considerare

[12] Alcuni di questi testi sono esaminati da WATT, « The Theory of Papal Monarchy ». I testi particolarmente importanti sono C. 23 q. 5 c. 18 (S. Agostino sulla natura del potere temporale); c. 20 (Isidoro sulla *disciplina terroris*); c. 23 (S. Gerolamo sulla protezione degli impotenti); c. 26 (Giovanni VIII sui pericoli del non usare la forza quando è necessario).

[13] C. 15 q. 6 c. 3 *Alius item*: « Alius item Romanus pontifex regem Francorum non tam pro suis iniquitatibus quam pro eo, quod tantae potestati non erat utilis, a regno deposuit et Pippinum Caroli Magni imperatoris patrem in eius loco substituit omnesque Francigenas a iuramento fidelitatis quam illi fecerant, absolvit ». Graziano attribuì il testo a Papa Gelasio I. Una discussione più esauriente con citazione si trova nello studio citato, n. 17.

la lunga serie di potenti reggitori-amministratori dopo Enrico II, Ruggiero II, e Filippo Augusto negli stessi termini dei loro predecessori. Mano mano che il re tendeva sempre più frequentemente a non mettersi di persona alla testa dell'esercito, a distribuire l'autorità giudiziaria tra giudici invece che usarla personalmente, udendo parlare da ogni parte di dominio della legge, consultazione, consiglio e rappresentanza, le vecchie distinzioni tra re giusto e tiranno divennero meno significative [14]. Mano mano che il potere personale privato del reggitore divenne impersonale e pubblico, i re cominciarono a circondarsi di un po' di quella mistica ecclesiastica e secolare che avrebbe poi dato origine agli *arcana imperii* del sedicesimo e diciassettesimo secolo [15]. La depersonalizzazione del potere politico e la conseguente nascita di concetti come « corona », « comunità del regno », considerati come sedi astratte del potere, ed il carattere soprapersonale del reggitore consacrato offuscarono i precedenti espliciti giudizi morali sugli individui e sollevarono nuove difficoltà sulla natura del potere sovrano.

Le difficoltà dei teorici della politica nel caratterizzare il governo di Ruggero II di Sicilia, come ha mostrato Helène Wieruszowski, furono risolte con la creazione sperimentale di un nuovo tipo politico, il *tyrannus utilis*, il tiranno che governa severamente ma sembra giovare al suo regno [16]. Nel 1245 su richiesta dei magnati e dell'alto clero del Portogallo, Innocenzo IV diede forma nel diritto canonico ad un altro tipo, il *rex inutilis*. Innocenzo designò Alfonso di Boulogne, fratello di Sancio II, come *curator* del regno del Portogallo con in mano la *cura et administratio generalis et libera* del regno, lasciando a Sancio soltanto il titolo reale e la *dignitas* di re [17]. Innocenzo riconobbe così, almeno in parte, che le teorie dell'insufficienza personale elaborate da canonisti quali Uguccione da Pisa e Giovanni il Teutonico per i prelati e applicate poi sperimentalmente anche ai maggiori reggitori temporali potevano essere ragionevolmente

[14] Il processo è stato tracciato con grande accuratezza e con ampie citazioni in KANTOROWICZ, *The King's Two Bodies*, cit. e POST, *Public Law and the State*, cit.

[15] V. E. KANTOROWICZ, « Mysteries of State: An Absolutist Concept and its Late Medieval Origins », « Harvard Theological Review », 47 (1955), 65-91.

[16] HELÈNE WIERUSZOWSKI, « Roger II of Sicily, *Rex-Tyrannus, in Medioeval Political Thought* », « Speculum », 38 (1963), 46-78.

[17] Ho tracciato la storia di Innocenzo IV e di Sancio II e di alcuni aspetti dello sfondo canonistico in uno studio intitolato « *Rex inutilis*: *Sancho* II of Portugal and Thirteenth Century Deposition Theory », *Studia Gratiana* 14 (*Collectanea Stephan Kuttner* IV), 1968, 253-305.

applicate nei casi di reggitori temporali i cui difetti non richiedevano la deposizione e che erano più incapaci che tiranni [18].

Tuttavia, stabilendo il *rex inutilis* come categoria formale del diritto canonico, Innocenzo dava in effetti un significato legale ad un tipo politico che era stato elaborato dall'ottavo secolo in poi nelle opere di cronisti, poeti e teorici della politica. Si trattava di un tipo che si era sviluppato da due fonti diverse: la spiegazione carolingia della sostituzione della dinastia dei Merovingi e le reazioni del nono e del decimo secolo di fronte a singoli reggitori che non erano stati capaci di conservare l'energico governo personale che di necessità aveva finito con il caratterizzare la regalità cristiana.

Si può così dire che la storia intellettuale del *rex inutilis* medievale comprenda vari e distinti sviluppi: la formazione di un tipo ideale del principe inutile o incapace corrispondente ai tipi ideali del giusto reggitore e del tiranno, i mutevoli criteri storici, per misurare l'attitudine dei re, criteri tratti tanto dall'esperienza storica e dalle mutevoli considerazioni politiche che dalle occasioni specifiche nelle quali singoli reggitori furono accusati di diventare inutili fornendo così una verifica delle teorie politiche poste in relazione con le esigenze della necessità pratica. Sarà dunque utile confrontare il processo attraverso il quale il tipo del reggitore inutile si formò nel pensiero politico degli inizi del medioevo con il mutevole carattere del governo reale e con l'esperienza storica dell'istituzione della regalità.

* * *

La storia della formazione di tipi politici ideali nel medioevo richiede lo studio di altre aree di pensiero oltre a quella puramente giuridica e politica. Le occasioni specifiche in cui ci si rivolse ai giuristi ed ai pensatori politici per razionalizzare la deposizione o la limitazione del potere dei re cambiarono quando le società acquisirono esperienza e consapevolezza politica e quando ne nacquero nuove possibilità di comportamento politico. I tipi politici non furono tuttavia facilmente esposti ai cambiamenti. perché non erano radicati esclusivamente nella teoria giuridica e politica ma anche nell'immaginazione sociale. Il potere sovrano era un elemento costitutivo non solo della politica medievale ma di una coerente visione del mondo in cui si univano etica e politica, ordine e rango, esperienza ed immaginazione.

[18] *Ibid.* 281-297.

In vari punti della sua storia il concetto del re inutile rivela sulla società medievale qualcosa di più che semplici atteggiamenti politici. Nel vocabolario molto formalizzato dei cronisti dell'ottavo e del nono secolo, per esempio, il re inutile era uno che aveva « falsamente » mantenuto il titolo — *nomen* — di re pur avendo perso il necessario complemento, la *potestas,* cioè la ricchezza, la forza militare ed il controllo politico necessari ad un « vero » re [19]. L'incapacità degli ultimi reggitori merovingi dei Franchi a conformarsi a questo modello assai immaginario di « vero » potere sovrano costituì almeno una delle basi che servirono più tardi a fondare il regno carolingio; altrettanto servirono l'importanza attribuita all'approvazione ecclesiastica della nuova dinastia che fece passar sopra alla illegittimità dinastica, e la preoccupazione di mantenere energicamente il potere politico al di sopra delle istituzioni spirituali e temporali, favorita ed accresciuta dal giudizio ufficiale sulla incapacità ed indolenza dei Merovingi [20].

Nel mondo politicamente tormentato del nono e del decimo secolo la vera e propria incapacità degli ultimi Carolingi a difendere il popolo e la *patria* fu razionalizzata dai cronisti e considerata come perdita di *virtus. Virtus,* un termine ambivalente che significa carisma e favore divino da una parte e potere effettivo dall'altra, ricevette così un senso notevolmente prammatico e fornì un fondamento sia filosofico che storico ai primi passi dell'ascesa al potere dei Capetingi e dei Sassoni [21]. Spesso poco propensi o incapaci a distinguere l'esperienza politica da quella etica, gli scrittori politici medievali elaborarono una tecnica per mezzo della quale poterono tradurre la prima in un vocabolario di categorie formalizzate che descrissero i nudi (e spesso sgradevoli) fatti dell'esistenza nei termini di tali categorie. Se nella storia essi non furono i soli a trovare la razionalizzazione dell'esperienza più importante degli eventi stessi, forse così

[19] Il più recente contributo in una lunga serie di comunicazioni accademiche sui significati rispettivi di *nomen* e *potestas* è quello di ARNO BORST, « Kaisertum und Namentheorie », *Festschrift Percy Ernst Schramm,* vol. I, Wiesbaden, 1964, 36-51. Altre ottime discussioni delle fonti si trovano in J. M. WALLACE-HADRILL, *The Long-Haired Kins,* N.Y., 1962; e negli studi di H. BUTTNER e R. BUCHNER in *Das Königtum* (*Vorträge und Forschungen,* vol. III), a cura di Theodor Mayer, Lindau-Konstanz, 1954.

[20] V., per es., il *Breviarium Erchanberti,* a cura di G. H. Pertz, MGH *SS* 2, 328.

[21] Per *virtus,* v. KARL BOSL, *Reges ex nobilitate, duces ex cirtute sumunt.* nel suo *Frühformen der Gesellschaft in mittelalterlichen Europa,* Münich-Vienna, 1964, 62-73; H. BEUMANN, *Widukind von Korvei,* Weimar, 1950, 205-265; *idem,* « Die Historiographie des Mittelalters als Quelle für die Ideengeschichte des Königtums », « Historische Zeitschrift », 180 (1955), 449-488.

facendo, furon loro ad avere una giustificazione etica e filosofica maggiore di tanti altri. La loro insistenza nel voler nobilitare le azioni violente di magnati brutali e di re favorì in un periodo difficile il mantenimento di una certa tensione etica nella politica ed una visione dell'uomo politico che è una delle poche caratteristiche attraenti dell'esperienza politica occidentale.

Anche alcune difficoltà ricorrenti agli inizi della società medievale contribuirono alla formazione di questo tipo. Nel complesso processo di sostituzione di vecchie dinastie con le nuove, quale che fosse il motivo della sostituzione, il potente senso germanico della legittimità dinastica poteva essere superato soltanto con l'assistenza e l'approvazione di strutture ecclesiastiche altrettanto potenti e con l'attribuzione alle vecchie dinastie di quella qualità di impotenza che rendeva i singoli membri inidonei a governare. Il mito della degenerazione merovingia utilizzato da Paolo Diacono e da altri pubblicisti carolingi, influenzò le successive teorie dell'inadeguatezza regale, come dimostrano le cronache e persino i trattati pubblicistici dell'undicesimo e dodicesimo secolo [22].

Il favore o la protezione accordata dal re a qualche uomo di chiesa o a qualche nobile inviso al popolo, l'acquisizione o la perdita dei pretesi poteri taumaturgici del re e l'istituzione della tregua di Dio potevano essere tutte occasioni per accusare il reggitore di impotenza [23]. Il costante orrore per i funzionari reali e per i cattivi consiglieri, tipico del feudalesimo, fece nascere anche un meccanismo psicologico secondo il quale uomini cattivi e dotati di forte volontà e di solito di umili origini avrebbero dominato il re dalla debole volontà e perciò tale solo apparentemente. Quando la visione politica di cronisti e scrittori satirici superò la rudi-

[22] Per le origini della leggenda, v. il resoconto di Clodoveo II nelle *Gesta Dagoberti Regis Francorum*, a cura di M. Bouquet, *Recueil des historiens des Gaules et de la France*, vol. II (Paris, 1739), 596; anche MGH *SS rer. Mer.* II, 425. Cfr. *Liber historiae Francorum*, MGH *SS rer. Mer* II, c. 44, p. 316; Paolo Diacono, *Historia Langobardorum*, a cura di G. Waitz, MGH *SS rer. Langob.* VI, 16, p. 218. Per l'uso che se ne fece nell'undicesimo secolo, v. l'anonimo *Liber de unitate ecclesiae conservanda*, a cura di W. Schwenkenbecher, MGH *Libelli de Lite* II, 173-284 e separatamente in MGH *SS in us. schol.* (Hannover, 1883), p. 36.

[23] V. Jean-François Lemarignier, « Structures monastiques et structures politiques dans la France de la fin du Xe et des débuts du XIe siècle », *Il monachesimo nell'alto medioevo*, Settimane di studio del Centro Italiano di studi sull'alto Medioevo, vol. IV, Spoleto, 1957, 357-400; Marc Bloch, *Les rois thaumaturges*, Paris, rist. 1961, 31, 146-157; Joel T. Rosenthal, « The King's 'Wicked Advisors' and Medieval Baronial Rebellions », « Political Science Quarterly », 82 (1967), 595-618.

mentale tipologia dell'ottavo e nono secolo, il tipo del *rex inutilis* finì spesso con l'essere legato alla funzione della fortuna nella caduta dei principi ed alla funzione dei vizi, in particolare l'*acedia* nei ritratti psicologici degli individui. Perfino l'utilità rispettiva del re che partecipava ad una crociata e di quello che non partecipava prestò caratteristiche al tipo, specialmente quando i criteri dell'« utilità » nei riguardi della patria originaria erano in conflitto con quelli dell'« utilità » nei confronti della causa comune della cristianità [24].

Anche la rappresentazione letteraria del potere sovrano fornì a tale tipo delle caratteristiche che non sempre avevano attinenza con criteri puramente politici. Le *chansons de geste* attribuivano spesso ed esplicitamente proprio quelle qualità che il pubblico dei nobili e dei *juvenes* giudicava più pericolose in un signore: la slealtà, l'inclinazione ingiusta ai favoritismi e la codardia [25]. L'incapacità di Carlo Magno nella *Chanson de Roland* ad imporre un unico piano di ritirata dalla Spagna riflette un giudizio sull'impotenza reale che sicuramente deriva molto più dall'opinione della nobiltà sui propri privilegi e sulla propria autorità che da sentimenti di ostilità verso la memoria del grande imperatore (sebbene la figura di Carlo Magno in più tarde *chansons* mostri sovente quei tratti di senilità, impotenza e codardia che sono invece più comuni ai reggitori minori) [26]. I re del ciclo arturiano erano poi d'altra parte reggitori di *aventure* che dovevano necessariamente essere inattivi nei momenti di crisi pubblica, per permettere all'eroico cavaliere di compiere la sua impresa vittoriosa

[24] V. la disputa fra i due re Eystein e Sigurdin *Heimskringla*, trad. di S. Laing, riv. da Peter Foote, London, 1961, p. 300. Il fallimento in una crociata poteva anche indebolire il prestigio in patria: ODO DI DEUIL, *De profectione Ludowici VII in Orientem*, a cura e con trad. inglese di V. G. Berry, Columbia Records of Civilization: Sources and Studies, no. 42, N.Y., 1948, xiv, 99.

[25] Per il carattere dei *juvenes*, v. GEORGES DUBY, « Dans la France du Nord-Ouest, au XIIe siècle: les 'jeunes' dans la société aristocratique », « Annales, Economies-Sociétés-Civilisations », 19 (1964), 835-846. V. A. EULER, *Das Königtum im altfranzösischen Karlsepos* in « Ausgaben und Abhandlungen aus der Gebiet der romanischen Philologie ». Heft 65 (Marburg, 1886); F. WERNER, « Königtum und Lehenwesen im französischen Nationalepos », « Romanische Forschungen », 25 (1908), 321-443; W. G. VAN EMDEN, « Isembart and the Old French Epic of Revolt », « Nottingham Medieval Studies », 8 (1964), 22-34; R. R. BEZZOLA, « De Roland à Raoul de Cambrai », in *Mélanges Hoepffner* (Paris, 1949), 195-213, ristampato anche nel suo *Les origines et la formation de la litterature courtoise en Occident* (500-1200), pt. II, vol. II, BEHE fasc. 113, Parigi, 1960, 495-517.

[26] V. E. AUERBACH, *Mimesis*, New York, 1953, 156 sgg.

o sventurata [27]. Anche le disavventure del *Roi Mehaignié* e del *Roi Pêcheur*, il re mutilato ed il re pescatore, fornirono una dimensione alle discussioni sull'impotenza reale nella società cavalleresca. Nelle cronache dei monaci e nell'agiografia, il re figura più sovente come benefattore o persecutore dell'istituto o del santo, in modi ora clamorosi ora striscianti, che come figura propriamente politica [28]. Nella retorica dell'invettiva e del panegirico, tanto fortemente e generalmente polarizzata, il re poteva sembrare lui stesso un dio, come negli scritti dell'Anonimo Normanno, oppure poteva essere letteralmente lo strumento vivente di Satana come appariva ad un papa come Gregorio VII.

La storia della tipologia politica medievale è essenzialmente quella di ciò che uno studioso ha chiamato recentemente « i modi della percezione » dell'esperienza politica [29]. Dati certi presupposti sulla natura umana (in particolare sulla sua fragilità), sul significato dell'esperienza umana nella sfera divina ed in quella umana e sulla natura della storia, gli uomini medievali trovarono più utile descrivere tipi ideali, modelli di caratteristiche ben compiute, che potevano essere realizzati da pochi eletti, essendo irraggiungibili per la maggior parte, proprio perché la natura umana, da sola, non aiutata dalla grazia, non poteva giungere fino ad essi. Non ci poteva essere continuità organica tra la natura umana ed il tipo perfetto, perché era proprio quello che c'è di umano nell'uomo che doveva essere superato. Il papa, il vescovo ed il re erano ritenuti *exempla* di quel tipo di perfezione, non in virtù della loro compiuta umanità, ma perché si erano imposti un carattere estraneo ad essa. L'atteggiamento pertanto che aveva la funzione di tener distinti, creativamente la persona dall'ufficio nella sfera legale finì anche con il creare una tensione tra la fragilità e l'incapacità umane poste continuamente in rilievo e la perfezione che le originarie teorie dell'ufficio presupponevano [30].

[27] V. E. KÖHLER, *Ideal und Wirklichkeit in der höfischen Epik*, « Beihefte der Zeitschrift für romanische Philologie », Heft 97 Tübingen, 1956; *idem*, « Le rôle de la 'coutume' dans les romans de Chrètien de Troyes », « Romania », 81 (1960), 386-397 (trad. « Die Rolle der 'Rechtsbrauch' [costume] in den Romanen des Chrestien von Troyes », nel suo *Trobadorlyrik und hôfischer Roman*, Berlin, 1962, 205-212.

[28] V. C. GRANT LOOMIS, « King Arthur and the Saints », « Speculum », 8 (1933); MARIE-CLAUDE BLANCHET, « Le double visage d'Arthur chez Layamon », *Studi in onore di Italo Siciliano*, vol. I, Firenze, 1966, 71-84; R. W. HANNING, *The Vision of History in Early Britain*, N.Y., 1966.

[29] W. J. BRANDT, *The Shape of Medieval History: Studies in Modes of Perception*, New Haven, 1966.

[30] V., per la separazione papale di titolo e ufficio, gli acuti studi di Walter Ull-

Perfino i più pratici ed i più prammatici dei teorici del diritto e della politica elaborarono una serie di presupposti sulla natura dell'uomo e sulla struttura della società. Il carattere chiaramente dialettico dei concetti ecclesiastici di *sacerdotium*, — il sacerdozio e l'autorità sacerdotale —, e di *imperium* o *regnum*, l'autorità temporale, dopo il pontificato di Gregorio VII, contribuì spesso alla determinazione delle qualità essenziali del reggitore idoneo. Molti canonisti, ad esempio, si servirono delle osservazioni di Gregorio sulla impotenza di Cilderico III per considerare i reggitori temporali come paralleli alla gerarchia dei prelati sotto la giurisdizione papale. Dopo i pontificati di Alessandro III e di Innocenzo III, le relazioni tra reggitori spirituali e temporali furono poste su di un fondamento giuridico più preciso e diedero origine alle teorie della necessità dell'approvazione papale di certi candidati al regno e di certi aspetti della condotta di tutti i poteri temporali e persino in certe circostanze della perseguibilità di tutti i reggitori, in caso di lagnanze, davanti al tribunale del papa stesso [31]. Il papa ideale di alcuni canonisti, pertanto, essendo al vertice di una gerarchia organizzata giuridicamente e con gradi ben precisi, avrebbe potuto tracciare criteri piuttosto ampi dell'« utilità » e dell'« inutilità », includendo in quest'ultima categoria non solo l'incapacità, ma la tirannia, il delitto, il peccato grave, e la negligenza criminale [32].

Tale opinione tuttavia non può essere riferita a tutto il periodo medievale così come non lo possono essere quelle dei poeti epici del dodicesimo secolo o quelle dei cronisti carolingi. Le minacce all'unità della cristianità costituite dalla crescita delle eresie nel dodicesimo secolo, dalle contrastate elezioni imperiali del 1198 e dalle crisi tra Filippo Augusto e i suoi vassalli e rivali attirarono un certo numero di forti dichiarazioni politiche da parte di Innocenzo III. Lo *Specchio per i Principi* di Innocenzo, quantunque spezzettato in una serie di lettere inviate a diversi reggitori ed ispirate da circostanze differenti e distribuito nelle sezioni della *Compilatio III* e del *Liber Extra* di Gregorio IX, ribadiva una considerazione

mann, specialmente *Principles of Government and Politics in the Middle Ages*, N.Y., 1966, 32-56, 87-116; M. J. WILKS, « *Papa est nomen jurisdictionis*: Augustinus Triumphus und the Papal Vicariate of Christ », « Journal of Theological Studies », 8 (1957), 71-91, 256-271, e il suo *Problem of Sovereignty in the Later Middle Ages.*

[31] V. gli studi citati da WATT, *The Theory of Papal Monarchy*, passim.

[32] V., per es., ULLMANN, *Principles of Government and Politics*; 57-86, *idem.* The Growth of Papal Government, Londra, 1955, 286-288; *idem*, « Law and the Medieval Historians », XIe Congrès International des sciences historiques, *Rapports*, vol. III, Uppsala, 1960, 34-74 a p. 44.

dell'autorità temporale che non tutti i reggitori e neanche tutti i canonisti erano pronti ad accettare nella sua totalità. Il più importante contributo che Innocenzo diede alla storia del *rex inutilis* fu la sua chiara e netta distinzione del concetto di negligenza criminale da quello di peccato grave o incorreggibilità tirannica. In seguito papi e canonisti come Innocenzo IV, Guglielmo Durante e Giovanni Andrea avrebbero poi completato la distinzione di Innocenzo III con la distinzione ulteriore tra il reggitore criminalmente negligente ed il meno cattivo *rex inutilis* [33].

Quando le monarchie territoriali e l'impero cominciarono ad avanzare le loro richieste come entità politiche separate, simili nei loro scopi ed organizzate secondo linee approssimativamente parallele, il loro *status*, *necessitas* ed *utilitas*, e non la semplice obbedienza o approvazione del papato, divennero più fermamente i criteri essenziali dell'utilità reale. La prerogativa papale di deporre i reggitori non idonei passò in altre mani, ma rimase il carattere legale che i canonisti avevano dato alle vecchie teorie della deposizione. Nel quattordicesimo secolo i re non potevano più semplicemente venir privati del titolo né i loro sudditi potevano essere liberati dal giuramento personale di obbedienza. Quello che Kern ha chiamato il passaggio « da una procedura ecclesiastica ad una costituzionale » fu pieno di tentativi di deporre vecchi reggitori e di insediarne dei nuovi nelle forme riconosciute del diritto pubblico [34]. Furono sperimentati (spesso in modo grossolano) metodi e teorie della resistenza che non erano, così si sosteneva, contrari alla legge ed erano invece in grado di sostenere l'esame ed il giudizio legale: così per lo meno sembrava ai baroni inglesi del 1308, 1327 e 1399, ai magnati dell'impero nel 1298 e 1400 ed ai canonisti ed ai pubblicisti che presero partito per una parte o per l'altra delle dispute sulla destituzione degli stessi papi nel 1294, 1378 e 1415. Quando la chiesa stessa cominciò ad essere discussa nei termini di quegli stessi principi di diritto pubblico che essa tanto aveva fatto per formare e per trasmettere alle nuove società politiche temporali, anche i titoli politici dei

[33] V. i commenti di Innocenzo IV citati sopra, n. 5; per Durante, v. il suo *Speculum Iudiciale*, 1ª *De Legato*, 17; per Giovanni Andrea, v. la sua glossa al *Liber Sextus* di Bonifacio VIII e il suo *Novella in Sextum*, Venezia, 1499, rist. Graz, 1963, 75-76.

[34] V. l'utile studio di G. Gaspary, « The Deposition of Richard II and the Canon Law », *Proceedings of the Second International Congress of Medieval Canon Law* (Monumenta Iuris Canonici, Series C: Subsidia, vol. I) Roma, 1966, 189-201. V. anche le interessanti osservazioni di H. G. Wright, « The Protestation of Richard II in the Tower in September, 1399 », « Bulletin of the John Rylands Library », 23 (1939), 151-165, che suggeriscono che non solo la casa di Lancaster ma il re stesso aveva dei canonisti come consiglieri.

papi furono sottoposti a considerazioni simili, come la serie di crisi ecclesiologiche dalla rinuncia di Celestino V al Concilio di Costanza avrebbe poi reso dolorosamente chiaro.

Il tipo del *rex inutilis* costituì uno fra i molti modi di affrontare il problema della non idoneità al potere sovrano a cui potevano ricorrere le nuove società politiche nel periodo formativo della loro esistenza. Gli attributi legali del re inutile tuttavia non sono gli unici tratti del tipo. Nelle disposizioni dell'imperatore Adolfo di Nassau e di Edoardo II e di Riccardo II d'Inghilterra nel 1298, 1327 e 1399 essi sono congiunti con accuse di delitti, peccati, incorreggibilità e riferimenti biblici al retto dominio [35]. Essi diventarono in breve parte di un'ampia varietà di approcci al potere sovrano che doveva ancora essere sistemata in un sistema coerente di diritto pubblico. Entro i nuovi sistemi essi tuttavia mantennero molte delle loro vecchie caratteristiche.

Dante si trova ad una svolta del processo attraverso il quale il diritto pubblico della Chiesa fu adottato, spesso rozzamente e con esitazioni, nel diritto pubblico delle monarchie territoriali. I suoi prìncipi negligenti nel settimo canto del *Purgatorio* riflettono la posizione ambivalente del *rex inutilis* sia nel vecchio sistema sia nel nuovo. Sebbene non sembrasse di poterlo condannare per la sua mancanza, neppure lo si perdonava completamente. Intorno al 1300 il vecchio senso della *dignitas* personale del reggitore era ancora abbastanza forte da impedire che questa si perdesse per ragioni che non fossero peccato grave o delitto. Nello stesso tempo tuttavia la gente sapeva benissimo che i re essendo uomini potevano essere anche loro inetti, trascurare l'amministrazione della giustizia e mandare in rovina il regno. Sebbene alcuni pensatori politici posteriori ritenessero tali mancanze meritevoli della deposizione, altri, e tra questi Dante stesso, erano meno sicuri [36]. Essi ribadivano che non si doveva condannare il *rex inutilis* perché serviva a ricordare i pericoli della *humana fragilitas* negli affari di governo. E tuttavia non lo si poteva discolpare completamente, perché il potere sovrano era uno strumento per raggiungere il benessere spirituale e temporale della società umana. Il re medievale ideale avrebbe dovuto essere un santo. Una delle tragedie della storia medievale

[35] Il processo istituito contro Adolfo di Nassau si può trovare in MGH *Const.* III, nos. 588-590, pp. 548-553. Quelli contro Edoardo II e Riccardo II in S.B. Chrimes e A. L. Brown, *Select Documents of English Constitutional History*, 1307-1485, N.Y., 1961, 33-38, 179-193.

[36] Per Agostino Trionfo e Ockham, v. WILKS, *The Problem of Sovereignty*, 223-250, 450.

è che così pochi dei suoi santi-re, con l'eccezione di Luigi IX, furono re capaci, mentre pochi dei suoi re capaci furono santi.

Non era compito dei pensatori politici e dei reggitori del medioevo ideare una scienza della politica o una interpretazione della storia secondo dimensioni umane invece che superumane. Tuttavia questi teorici e reggitori riuscirono, ponendo altissimi ideali metafisici alle strutture ed agli individui al governo, a far mantenere un alto senso del valore della società e delle sue forme e delle libertà dell'individuo. Tale senso poté essere ripetutamente invocato per ammonire i reggitori criminali o deboli a non dimenticare gli obblighi della *via regia*. Gli stessi reggitori, identificando le loro persone con l'equità e la giustizia, la responsabilità per il bene pubblico e i più alti ideali della società, contribuirono a fare della *via regia* la *via politica* della cristianità medievale.

(Traduzione di Adalberto Chiesa).

XII

Pars, *Parte*: Dante and an Urban Contribution to Political Thought

Of all the constituent parts of political communities, none has had to overcome as intense and enduring an opposition on the part of political and constitutional thinkers, from antiquity to the nineteenth century, as the institution of party. On the other hand, none has seemed so essential in the eyes of political analysts for the effective functioning of modern republican or democratic governments and political communities. Ignored or condemned by classical political theorists from Aristotle to Cicero, the concept of party was semantically tainted by association with such terms as *factio* and *secta*. Later, it was set systematically in opposition to such compelling images as *unitas*, *concordia*, and *corpus* by medieval political theorists.[1] The very idea of organized, constructive political conflict

1. On the development and terminology of social and political conflict in the Roman Republic, see P. A. Brunt, *Social Conflicts in the Roman Republic* (London, 1971) and A. W. Lintott, *Violence in Republican Rome* (Oxford, 1968). The most thorough study of the semantics of the Roman usage of "pars" and "factio," however, is the study of Lily Ross Taylor, *Party Politics in the Age of Caesar* (Berkeley and Los Angeles, 1949), esp. pp. 7–24, 176, 188–90. Under Augustus and afterward, both pars and factio "became practically synonymous with *seditio*" (Taylor, p. 190, n. 40). My colleague Robert E. A. Palmer has kindly informed me that the terms long retained this meaning in Latin belles lettres. In his *Etymologiae*, ed. W. M. Lindsay, 2 vols. (Oxford, 1911), Isidore of Seville defines *factiosus* (X, 106) as "inter opprobria, cum seditiosum accipi volumus: cum vero gratiosum ac potentem et quasi magnae factionis." *Seditio* (V, xxvi, 11) is defined as "dissensio civium, quod seorsum alii ad alios eunt." In Book VIII, *De ecclesia et sectis*, (VIII, iii, 4–5) both *secta* and schisma, particularly the latter, are regarded as fundamentally pejorative: "Schisma ab scissura animorum vocata. Eodem enim cultu, eodem ritu credit ut ceteri; solo congregationis delectatur discidio." With Isidore, factio, secta, seditio, and schisma have become virtually identical, pejorative terms. St. Augustine's treatise *Contra partem Donati*, written in 397 and no longer extant, suggests that among the Church Fathers the social sense of pars too had gone the way of factio and secta. For Byzantium, see Jacques Jarry, *Hérésies et factions dans l'Empire Byzantin du IVe au VIIe siècle* (Cairo, 1968), esp. pp. 95–188. On the vocabulary of society and its parts, see Pierre Michaud-Quantin, *Universitas: Expressions du mouvement communautaire dans le moyen-âge latin* (Paris, 1970), particularly pp. 271–80 for a discussion of another, and perhaps related usage of pars, that in ecclesiastical elections. There is further literature and discussion in Walter Ullmann, *The Individual and Society in the Middle Ages* (Baltimore, 1966), pp. 34–35. There is an extensive literature on the ecclesiastical concept of *unitas*, from Cyprian on.

within a single community failed to acquire theoretical respectability until it was taken up (cautiously, to be sure) first by English thinkers of the seventeenth and eighteenth centuries and then (even more cautiously) by political theorists in the North American colonies and the new republic, notably James Madison. In spite of a growing willingness to tolerate a politics of parties in the work of such thinkers as Barrington, Hume, Burke, and Madison, political theorists' acceptance of the idea of party was slow and tangled in semantic difficulties. Even into the nineteenth century theories of party oppositon and party government made difficult headway against what both theorists and the political public persisted in conceiving of, and indeed experiencing, as factionalism—divisive, corroding, and ultimately destructive of the unity of the state.

The history of the idea and institution of party has been further obscured by historians' and political scientists' reluctance to agree on the nature of party and faction, the nature of organized political conflict, and the social origins of the modern party system. In this essay I propose to take a position far less rigid and analytical than is often found in discussions of the nature and history of parties and approach the history of the idea in terms of both semantics and political theory, particularly as they offer evidence for the concept of the term in two different periods and places, the first in the northern Italian cities between 1200 and 1500, and the second in England and North America between 1649 and 1800. For only once in European history before the English and North American experiments of the eighteenth and early nineteenth centuries had anything resembling a theory of the legitimacy of party acquired any currency. This phenomenon occurred in the northern Italian city-republics between the thirteenth and the fifteenth centuries. Its opening phase was signaled by the use of the term *pars* (*parte* in Italian) in reference to the Guelf and Ghibelline conflicts early in the thirteenth century. Its closing phase was typified by the brooding political meditations of Machiavelli and Guicciardini in the first half of the sixteenth. After the mid-seventeenth century, political factionalism in England, colored in some quarters by the attraction of republican political ideals, gained ground slowly as political thinkers were once again compelled to face the question of conflict and opposition not only as a theoretical problem, but as an enduring fact of political life. I shall risk the suggestion that in the experience of party the world of Dante and his contemporaries and successors anticipated in several important ways the problems of political conflict and opposition within the civil community and in some instances, particularly in the writings of

Leonardo Bruni and Niccolò Machiavelli, came close to finding a rationale for party conflict and conciliation that was not dissimilar from the views of several eighteenth-century constitutional theorists.[2]

Dante, "a great scholar in almost every branch of learning, albeit he was a layman," was also, as he once called himself, "a man preaching justice," a prophet. The motif of prophecies, adumbrated, partial, misguiding, obscure, and malevolent, constitutes one of the great themes connecting Heaven and Hell. In the *Paradiso* most of the earlier prophecies are finally stated explicitly, in both love and sorrow, and none of them is more troubling than that made by Cacciaguida in *Paradiso*, 17. Dante has said,

> While I was in Vergil's company upon the mountain that heals the souls, and descending into the dead world, grave words were spoken to me of my future life, though I feel myself set foursquare against the blows of chance; so that my desire would be met if I knew what approaches me, for an arrow foreseen comes more gently.

And Cacciaguida, addressed in the first place because he is a respected relative, a saint, and one "who sees contingent things before they are in themselves," "without dark sayings," as in pagan antiquity, and "in plain words and express terms," out of Christian love, utters the memorable, sonorous prophecy of Dante's exile, a prophecy that reflects Dante's sense of his own solitude as he had expressed it to the Italian cardinals in his letter of 1313: "*una sola vox, sola pia, et hec privata, in matris Ecclesie quasi funere audiatur*" :

> And that which will weigh heaviest on thy shoulders is the wicked and senseless company with which thou shalt fall into that valley, which shall become wholly ungrateful, quite mad and furious against thee; but before long they, not you, shall have the brows red for this. Of their brutish folly their doings shall give proof, so that it shall be thine honor to have made a party by thyself.

In spite of Dante's twenty years of philosophical and political solitude, Cacciaguida's prophecy is still painful. And the content of that prophecy, "Si ch'a te fia bello/averti fatta parte per te stesso," that Dante will

2. See Frederic C. Lane, "At the Roots of Republicanism," *American Historical Review 71* (1966), 403–20, for a discussion of other relationships between Italian and American republicanism and the citation of extensive literature. See also Ullmann, *The Individual and Society in the Middle Ages*, esp. pp. 101–51.

make a party unto himself, is *not* honorific. It is certainly not, as some commentators have read it, a kind of paean to Dante's romantic political individualism. Dante's becoming a parte is of a piece with the salty taste of other men's bread, the steepness of other men's stairs, and the bestiality of the exiled White Guelfs. Being a parte will be to Dante's honor, because in the upside-down moral world of early fourteenth-century, there is no hope of a restored political community. Parte, which is used in an unremittingly pejorative sense throughout the writings of Dante, Remigio de' Girolami, Compagni, and Villani, is a condemnation to continued political impotence, an ironic commentary on the political divisiveness that Dante so uniformly condemns throughout the *Commedia*.

A party was not even a legitimate part of a *popolo*, and, as Dante remarks in *Paradiso*, 31, the only "popol giusto e sano" is that of Heaven, where there are no parties. The honor of which Cacciaguida speaks in *Paradiso*, 17, is the honor that exists in the face of the shame of factionalism, not an honor that justifies it. It was this sense of pars, parte, and factio that the citizens of the northern Italian city-republics sharpened and tasted first, and yet could not avoid. Other before and after Dante had perceived and denounced the evils of factionalism, but few put their denunciations into great poetry, and few could work it as sharply into the counsels of Heaven as Dante. "Questo tuo grido" (this cry of yours), Dante's "molesta voce," Cacciaguida says, was not made to benefit Dante himself, but to lacerate Dante's world. In that perverted world, Dante's own future could be at best dismal, and the badge of "parte per te stesso" was not a badge otherwise worn in honor.

The apparatus of Dante's assault on the concept of parte as the sign of civic discord appears early in the *Inferno*, probably as early as the whirling banner and its aimless followers in canto 3. In canto 6, the bestial Cerberus introduces a number of motifs that are developed in Dante's discussion with the Florentine Ciacco, and Florence, "la città partita," full of discord, is divided by "la parte selvaggia" and "the other." Throughout much of the *Commedia*, bestiality is associated with civil discord, probably from the frequency of the image in Aristotelian sources and commentaries, and very frequently it is associated with the form of discord taken by party and factional opposition.[3] Ciacco's is one of the prophecies taken up and expanded by Cacciaguida in *Paradiso*, 17. Farinata, in *Inferno*, 10, speaks of Dante's ancestors' hostility "to me, to my forebears, and to my party,"

3. See, e.g., Pierre Michaud-Quantin, *Études sur le vocabulaire philosophique du Moyen Age* (Rome, 1970), p. 51, citing Jean Buridan's *Quaestiones in decem libros Ethicorum Aristotelis*, VII, q. 1.

and is saddened by his own party's failure to have learned the *arte* of returning to power. Farinata too, dimly prophesies Dante's inglorious future, and with him in the tombs of the heretics are other great Ghibellines, including Frederick II and Cardinal Ottaviano degli Ubaldini, the *sectae* of the heretics here explicitly identified with the *pars Gebellina.* In canto 15, Brunetto Latini, who himself had inveighed against partisanship in his *Livre dou Trésor*, takes the divisions of Florence still further back in time. Ciacco had spoken of the Black and White Guelfs, Farinata of the Guelfs and Ghibellines, and Brunetto of the legendary beginnings of factionalism in Florence, the intrusion of new people from Fiesole, an "ingrato popolo maligno ... tiene ancor del monte e del macigno." "Thy fortune holds for thee such honor," Brunetto tells Dante, "that one party and the other shall be ravenous against thee." In canto 16, the three Florentine sodomites elicit yet another condemnation of factionalism from Dante. Thus, halfway through the *Inferno*, Dante's condemnation of party strife and its origins has been repeatedly and extensively articulated. In canto 19, Dante, having explored the domestic, political, and social origins of civil discord, begins his depiction of the Church's role in fomenting and extending party divisions. In canto 28, the party feuds of Dante's own Italy are linked with ecclesiastical and domestic schism, through Mohammed, Piero de Medicina, Curio, Mosca, and Bertran de Born. Ecclesiastical schism and family discord are here linked to the political struggles in Florence and in other city-republics. Even the association of the giants, in canto 31, with the towers of city factions, particularly in the image of linguistic discord in Nimrod, echoes Dante's systematic depiction of party rivalry in its multiple dimensions. The reference in canto 31 completes its exposition in the *Inferno*.

The *Purgatorio* takes up the theme of discord on a grander scale, from Dante's majestic invective in canto 6, with its references to Marcellus and partisanship and the perversions of rapid and contrary changes in law and custom, and with the reference to *rinovate membre*, a grotesque image of recalling citizens that echoes some of the physical transformations in the lower *bolge* of the *Inferno*. In canto 14 and canto 15, Guido del Duca and Vergil discuss communal affection in the context, first, of the politics and rivalries of the Romagna, and, second, in the larger context of charity in Vergil's discourse. Canto 16, extending Brunetto Latini's discourse in *Inferno*, 15, and pointing toward Cacciaguida's revelations in *Paradiso*, 17, answers the last of Dante's civic questions, and when, in canto 27, Vergil "crowns and mitres" Dante over himself, he anticipates Cacciaguida's prophecy of Dante's becoming a "party unto himself" in *Paradiso*, 17.

In *Paradiso*, discord and party strife appear in sharper contrast to the background, partly because of their inappropriateness, both in Paradise itself and in the long political meditation that runs through the *Commedia*, with its beginnings in *Inferno*, 6. In *Paradiso*, 6, Justinian scornfully describes the futile and avaricious competition waged by the yellow lilies against the *pubblico segno* on the one hand, and the imperialists' claiming the *segno* itself as an emblem of a mere party cause. Carlo Martello in *Paradiso*, 8, reconciles the diversity among individuals and explains the biological violations committed by the divided society of Florence. In *Paradiso*, 15–17, of course, the discussion of parties is taken up at its most extended level and traced back to Florence's fall from "il buon tempo antico" and the intrusion of new people with lower standards. St. Peter's invective in *Paradiso*, 27, accuses the papacy and echoes Justinian's earlier denunciation:

Non fu nostra intenzion ch'a destra mano
   de' nostri successor parte sedesse,
   parte dall'altra del popol cristiano;
nè che le chiavi che mi fuor concesse
   divenisser signaculo in vessillo
   che contra battezzati combattesse;
nè ch' io fossi figura di sigillo
   a privilegi venduti e mendaci,
   ond' io sovente arrosso e disfavillo.

Paradiso, 27, 46–54

Dante, it should be pointed out, like many other medieval writers, knew many uses of "pars" and its synonyms and cognates. His most frequent usage of the terms are not, in fact, in the pejorative political sense, but in that range of geographical, philosophical, logical, and geometrical terminology in which the word had a strictly neutral meaning. The contrast between Dante's commonest use of the term and his pejorative use of parte in politics is striking precisely because Dante rarely uses factio or secta. When he denounces civil discord, it is parte he denounces, almost as if the word took on a stronger meaning in contrast with its more frequent subordination in spatial and logical discourse. It is the parte that the poet attacks, and indeed it is Dante's perception of the party as the chief object of his denunciations that suggests the particularly odious connotations the term, and the institutions it designates, have for him. Parte, the product of the Devil, of avarice, of biological and genetic mishaps, of injustice in all its forms, and of social degeneration, bears the semantic brunt of Dante's outrage.

Dante's invective against parte was not simply the result of his philosophical ideas, but a direct attack upon the use of the term to designate political opposition in the city-republics themselves. For the term pars had come into wide use in the thirteenth century to designate political opposition, and contending groups on opposite sides of issues and cities used the term to refer to both themselves and their enemies.[4]

Many scholars have studied the origins of political conflict in twelfth- and thirteenth-century Italy, and many have observed Dante's particularly intense and unremitting invective against civil discord, which echoes similar expressed attitudes on the part of other writers, most frequently Remigio de' Girolami, Dino Compagni, and Giovanni Villani.[5] Few, however, have paid much attention to the terms pars and parte in themselves and to their appearance in the thirteenth century to designate political groupings. What is particularly striking about the term pars is its initially value-free usage. It is one thing to denounce party universally, as Dante does, or to use the term only as a epithet to describe one's enemies, as did many writers in seventeenth- and eighteenth-century England and the North American colonies. The partes in thirteenth-century Italy appear to have been the first to apply the term *both* to themselves and to their opponents, thus using it to designate subgroups within a wider political community. Many historians have properly observed that the content of the terms Guelf and Ghibelline waxed and waned between the early thirteenth and the early fourteenth centuries, possessing various meanings that could be understood only in terms of particular localities and particular times (even Bartolus threw up his hands in distraction when it came to explaining the differences between Guelf and Ghibelline). Nevertheless, the use of the term pars to designate the two groups and the survival of pars as a political construct well beyond the age when Guelfism and Ghibellinism had wholly lost the last of their ideological content has a great deal of significance.

4. The standard collection of references is Robert Davidsohn, *Forschungen zur Geschichte von Florenz* (1908; reprint ed., Turin, 1964), III, 29–67. See also R. Caggese, "Sul l' origine della parte guelfa e le sue relazioni col Comune," *Archivio storico italiano*, 5th series, *23* (1903), 265–309; G. Glotz, ed., *Histoire générale: Histoire du moyen age* (Paris, 1939), vol. IV, pt. 1, E. Jordan, *L'Allemagne et l'Italie aux XIIe et XIIIe siècles*.

5. Most recently, Charles T. Davis, "Ptolemy of Lucca and the Roman Republic," *Proceedings of the American Philosophical Society*, *118* (1974), 30–50; Charles T. Davis, "An Early Florentine Political Theorist: Fra Remigio de' Girolami," *Proceedings of the American Philosophical Society*, *104* (1960), 662–76; L. Minio-Paluello, "Remigio Girolami's *De Bono Comuni*," *Italian Studies*, *11* (1956), 56–71; Louis F. Green, *Chronicle into History: An Essay on the Interpretation of History in Florentine Fourteenth-Century Chronicles* (Cambridge, 1972).

Few scholars now accept the older views of class conflict and urban-rural rivalries that were once invoked to explain the factionalism of the Italian cities from the eleventh to the fourteenth centuries. The growth of town populations, wealth and physical fabric, and autonomy increased dramatically from the tenth century on. The unpredictable rivalries fashioned and discarded throughout the Investiture Conflict altered not only traditional town authority relationships, but also the relative importance of different groups within each town. From the early twelfth century on, the towns of northern Italy created a kind of social, material, and political life that had not before been seen in the history of the West. Not the city-states of Greece or Rome, not even the closely governed cities of Byzantium or the Islamic east, had been quite like them, and a number of their unique circumstances deserve re-emphasis.

First, after the early twelfth century, the distance between the Italian cities and their nominal legal overlords, the Holy Roman Emperors, varied considerably. Deprived of the ultimate authority of state organization, many of their institutions were developed to deal with practical problems on a level that put the question of absolute authority to one side. They and their territories were compact, densely populated, and extraordinarily diversified socially. These three features set them apart from other contemporary political structures, which were hampered by problems of communications, size, and social homogeneity. Finally, the city itself took a long time to attract and hold the loyalty and identification of its citizens, partly because the question of urban governmental authority was always ambiguous, and partly because most city-dwellers felt more loyalty to the innumerable *societates*, the lesser communities from the neighborhood to the *arte*, to the military association, to the clan, or to the religious confraternity than they did to the city itself. The fractionalization of loyalty, economic interests, status, and family generated much dissension and insecurity, as well as civic instability, and political turbulence was a constant of life under these conditions.

It is one thing to look back at the history of the towns from this side of the watershed constituted by the modern theory of the sovereign state and regard them as politically incomplete communities. It is another to look at the problem of political power within the towns from the point of view of those who had to live with it and possessed virtually no political theory at all to justify their public activities. In a brilliant study, Nicolai Rubinstein has shown how, in the case of Florence, political theory grew up in the chronicles concerning the origins of the city and was the result of several writers' attempts to understand the rapid economic, social, and political changes that had taken place during the thirteenth century.[6] Although several chroniclers attributed much to Fortune and to cycles of progress and decline determined astrologically, Rubinstein has elsewhere shown how, in the case of Albertino Mussatto's account of Paduan history, "by blending Roman ideas on history with contemporary astrological speculations and the political experience of changes and instability, Mussatto was able to present his contemporaries with an interpretation of Paduan history which would help to explain the fateful events of the last years of the Paduan republic."[7]

Neither Mussatto's nor Dante's dismay at the prospect of understanding the rapidly changing course of local history, with the confines of the city as its object, is surprising, considering the rapidity of that change, the diversity of the elements active in it, and, until quite late, the lack of any widely accepted theory or institutional structure supporting the organic polity. In the eyes of neo-Aristotelians and other theorists of the organic polity, discord and factionalism seemed the only explanations for turbulent histories in city after city. In the eyes of those who, in the late twelfth and thirteenth centuries, lived through the changes that later histories tried to make sense of, discord and factionalism were hardly objectified at all, but were rather the normal horizons of political life.

The terms by which the various societates acquired a voice in affairs that they saw as touching *them* alone, far more than as touching the city as a whole, usually entailed deference to some group of nobles and division among groups of nobles themselves. Within the cities there was virtually no limit to the extent to which division on these terms could occur. The multiple affiliations and interests of the nobles (whether older nobility, *magnati*, or *popolani grassi*) were continued in the oligarchies that replaced them and ruled the governments of the popolo. Within these successive governments, there was room for rivalries, but hardly for opposition on a "constitutional" basis.

Within this framework of family, societates, confraternities, and even more amorphous interests, the administrative officials of the cities, the *podestà*, sought to maintain both the rights of the communes and the stability of the public order. Commune, *consorterie*, arti, *vicinanze*, popoli—such subsocieties as these made the medieval Italian city rather like a nest of ill-fitting Chinese boxes, no one of which was able to turn the *civitas*

6. Rubinstein, "The Beginnings of Political Thought in Florence," *Journal of the Warburg and Courtauld Institute*, 5 (1942), 198–227.

7. Rubinstein, "Some Ideas on Municipal Progress and Decline," *Fritz Saxl: A Volume of Memorial Essays* (London, 1957), pp. 165–83, at 183.

itself into a political unit. In this world, whose political conditions pointed toward the experience of later territorial states, civil administration did little to create a state framework except by trying to prevent the undue exercise of informal power by one contending group or another. Thus the appearance of Guelf and Ghibelline parties in the early years of the thirteenth century is less important as a chapter in the history of the papal-imperial conflict than as the opportunity to grasp the form of a societas that could claim a degree of legitimacy denied to the contending groups within the city itself.

Édouard Jordan, in his account of the origins of the Guelf-Ghibelline struggle, shrewdly remarked:

> We must recall that at the beginning the Italians were not set to fighting one another because they supported the Empire or the Church; it was because they were already struggling for local interests that they had chosen in different ways between two powers who fought each other over and around their heads. It is necessary to be a bit more sceptical of that reproach, addressed since the thirteenth century at the popes and above all at the emperor for having set discord into Italy. It existed there already.[8]

The attractions of the Guelf and Ghibelline causes were many. Each side could claim the sanction of a superior authority and count on the aid of people of like sympathies in other towns. Each could attack the other with new and formidable weapons, new arms, confiscated property, declarations of enemies as traitors, if Guelfs, or as heretics, if Ghibellines. These larger causes offered a wider base of support than the more parochial societates. Nevertheless, they did not become identical with the civitas itself, and they emerged, as Romolo Caggese long ago put it, "as two great associations which joined themselves to the skeleton of the organism of the commune as a vertebral column."[9] With local, particularistic antagonisms translated to a larger sphere, both parties organized themselves so successfully that whichever of them dominated a city could determine communal policy while remaining separate from the commune itself. However unstable particular communal governments might be, the resouces of one of the great partes provided both a degree of stability and a powerful force for instituting change. In short, the partes offered another channel for the political life of the divided communes, one with greater claims to

8. Jordan, *L'Allemagne et l'Italie*, p. 257.

9. Caggese, "Sul l' origine", p. 281.

legitimacy, greater financial and juridical strength, and a wider basis of participation. Because the commune had failed to reconcile the diverse interests of its multiple subcommunities, the partes came to dominate the commune. Finally, during the period of Dante's youth, when organic notions of the civitas were beginning to be circulated, the ideology of the partes, particularly of the *parte guelfa*, played no small role in shaping the idea of a complete and ordered community. Thus, in spite of the distracting aspect of papal or imperial sympathies and the tangle of foreign relations, the multiplicity of interests that made up each party in each city, and the garbled versions of party opposition that later chroniclers laid out, the partes, particularly the Guelf party, played a role in urban political development that contributed substantially to the organization of the civitas as it emerged in Dante's lifetime and was reflected in the preaching and the writing of such powerful civic theorists as Remigio de' Girolami.[10]

By significantly expanding the character and composition of their support, however, the partes actually intensified the contentious character of urban life at the same time as they strengthened the legitimacy of their claim to a larger and larger role in communal affairs. Not only did party ideology and propaganda run the risk of deepening political opposition within the towns, however, but party affiliation with papal or imperialist causes, however nominal and intermittent, could not fail to be affected by shifts on the larger political scene. Papal attempts to control the Angevins of Naples after the astonishing successes of the 1260s, the arrival of Henry VII in 1310, the new round of papal-imperial conflicts between John XXII and Louis of Bavaria, and the papal rapport with Charles IV are the major shifts of alliances and intensifications of conflicts on the larger scale that influenced the policy of parties within the towns themselves. In spite of the vulnerabilities and risks that party domination of the communes entailed, however, it is hard to avoid the conclusion that the appearance and development of the partes themselves constituted a new arena for political awareness and political activity in the north Italian city-republics. At the very least, the partes offered a rationalization for the control of communal institutions, laws, and policies considerably stronger than any

10. The best general survey of this period is that of Marvin B. Becker, *Florence in Transition*, 2 vols. (Baltimore, 1968–69). In the wider context of the world of the city-republics, see J. K. Hyde, *Society and Politics in Medieval Italy* (New York, 1973), pp. 65–152; D. P. Waley, *The Italian City Republics* (New York, 1969), pp. 164–220. On the specific problem of political and social conflict, see J. K. Hyde, "Contemporary Views on Faction and Civil Strife in 14th Century Italy," in *Violence and Civil Disorder in Italian Cities, 1200–1500*, ed. Lauro Martines (Berkeley and Los Angeles, 1972), pp. 273–307, as well as the other studies in that volume; Lauro Martines, "Political Conflict in the Italian City States," *Government and Opposition*, *3* (1967/68), 69–91.

political movement before the growth of an organic theory of political unity. As Jordan concludes, emphasizing the strength of party organs, particularly in Florence:

> The factions that the labels designated were not spontaneous and diffuse groups analogous to our modern parties; but, by a transformation that had as one of its gravest consequences the continuation of that division, they constituted themselves as *partes*, associations powerfully organized, highly disciplined, provided with administrative organs, governed by regularly elected chiefs, ruled by statutes, disposing of considerable resources, animated by a lively *esprit de corps*, and, banished or readmitted, understood the need to remain distinct from the commune in order to control it.[11]

Surely the remarkable organization of the parte guelfa in Florence, for example, influencing as it did the political life of virtually the whole of Tuscany, constitutes something more than mere factionalism, constitutes, in fact, a new kind of political organization that influenced the shape of political consciousness as much as the neo-Aristotelianism that has often received much of the credit.

"Political culture" in the Italian cities was, of course, an inseparable part of the rest of civic culture, and as a number of important and stimulating studies have recently shown, the cultural life of the cities was also rapidly changing during Dante's lifetime. The religious experience of the cities, long considered separately from their political and economic life, the optimism that marked much of civic life and institutions, and the glowing paeans to communal solidarity reflected in sources as diverse as the works of Remigio and Lorenzetti were all part, with formal political theory, of the new intellectual development of the idea of a *vita civile*.[12] The solidarity and broad diffusion of Guelf or Ghibelline party membership contributed to such a movement, although that contribution is often not recognized. But the last years of the thirteenth century and the first decades of the fourteenth saw such a notion of civic solidarity develop only slowly, and up through the beginnings of the critical period 1343–78, the institution of party took up the slack in the constitution of the polity that endured into the second half of the fourteenth century.[13]

11. Jordan, *L'Allemagne et l'Italie*, p. 330.

12. Generally, see John Larner, *Culture and Society in Italy, 1290–1420* (New York, 1971); Marvin Becker, "Dante and His Literary Contemporaries as Political Men," *Speculum, 41* (1966), 665–80; Charles T. Davis, "Education in Dante's Florence," *Speculum, 40* (1965), 415–35.

13. For the period, Gene A. Brucker, *Florentine Politics and Society, 1343–1378* (Princeton, 1962).

The rapid development, organization, and rise to power of the Guelf and Ghibelline parties and, in the famous case of Florence, the division between the Black and White Guelfs gave a structure, a new source of legitimacy and power, and a new direction to major elements in the cities, even though their opposition derived more from the particular and varied alignments of interests in the city-*contado* and from the unique constitutional structure of governmental authority than from the great conflicts between the Hohenstaufen and the papacy. Dante's denunciation of parte recognizes both the local and the external pressures that helped to create the parties, but his subordination of political theory to moral and philosophical vision only made him condemn the factionalizing all the more fiercely. Of all the villains in Dante's political world, only Henry VII is spared the poet's denunciation of the divisive and avaricious forces within the urban ruling classes and the Church for having usurped the pubblico segno and the papal keys for use as mere party emblems.

Dante was one of the first, and one of the most articulate writers to challenge the factionalism of the parties in the name of the organic polity. Although Dante's ideal polity was the universal Empire, other writers conceived of it as the city itself. And slowly in the course of the fourteenth century in Florence, the parte guelfa both strengthened that new idea of polity and came to be a component part of it. While fifteenth-century writers looked back to the Guelfs with a lack of sympathy and understanding, they also expressed a nostalgia reminiscent of Dante's nostalgia for "il buon tempo antico." Furthermore, in the invective with which later writers, from Dino Compagni to Villani and Marchionne di Coppo Stefani, denounced party and factional conflict, the Guelf achievement came to be denounced indiscriminately with other manifestations of civil discord. And in areas as diverse as eschatology, political theory, law, historiography, and art, and, as some scholars have suggested, the changing social and political circumstances within such cities as Florence itself, the concept of the importance of the parte guelfa as a party waned in the later fourteenth and fifteenth centuries, surviving only as a vaguely understood element in Florentine political ideology, as a constituent part of what Donald Weinstein has recently called "The Myth of Florence," and in the white shields with red crosses of the Guelf party that were absorbed into Florentine political iconography.[14]

14. Donald Weinstein, "The Myth of Florence," in *Florentine Studies: Politics and Society in Renaissance Florence*, ed. Nicolai Rubinstein (Evanston, 1968), pp. 15–44, with extensive literature cited. See also George Holmes, "The Emergence of an Urban Ideology at Florence, 1250–1450," *Transactions of the Royal Historical Society*, 5th series 23 (1973), pp. 111–34.

Weinstein's important study traces the historical development of the eschatological Florentine political and religious ideology around the time of Savonarola. According to this ideology, Florentine religion, civic order, and virtue would soon constitute a compelling model for the whole world. As Weinstein convincingly demonstrates, elements of this view had been present even in the earliest thirteenth-century chronicles of Florentine history and had been kept alive and developed by various writers and groups, from lay and clerical religious visionaries to humanist historians like Bruni. The external threats from Milan and the internal turmoils of the late fourteenth century had combined to create an elaborate vision:

> So it was that under the double pressure of civic strife and foreign aggression the mythic Florence of the Guelfs tended to coalesce with the prophetic Florence of the Ciompi. Good government and piety, social justice and power, temporal and religious leadership—Rome and Jerusalem—were blended in a single vision which seems to have functioned both as a model of a civic ethos and as a promise of ultimate rewards.[15]

Florentine civic humanism and "the new assertion of Florence's mystical destiny to religious and political supremacy" served as diverse political powers, as Weinstein notes, as Cosimo de' Medici, his opponents in the 1460s, Lorenzo the Magnificent, the post-Laurentian reactionaries, Savonarola, and the restored republic of the early sixteenth century.

If eschatology is at once the most capacious and the vaguest area in which the decline of party legitimacy may be traced, legal theory may be considered the most narrow and precise. Yet the views found in both between 1300 and 1400 are remarkably similar. In the various works of Bartolus, particularly in the well-known treatise *De Guelphis et Gebellinis*, the question of the legitimacy of party power is treated as both a historical and a juridical reality. One of the first writers to suggest a twelfth-century origin (and perhaps a kind of prescriptive right) for the party feuds of the thirteenth century, Bartolus argues that both parties represent "duas affectiones, quiddam . . vocatur Guelphi, quiddam Gebellini," and these

15. Weinstein, "The Myth of Florence," pp. 34–35. On the origins of the Black-White feud, see Gino Masi, "La struttura sociale delle fazioni politiche fiorentine ai tempi di Dante," *Giornale dantesco, 31* (1928), 1–28; Masi, "Sull'origine dei Bianchi e Neri," *Giornale dantesco, 30* (1927), 124–32. On the use of the term pars in other cities, as well as an account of party organizations under other designations, see J. K. Hyde, *Padua in the Age of Dante* (New York, 1966), pp. 193–219; Gina Fasoli, "Guelfi e Ghibellini di Romagna nel 1280–1281," *Archivio storico italiano, 94* (1936), 157–180; Davidsohn, *Forschungen*, III, 39–45; William Bowsky, "Florence and Henry of Luxemburg: The Rebirth of Guelfism," *Speculum, 33* (1958), 177–203.

affectiones in turn derive from the *magna discordia* between Frederick Barbarossa and the Roman Church. Bartolus's particular concern, however, is to determine whether or not the legislative enactments taken by the council of a city (specifically, the commune of Todi), from which the members of one of the two parties are absent, are valid. Bartolus asks whether the missing party's absence was voluntary or involuntary, whether, if the absence is involuntary, the absent party had the *ius condendi statuta* or not, and, if it had, whether its absence was *ex justa causa* or not. In Bartolus's view, each party appears to have shared some part of the total public authority of the commune of Todi, and, if one party was exiled, even though the other, or both, were *collegia approbata* and lawful as long as they tend to further the *bonum publicum*, it was nearly impossible for a single party to rule legally. Bartolus goes on to say that no honorable man in any case should assume a party name or affiliation, *nisi ex magna causa*. There is, according to Bartolus, a theoretically legal justification for parties, but the weight of experience suggests that in practice and, more important, in law, extensive party power is dangerous and raises serious constitutional questions.[16]

The successors of Bartolus, including Baldus, continued to maintain the technical legality of party authority, but increasing juridical hostility grew up in the course of the fourteenth century. Walter Ullmann has suggested that lawyers increasingly swung toward the opinion that all political parties were illegal. He cites the remarkable opinion of the jurist Raynerius de Forlivio, who took that view, because, as Ullmann puts it, "[parties] were disruptive of political unity and stability within the body politic; that, in other words, they were factors disturbing the smooth and peaceful internal development and, consequently, might unduly upset the political and social balance within the state."[17]

The sweeping and vague claims of eschatology, on the one hand, and the narrow technical world of juridical opinion, on the other, both reflect a similar rejection of the legitimacy of party in the political life of the north Italian city-republics during the course of the fourteenth and fifteenth centuries. The immediate historical experience of the early fourteenth century turned other kinds of thinkers toward a similar opinion. The most famous of these is Marsiglio of Padua, whose *Defensor Pacis*, completed in 1324, also focused directly upon the causes of discord within the city-

16. See the discussion in C. N. S. Woolf, *Bartolus of Sassoferrato* (Cambridge, 1913), pp. 189–95 and John H. Mundy, *Europe in the High Middle Ages, 1150–1309* (New York, 1973), pp. 440–42.

17. Walter Ullmann, "The Mediaeval Theory of Legal and Illegal Organizations," *Law Quarterly Review*, *60* (1944), 285–91.

republics of northern Italy. In Marsiglio's analysis of the ideal state, the very word pars is functional, describing various offices within the republican regime, not contending groups or a single triumphant group in power. The organic political theories of Aristotle, passed through St. Thomas, Remigio de' Girolami, and Ptolemy of Lucca (and, as Nicolai Rubinstein has pointed out, through the Lorenzetti frescoes in the Palazzo Pubblico in Siena) and urbanized to suit the particular character of the city-republics in the process, could be set over against the theme of discord and faction and invoked to justify either a republican or a signorial regime.[18] In Marsiglio's eyes, as in Dante's, the intervention of external powers, particularly the interference of the papacy, had fomented discord within the cities and prevented the collective authority of the citizens from disposing of executive power within its proper limits. Neither party nor signory satisfy the constitutional requirements of the *Defensor Pacis*. Marsiglio instead develops a sophisticated and articulate expression of the idea of a common good and of the institutional details that supervise its maintainance.

The new emphasis upon the organic character of the political community was reflected in historiography as well as political theory. In the *Chronica* of Giovanni Villani, both the Guelfs and the Ghibellines come under heavy attack, the former because they have forfeited their right to rule by the avarice of their members, and the latter because their actions lead toward inevitable tyranny. Later in the century, the chronicle of Marchionne di Coppo Stefani attacks both parties equally and sees in them nothing more than factionalism and occasions for civil strife, reflecting, far more than even Villani, the view that parties represent a division of an originally unified people. He thus reverses Dante's thesis of the mingling of two separate peoples, but emerges with no less devastating a criticism of party politics.[19]

By the first half of the fifteenth century, when Leonardo Bruni undertook to write the history of Florence on a larger scale and from a more complex point of view, he recognized for the first time the essentially competitive character of republican institutions and the danger of the republic's tendency to dissipate its energies in factional struggles for power. Envy

18. Nicolai Rubinstein, "Marsilius of Padua and Italian Political Thought of His Time," in *Europe in the Late Middle Ages* ed. John Hale, Roger Highfield, Beryl Smalley (Evanston, 1965), pp. 44–75; Rubinstein, "Political Ideas in Sienese Art: The Frescoes by Ambrogio Lorenzetti and Taddeo di Bartolo in the Palazzo Pubblico," *Journal of the Warburg and Courtauld Institutes*, *21* (1958), 179–207; Helène Wieruszowski, "Art and the Comune in the Time of Dante," *Speculum*, *19* (1944), 14–33.

19. Green, *Chronicle into History*, is a good general introduction.

and contention, Bruni admitted, are a necessary accompaniment of liberty, and in the good republic they will be kept under control. The discord among noble families, the accessibility of an arena for the demonstration of outraged honor and social influence, and the absence of a constitution that could control the competitive spirit of the magnates and release the psychological energies of the citizens—all accounted for Florence's grim history of party domination. The determination of public policy by private interests, social passions, and factionalism were for Bruni the results of a failure to control the dangers of republicanism. Bruni goes on to point out that bringing in foreign lords, excluding large segments of the powerful from office, and the widespread practice of imposing exile on dissidents do not merely suppress fundamental discords. They weaken the city, while strengthening its enemies. For Bruni, then, factionalism and party preponderence are the result of the commonwealth's failure to control the human passions that threaten to erupt while it preserves a constitution that encourages eruption but brings other political and cultural advantages. Bruni's aphorism sums up his criticism of factionalism: "Cives enim sic odendi sunt, ut tamen cives illos esse meminerimus".[20] The *inane partium studium*, Guelf or Ghibelline, is no proper passion of the constitutional state nor a proper outlet for republican civic concerns. Yet Bruni, as Donald Wilcox has shown, recognized better than any earlier writer the coincidence of factionalism with republican liberties. On a number of occasions Bruni speaks against the excesses of factionalism rather than against factionalism and competition for honors (what earlier writers had called the *gara d'ufici*) itself. Neither private gain nor private injury must take place if factions are to be balanced. In short, unlike his predecessors who praised the virtues of the organic polity, from Brunetto Latini to Marchionne di Coppo Stefani, Bruni is sufficiently perceptive to see the intimate, tangled relationship between various forms of political conflict and the good of the republican state itself. For all of his reverence for the polity, however, Bruni does not scorn the parties as his predecessors had, and his appreciation of the parte guelfa strongly suggests that he is coming to terms with a theory that accorded the parte a place in the republic.

Casual and frequent denunciations of factionalism appeared throughout the late fifteenth and early sixteenth centuries, heightened, surely, by the vicissitudes of Florentine internal history, particularly the circumstances surrounding the career of and contributing to the impact of Savonarola.

20. See the extended discussion in Donald J. Wilcox, *The Development of Florentine Humanist Historiography in the Fifteenth Century* (Cambridge, Mass., 1969), pp. 71–83. See also Franco Gaeta, *Il vescovo Pietro Barozzi e il trattato "De factionibus extinguendis"* (Rome, 1961).

Once again a historian, this time Machiavelli, was one of the few voices that echoed Bruni's recognition of the close relationship between faction and republican government. In his analysis, Machiavelli tried to account for a positive containment of contention; he did not condemn it categorically.[21] Yet Machiavelli, careful as he is, envisions nothing on the scale of the earlier parte guelfa; indeed, he rarely uses the term *parte* at all, favoring *sette*, and attempting to distinguish those organized conflicts that preserve the republic by balancing rival interests from those (usually factions and sects) that threaten to undermine it. Machiavelli may represent one of the earliest attempts to secularize the term *secta*. Machiavelli's *divisioni*, unlike Dante's, have two meanings, one productive and the other destructive. In his repeated proposals for a framework of laws and institutions that could check the destructive aspects of political conflict and his emphasis upon the competing interests of all citizens and the equal distribution of offices and state rewards, Machiavelli touched on two of the most striking developments of the next three centuries, a new concept of the constitution and an expanded political public.

The society of fifteenth- and sixteenth-century Florence, in spite of the leads offered by Bruni and Machiavelli, looked more toward division-free concord and political autonomy. It regarded the city not only as *sibi princeps* but as *sibi magister* and perhaps, as Weinstein suggests, *sibi salvator*. Increasingly, a more sophisticated awareness of economic and social differences replaced the mechanistic moral denunciations of Dante and Villani. And the names as well as the natures of old political divisions, Guelfs and Ghibellines, Blacks and Whites, Amidei and Buondelmonte, were eventually relegated to the status of moral exempla in the archaic history of Florence. In other respects, of course, much of the earlier rationale

21. The best study of Machiavelli's concept of division and political conflict is the work of Alfredo Bonadeo, *Corruption, Conflict, and Power in the Works and Times of Niccolò Machiavelli* (Berkeley and Los Angeles, 1973), esp. pp. 35–71, 98–105. Bonadeo cites most of the relevant primary and secondary literature. In addition to Bonadeo's work, however, it is useful to note two studies of other justifications of factionalism in late fifteenth- and early sixteenth-century Florence: Felix Gilbert, "Florentine Political Assumptions in the Period of Savonarola and Soderini," *Journal of the Warburg and Courtauld Institutes, 20* (1957), 187–214, and Felix Gilbert, "Bernardo Rucellai and the Orti Oricellari: A Study on the Origin of Modern Political Thought," *Journal of the Warburg and Courtauld Institutes, 12* (1949), 101–31. On Machiavelli and the early period of Florentine history, see Nicolai Rubinstein, "Machiavelli e le origini di Firenze," *Rivista storica italiana, 79* (1967), 952–59. There are a number of interesting studies on Machiavelli by modern political scientists in Martin Fleischer, ed., *Machiavelli and the Nature of Political Thought* (New York, 1972). The paper by Harvey Mansfield, Jr., "Party and Sect in Machiavelli's *Florentine Histories*," (pp.209–66) deals directly with the problem addressed in this essay, but does so very unfortunately. See the comments of Mark Phillips and J. A. Gunn following Mansfield's paper, pp. 277–81.

for the emergence of parties had become unnecessary by the late fifteenth century. A complex view of the polity, the resurgence of religious groups linking different social ranks and channeling ecclesiastical and devotional influences throughout Florentine society, and the depoliticization of much of public life under the Medici had reduced the grounds for division and factional strife. The restoration of Medici rule in the person of Cosimo the Younger slowly transformed the contentious republic of Bruni and Machiavelli, "the worn-out republic," as Eric Cochrane calls it, "into a well-run monarchy."

With Machiavelli's concept of *vivere civile* and his dogged insistence on the legitimacy of party opposition in a well-ordered state, even in the last Florentine republic, battered by Fortune, Frenchmen, Spaniards, and popes, the first extended European experience of party and polity came to an inglorious end. The city itself became the principality, and the adventurous monarchies of the sixteenth century had little use for Machiavelli's delicate orchestration of competing powers within the small political community. Machiavelli himself became the symbol, ironically, of the destructive and cynical attempts to divide the political community that sixteenth- and seventeenth-century writers and rulers identified with parties and factions.[22]

The political experience of sixteenth- and seventeenth-century Europeans intensified the revulsion against divisions within the polity. The social tensions that most political structures of this period only seemed to exacerbate produced *ligues*, *frondes*, and rebellions, movements against which virtually every political theorist and political authority savagely turned. The Reformation, by once more raising in its original sense the specter of schism and sectae, particularly in political and ecclesiastical polemics, contributed further to the unrelievedly discordant character that any concept of party or faction possessed.

Sixteenth- and seventeenth-century dictionaries reveal these attitudes as sharply as any polemics, perhaps, because of the commonplace character of their definitions, more sharply. As Alison Gilbert Olson has pointed out, the 1559 edition of *Bibliotheca Eliotal*, *Eliotes Dictionarie* offers a characteristic definition:

22. See Mario Praz, "The Politic Brain: Machiavelli and the Elizabethans," reprinted in *The Flaming Heart* (New York, 1958), pp. 90–145; Felix Raab, *The English Face of Machiavelli* (Oxford, 1964); Friedrich Meinecke, *Machiavellism* (reprinted., New York, 1965).

> Factio factionis, f.g. a division of people in sundry opinions . . . also a companie or bande of men, sometyme rychesse, authoritee, or estimacion in a citee. Factionum principes, the heads of rebellion or sedition . . .[23]

Many other similar definitions could be cited from other dictionaries of the same period and for much later. Not until the eighteenth century did the opprobrium in which the concept of party was held, which included Machiavelli as one of its chief targets, begin to give way to a new concept of *vivere civile*. Ultimately, something of the Florentine secretary's guarded enthusiasm for the constructive virtures of controlled opposition within the state acquired greater strength and ultimately won a major place within eighteenth- and nineteenth-century political communities. Of Machiavelli's intellectual legacies to later political theory, the themes of *raison d'état* and anti-Machiavelism have received by far the most attention from historians. Yet Machiavelli's unremitting attention to the nature of the political societies he observed in ancient Rome and in his own Florence had seen something legitimate in the character of conflict in these societies that acquired new meaning, not for the princely states of the sixteenth and seventeenth centuries, but for the contentious civil communities of eighteenth-century England and the North American colonies. Between the implacable hostility universally felt toward the idea and the term party and faction as late as the end of the seventeenth century and the general acceptance of both a century later, there lies a complex process of transformation. The political experience and constitutional theory of this period has generated a large and competent but often diffuse and conflicting literature. A brief discussion of some of the circumstances that led to the legitimation of the concept of party in the political communities of England and North America in this period may suggest one further instance in which the experience of the medieval city anticipated that of its later and larger political successors.

The very proliferation of the various forms of sectae in sixteenth and early seventeenth-century Europe may well have contributed to one aspect of the grudging acceptance of faction and sectarianism by seventeenth-century political theorists. Not only did the Reformation and its social and political consequences not disappear, as many theorists seem to have hoped they would, but even the principles of the Peace of Augsburg, "cuius regio, eius religio," became strained almost beyond the resources of many political communities between 1550 and 1650. The general ap-

23. Olson, *Anglo-American Politics, 1660–1775* (Oxford, 1973), pp. iv-viii.

proaches toward a degree of toleration on essentially utilitarian grounds, first adumbrated by the Politiques during the French wars of religion, soon made their way into the pamphlet literature of seventeenth-century England. It appears, in fact, that the first steps toward the acceptance of religious sectarianism, a fundamental condition for the tolerance and legitimation of political parties, were taken by theologians in the seventeenth century.[24] As J. A. W. Gunn has convincingly demonstrated, one of the earliest and most sophisticated of such approaches was that of John Shute, later Viscount Barrington, who early in the eighteenth century urged the rights of full citizenship for Nonconformists in order to ensure their loyalty to the Crown. Barrington then went beyond the familiar contemporary notions of balancing competing interests to argue something very close to the idea of the *concordia discors* of Machiavelli, Sidney, and Montesquieu:

> The constitution of England consists in a ballance of parties as the libertys of Europe do in a Ballance of power. . . . So when we allow one of the parties in England to be above the check of the other, we bid farewell to its liberties too.[25]

Against the familiar eighteenth-century notion of balance and concordia, on which several of his principles are based, Barrington set the much more active image of the essential conflict of undeniable and indestructible elements—religious Conformity and Dissent—"in the context of the party struggle." And he appears to have emerged with a doctrine of the legitimacy and necessity of party politics that anticipated those promulgated at the end of the eighteenth century.

Barrington is one figure of several whose view of politics was of sufficient

24. Although it focuses primarily upon the debates over the nature of sovereignty on the part of English thinkers of the seventeenth century, J. H. M. Salmon, *The French Religious Wars in English Political Thought* (Oxford, 1959) suggests the importance of theories of natural law and toleration, the exhaustive discussions of political liberties in the tracts of the 1670s and 1680s, and the new role of the individual and his rights in the theory of Sidney and Locke in the complex political theory that emerged in England in the late seventeenth century, particularly in their cosmopolitan origins: "[The strands of thought woven into the pattern of liberalism] have been regarded as the specifically English products of the seventeenth century, but at every stage of their English formulation it has been possible to trace the debt of English politics to the examples and ideas of the French Religious Wars" (p. 170). More recently, J. A. W. Gunn, "Party Before Burke: Shute Barrington," *Government and Opposition*, *3* (1968) offers a detailed study of the complex intellectual origins of Barrington's theories of party legitimacy in the early years of the eighteenth century.

25. Gunn, "Party Before Burke," p. 228. For other aspects of the legitimation of the idea of party in seventeenth-century England, see Caroline Robbins, "'Discordant Parties': A Study of the Acceptance of Party by Englishmen," *Political Science Quarterly*, *73* (1958), 505–29. Both Robbins and Gunn cite an extensive literature, and further documents may be found in Alan Beattie, ed., *British Party Politics* (London, 1970), I, 1–57.

width to embrace social and religious divisions and to force their solutions into the political arena. For what characterizes many of Barrington's views, as it does those of later political thinkers, is as much a new image of the psychology of the political community as a new theory of politics per se. Much has been written of Machiavelli's and Guicciardini's cynicism regarding the possibility of concord within a fractious and passionate polity. However, less note has been taken of the revival of this and analogous views of human society in the late seventeenth and eighteenth centuries. In the writings of Algernon Sidney, for example, the same view of an imperfect, potentially brutalized and licentious human condition that had led Hobbes to posit the authority of a centralized monarch is turned inside out and made the rationale of effective, productive republican government.

The new psychological orientation of eighteenth-century political theorists from Montesquieu on suggests a new image of *homo politicus*, one perhaps adumbrated by Machiavelli and Hobbes (and perhaps more sympathetically conceived by the former). This view's essential characteristics are a degree of voluntarism, a belief in the endemic nature of social conflict, and the conviction that opposing elements must be balanced. Such a new *imago hominis* makes its appearance in other fields as well, from biography to the historical study. Montesquieu's political theory depends upon such a view of the human passions and the role of social conflict in adjusting them to suit the needs of the political community at large.[26]

Such transformations of political theory did not, of course, occur in a social vacuum. If the devastating sectarianism of the sixteenth and seventeenth centuries instilled an absolute, undeviating horror of faction and division within political and religious communities, it may also have made thinkers receptive to the fact that such divisiveness could never be suppressed and that it must needs be contained in some sort of commodious political framework. The insertion of religious toleration into the constitutional framework of European states, with England in the lead, widened the concept of constitutionalism and thus prepared the way for a broader role for political diversity. Thus, political and social experience, new attitudes toward the psychology of human behavior and its relation to the collective character of the political community, and a new theoretical appreciation of social conflict, later embodied in the theory of contending political parties—all contributed toward the legitimization of the theory

26. On these and the following remarks, see Neal Wood, "The Value of Asocial Sociability: Contributions of Machiavelli, Sidney, and Montesquieu," in Fleischer, *Machiavelli and the Nature of Political Thought*, pp. 282–307, and Wood, "Some Reflections on Sorel and Machiavelli," *Political Science Quarterly*, *83* (1968), 76–91.

of party in the period between 1660 and the beginning of the nineteenth century. The course of this history, from Algernon Sidney and Barrington to Burke, is reflected in the experience of real political parties in the political life of England under the last Stuarts and the first Hanoverians.[27]

Britain's North American colonies were also involved in the theory and practice of party opposition and conflict during the same period. The first colonists were, if anything, even more scornful of party and faction than their English contemporaries. John Winthrop, with John Smith's *Advertisements for the Inexperienced Planters of New England* in hand and mind, appears to have designed his colony specifically to avoid that propensity to factionalism that Smith had denounced as the greatest danger to colonial stability and success. For Winthrop, faction and division were devices used only by those political forces he detested the most, "the rules of Matchiavell and the Jesuits," the Devil, and "the council of England and other states who walk by politic principles only." Harmony, mediation, compromise, and, above all, the Covenant dominated the thought and language of seventeenth-century colonial political figures from Winthrop to Mather and beyond.[28]

Yet, as Dante and Machiavelli had long ago remarked of Florence and other city-republics, factions in the colonies existed and even made their impact upon the mother country. Similarly, after 1649, English political factionalism made its own impact upon the life of colonial society. Various aspects of colonial life, in fact, generated factionalism even more quickly and intensely than life in England itself. Mobility produced dissenting factions under many colonial administrations. The multiple interests and roles of the colonial gentry tended to make quarrels and rivalries in one area of activity spill over into others, including politics. Dissidents and factions could look to sympathizers in neighboring colonies and in England, and until 1765 colonial interests often served as a focus for English opposition to the government.

The philosophical acceptance of political opposition in England and the pragmatic experience of factionalism in the colonies stands at the beginning of the historically and historiographically complex problem of the modern history of parties, particularly as that history has been regarded by scholars who take the nineteenth-century norms of English and

27. The literature on the subject of parties in English political life in the eighteenth century is extensive. Most of it is available in the studies of A. S. Foord, *His Majesty's Opposition, 1714–1830* (Oxford, 1964), Clayton Roberts, *The Growth of Responsible Government in Stuart England* (Cambridge, 1966), and J. H. Plumb, *The Growth of Political Stability in England* (London, 1967).

28. In general, see Olson's controversial and provocative study, *Anglo-American Politics, 1660–1775*. For Winthrop, see T. H. Breen, *The Character of the Good Ruler* (New Haven, 1970).

American political parties as their primary—and sometimes sole—criterion for the definition of party. According to such a view, party and faction are separate and distinct, thus leaving the political organization and groupings of the early nineteenth century virtually without a past, springing fully armed, as it were, out of the circumstances of political life in the first quarter of the nineteenth century. Many scholars have tirelessly pointed out that factions were too ephemeral, too oriented toward single issues, and tied too firmly to deferential politics to qualify as true parties. In one of the fundamental works on the idea of party in revolutionary America, Richard Hofstadter elaborated upon this argument. He considered the importance of the fact that whole legislative programs were not necessary in the eighteenth century; the role of the politics of deference in selecting leaders because of family, status, character, generosity, or personal reputation; and the lack of a sustained commitment to issues or policies, and concluded that political parties had no history, in effect, before the 1790s.[29] Hofstadter's conclusion is supported by the work of many scholars, and indeed by much of the language of the sources, in which the terms party and faction are virtually interchangeable and consistently pejorative. Even Madison, when read in this light, can appear to be interested in controlling conflict rather than in recognizing an integrated role for political opposition within a constitutional framework.

Yet much of the support for this view of the rise of parties depends upon a very narrow focus upon party experience after the beginning of the nineteenth century. Such a view was once responsible for the theory of "New Monarchies" that were alleged to have arisen in the sixteenth century, as well as a view that once held, largely by misreading the impressionistic and tantalizing works of Max Weber, that capitalism appeared in Europe as an inevitable consequence of the character of the Protestant concept of vocation. Ronald Formisano, in a critique of the scholarship in the history of parties, criticizes both the celebrants of party and its critics as possessing "an exaggerated view of parties as electoral machines unrelated to conflicts over values and social belief-systems. . . . The critics tend to empty party politics of its social, cultural, and ideological content."[30] Parties, even in the early nineteenth century, played a partial role in government, and were largely dependent, during their emergence,

29. Richard Hofstadter, *The Idea of Party* (Berkeley and Los Angeles, 1969). A short abstract of Hofstadter's arguments has circulated widely: "A Constitution Against Parties: Madisonian Pluralism and the Anti-Party Tradition," *Government and Opposition*, *4* (1969), 345–66, reprinted in *Political Parties in American History*, ed. Winfred E. A Bernhard, I, *1789–1828* (New York, 1973), 34–58.

30. Ronald P. Formisano, "Deferential-Participant Politics: The Early Republic's Political Culture, 1789–1840," *American Political Science Review*, *68* (1974), 473–87. I am grateful to my colleague Richard R. Beeman for suggesting this study to me.

on changing modes of patronage from clients and family to interest groups and constituents, on the spirit of subcommunity unity as exemplified by such voluntary associations as militia companies, and perhaps on the increased popular interest in politics and the diversity of those interested. In these terms, the history of party, freed from the narrow constraints of focus upon electoral issues, may be regarded as a direct continuation of that often denounced factionalism of the eighteenth century. Freed from the narrow and restrictive focus upon electoral and organizational forms after 1800, the history of parties may well be more productively considered as a chapter in the history of how lesser communities within larger communities reconciled their immediate, temporary, parochial needs with the problem of the government of the larger community as a whole. In this light the history of modern political parties touches the history of the violent conflicts of opposing forces in the Italian city-states in the thirteenth and fourteenth centuries, for they too faced the same problem, although with very different conceptual frameworks and social and economic resources. Both societies were, after all, a part of what some historians have come to call "traditional Europe," and in both the heady experience of the proximity of public power to private needs, wants, and aims was remarkably similar.

In a sophisticated and extensive review article of the historiography of early American politics, Jack Greene suggested "a rough typology of political forms into which, after the elimination of certain individual variants, most pre-1776 colonial political activites can be fitted":

> . . . *chaotic factionalism*. . . . involved a ruthless competition for dominance, power, and economic advantage among rival groups of leading men, groups which were largely ad hoc and impermanent. . . . *stable factionalism* . . . was distinguished by the emergence of two semi-permanent opposing interest groups with relatively stable memberships and representing explicit regional . . . economic, religious, or kinship rivalries. . . . *domination by a single, unified group* . . . [involved] all the avenues to political power and most of the primary sources of wealth . . . monopolized by a dominant elite. . . . *faction free with a maximum dispersal of political opportunity within the dominant group* . . . depended upon a homogeneity of economic interests among all regions and all social groups, a high degree of social integration, and a community of political leaders so large as to make it impossible for any single group to monopolize political power.

Greene remarks, "[this typology] may by providing a general frame of reference at least make it easier to discuss early American politics. Hopefully, it may also be a first step toward the development of new, less abstract categories which will more accurately reflect the political life they seek to describe."[31] Such forms could well, it may be suggested, be extended to the period before 1776 to help break the semantic and conceptual barriers that now exist between faction and party in contemporary historical literature and thought.

After 1745 the coalition governments of England drew heavily upon party distinctions and cooperation, and at the same time they brought colonial affairs more prominently into the forefront of governmental concerns. In turn, English interest in them sharpened party rivalries within the colonies themselves. But the inability or willingness of royal officials to support favorable loyalist parties in North America and the demise of colonial affairs as a rallying point of opposition in English government led to a separation between English and American parties that turned out to be irreparable. By 1769 some Americans could assume naturally that parties were fundamental and essential parts of English government. At the same time, the American experience of faction became, as it were, independent of English forces. The political public in the colonies had expanded beyond the narrow framework of governors and assemblies and embraced the "out of doors," where the role of colonies as pawns of British factions declined. In addition, "the longer tradition of legitimate opposition to royal authority [in the North American colonies] gave the colonists more experience than their British counterparts in working with political factions."[32] Without the experience of factions, and except for those lesser groupings formed for hosts of different reasons, unstable and short-lived, the acceptance of party a quarter-century later might have turned out differently. Emotions, wills, and experience of loyalty to small groups in a political context, with the experience of success, failure, and impact of those groups on the larger political community was, for the Americans, as for the Italians and British before them, a prerequisite to more sophisticated and precisely defined party organizations.

In this respect, it is possible to read such documents as *The Federalist*, X and L, in a different light. Could Madison's views on party have depended less up on his reading of English political theory than upon his and others' experience of "faction"? The hard and bitter disputes that raged on, and often increased in intensity after 1783, may well have been weathered, not primarily by innovation and invention, but by the very

31. Jack P. Greene, "Changing Interpretations of Early American Politics," in *The Reinterpretation of Early American History: Essay in Honor of John Edwin Pomfret*, ed. Ray Allen Billington (San Marino, Cal., 1966), pp. 151–84. I am grateful to my colleague Vincent Conti for pointing out Greene's study to me.

32. Olson, *Anglo-American Politics*, pp. 142–82, at 180.

experience of hated faction that American writers, no less intensely than their Italian predecessors, had denounced so bitterly.[33]

Machiavelli's Florence had not weathered its own storms, although it had succeeded for four centuries partly through a skillful diffusion of political powers. Indeed, it is anachronistic to expect that it might have. It existed at the beginning of an age of princes, just as the United States was created at that age's end. Yet the experience of both societies had much in common. Intrasocietal rivalry, the proliferation and confused interaction of many lesser, often overlapping communities within the larger community of the colony or the city-republic, and the communications between local dissidents and like-minded supporters in other regions were certainly common to both societies. The fragmentation of dominant oligarchies in the face of social, religious, and economic pressures and the deferential attitudes toward the leaders of individual families and *consorterie* made groups in both societies seek out larger communities of interest, effective factions or temporary parties. Troublesome citizens or disenfranchised magnates might be sent into exile or made to stand surety for their good behavior, and the *fuorusciti* of Massachusetts made as much difficulty in London as did those of Florence in Pisa or in imperial or papal camps. Superior authorities could and did often intervene in local disputes, and religious conflicts often spilled over into the political arena. At times exiles could threaten to drain off so much population or economic strength as to weaken the remaining society. There were few barriers between the intensity of family quarrels and the wide scope of civic polity. In both societies thinkers recognized that political factionalism only represented one aspect of more fundamental social divisions, and, most important of all, both societies experienced that shortened distance between private and public conflicts that made conflict itself an endemic characteristic of political life.

Finally, in both societies, an absolute, unquestioned, unambiguous, single-willed authority was absent. In these circumstances, the role of faction and party offered strength and a kind of superior legitimacy to a constitutionally incomplete polity, transcending the narrow constraints of local, sectarian, or purely private interests, at least in theory, and remaining

33. On Madison, see Marvin Meyers, "Founding and Revolution: A Commentary on Publius-Madison," in *The Hofstadter Aegis: A Memorial*, ed. Stanley Elkins and Eric McKitrick (New York, 1974), pp. 3–35, and Meyers, *The Mind of the Founder: Sources of the Political Thought of James Madison* (Indianapolis, New York, 1973). A different approach to the similarities, if not the links, between Machiavelli and Madison is that of David E. Ingersoll, "Machiavelli and Madison: Perspectives on Political Stability," *Political Science Quarterly*, *85* (1970), 259–80.

vulnerable to claims made on behalf of the higher authority which gave it its legitimacy in the first place. In the period between 1783 and 1840, the United States witnessed a similar ambiguity in the character of central governmental authority. And that milieu shaped the later system of party opposition and gave it a new organization and legitimacy. This experience, like Britain's in the eighteenth and nineteenth centuries, turned out far differently from that of Florence and the other medieval towns. Nevertheless, medieval cities were among the first, and most adventurous polities in modern European history. In the role of faction and party as well as in other aspects of the exploration of the variety and range of human political and social experience, they launched the political adventure of modern Europe.

XIII

THE FROWNING PAGES: SCYTHIANS, GARAMANTES, FLORENTINES, AND THE TWO LAWS

Dante was a poet who paid particular attention to his own script and conscientiously attended to the architecture of canto and page. It is therefore not surprising that, from the first chapter of the *Vita Nuova* to the final *canti* of the *Paradiso*, Dante also displayed a considerable interest in the use of book and page as metaphor. Images of codices and folios, leaves and volumes, occur frequently in the *Commedia* and often illuminate its most profound and touching moments. In *Par.* xxxiii, for example, as he approaches the great vision that concludes the poem, Dante finds just such an image to illuminate his prepared understanding:

> In the depth of the Infinite Goodness, I saw that it contained, bound by love in one volume, that which is scattered in leaves throughout the universe, substances and accidents and their relations.

At its most touching, the image springs from the lips of Oderisi da Gubbio (*Purg.* x. 73-108), who purges himself of the — then — unusual sin of artistic pride:

> Brother, more smiling are the pages that Franco of Bologna paints; the honor is all his now — and mine in part.

Oderisi's discovery that artistic reputation is no more than a breath of wind — *un fiato di vento* — is eloquent testimony both to Dante's perception of his own age and to the psychology of the repentant artist, a topic elegantly considered by Millard Meiss in an essay called "The Smiling Pages."[1]

Elsewhere in the *Commedia* the same imagery turns up "frowning" pages — those containing the quibbling sophismata of the dialecticians and the deceptive messages of lust that so stirred Paolo and Francesca. But the least smiling pages are those which Dante associates with the perversion of * justice and law, bluntly and contemptuously dismissed by Carlo Martello in *Par*. ix, 133-5:

> For this the Gospel and the great Doctors are deserted, and only the Decretals are studied, as may be seen by their margins.

This is one of Dante's best know indictments of some, at least, of the most influential jurisprudence of his own age, the canon law based upon the great collections of papal decretal letters and canons of church councils, from the early thirteenth-century *Compilationes Antiquae*, through the *Liber Extra* of Gregory IX of 1234, to the *Liber Sextus*, issued by Boniface VIII in 1298. Elsewhere, Dante also condemns some of those who commented upon and taught — and some of those also who studied — this material, citing Guilelmus Durantis, Hostiensis, and Innocent IV. In the last decade of Dante's life, Clement V compiled yet another lawbook of papal decretals, the *Extravagantes*, which was published in 1317 by yet another pope, John XXIII. This too was quickly thumbed, read, and covered by the marginalia of legists and practicing lawyers. Of the making of decretals and marginal glosses to them, there seemed indeed to be no end. And for Dante, none of their pages smiled.

Yet it will not do simply to take Carlo Martello's complaint as "Dante's attitude toward canon law." For Dante here uses the manuscripts of the decretals as synecdoche for the larger disorder of his world: the successful envy of Satan, the papal neglect of the Holy Land, and the corruption of Florence. Dante contrasts the Rome of the pilgrims — the Vatican and St. Peter's, *Roma sacra* — implicitly with administrative Rome, the Lateran, and, by the time of the *Paradiso*, Avignon.[2] These images suggest that any consideration of Dante's ideas about, and treatment of jurisprudence must first take into account the context of fundamental disorder which he perceived in the world about which he wrote.

In Dante's encyclopedia of the arts and sciences law has primarily an ethical function and is therefore linked directly to the individual and to the elementary constitution of human society. Any consideration of Dante's concepts of law must start with these areas rather than individual citations of legal questions, particularly when these are closely linked with other imagery and perform a poetic function. The "two laws" of my title refer, of course, to canon and civil, or Roman, law, and the references to Scythians, Garamantes, and Florentines indicate Dante's concern for the legal character of societies either distant from or subordinate to that world of western

* Note: *For* Carlo Martello *read* Folco and *passim*.

Europe in which the two laws are, or should be, supreme. All of Dante's observations on the theory and practice of jurisprudence derive from his philosophical concept of justice, as do his ideas about politics and ethics. To begin with, something must be said about that broader and governing idea of Dantean justice.

I

Dante's concept of justice was inspired by a long tradition of Christian social and legal thought and by the Christianizing of the fifth book of Aristotle's *Nichomachean Ethics* on the part of thirteenth-century thinkers, notably St. Thomas Aquinas.[3] The particular Christian contribution to the latter dealt with the relation between humans and God and linked justice to the theological virtue of charity, of which Aristotle had made no mention. Even the place of justice in the divine plan, however, was considered from a perspective of Christian Aristotelianism.

The highest expression of Dante's concept of justice, as defined in *Par.* xix, 67-90, is its identification with the will of God. Justice among the creatures is achieved to the extent that their own desires and wills accord with that primal justice (*Par.* xix, 88). Like Aquinas, Dante recognized two ways by which the creatures may align their wills to divine justice: participation and revelation. Participation of the rational creature in eternal law is achieved through the natural law, which is the link between Creator and creatures. Humans, possessing reason and will, participate in the eternal law more perfectly, because more rationally and voluntarily, than the rest of creation. Revelation is the second route toward divine justice. As Aquinas observed,

> By natural law the eternal law is participated proportionally to the capacity of human nature. But to his supernatural last end man needs to be directed in a yet higher way. Hence the additional law given by God, whereby man shares more perfectly in the eternal law. (*ST* II. 1. 91. 4 ad 1)

Both participation and revelation, of course, still limit the ultimate human understanding of eternal law. Its essence is impenetrable to the human intellect, often making it seem unjust (*Par.* iv, 67-69). Dante likens the human intellect's attempts to probe the eternal law more deeply than is possible to an eye trying to peer to the bottom of the sea — *com' occhio per lo mare* (*Par.* xix., 60).[4]

Human justice, positive law, then, stands lowest in a hierarchy that ascends through natural law and revelation (divine law) to the eternal law.

That hierarchy defines and identifies the justice in human law and limits its freedom (or, to put it in Dante's terms, gives it the freedom to align itself with the natural, divine, and eternal laws). When human jurisprudence fails to accord itself with the laws of nature and God, it perverts justice. Some of Dante's harshest criticism of human society, indeed, one must say, the organizing ethical principle of the *Commedia* and the *De Monarchia*, focuses precisely upon what Dante considers the grand perversions of justice as manifested in the misuse of law by human lawmakers, signalled by the great vice opposed to justice and charity, avarice.[5]

Following thirteenth-century Aristotelian thought and several important twelfth-century thinkers, Aquinas and Dante also posited the naturalness of organized human society and therefore the obligation upon all human societies to ordain and follow the principles of natural (and hence divine and eternal) justice.[6] Such a view contrasted with the more traditional idea that civil society had arisen as a defect resulting from the corruption of nature and the Fall. But Dante takes the idea of the naturalness of society even further than Aristotle and Aquinas. Aristotle had argued that the intrinsically human quality of human beings was social and civil life. The Greek is quite explicit: humans were *zoon* made distinctively human only by *politike techne*. The civil life of humans thus defined and identified human nature. Communities therefore had to possess laws and governments in order to guarantee not only civil, or common interests, but a distinctively human nature itself. The good of the individual, a principle agreed upon by Aquinas and other thirteenth-century commentators, had necessarily to be subordinated to the principle of the preeminence of the common good.[7] Toward the end of the *Commedia*, however, and throughout the *De Monarchia*, Dante extended this notion and spoke of an "earthly," or "human" beatitude to be achieved in earthly societies. This secondary beatitude was subordinate to, but essential for, the salvation of the human soul. Without the proper ordering of civil life on earth, the conditions by which humans could achieve spiritual salvation became more difficult, since a perfect human, or civil, life provided the conditions for a perfect spiritual life. Because Dante felt so strongly that the world was greatly disordered in his own lifetime, it may be assumed that the saved souls in the *Purgatorio* and the *Paradiso*, at least those who had died during the period of disorder and avarice, managed to achieve salvation in spite of, not because of the present mis-ordering of the world.

Dante also went further than Aquinas in his concept of human law.

Aquinas and Aristotle both recognized the legitimacy of the differences between the particular laws of particular communities. But for Dante, Roman law was, or ought to have been, a particular gift of God to humans, a perfect positive law for all mankind, and the Roman Emperor was the ideal single ruler of the world. In Dante's eyes Roman law was that human institution which best aligned itself with the law of nature and created the ideal conditions by which the divine law of revelation might be followed. Canon law, therefore, had to be derived from the divine law and administered only for man's spiritual end, and not for his temporal affairs.

Although several of these topics will be discussed again below, there is one episode that so succinctly illustrates the relative characters of Roman and canon law that it may be usefully cited here. In *Par.* vi, and again in *Par.* xix, the word "justice" itself serves as a signal of the value of imperial rule and imperial law. In *Par.* vi Justinian, whose very name — *nomina sunt consequentia rerum* — suggests in this one great case the identity of Caesar, Justinian the individual, and Justice — *Cesare fui, e son Iustiniano* — identifics himself as one,

> who, by the will of the Primal Love which I feel, removed from among the laws what was superfluous and vain.

But Justinian could not sense correctly the will of the Primal Love until Pope Agapetus had played his own part:

> And before I put my mind to this work, one nature and no more I held to be in Christ, and with that faith I was content; but the blessed Agapetus, who was the supreme pastor, directed me to the true faith by his words.... So soon as with the Church I moved my feet, it pleased God of his grace to inspire me with this high task, and I gave myself entirely to it, committing arms to my Belisarius, with whom Heaven's right hand was so joined that it was a sign for me to rest from them.

In this passage, perhaps the only one in Dante in which a pope and an emperor function as they ideally should, Agapetus reforms Justinian's dogmatic heresy of monophysitism, exercising a sacerdotal and magisterial role concerning Christian belief, so that Justinian was able, as no human had been before or after, to follow the will of the Primal Love and shape the most perfect of all human laws, a law so perfect, in fact, that it ought to be the single law that directs all human society.

A Roman emperor, whose task was to wield laws and arms — *legge ed arme* — was so perfectly taught by a perfect pope that he could even leave his concern with arms to a perfect general. In Dante's view this remarkable and happy coincidence had occurred only once, but its occurrence set forever the standard by which subsequent law, civil and canon as well as the laws of remote or subordinate peoples, should be judged. It only remained for human society to re-establish those relationships and align itself with the perfect human law, of which Dante himself was to be the prophet. This is the background, not, to be sure, throughout all of Dante's works, but from the *Convivio* on, of Dante's idea of Roman law and his vision of it as the supreme instrument of human civil reason and therefore an agent of salvation.

Thus, in their broadest senses, law and justice were for Dante metaphysical concepts, intimately linked to ethics, and thus, when applied rightly and equitably by the legitimate earthly law-giver, the emperor, they became, as G.R. Sarolli has nicely observed, a para-sacrament.[8] When Dante spoke of law, therefore, he spoke of a wider range of topics than jurisprudence alone. He also connected jurisprudence and justice to all other areas of human activity.

Dante's test of any jurisprudence, or indeed of the legitimacy of any lawmaker or magistrate, was also based upon the Aristotelian designation of justice as the highest of the political virtues (which allowed Dante to link it to the highest of the Christian theological virtues, charity), as Helene Wieruszowski observed, "organizing, ruling, and embracing the other laws, sciences and virtues."[9] In *Convivio* II. 14, for example, Dante explains how the heavens resemble the sciences. The planetary heavens correspond to the *trivium* and the *quadrivium*, the seven liberal arts. To the eighth sphere, the *stellatum*, correspond physics and metaphysics. To the ninth, or crystalline sphere corresponds Moral Science, and to the unmoved and unmoving tenth sphere corresponds theology. Explaining the correspondence between the ninth sphere and Moral Science, or *Giustizia*, Dante cites the fifth book of the *Nichomachean Ethics*:

> For...legal justice disposes the sciences for our learning, and in order that they may not be forsaken, commands that they be both learned and taught.

The heaven of Mercury, in which Justinian explained the genesis of Roman imperial law to Dante, besides being the heaven corresponding to rhetoric among the liberal arts, is also the heaven of the arts and sciences generally, and the heaven of law, thus linking the particular subject of justice to the particular heaven of Justinian. Justice in civil society preserves, develops, and cultivates those arts and sciences that exercise and shape human reason and therefore shape human nature.

From the organizing principle of the proper relationship between God and the created order, through the natural and therefore necessary experience of civil society, to the organization and training of human reason itself, Dante's concept of justice can be seen to have informed all of his thought. It also informed Dante's anthropology.

Thus far, we have considered the Dantean idea of justice from the point of view of the ordering of the divine will and the cosmos. But Dante also fitted the idea to his anthropology, and that too casts light on his ideas of jurisprudence. In *Convivio* I. 12. 72-74 Dante observes that justice is the most human of virtues because it exists "only in the rational or intellectual part of a man, that is in his will," and although Dante had a great deal of difficulty with the problem of free will and physiological and astrological determinism, his repeated assertion of the freedom of the will and the power of disciplined reason culminates in the great speech of Marco Lombardo in *Purgatorio* xvi, at the exact center of the *Commedia*:

> From His hands, who fondly loves it before it exists, comes forth after the fashion of a child that sports, now weeping, now laughing, the simple little soul, which knows nothing, save that, proceeding from a glad Maker, it turns eagerly to what delights it. First it tastes the savor of a trifling good; there it is beguiled and runs after it, if guide or curb bend not its love. Wherefore it was needful to impose law as a bridle, it was needful to have a ruler who could discern the tower at least of the true city. Laws there are, but who puts his hand to them? None, because the shepherd that leads may chew the cud but has not the hoofs divided. Wherefore, the people, who see their guide snatch only at that good whereof they are greedy, feed upon that and seek no other. Well can you see that ill guidance is what has made the world wicked, and not nature that is corrupt in you. Rome, which made the world good, was wont to have two suns, which made visible both the one road and the other, that of the world and that of God.[10]

Because of the delight (undiscriminating in the creature, perfect in the Creator) that is the very first experience of the created soul, delight in things is the fundamental characteristic of human nature. Untrained and undisciplined, that delight may be lavished upon any object indiscriminately. Law, administered by a wise ruler, thus shapes the very essence of human personality. Without it, the soul still possesses delight, but in improper objects, unaware of their relative value. The evil guidance (in this case) of pastors, who themselves take indiscriminate delight in subordinate goods, inspires their flock to do no more than the same thing. Human reason and will, properly guided and bridled, can overcome any material predisposition at all, but it cannot, at least for most people, overcome the effects of misdirected rule. Under a proper world order, Dante's "myth of Rome," both ends of humanity, earthly and spiritual beatitude, were once, Dante thought, achieved; but now:

> The one has quenched the other, and the sword is joined to the cross: and the one together with the other must perforce go ill — since joined, the one does not fear the other.

With the failure of law and rule, misdirected delight and self-love people the rings of hell and delay the purgation of the sinful in Purgatory. It is this view of both ethics and anthropology that gives the problem of justice its central place in Dante's thought and colors his treatment of human jurisprudence.

II

The discussion of Dante's concepts of justice in the preceding section necessarily consisted of a synthesis of ideas that are evidenced in his writings, generally from the *canzone*, *Tre donne*, around 1305, through the *Paradiso*, completed in 1321. Although virtually every detail of the dating of Dante's major works as evidence of the development of his thought, has been (and probably will continue to be) disputed, a brief consideration of general ideas about jurisprudence in Dante's lifetime and of Dante's own experience before 1305 or so may establish some framework for a discussion of Dante's attitude toward Roman and canon law in later life, as well as toward the legal structures of smaller or more distant societies.

The juridical world of Dante was in large measure a continuation of that of the twelfth century. The slow assembling of laws and customs within hundreds of independent jurisdictions, the "deadly pressure," as Julius Goebel called the phenomenon in an earlier period, "of social change upon outmoded structures of rights and remedies," the partial survival and great rediscovery of Roman law around 1100, the formulation of canon law, and the growth of legal education and learning in place of semiprofessional routine drastically transformed the earlier legal history of western Europe and have, in this century alone, been the subject of a large literature from Charles Homer Haskins to the present.[11]

In addition to the institutional and formal aspects of the legal revolution of the twelfth century, there were other elements as well. As Stephan Kuttner has recently described them,

> There were not only the "two laws," Roman and canon, that were professionally explored by the scholars of the twelfth century. There were the statutes and customs of the feudal law, codified and acknowledged by the end of the twelfth century as a subject of legal study. Some of the new learning found its way into the *Usatges* of Barcelona with their far-reaching influence in the western Mediterranean, some found its way into the treatise on the laws and customs of England that goes under the name of Glanvill. There was above all Lombard law, now systematically reorganized from the *Liber Papiensis* as (*lex*) *Lombarda* in the age of the glossators...In all these areas of twelfth-century law that were essentially outside the Roman and canonistic jurisprudence, much remains to be explored about the way legal doctrines took shape and almost unwittingly absorbed — some more, some less — terms and methods of the new learning.[12]

As important and influential as it was, however, neither professional jurisprudence alone, nor applied jurisprudence of any kind, was the sole carrier of the results of the twelfth-century revolution. Part, at least, of the new study of Roman law had grown out of the study of rhetoric, and the art of rhetoric was in turn influenced by new developments in law and legal thought. As Arrigo Solmi put it long ago,

> After the renaissance of Roman law, even the schools of the liberal arts undertook a new scientific approach to this discipline, and the preparation of notaries, judges, lawyers, and other public officials had as its basis [the study of] Roman law. Not only in Bologna, but in all the public and episcopal schools in the Italian cities, Roman law was the subject of study and provided the material for both dialectical disquisition and the *ars dictandi*.[13]

The mid-thirteenth century rhetorician Buoncompagno called the *ars dictandi* the *juris utriusque alumna*, and Buoncompagno was widely read throughout the rest of the century, including most probably by Dante.[14] In one sense, it is unlikely that anyone who grew up and was educated in a northern Italian commune could have avoided one stream or the other of the influence of legal thought in the late thirteenth century. In addition, of course, the developing juridical consciousness of the communes themselves led to a proliferation of statutes, customs, *ordinamenti*, institutions, policies, and personnel that further sharpened the legal consciousness of their citizens. These changes also created a juridical approach toward politics and governance, as the influence of Buoncompagno or, even more directly, that of Brunetto Latini, makes clear.

In a stimulating recent essay based chiefly upon the work of such scholars as Plesner and Ottokar, Jeremy Catto has emphasized the extent to which Florentine thought at the end of the thirteenth century was still closely tied to the smaller sub-societies of clan, *consorteria*, and *sesto*.[15] What, according to Catto, distinguished Dante and a few others from this parochial mentality was,

> no civic spirit, but his intellectual and moral vision which raised him from the state of nature in which [the other Florentines'] limited outlook kept them; and if, as here suggested, Florence and other cities had no distinctive [civic] social structure or cultural values, the range and quality of Dante's highly conscious art may indicate in what their true distinction lay.

From the *Convivio* through the *Paradiso*, Catto argues, Dante's purpose was to use highly developed and intellectualized poetic forms to raise his fellow citizens' vision, to enable the Florentines to acquire "certain moral qualities, dispositions, or habits," necessary to pursue the arts, *pratiche*, of commerce and government by co-operating, "sinking purely clannish loyalties in the pursuit of the common good," and developing a "certain intellectual curiosity, a willingness to understand events beyond the horizon of family and the horizon of Florence." Following in the recent tradition of Brunetto Latini and others, Dante addressed the *Convivio* to the "principi, baroni, cavalieri, e molt'altra nobile gente, non solamente maschi ma femmine, che sono molti e molte in questa lingua, volgari e non litterati" (*Conv*. I. 9). These, presumably the audience of the *Commedia* as well, were thus to be elevated by inspired instructive poetry above the level of clan and *sesto*, even above the level of *città*, to that of a cosmopolitan, ethical, imperially ruled and rationally regulated world. Only in such a world could Florentines or anyone else achieve, first, earthly beatitude, and second, spiritual salvation.

Such an attitude on the part of Dante, however, surely grew out of his experiences in the early study of the liberal arts in Florence, his own intellectual and political career, his exile, and his reflections upon his exile. Giovanni Boccaccio, unhappily neither the most thorough, nor the most reliable of biographers, notes that Dante pursued the intense study of liberal arts in Florence, rather than those arts "that bring gain," i.e., medicine or law. From his early studies, Boccaccio continues, Dante went on to study further at Bologna, probably during the period between late 1286 and the end of 1287. Dante certainly knew Bologna well, but there is a question of the extent to which he was familiar with the study of law at Bologna, then the greatest center of legal studies in Europe.

Leonardo Bruni's *Life of Dante* thoroughly discusses Dante's civic activities and ideas, but says nothing about Dante's own study of the law, even though it does remark that Dante's son Pietro did study law and achieved a distinguished legal career. As Solmi, Wieruszowski and others remind us, however, Dante certainly became acquainted with legal ideas and perhaps even legal methods, if only in his early and advanced study of rhetoric and in his own political activities in the 1290s in Florence. For Florentine law was the first law that Dante knew, and in his youth and young manhood that law was the object of violent and partisan change and ambitious revision and reform.

For twelve years between his return from Bologna around 1288 and the political crises of 1300, Dante had ample opportunity to familiarize himself not only with Florentine political and legal affairs, but with the relations among law, ethics and politics that were discussed, not only by Brunetto Latini, but in the convents of Santa Croce and Santa Maria Novella.[17] 1293 was the year not only of the *Vita Nuova*, but of the first Ordinances of Justice. The death of Brunetto Latini in 1294 was followed by the revision of the Ordinances in 1295 and Dante's entry into political life in the same year. By 1296 Dante had read Aristotle's *Ethics*. Between 1300 and 1302, of course, there occurred Dante's priorate, the personal disaster of exile, Dante's initial sojourn among the other exiles, and finally after 1304 the long years of solitary exile and poetic and political reflection upon what he had seen.

What had he seen? At the time of his reading about law in rhetorical studies and discussing it with Latini and others, Dante also witnessed the early communal pride in legality and legal order. This must have seemed a pretentious pride on the part of Florentines, claiming the high name of justice for policies that seemed to Dante, at least in retrospect, to stem as much from private rivalries and enmities as from the parochial intellectual horizons of those who made them. For Florentines and citizens of other communes also found in the figure of *Giustizia* the symbolic representation of the commune itself, not only in public statements, but also, as Wieruszowski has eloquently pointed out, in visual representations as well.[18] In many cities, a personified female figure or a judge, as *Giustizia*, represents the commune itself. The disparity between such high claims and representations and the parochial horizons of actual political practice may well have outraged Dante further and inspired his general harshness later toward the communes' pretensions to legal and juridical autonomy in regard to Roman imperial law.

These, then, seem to be the roots of Dante's concerns about jurisprudence: the legal and ethical dimension of rhetorical study, the discussions with Brunetto Latini and others, and his own experience of Florentine political life in the five years 1295-1300. There is no evidence that he became at all a professionally qualified lawyer, at Bologna or anywhere else.[19] For Dante's resentment in his later work is not that of a professional jurist, but of an ethical philosopher and lay theologian. Florentine law, for all of its pretentions to justice, had in fact degenerated from its earlier character of communal trust and sobriety. Dante's portrait of Florence "in the good old days" painted by his ancestor Cacciaguida in *Par*. xv, suggests the idyllic past before Florentines had learned to use the law to advance their private quarrels:

> To so reposeful, to so fair a life of citizens, to such a trusty community, to so sweet an abode, Mary, called on with loud cries, gave me, and in your ancient Baptistery I became at once a Christian and Cacciaguida.

Now, after 1305, while many others have justice at heart and deliberate about its course over time, "for the shaft does not come without counsel to the bow"(*Purg*. vi. 131), Florentines proclaim their justice quickly and loudly, but in fact possess none.[20] The last verses of *Purg*. vi contain the famous denunciation of Florentine fickleness and instability, preserving none of the noble *antichi costumi* permitted within imperial law, but shaming ancient Athens and Lacedaemon themselves, making

> such subtle provisions that what you spin in October lasts not till mid-November. How many times within your memory have you changed laws, coinage, offices and customs, and renewed your members!

From the perspective of the years after 1305, the 1290s in Florence must have been years of sharpest incongruity between the studies in legal philosophy and the actual practice of the Florentine government, and the disasters of 1301-2 must have seemed virtually inevitable.

For all of the misgivings that Florentine affairs between 1295 and 1301 may have engendered in Dante's thought, much of his experience of Florentine, and general civic law, finds an echo in his writings after 1305 virtually unaltered. In his discussions of marriage, for example, the obligations of family membership and inheritance, the rights of officeholders, and particularly the vast spectrum of most criminal law, he echoes without criticism the operation of municipal ordinances and customs. He recognizes *infamia* and may have been strongly influenced, particularly in the *Inferno*, by the *pitture infamanti*, the bold frescoes of criminals, their crimes, and their punishments that were painted at public command through the thirteenth and fourteenth centuries.[21] Cacciaguida's discourse echoes Florentine sumptuary laws, and Dante's letter to a Florentine friend mentions the custom of *oblatio*, the ceremonial ritual of reconciling criminals to the republic — and Dante objects to its use only in his own case, not generally.[22]

And yet although much of Florence's law operates routinely in Dante's treatment of jurisprudence in the *Convivio* and the *Commedia* and *De Monarchia*, even in this area the connection to his philosophical jurisprudence is not clear. It is odd that Dante does not mention the Ordinances of Justice of 1293 and 1295, and it is not clear whether or not he mentions Giano della Bella, their creator. Stripped of their later constitutional significance in the "Myth of Florence," the ordinances and their creators may well have seemed less noble to Dante than they have to later historians, and less public minded.[23] Nicola Ottokar has shown how little the Ordinances affected Dante and his family, and for the poet, looking back from 1305 and later, their character may have seemed simply one more instance of private, family rivalry using urban statutes and the name of justice to punish political and personal enemies.[24]

There are also other, less readily noticed aspects of Dante's thought on local law. He seems to have approved of the judicial duel and argued in *Monarchia* II. ix. 1 that it indeed revealed divine justice. Although the context is Dante's justification of the Romans' conquest of an Empire, he nowhere indicates that he limits the effectiveness of the judgement of God to imperial issues alone. In *Monarchia* II. vii. 7. Dante also includes some forms of *sortes* along with judicial combat. His references in these locations are chiefly scriptural and classical, and they may be deliberately so in order to avoid the canon against judicial ordeals of the Fourth Lateran Council of 1215. Such a view, however, is consistent at least with the idealized ancient world of Cacciaguida and the simpler, older nobility to whom God might still speak his will in the ritual forms of judicial combat.[25]

If I have emphasized Dante's awareness of Florentine laws first, it is because Dante's Florentine experience forged his later attitudes toward the law and his thought about Roman and canon law. I would not be too quick to deny that the troubles of the small juridical world of the city-republic did not lie at the root of Dante's later and grander speculations about jurisprudence.

Nor should Dante's denunciation of the jurisprudence and legal practices of the Florentines and his admiration of imperial law obscure his attitudes toward the laws of peoples elsewhere inside the Empire, and particularly outside it. Around 1250 the Roman lawyer Accursius addressed the Digest text *Omnes populi* — which stated that all people are ruled by the civil law or the law of nations. When he raised the question of people who are not so ruled, Accursius replied that such men were not civilized. By the end of the thirteenth century, however, and in the fourteenth, a number of Roman lawyers recognized extreme latitude on the part of individual communities to make their own statute law. As Donald Kelley has shown, the thought of Bartolus and Baldus on these questions greatly strengthened the claims for making law on the part of city-republics and other regions within and outside the Empire.[26]

Although Dante would not have gone as far as Bartolus and Baldus, he was, nevertheless, more liberal than Accursius, although he preferred to keep the discussion remote from imperial territory. Thus, he approached one aspect of local independence in lawmaking from the point of view of the ethnographer as much as from that of the jurist:

> Municipal laws do fail at times and have need of regulation, as the Philosopher shows in his commendation of equity in the fifth book to Nicomachus. Nations, kingdoms, and cities have individual conditions which must be governed by different laws. For law is the directive principle of life. The Scythians...must rule their lives in one way...and the Garamantes must do otherwise.[27]

In Dante's eyes, part of natural law was unique, leading to the civil law of Rome, and partly common to all mankind, to the extent that it was perceived by natural reason, which all humans share. In the latter case, it was expressed as the law of nations, the *ius gentium*. The civil law of Rome and the *ius gentium* shaped the laws of different peoples and places both in and beyond Europe. Yet the Scythians and Garamantes, about whom Dante had heard from classical and medieval ethnographers, were easy to discuss in this context. They were, respectively, the northernmost and southernmost peoples of Dante's world, living in bitter cold and torrid heat, obvious examples of a naturally dictated special circumstance that literally illustrated Dante's thesis. But the Scythians and Garamantes are rhetorical subjects; they are easier to discuss in this context than Florentines, say, or Swabians, or the French — precisely the kinds of groups that some Roman lawyers were entitling to make their own laws.

Closer to home, however, Dante grew more conservative. As he looked back from 1305, Dante saw that Florence had no justification in acting like the Scythians or Garamantes. *Civilitas* derived, for Dante, from Justice. Within the Empire, justice derived from Roman law alone. In his letter to the Florentines, Dante accused them of trying perversely to erect a *Florentina civilitas* in rivalry, rather than submission, to the Empire.[28] Such an attempt is the establishment of a *regnum novum*, wholly outside the order of reason and justice. Unlike the Scythians and Garamantes, then, Florence did not merely enact laws suited to unique and extreme circumstances, which she might have been permitted to do, but rather she ceased to behave like a *provincia* (within Italy, the *regina provinciarum*), and dared to rival the Empire itself. Such pride was to Dante a form of *impietas*.

In the matter of Scythians, Garamantes and Florentines, then, Dante formulated both a recognition of a certain degree of local autonomy in law-making and a sharp criticism of local communities that tried to make too much law too independently of the Empire. For the remotest northern or southern peoples, local idiosyncrasy might be permitted a great leeway; but for *provinciae*, local lawmaking was greatly constricted, lest it dare to reject the imperial law, *ratio scripta*, the divine gift itself. When this happened, the result was a debased, imperfect attempt at the embodiment of reason in a local, and hence impossible, even blasphemous *Florentina civilitas*.

III

On the long track of his exile after 1302, separated from his fellow exiles after 1304, Dante had little hope for the juridical good sense of either Black Guelfs in Florence or White Guelfs and Ghibellines in exile. Having washed his hands of both, Dante became, as he said of himself in the letter to the Italian Cardinals of 1314,

> *una sola vox, sola pia, et hec privata, in matris Ecclesie quasi funere audiatur,*

or, as Cacciaguida prophesies for him in *Par*. xvii, 68-9, a party unto himself. Yet Dante, like St. Augustine when he turned directly to *philosophia* in the *Confessions* rather than to one or another contending school of philosophy, rejected the *inane partium studium*, as Leonardo Bruni later called it, and aimed directly at Reason and Justice themselves.[29] The city-republics, the *provinciae*, had failed him, and their impious misuse of the law had created a grand perversion which made those who should love each other the most — fellow citizens — gnaw at each other:

> and now in [the cities] your living abide not without war, and of those whom one wall and one moat shut in, one gnaws at the other!

The reason for this is that the cities have turned their backs upon the living law, and the living emperor who must apply it:

> What avails it that Justinian should refit the bridle, if the saddle is empty?

From Cicero, Aristotle, Brunetto Latini, and Remigio Girolami, Dante now took up the ideal of the obligations of a harmonious universal social order and civil life and their role in the full development and expression of *humana civilitas*.

As Charles Davis has shown, Dante was not the only Italian thinker of the thirteenth and fourteenth centuries who held this opinion of Justinian and Roman law, nor was he the last.[30] Davis cites Gioacchino Volpe to the effect that even though "the inhabitants of a free city might in practice make or repeal laws, and obey or resist particular emperors, according to their pleasure...the source of law was for them always Caesar, and (recognizing their practical autonomy) they never negated that fact."[31] The paradox of universal, eternal, continually binding Roman law and its ethical necessity on the one hand, and the disappointing practice of individual city-republics and kingdoms on the other, was resolved by Dante in favor of the former, more philosophically, but no less emphatically than it was by contemporary jurists themselves, notably Dante's friend Cino da Pistoia. A.P. d'Entrèves' observation that Dante's attitude toward Roman law was the first key to Dante's "discovery of the Empire," has much to recommend it, and he may well have been led to it by his experience of what he perceived to be the privatized, corrupt, and impious legal practice of the Florentines and other city-republics.[32]

Any consideration of Dante's knowledge of and developed acquaintance with Roman law would be vastly improved by a systematic study of Dante's citations, particularly in the *Convivio*, the *De Monarchia*, and *Commedia*, in relation to the thought of Cino da Pistoia. Cino, one of the most eminent and intellectually adventurous civil lawyers of his age (1270-1326), knew Dante well, exchanged poems and literary and aesthetic questions with him, and is often mentioned in Dante's *Rime*.[33] It is likely that the Letter to a Pistoian exile (*Ep*. III) was sent by Dante to Cino, and Cino mentions Dante in his own verse, for he was an accomplished poet as well as a lawyer. Unfortunately, no such study has been made, for two reasons: first, there is not a word of law in any of the numerous exchanges we know of between Dante and Cino; second, Dante's most numerous references to Roman Law in the *Convivio* are to the *Digest*, and until very recently, only Cino's early commentary to the first part of the *Digest* had been thought to survive — only in 1963 did Domenico Maffei reconstruct Cino's *Lectura*. It may be that a systematic comparison might reveal some mutual influence. But for now the problem remains unresolved.

Nowhere does Dante sum up his own admiration of Roman law as in the opening words of *Ep*. VI, of 1311, to the Florentines:

> The pious providence of the eternal king, who in the heavens is eternal goodness, yet does not cease to look down on our affairs here below, committed to the holy governance of the Romans (*sacrosanctum romanum imperium*) all human affairs, so that humankind might have peace under the guidance of such a serene rule, and so that everywhere, as nature demands, men might live *civiliter*.

This is a strong and relatively early statement, but what is interesting is the context of the proof for it that Dante cites. This truth had been discovered independently by the ancients' use of natural human reason, revealed in scripture, and shown by experience — whose experience?

> *Italia misera, sola...privatis arbitriis derelicta, omnique publico moderamine destituta.*

"Wretched, lonely Italy, abandoned to private wills, destitute of all public moderation"...This is an odd array of proofs if considered simply in traditional philosophical and ethical terms, but it is not an odd array in terms of Dante's own perception of his experience in the city-republics.

In the *Commedia* and the *De Monarchia* Dante's concern with Roman law is chiefly in terms of its role as the constitutional law of Christendom; that is, it operates on that level at which philosophy, ethics, and justice touch. It becomes the standard by which human societies and the Church itself are judged. Dante holds it out to correct the shortcomings and errors of the former, and the transgressions and misdirections of the latter. In terms of Dante's own philosophical development, Roman law is the particular manifestation of the generalized Aristotelian dictum that civil laws permit the other arts and sciences to flourish and therefore permit humans to become fully human. Neither Aristotle (nor St. Thomas himself) had, of course, cited Roman law specifically in this role. Thomistic anthropology was closed to Dante's second reason for insisting upon the centrality of Roman law, the depravity of untaught and misled humans. In the latter sense, the absence of law made salvation itself difficult, if not impossible. For, as the next section will consider, the Church itself, without obeying or recognizing Roman law, was in no position to substitute its own law for the laws of the emperors. In doing so it had only contributed to the misdirection of human society and the triumph of avarice.

Despite the lofty plane upon which Dante conducts much of his discussion of Roman law in the *Convivio*, the *Commedia* and the *De Monarchia*, the link between Dante's Florentine experiences and his prescriptions for rectifying Italian society after 1305 is clear. As Solmi once pointed out, unlike Aquinas, who passed from the study of theology to that of law without ever becoming committed to a fundamentally juridical view of human society, Dante went straight to Justice itself as an expression of supreme reason, and to law as *ratio scripta*, elevating what had become a commonplace of jurists to a philosophical principle.[34]

Although there was indeed a powerful literary tradition among twelfth- and thirteenth-century civil lawyers which praised Roman law as highly as Dante himself did, no Roman lawyer had ever precisely placed imperial law within a cosmological framework as spacious and detailed as Dante's.[35] Dante's attitude toward Roman law was not the predictable exclusivity of a professional with an exaggerated degree of *Berufsbewusstsein*, but that of an ethical philosopher who found in the law a concrete program for specific reforms, just as he sought specific solutions elsewhere. What mattered to Dante was that the imperial law, with all that it stood for in his thought, be in place and properly acknowledged and administered. When that happened, the natural variations among communities — cities, *provinciae*, kingdoms, and regions — could readily be accommodated by local decision, and the Church itself could turn to the end for which God had designed it instead of assuming a prerogative that God himself had intended for the emperor alone.

Nor did Dante regard all civil lawyers as his natural allies. Boccaccio tells us that Dante himself undertook no lucrative studies, and Dante had little respect for those, even Roman lawyers, who did. In *Monarchia* II. 10.9 Dante refers to "presumptuous jurists" who argue against the justice of the Roman conquest of the Empire. These jurists squat far below the watch-tower of reason from which "the human mind gazes out at these abiding principles," and they should restrict themselves to proper counsel and judgement and not assume that the law is merely a reflection of their own opinions. This passage is sometimes taken to refer to canon lawyers, but it seems in fact to refer to Guelf or otherwise anti-imperial practicing Roman lawyers who are not, in Dante's opinion, legitimate legal scholars but rather mere practitioners. Here Dante joined a host of other satirists of the professions, and one of his sharpest criticisms of the canon lawyers was that they too worked for gain and not for the sake of the common good.[36] When professionals worked for the sake of avarice, they misled those in whose power it was to influence society as a whole, and thus they contributed to its great disorder. As the next section will suggest, much of Dante's criticism of canon lawyers was based on similar grounds.

Dante had arrived at his concept of the necessity of Roman law from two different directions: one leading from the avarice and injustice of Florence and the misdirection of the Church, the other leading from ethical philosophy, chiefly Aristotle via Aquinas, but, as Ernst Kantorowicz demonstrated, also from the transformation of the old ecclesiological image of the *corpus mysticum* by both lawyers and theologians, through Godefroid des Fontaines — and Cino da Pistoia — to Dante's concept of a universal *humana civilitas*.[37]

That Roman law was the written reason of this *humana civilitas* was Dante's original contribution to political thought and jurisprudence. He did not make it in the role, or with the expertise, of a professional jurist, but as an ethical philosopher who unquestionably knew enough Roman law to recognize that it, and it alone, served his high purpose. As Dante remarked of the world, as he looked down upon it from the heavens in *Paradiso* xxii, the smaller societies were each like a little threshing floor "which makes us so fierce."[38] Corporate and individually distinctive though they might be, they were nevertheless too small, too proud, and too liable to disorder to constitute the essential human society. To achieve this, a necessity, not an ideal, and to overcome avarice and restore the order of charity and justice, only Roman law and only the emperor were left, and to these, in both his political theory and his jurisprudence, Dante turned in his exile.

Against the presumptuous pictorial representations of *Justitia* in civic iconography during Dante's lifetime, we may set two other sets of pictures. In the church of San Vitale at Ravenna Dante could observe, glowing in the light of the apse, the seventh-century mosaics showing the court of Theodora and Justinian.[39] In Rome, as Dino Compagni tells us, Dante also observed, in the Sylvester Chapel of the church of the Quattro Coronati, the crude and clumsy frescoes that represented the Donation of Constantine.[40] The artistic differences between these two sets of images conform to Dante's estimation of the events that each represented. And Justinian's long discourse in *Paradiso* vi joins the two. Although Constantine is indeed in Paradise himself, he is not there because of the Donation, but in spite of it; it remains for Justinian — and Justice — to put that great error right, and it must be done by the successful reassertion of the rightful primacy of Roman law and Roman imperial rule.

IV

Any essay that begins by referring to Dante's "frowning pages" on the subject of jurisprudence must begin its discussion of canon law with a reference to the only smile in Dante's treatment of the subject, that of Gratian, in *Paradiso*, x,

> who served the one and the other court so well that it pleases in Paradise.

Any consideration of the place of canon law in Dante's jurisprudence must begin with Gratian and conclude with the *decretalisti* of *Paradiso* ix and the *Extravagantes* of Clement V. The way is not entirely clear, since it runs, not through the history of the classical period of canon law (1140-1378), but through the mind of Dante, and the two are far from synonymous.[41]

There are two possible ways of interpreting Dante's reference to Gratian and *l'uno e l'altro foro*. Either (to be more correct in the technical terminology of canonists) the two *fori* are the interior forum of conscience and the confessional and the exterior forum of the ecclesiastical tribunal, or they are the *fori* of Peter and of Caesar, that is, spiritual and temporal powers. An expert canonist would choose the first of these as the proper interpretation of Dante's reference, but it is possible, and even more probable, that Dante intended the second. The only other use of the term *foro* in the *Commedia* occurs in *Par*. xxx, in a reference to Clement V as the

> *prefetto nel foro divino,*

opposed to the emperor Henry VII, whose *alma agosta* is anticipated in Paradise by a glorious throne and crown. In the *Paradiso* reference, the division between spheres of competence of pope and emperor, and the subordination of the former to the latter, is explicit.[42]

Our interpretation of Dante's reference to Gratian would be clarified if we knew more about the way in which Gratian was regarded at the beginning of the fourteenth century, both by literate layfolk and professional jurists. Dante may well have regarded Gratian, not as "the father of the science of canon law," but as a theologian whose *Decretum*, if it neglected Roman law, nevertheless expressed an admirable restraint concerning the character of papal authority, emphasized the priestly and magisterial role of the pope, and firmly outlined a hierarchy of authoritative sources of dogma and law, one in which papal decretals did not yet occupy the pride of place attributed to them by later popes and *decretalisti*.

The question of Dante's reading of Gratian on the sources of law is further complicated by the fact that although professional jurists accepted Gratian's hierarchy, they were prepared, both theoretically and pragmatically, to accept the precedence of decretals over canons on the grounds that the popes issued decretals "from certain knowledge, according to law." It is perhaps in this difference of perception on the part of literate laymen like Dante and professional canonists that Dante's attitude toward canon law is most clearly to be seen. Although canonists themselves acknowledged the great *auctoritas* of the Fathers and the canons, as did Dante, they also recognized, as Dante did not, that *decretalis prevalet canoni*.[43] For practical reasons, such an attitude is understandable within the realm of professional practice, but it is not an attitude with which Dante had any sympathy, and, as a layman, he would probably not have understood the canonists' reasons for according precedence to decretals, particularly if these were expressed categorically and mechanically — as, it must be admitted, they occasionally were.

It is chiefly the problem of the decretals and the *decretalisti*, then, that contained the seeds of Dante's criticism of canon law.

For it must be remembered that in most of Dante's corpus canon law operates routinely, almost unnoticed, in discussions of vows, penitence, retributive justice, degrees of consanguinity, and even in such changing areas as the translation of bishops, direct papal authority in some temporal affairs, and in reserved causes. A premature decision on the question of Dante's attitude to canon law cannot be made, as I suggested above, simply from Carlo Martello's bitter reference to *decretalisti* in *Paradiso* ix. Even when he himself comes to the tender point of papal decretals, Dante pointedly mentions that he venerates them. Thus, the problem of canon law in Dante's jurisprudence is broader than a glance at Dante's customary invective suggests.[44]

In a recent study Richard Kay ingeniously interprets Dante's DXV

(*Purgatorio* xxxiii, 40-45) prophecy as referring to *Distinctio* XV of Gratian's *Decretum,* a series of texts that deal with the authority of different sources of canon law, one of which places papal decretals generally low in the hierarchy of sources for the faith and the divine law.[45] Such an interpretation has the virtue of being absolutely consistent with Dante's own interpretation of the sources of law elsewhere, although Dante would read that hierarchial position differently from a professional canonist. If we consider, for example, *Monarchia* III. 3, a parallel passage to the one condemning the *decretalisti* in *Paradiso* ix, we find overwhelming evidence in favor of the superior authority of the ignored fathers and doctors to the statements of individual popes.[46] Of the six fathers and doctors whose works are cited as being ignored by canonists in Dante's letter to the Italian Cardinals of 1314, two actually appear, one is clearly referred to, and one is mentioned in *Paradiso* x. The remaining two, Gregory the Great and St. John of Damascus, do not appear in this canto, but the former is mentioned in *Purgatorio* x and in *Paradiso* xxviii. Only John of Damascus is not explicitly mentioned in the entire *Paradiso*, and only he and Gregory are not explicitly referred to in the heaven of the Sun. (There is some uncertainty whether the unnamed figure in *Paradiso* x is Orosius or St. Ambrose.)

On several different occasions Dante clearly contrasts unfavorably his contemporaries' consultation of papal decretals with their simultaneous neglect of the fundamental authorities of Christian doctrine and law. As the text of Gelasius stated, papal decretals are indeed to be venerated (and in *Monarchia* III. 3, Dante explicitly states, surely echoing the Gelasian text, "and I venerate them myself"), but only after Scripture, the Four General Councils, other Councils, the writings of Church Fathers including the *Epistola* of Leo I, and the works of other Fathers who did not deviate from the faith. In the full Gelasian text the decretals are followed in authority by the deeds of the martyrs, the lives of the desert fathers, those works of Origen not repudiated by St. Jerome, and the Chronicle and *Historia ecclesiastica* of Eusebius. Dante's reiterated emphasis in the *Commedia* and other works upon the authority of Scripture, Councils and Fathers, his treatment of Pope Agapetus, and, as Kay points out, the restriction of the exercise of the power of the keys in the *Commedia* only to cases of conscience, all suggest Dante's idea of the papacy and the nature and limits of its authority.[47]

Dante is thus, in one respect at least, very hard, not only upon individual popes but also upon the early fourteenth-century supporters of papal authority. He treats the *decretalisti* very harshly, as if they, more than the popes themselves, were responsible for the misdirection of canon law. Eager for gold (and by implication insufficiently learned in the true sources of the law), they pervert the very sources of the law and in fact invert them. Further, they have misled popes themselves and have therefore contributed to the great struggle between *papato* and *impero*.

Although Dante takes this theme very far, farther in fact than his most adventurous contemporaries and farther than anyone else before Marsiglio of Padua, it was not original with him. During the exile of Thomas Becket, a century and a half before the *Commedia*, John of Salisbury had written to his master, urging Thomas to mitigate the increasingly juridical character of his dispute with King Henry II:

> The laws and canons are useful to us, but...they excite curiosity rather than devotion. Do you not remember how it is written, "The priests and ministers of the lord shall mourn between the vestibule and the altar, saying, 'Have mercy, O Lord and spare Thy people' [Joel 2. 17]?" ...Whoever rises up from the study of the laws, or even the canons, stricken with remorse? I say more: the exercises of schools sometimes puff up knowledge, but they rarely, or never, inflame virtue.[48]

St. Bernard gave similar advice to Pope Eugenius III.[49] As Michael Wilks has suggested, "decretalism" was challenged again by the Thomists in the thirteenth century, and other thirteenth-century sources indicate that the theme struck by John of Salisbury became a leitmotif of papal criticism,[50] culminating in the attacks of Dante. The chief targets of Dante, besides the *decretalisti*, were the *Speculum* of Gulielmus Durantis and the work of Hostiensis and Innocent IV, the pope who was also an influential canon lawyer. All three are targets of a generation earlier than Dante's own. Of these, Hostiensis was criticized from both camps, since Aegidius Spiritalis criticized him for his restraint in discussing the casual jurisdiction of the papacy.[51] Although the research of Davidsohn and of Charles T. Davis has not revealed any contemporary sources of great importance in the canon law libraries of Florence, one suspects that Dante did not need Riccardo da Siena, Guido de Baysio, or Johannes Andreae to attack. He took up an older argument, refitted it with a specific context, and pursued it in new circumstances — for a lay audience.

It is customary in modern scholarship to consider Dante's jurisprudence in the context of his larger political thought. In this study I have attempted to keep the subject isolated as much as possible from political theory and to focus instead upon Dante's view of the juridical character of different societies — those of the city, the region, kingdom, Church, Empire, and land temporarily or ethnographically beyond the Empire. Ultimately, of course, Dante's jurisprudence does lead to political theory, and this conjunction has been widely described.[52] But his jurisprudence is not an idea derived from the grander idea of Empire, or at least not exclusively. Both his early study of rhetoric and his early political life showed him the law, the former as it shoud be and the latter, for all of what he considered its pretensions to Justice, the law as it was. During his exile, *provinciae* showed him no better. For Dante, a greater polity and a greater law were needed, both to impose peace and to assert the true hierarchy of the sources of the law.

Like Petrus de Vinea and Romeu de Villeveuve (whose very name invokes the Rome of the pilgrims, *Roma sacra*, the Rome that is forgotten by popes and *decretalisti*), both of whom suffered from the disorder of particular noble and royal households, Dante turned to the great law in order to regulate the little laws, so that Florentines, like Scythians and Garamantes, might live in a justly ordered world.

In such a world pious pilgrims, royal advisers, and philosophical lovers would not be expelled, driven to suicide, and flung out into unjust exile.[53] Nor would Dante, as Villani said of him, have seemed to "delight to denounce and cry out after the manner of poets, perhaps in certain places more than was fitting." The key moment in his idea of the law seems to have arrived in 1304-1305, when the fact of his exile seems to have sunk in and any ideal of local justice rapidly receded. As Villani concludes, "maybe his exile was the cause of this." Maybe it was.

NOTES

1) Millard Meiss, "The Smiling Pages," in Peter Brieger, Millard Meiss, and Charles Singleton, eds., *Illuminated Manuscripts of the Divine Comedy*, 2 vols. (Princeton, 1969), I, 31-80. For Dante's delight in his own hand, see P. Toynbee, *Dantis Alagherii Epistolae* (rpt. Oxford, 1966), xix, xxviii-xxix. The translation of the *Commedia* cited here is that of Charles S. Singleton, 6 vols. (Princeton, 1975); the ed. of *Convivio* is that of G. Busnelli and G. Vandelli, 3 vols. (Florence, 1934); that of the *Monarchia* is that of P.G. Ricci (Florence, 1965), and that of the *Epistolae* that of Toynbee, cited above. I am grateful to Kenneth Pennington and Charles T. Davis for their advice on this essay.

2) See *Par.* xxvii, 22-25 for a further specific reference to the character of Rome as the sacred burial ground of St. Peter. See also A.P. d'Entrèves, *Dante as a Political Thinker* (Oxford,

1952), 28-9, and J.H. Whitfield, "*Paradiso* VI," in David Nolan, ed., *Dante Commentaries: Eight Studies of the Divine Comedy* (Dublin, 1977), 143-158; Charles T. Davis, "Rome and Babylon in Dante," in P. Ramsey, ed., *Rome in the Renaissance: The City and the Myth* (Binghamton, 1982), 19-40.

3) The most extensive treatment of the general subject is still that of Alan H. Gilbert, *Dante's Conception of Justice* (rpt. New York, 1965). For Aristotle's treatment of justice in relation to the distribution of power within communities, see R.D. Cumming, *Human Nature and History: A Study of the Development of Liberal Political Thought*, 2 vols. (Chicago, 1969). A recent treatment of the theme in terms of the poetic is that of Anthony K. Cassell, *Dante's Fearful Art of Justice* (Toronto, 1984).

4) Cf. *Par*. vii, 58-60; xx, 91-3.

5) *Mon*. I. 11. 69-105; I. 13. 47-55; *Conv*. IV. 22-44; *Ep*. VI. On Dante's concept of true freedom, see *Ep*. V. 6; *Mon*. I 12; *Ep*. VI. 5; *Ep*. VI. 2.

6) On the tradition, see Gaines Post, *Studies in Medieval Legal Thought: Public Law and the State, 1100-1322* (Princeton, 1964), 494-561.

7) See I. Th. Eschmann, O.P., "A Thomistic Glossary on the Principle of the Preeminence of a Common Good," *Medieval Studies* 5 (1943), 123-165; *Mon*. II. 5. 1-21.

8) G.R. Sarolli, *Prolegomena alla 'Divina Commedia'* (Florence, 1971), 412- 414.

9) Helene Wieruszowski, "An Early Anticipation of Dante's *Cieli e scienze*," in Wieruszowski, *Politics and Culture in Medieval Spain and Italy* (Rome, 1971), 503-514. Now, see the bibliographies in David L. Wagner, ed., *The Seven Liberal Arts in the Middle Ages* (Bloomington, 1983).

On Mercury, the planet of *Par*. vi, as signifying the planet of the lawgiver, see Giuseppe Mazzotta, *Dante, Poet of the Desert* (Princeton, 1979), 180.

10) Cf. *Conv*. IV. 12. For Aquinas on law and reason, see St II. II. 55. 4. Further, A.P. d'Entrèves, *Dante as a Political Thinker* (Oxford, 1952), 76-97.

11) Much of the recent historiography is conveniently reviewed in Stephan Kuttner, "The Revival of Jurisprudence," and Knut Wolfgang Nörr, "The Institutional Foundations of the New Jurisprudence," both in Robert L. Benson and Giles Constable, eds., with Carol D. Lanham, *Renaissance and Renewal in the Twelfth Century* (Cambridge, Mass., 1982), 299-323, 324-338. For wider bibliography, see Walter Ullmann, *Law and Politics in the Middle Ages* (Ithaca, 1975), and Helmut Coing, ed., *Handbuch der Quellen und Literatur der neueren europäischen Rechtsgeschichte*, Vol. I, *Mittelalter* (Munich, 1973). See also Armin Wolf, "Gesetzgebung und Kodifikation," in Peter Weimar, ed., *Die Renaissance der Wissenschaften im 12. Jahrhundert* (Zurich and Munich, 1981), 143-171. For our subject still classic are the works of Woldemar Englemann, *Die Wiedergeburt der Rechtskultur in Italien* (Leipzig, 1939), and particularly for criminal law, Hermann Kantorowicz, *Albertus Gandinus und das Strafrecht der Scholastik*, 2 vols. (Berlin and Leipzig, 1907, 1926).

12) Kuttner, "The Revival of Jurisprudence," 305-306. To anticipate somewhat a point made below, it is necessary to point out that, ironically, the *decretalisti* whom Dante criticized were attempting to model their interpretation of canon law upon the scientific jurisprudence of Roman law.

13) Arrigo Solmi, "Dante e il Diritto," Ch. VII of his book *Il Pensiero Politico di Dante* (Florence, 1922), 219-252, at 224. Solmi's study recapitulates the argument two decades earlier

between Luigi Chiappelli and Mario Chiaudano in regard to Dante's first-hand knowledge of the texts of Romance law. Solmi sides with Chiappelli. There is a bibliography of the dispute in the study by Giuseppe Lumia, cited below, n. 19.

14) I am grateful to Robert L. Benson for this suggestion. See also Charles T. Davis, *Dante's Italy* (Philadelphia, 1984), 169-70, with further references. See below, n. 50.

15) Jeremy Catto, "Florence, Tuscany, and the World of Dante," in Cecil Grayson, ed., *The World of Dante* (Oxford, 1980), 1-17. On the intellectual background, I cite only Charles T. Davis, "Education in Dante's Florence," *Speculum* 40 (1965), 415-435, rev. in Davis, *Dante's Italy* (Philadelphia, 1984), 137-165, and Wieruszowski, "Rhetoric and the Classics in Italian Education," in *Politics and Culture*, 589-627. See also Robert Davidsohn, *Geschichte von Florenz*, Vol. IV, *Die Frühzeit der florentiner Kultur*, Pt. 3, "Kirchliches und geistiges Leben, Kunst, offentliches und hausliches Dasein," (Berlin, 1927), 128, 142-7, 162-9; Peter Herde, *Dante als florentiner Politiker* (Wiesbaden, 1976).

16) There are many detailed biographical surveys of Dante. See, e.g., Giuseppe Lando Passerini, *Dante et son temps*, 1265-1321 (Paris, 1953). For the biographies discussed in this and the next paragraph, see Philip Wicksteed, trans., *The Early Lives of Dante* (London, 1904). Documents concerning the legal career of Pietro di Dante are printed in Renato Piattoli, *Codice Diplomatico Dantesco* (Florence, 1950), 319-324, which also prints the life-records of Dante and his family.

17) See Davis, "Education in Dante's Italy," and the references in Brunetto Latini, *Il Tesoretto*, ed. and trans., Julia Bolton Holloway (New York and London, 1981), and Bianca Ceva, *Brunetto Latini, l'Uomo e l'Opera* (Milan-Naples, 1965).

The *canzone* 'Tre donne,' written in 1304-5, is not only Dante's earliest consideration of the relation between justice and the various laws, but a remarkable lyric poem in itself, unique in the history of European vernacular literature. It probably was intended to be the *canzone* for the promised discussion of Justice in the penultimate section of the unfinished *Convivio*. (*Conv.* IV, 27). As its most recent English translator says of it, "Who else could have successfully presented the concepts of divine law, the unwritten law of humanity (*ius gentium*) and actual law and the theme of human transgressions against justice in the form of a conversation between Love and three outcast, wandering women?" Patrick S. Dihl, trans., *Dante's 'Rime'* (Princeton, 1979), p. 5. See further, Kenelm Foster and Patrick Boyde, *Dante's Lyric Poetry* (Oxford, 1967), and Patrick Boyde, *Dante's Style in his Lyric Poetry* (Cambridge, 1971). There are a number of important studies of the legal aspects of late thirteenth century rhetorical study in Wieruszowski, *Politics and Culture*.

18) Wieruszowski, "Art and the Commune in the Time of Dante," in *Politics and Culture*, 475-502, and see below, n. 21. On Florentine political ambition and conceit, see the Bargello inscription, discussed in Patrick Boyde, *Dante: Philomythes and Philosopher: Man in the Cosmos* (Cambridge, 1981), p. 20. See also Samuel Y. Edgerton, Jr., "Icons of Justice," *Past and Present* 89 (1980), 23-38.

19) The literature on this subject is conveniently summed up in the synthesizing article of Giuseppe Lumia, "Legge, Diritto e Giustizia nel Pensiero di Dante," in *Atti del Convegno di Studi su Dante e la Magna Curia* (Palermo, 1967), 563-568, at 568, n. 1. See also the art. "Legge," *ED* III, 613-617. There is no serious scholarly argument today that Dante either completed a course of legal studies at Bologna or anywhere else or was a professional jurist in any sense of that term. The debate between Chiaudano and everyone else centers simply on the question of whether Dante had first-hand knowledge of Roman legal texts, and the current con-

sensus is that he did.

20) On haste in intellectual effort in Dante, see *Par.* x, 121-9, xiii, 112-29, as well as Robin Kirkpatrick, *Dante's Paradiso and the Limitations of Modern Criticism* (Cambridge, 1978), p. 28ff. See also Raffaello Ramat, *Il mito di Firenze* (Florence-Messina, 1976), 147-165. Dante frequently denounces the Florentines' use of law for vicious or private purpose, e.g. *Inf.* vi, 74-5; *Inf.* x, 83-4.

21) On *infamia* see Samuel Y. Edgerton, Jr., *Pictures and Punishment: Art and Criminal Prosecution during the Florentine Renaissance* (Ithaca, 1984), and Gherardo Ortalli, *Pingatur in Palatio: La pittura infamante nei secoli XIII- XVI* (Rome, 1979). I am grateful to Samuel Edgerton for these references. For *infamia* in canon law, see J.M. Livingston, *Infamia in the Decretists from Rufinus to Johannes Teutonicus* (Ph.D. Diss. University of Wisconsin, 1962), and Peter Landau, *Die Entstehung des kanonischen Infamiebegriffs von Gratian bis zur Glossa Ordinaria* (Cologne-Graz, 1966). In general, see *Enciclopedia del Diritto*, ed. C. Mortati and S. Publiatti, Vol. XXI, Giuseppe Dalla Torre, Jr., art. "Infamia," 382-391.

22) *Ep.* IX. 2. See the long note by Toynbee, pp. 154-5.

23) Donald Weinstein, "The Myth of Florence," in *Florentine Studies: Politics and Society in Renaissance Florence*, ed. Nicolai Rubinstein (Evanston, 1968), 15-44; George Holmes, "The Emergence of an Urban Ideology in Florence, 1250-1450," *Transactions of the Royal Historical Society*, 5th Series 23 (1973), 111-134. Davis, *Dante's Italy*, 71-93.

24) On the Ordinances, see Nicola Ottokar, *Il Comune di Firenze alla fine del dugento*, 2nd ed., by Ernesto Sestan (Turin, 1962), 199-215. On Dante and the Ordinances, see Ottokar, *Studi Comunali e Fiorentini* (Florence, 1948), 127- 132; Catto, "Florence, Tuscany, and the World of Dante"; Peter Herde, *Dante als Florentiner Politiker* (Wiesbaden, 1976), and idem, "Dante in seiner sozialen Umwelt (Zur Genesis seines politischen Denkens in Florenz)," *Deutsches Dante-Jahrbuch*, 51. 52. Band (1976/77), 32-64.

25) Solmi, in "Dante e il Diritto," argues that Dante's chief theme in his treatment of jurisprudence is his recognition of proportion and equilibrium, established by Roman law, as essential to true humanity. It is thus that he offers an original explanation for Cacciaguida's praise of old Florence in *Par.* xv: "Dante saw [within the old circle of Florence's walls] the triumph of proportion and equilibrium which were secured to the citizens by a sober and modest peace." This rather than conservative reactionariness, accounts for Cacciaguida's Florence.

26) Donald Kelley, "*Gaius Noster*: Substructures of Western Thought," *American Historical Review* 84 (1979), 619-648, at 627-8.

27) *Mon.* I. 14. 35-47. The Scythians and Garamantes live by law naturally. Cf. *Mon.* I xiv. 5; *Conv.* IV. 9. 150-167; IV. 15. 175-8. The Scythians turn up again in *Mon.* III. 3. See now Robert L. Benson, "*Provincia = Regnum*," in George Makdisi, Dominique Sourdel, Janine Sourdel-Thomine, eds., *Preaching and Propaganda in the Middle Ages / Prédication et Propagande au Moyen Age*, Penn-Paris-Dumbarton Oaks Colloquia III (Paris, 1983), 41-70.
On a similar problem in Ockham, see Arthur Stephen McGrade, "Ockham and the Birth of Individual Rights," in Brian Tierney and Peter Linehan, eds., *Authority and Power: Studies on Medieval Law and Government Presented to Walter Ullmann on His Seventieth Birthday* (Cambridge, 1980), 149-165, at 161, with further references.

28) *Ep.* VI. 2; V. 3. See Michael Richter, "Dante the Philosopher-Historian in the *Monarchia*," in David Nolan, ed., *Dante Soundings* (Dublin, 1981), 164-87, at 176, 181. On the early history of the identification, see Robert L. Benson, "*Provincia = Regnum.*"

29) For Augustine, see *Confessions*, III. 4; for Bruni, see Edward Peters, "*Pars, Parte*": Dante and an Urban Contribution to Political Thought," in David Herlihy et al., eds., *The Medieval City* (New Haven, 1977), 113-140, at 129.

30) Charles Till Davis, *Dante and the Idea of Rome* (Oxford, 1957), 73-100.

31) Davis, *Dante and the Idea of Rome*, 170.

32) *Dante as a Political Thinker*, 27.

33) On Cino, see Davis, *Dante and the Idea of Rome*, 141, 170. Cino and Dante shared a number of ideas. Cino recognized very early in his commentary on the code the problem of diverse laws within the Empire. See *Cyni Pistoriensis in Codicem...Doctissima Commentaria* (Frankfurt, 1578; rpt. Turin, 1964), I. 1. p. 2; cf. *Monarchia* I. xiv. 4. On Cino's sources, see W.M. Gordon, "Cinus and Pierre de Belleperche," in Alan Watson, ed., *Daube Noster: Essays in Legal History for David Daube* (Edinburgh and London, 1974), 105-118. On Maffei's discovery of the commentary on the digest, see Domenico Maffei, *La 'Lectura super digesto veteri' di Cino da Pistoia* (Milan, 1963). For Cino's use of the same non-professional sources as Dante, particularly St. Augustine and Cicero, see p. 34, n. 98.

34) For *ratio scripta*, see *Conv*. IV. 9. 8; IV. 19. 4; IV. 24. 15; *Mon*. II. 5. III. 10f. Justinian had stated that the science of the law represented true wisdom, *Dig*. 1.1.1. The phrase is frequently used after the early twelfth century.

35) Solmi, "Dante e il Diritto," 238-9, cites the description of the glorious temple of Justice at the beginning of the *Questiones de iuris subtilitatibus*, once attributed to Irnerius, and observes that the text circulated widely in thirteenth-century Tuscany. See Ginevra Zanetti, ed., *Questiones de iuris subtilitatibus* (Florence, 1958).

36) See the excellent discussion in Alexander Murray, *Reason and Society in the Middle Ages* (Oxford, 1978), 218-227, and Richard Kay, *Dante's Swift and Strong* (Lawrence, 1978), 39-66, revision of Kay, "Dante's Unnatural Lawyer: Francesco d'Accorso in *Inferno* XV," *Studia Gratiana* 15 (1972), 147-200; Stephan Kuttner, "Dat Galienus opes et sanctio Justiniana," rpt. in Kuttner, *The History of Ideas and Doctrines of Canon Law in the Middle Ages* (London, 1980), X, 237-246; *Conv*. III. 11. 10. Kay's study portrays a Roman lawyer who is incompetent, greedy for money, dependent upon his father's reputation, and treacherous to the emperor. See Kay's further references, "Dante's Unnatural Lawyer," p. 160n.

37) Ernst Kantorowicz, *The King's Two Bodies* (Princeton, 1957), 207-212. There is interesting use of this idea in Giuseppe Mazzotta, *Dante, Poet of the Desert* (Princeton, 1979), 134-35. The most comprehensive study of the organological metaphor in medieval political thought is now Tilman Struve, *Die Entwicklung der organologischen Staatsauffassung im Mittelalter* (Stuttgart, 1978).

38) Cf. *Par*. xi, 1-12.

39) The point is well made in Whitfield, "*Paradiso* VI."

40) Dante and the frescoes are briefly discussed in Bruno Nardi, *Dal Convivio alla Commedia* (Rome, 1960), 240-1. The section of the book is Nardi's long study, "Intorno ad una nuova interpretazione del terzo libro della *Monarchia* dantesca." See next note.

41) Just how far may be seen in the difference between Nardi's article cited in the preceding note and the studies which triggered it, Michele Maccarrone, "Teologia e Diritto Canonico nella *Monarchia* III. 3," *Rivista di Storia della chiesa in Italia*, 5 (1951), 7-42, and idem, "Il terzo libro della Monarchia," *Studi danteschi* 55 (1955), 5-142.

42) I have considered the passage in "The Failure of Church and Empire: *Paradiso*, 30," *Medieval Studies* 34 (1972), 326-335.

43) These canonist attitudes are cited from Huguccio and the *Glossa Palatina* in G. Le Bras, C. Lefebvre, and J. Rambaud, *L'Age classique* (see next note), p. 133 n. 3. The topic is generally discussed ibid. 133-166.

44) Besides the references above, n. 11, there is a brief discussion of the criticism of Dante and others of the *decretalisti* in G. Le Bras, Ch. Lefebvre, J. Rambaud, *L'Age classique, 1140-1378. Sources et théorie du droit*, Vol. VII of G. Le Bras, ed., *Histoire du droit et des Institutions de l'Église en Occident* (Paris, 1965), 353 n. 2. Dante was not alone in perceiving a juridical turning away from scripture and the Fathers to papal decretals in the thirteenth century. See also ED II, 332-4, arts. "decretali," "decreto," and below, nn. 46-48. In his article, "decretali," in ED II, 332-3, Raoul Manselli emphasizes the strong anti-legist current in Franciscan thought and literature, suggesting the influence upon Dante of Peter John Olivi's *Lectura super Apocalipsim* of 1297, known in Florence, and condemning the "*multiplex enormitas...causidicationum, litigiorum, et rapinarum ex ipsis occasionaliter accepta*."

Mon. III. 4-12 in fact consist of examples of decretalist opinion and Dante's refutation of them.

45) Richard Kay, "Dante's Razor and Gratian's DXV," *Dante Studies* 97 (1979), 65-95. I am grateful to Richard Kay for a number of illuminating discussions of this and related topics.

46) In *Mon*. III. 3. 9-18, Dante lists the three classes of men who make mistakes about the true relationship of pope and emperor: the popes themselves, temporal rulers of territorial monarchies, and the *decretalisti*, who are ignorant of both theology and philosophy, both of which would have told them of the place of papal decretals in the hierarchy of divine law. Dante then explains the nature of the hierarchy of law, the *lex ante ecclesiam* and the *lex cum ecclesia*, and argues that the original charge to the Church antedates the Church's traditions, *traditiones qua decretales dicunt*, and the latter cannot therefore assume greater authority than the original sources of ecclesiastical authority. The Fathers mentioned in *Ep*. XI. 16 are: Gregory the Great, Ambrose, Augustine, Dionysius the Areopagite, John of Damascus, and Bede.

47) For Dante's attitude toward the papacy and its transformation over time, see George Holmes, "Dante and the Popes," in *The World of Dante*, ed. Cecil Grayson (Oxford, 1980), 18-43. See also Kantorowicz, *The King's Two Bodies*, 451-495. On Dante's prophetic urgency, see Sarolli, *Prolegomena alla 'Divina Commedia'*, 381-419.

48) I have discussed this text in my article, "The Archbishop and the Hedgehog," in Kenneth Pennington and Robert Somerville, eds., *Law, Church, and Society: Essays in Honor of Stephan Kuttner* (Philadelphia, 1977), 167-184.

49) *De consideratione*, I. iv. 5.

50) Michael Wilks, *The Problem of Sovereignty in the Later Middle Ages: The Papal Monarchy with Augustinus Triumphus and the Publicists* (Cambridge, 1963), 305. Early in the thirteenth century Buoncompagno da Signa described decretals in terms strikingly similar to Dante's: *Decretum est sacer canon ex auctoritate summi pontificis et assensu concilii promulgatus.... Decretista est canonici iuris prolator.... Decretalis est primogenita decretorum. Unde dicatur: Decretalis dicitur a decreto et est eius diminutivum; sed modo parificari sibi attentat*. That is: a decretal is the diminutive of a *decretum* but now tries to be its equal. *Rhetorica novissima*, ed. A. Gaudenzi, *Bibliotheca iuridica medii aevi*, 3 vols. (Bologna, 1888-1901), Vol. II, 258. There is a discussion in John H. Mundy, *Europe in the High Middle Ages 1150-1309* (New York, 1973), 346-56, at 349.

51) Ibid.

52) Most recently and articulately done by Joan M. Ferrante, *The Political Vision of the 'Divine Comedy'* (Princeton, 1984).

53) See now Randolph Starn, *Contrary Commonwealth: The Theme of Exile in Medieval and Renaissance Italy* (Berkeley and Los Angeles, 1982).